Myths about the Powerless

EDITED BY

M. Brinton Lykes
Ali Banuazizi
Ramsay Liem
Michael Morris

Myths about the Powerless

Contesting
Social Inequalities

TEMPLE UNIVERSITY PRESS

PHILADELPHIA

Temple University Press, Philadelphia 19122
Copyright © 1996 by Temple University
All rights reserved
Published 1996
Printed in the United States of America

⊛ The paper used in this publication meets the requirements of the American National
Standard for Information Sciences—Permanence of Paper for Printed Library Materials,
ANSI Z39.48-1984

Text design by Kate Nichols

Library of Congress Cataloging-in-Publication Data

Myths about the powerless : contesting social inequalities / edited by
    M. Brinton Lykes . . . [et al.].
        p.   cm.
    Includes bibliographical references and index.
    ISBN 1-56639-421-X (cloth : alk. paper). — ISBN 1-56639-422-8 (pbk. : alk. paper)
    1. Social classes—United States.   2. Poor—United States.   3. United States—Social
policy—1993–   . 4. United States—Social conditions—1980–   . 5. Ryan, William,
1923–   . I. Lykes, M. Brinton, 1949–
HN90.S6M97   1996
305.5'6'0973–dc20   95-47188

To William Ryan, whose life work as a scholar and committed activist for the cause of justice and equality has enlightened and inspired us all as his students, colleagues, and friends. And to Phyllis, his lifelong companion, who has shared equally in his struggles, setbacks, and many achievements.

Contents

Foreword

George W. Albee

DURING THIS PAST YEAR I HAVE BEEN SORTING THROUGH FORTY-SOME BOXES of papers, correspondence, and other materials related to my long history with the American Psychological Association (APA). I have also sorted and donated hundreds of books accumulated during nearly fifty years in psychology. It has been a daunting experience. I have taken two truck loads of paper to the town dump, and I have packed innumerable boxes of materials to be shipped off for sorting and classification for the APA archives and the new APA library in Washington, D.C. I have kept only a small number of books that are especially precious to me and that I want to take with me to Florida, where I hope to continue writing. The books I am keeping are like old familiar friends.

Three books, especially, I cannot part with: those written by William Ryan. These books have had the most profound and lasting effect on me, and have helped to shape my thinking about psychology and my whole intellectual world.

Bill Ryan and I have known each other, and each other's work, for at least thirty years. I met him for the first time back in the early 1960s, when I was asked to give a talk at a mental health center in Connecticut where he was the senior person on the staff. At that time he was in trouble, as usual, because he had encouraged a group of welfare mothers to confront the local welfare establishment. At that time I was picketing the Cleveland Board of Education, which had insisted on building new schools in the poverty-stricken ghettos of that city rather than integrate schoolchildren. We were both committed to the civil rights struggle, and we continued to send each other papers and accounts of our respective activities.

In 1959, I had written a book, *Mental Health Manpower Trends,* as part of the Joint Commission on Mental Illness and Health established by President Dwight D. Eisenhower with major support from Senator Lister Hill and a variety of national organizations in the field. In my book I had been able to show that there was a vast shortage of psychiatrists, clinical psychologists, social workers, and nurses to staff mental hospitals and clinics. No amount of effort at training more professionals to work on a one-to-one basis with clients could ever begin to meet the nation's needs. The Joint Commission's final report, *Action for Mental Health* (1960), had called for the establishment of two thousand community mental health centers whose purpose would be to provide interventions for individuals with mental and emotional problems. These proposed centers were to intercept people headed for the big old state hospitals and were to receive persons being discharged from those terribly inhumane places.

The proposed mental health centers were not embraced enthusiastically by the American medical establishment. Indeed, Greer Williams wrote an article in the *Atlantic Monthly* in 1962 telling how the leading members of Congress had received personal phone calls from their own physicians telling them that it was okay to appropriate money to *construct* these centers but not to *staff* them, because this was a first step down the long road toward socialized medicine! About seven hundred of the centers eventually were built, but it was several years before any federal money was available to staff them, and staffing funds were always uncertain and insufficient.

I first read Bill Ryan's *Distress in the City* (1969) when it appeared as a monograph that summarized his detailed analysis of Boston's system of dealing with the problems of people experiencing emotional difficulties. That book clarified my efforts at thinking about the faults and failures of the whole mental health system. It described how Boston, a city with more mental health professionals, more "psychiatric" clinics and hospitals, more private mental health practitioners, more of everything related to mental health than any city in the world, and with at least five universities turning out mental health professionals, was not reaching the people who most needed help. Bill Ryan identified five groups barely touched by the system: seriously disturbed children, particularly those in need of residential treatment; seriously disturbed adolescents; families who were called "multi-problem"; elderly people with mental problems; and people who had been discharged from the public mental hospitals. If Boston, with all of its resources, was neglecting these five groups, how could other parts of the country deliver care?

Distress in the City had had only a limited printing and soon became difficult to find or even unavailable. I encouraged the Press of Western Reserve

University to publish a hardcover edition of Ryan's monograph, and we recruited a dozen commentators to write their perceptions and insights based on his study, all included in one volume. This effort kept the work in print for a number of years and helped spread Ryan's message.

The answer to the quandary about treatment came to me gradually over several years: the only hope was effective prevention. While working for the Joint Commission on Mental Illness and Health I had had frequent conversations with John Gordon, who was then professor of epidemiology at the Harvard School of Public Health. Gordon explained to me in terms I could understand that public health had primary prevention as its core concept. He explained that no mass disease (or disorder) afflicting humankind had ever been eliminated or brought under control by attempts at treating the affected individual. Only through effective efforts at primary prevention were the great plagues ever controlled.

Bill Ryan understood this, demonstrated it, and helped me understand the reasons that led the professional political system to find problems inside individual victims and not in an unjust social order. His *Blaming the Victim* (1971) clarified for me, and for thousands of other people, the strategy of the dominant voices in government and the academy: emotional problems were attributed to individual defect, and not to an unfair and inequitable social-economic-political system. Real prevention meant social change and so threatened the power structure. This threat was further compounded by the enormous appeal of Bill's insight into the ideology of inequality to virtually every sector of the movement for social change born in the turbulent period of the 1960s.

A decade later, his book *Equality* (1981) further clarified how the establishment pretended to give everyone the same chance of success but without removing the economic and social barriers that kept large groups of people captive to major economic and social inequalities. Bill clarified how society could establish a system that protects the powerful by pretending that everyone has the same opportunity, and that sheer individual ability and effort determine who achieves health and happiness. But they kept the playing field tilted. In contrast to the existing system that operates on the basis of "Fair Play," Bill argued for "Fair Shares." His critics frequently challenged him, arguing that he was advocating equality of outcomes. Bill countered by clarifying that a "Fair Share" refers rather to each citizen's right to expect a reasonable share of material resources, education, health care, etc., and does not refer in any way to equal results or to uniformity of resources. This argument went further than his earlier claims in *Blaming the Victim* and further challenged the power structure.

Bill Ryan's three books have had a major influence on community psychology, on the social sciences, and on the political awareness of many who
have struggled for social justice and social change. He is a giant in his field,
someone whose ideas, unlike those that languish in esoteric, academic journals, have made a difference in the ability of many of us to glimpse the myriad ways that power and privilege reproduce and sustain themselves.

Acknowledgments

During the 1960s and 1970s, the provocative insights of William Ryan, in such well-known works as *Distress in the City* (1969), *Blaming the Victim* (1971), and *Equality* (1981), helped to reframe the problems of social inequality and racial injustice in the United States. Ryan's insights are no less pertinent for a critical analysis of the social problems that our society faces today, and in different ways, the contributors to this volume address the social costs of inequality by extending his ideas about victim-blaming, social inequality, and social welfare. What has emerged, we believe, are fresh insights that bear the unmistakable imprint of Ryan's gift for making the obvious problematic and the natural, unnatural.

A book focusing on social issues may fail to capture innumerable, more personal experiences of William Ryan. Some of us met him first as graduate students, struggling to keep up with the breadth of his knowledge. Others, who have taught or collaborated with him for many years, never cease to wonder at his insights into the subtleties of contemporary forms of "Fair Play" ideology and his ability to draw connections among texts that analyze social practice across diverse situations and at very different historical moments. His passion, wit, and deep-running commitment to "ordinary people" are well known to all of us.

His wife Phyllis, widely recognized and respected in Boston for her activism in the Civil Rights Movement, has been a constant companion to him and a source of inspiration to all of us. The two of them continue to be key resources to many friends and associates, both within and beyond the academy, who work for the cause of social justice and progressive social policies.

Collectively the four editors of this volume have been students and colleagues of Bill's since the mid-1960s. As such we have been nurtured and nudged and challenged and criticized. The preparation of this volume has brought us together in new ways. It has allowed us to appreciate more fully the individual and shared stories of our own formation as scholars and activists, and of how our lives have intersected with Bill's. We have laughed and cried as we remembered many of those experiences. Although Bill has accompanied each of us, and we thank him for the many contributions he has made to our lives, we alone are responsible for the ways in which we have reinterpreted those relationships through our scholarship and activism. We hope that the essays and conversation with Bill gathered in this volume will serve as a resource for our peers while also introducing a new generation of scholar-activists to the work of William Ryan.

Part I

Introduction

THE SHARP CONSERVATIVE TURN IN U.S. POLITICS IN THE MID-1990s, heralded by its partisan enthusiasts as the "Republican Revolution," promises not only to undo many of the progressive social policies that had been fought for and won during the 1960s and early 1970s, but, more ominously, to undermine a core assumption in our system of social welfare for the past two generations: that to guarantee a minimum standard of living for all citizens is a fundamental task of government. From the most basic welfare programs like Aid to Families with Dependent Children (AFDC), food stamps, and Medicaid, to school lunches, subsidies for public housing, and aid for basic education and job training, "reform" has come to mean shifting the "burden" of social welfare to the states or the voluntary sector, making deep budget cuts, or outright scuttling the programs. The main targets of such cuts, at both the federal and state levels, are the poorest and most vulnerable segments of the population.

Paradoxically, the above regressive social agenda comes on the heels of a decade of unprecedented prosperity for the most affluent American families. While extraordinary wage and salary differentials, entitlement programs like farm subsidies, mortgage interest deductions, massive government bailouts, and generous tax cuts in the 1980s helped the more privileged reap the lion's share of the gains of the Reagan-Bush era of "trickle down" economics, the bottom 40 percent lost ground during the same period. Today, contrary to our cherished national image, the United States has the dubious distinction of being the most economically stratified society among the industrial nations, whether one uses income or wealth as a yardstick. According to recent studies, the wealthiest 1 percent of U.S. households owns nearly 40 percent of the nation's wealth, and the top 20 percent owns over 80 percent. Similar disparities exist with respect to the distribution of family income, with the top 20 percent of households receiving 55 percent of all after-tax income, and the lowest-earning 20 percent, only 5.7 percent (Bradsher, 1995, p. D4).

An ideological crusade by the neoconservatives has sought to persuade the middle and working classes that their stagnant economic position is due not to the unfair advantages accorded to the privileged groups but to the slothfulness of "welfare mothers," the overburdening of our schools and social service agencies by immigrants, and the undue advantages enjoyed by those who have been helped by affirmative action programs. Social justice, equality, the redressing of grievances of the past or present, and basic rights to food, shelter, health, and education—even for children—are less and less a part of the current discourse on national priorities and social policy.

The contributions to the present volume are by policy analysts, academics, and activists who have long been concerned with the plight of those with limited access to economic, social, and political resources or otherwise marginalized from the mainstream society. The contributors draw on and extend the penetrating insights of William Ryan into the structural roots of social inequality, the ideological rationalizations that help to sustain it, and the collective actions that are needed to revitalize movements for progressive social change. As such, they hope to affirm Ryan's lasting contribution to the analysis of social inequality and enhance the prospects of a new agenda for a more just society.

II

The chapters in the second section of this volume address several aspects of the debate on social inequality and poverty in the United States today. They range from a provocative analysis of the role that moral claims can play in strategies to reduce inequality, to richly detailed critiques of dominant perspectives on the underclass, the homeless, and welfare policy. Drawing on Ryan's work, they attempt to wrest social policy from a discourse that views an unequal distribution of resources, no matter how lopsided, as either a reflection of the "natural" limitations of those at the bottom of the system or as a sociological imperative.

In *Equality* (1981) Ryan offered an assessment of the pernicious effects of the highly skewed distribution of income, wealth, and other resources in our society, and juxtaposed two conceptions of equality that are prevalent in the professional and lay discourse on the topic. Most Americans, he argued, exalt a "Fair Play" version of equality, one that emphasizes equal opportunity and the right of each individual to pursue happiness and obtain resources on the basis of his or her own efforts and merits. This conception of equality, he argued, stands in contrast to what he termed the "Fair Shares" idea, one that stresses the need for an egalitarian distribution of and access to resources that are necessary for sustaining life and preserving liberty.

Anticipating his critics' characterization of Fair Shares as unnatural, stifling of individual initiative, threatening to excellence and efficiency, and ultimately un-American, he wrote:

> the idea of equality as Fair Shares has had the misfortune of being defined to a large extent by its opponents, who have been remarkably successful in lampooning it as the recipe for a ridiculous, bizarre, and inhuman world. In current writing and rhetoric, the advocates of Fair Play like to set forth the artificial choice between "equality of opportunity and equality of results." They present this stark dichotomy as though the contrasted terms were mutually exclusive, as though it were an either/or proposition. Logically, of course, the terms are not at all contradictory: more important, defining the issue in this oversimplified fashion obscures and dismisses most of the relevant questions. (Ryan, 1981, pp. 26–27)

He was careful to distinguish his idea of Fair Shares from the notion of "equal results"—the catch phrase used mostly by antiegalitarian Fair Players to deride the views of their opponents—which he viewed to be a straw man. Ryan described the perspective of the Fair Shares advocate this way:

> A Fair Shares egalitarian would hold that all persons have a *right* to a reasonable share of material necessities, a right to do constructive work, and a right to unhindered access to education, to gratifying social memberships, to participation in the life and decisions of the community, and to all the major amenities of society. This principle doesn't lend itself to the calculation of "equal results," and it certainly doesn't imply a demand for uniformity of resources. (Ryan, 1981, p. 29)

A baleful consequence of the neoconservative backlash against the economic programs and social legislations of the 1960s has been the "assigning" of a segment of the poor to a permanent economic status popularly referred to as the "underclass," reminiscent of the earlier notion of the "culture of poverty." The concept of the underclass has been reified through social and economic policies that make invidious distinctions between the deserving and undeserving poor. Some can be rehabilitated, others cannot. However, in both cases the message is the same: life style, values, and personal attributes are the primary determinants of economic status.

In his essay on the moral underpinnings of the relationship between equality and democracy, S. M. Miller suggests that the most effective argument for promoting equality is one that would show that the present-day economic and social stratification endangers the nation's political ideals. Although the American public may be ambivalent about the possibility or desirability of greater economic equality, it passionately subscribes to a model of political democracy in which each person counts only as one and has equal impact on political decisions. Miller examines how the distribution of income and wealth is linked to rates of voting and political influence, thus arguing that economic inequality severely constrains political democracy. He concludes that reducing economic disparities is essential if genuine democracy is to be achieved.

Current images of the poor are examined critically in the contributions of Michael Morris and Dennis P. Culhane to the present volume. Morris views the current discussions of the concept of underclass as the continuation of the long-standing debate over the individualistic versus environmental aspects of "disreputable poverty." He uses Ryan's analysis of the belief systems that impede progress toward greater equality to highlight the limitations of underclass-oriented policy proposals emanating from both the right and the left of the political spectrum. Focusing on the most deprived and visible segment of the underclass—the homeless—Culhane places the contemporary shelters approach to the problem of homelessness within the historical context of other attempts to deal with the disenfranchised, such as the poorhouse solution. A preoccupation with breaking the dependency of those in need and the use of psychiatric services as the first line of defense, in his view, divert attention away from the structural roots of the problems and will ultimately cause the failure of homeless shelters in much the same way that poorhouses failed a century ago.

The latest wave of political rhetoric concerning welfare policy in the United States is the subject of the essays by Frances Fox Piven and Richard P. Cloward and by Herbert J. Gans. Piven and Cloward point to the processes by which AFDC mothers have been scapegoated, in quintessentially blaming-the-victim fashion, as part of the reason for society's inability to address the serious structural problems that affect labor market functioning and the distribution of economic resources. As a result, coercive work requirements are being directed at these women in the name of enhanced self-sufficiency, even though the available evidence indicates that such proposed policies are unlikely to achieve this objective on a sustained basis. Looking at the future of antipoverty programs more generally, Gans considers the question of what strategies should be advocated in an attempt to shift the focus of the welfare debate from scapegoating the underclass for their undeservedness to a genuine search for effective antipoverty policies. While acknowledging the difficulties involved in combating the negative perceptions of the underclass, Gans outlines several strategic paths toward a more effective antipoverty policy.

III

The third section of the book focuses on the ideological and institutional construction of marginality. William Ryan's *Blaming the Victim* (1971) appeared at the end of a turbulent decade of social change and at a time when an emergent neoconservative movement had begun to challenge, on both ideological and public policy grounds, some of the modest gains made by the 1960s Civil Rights and War on Poverty movements. His now classic analysis, however, was at once a polemical attack on the conservative opponents of these reforms as well as a powerful critique of the then dominant professional ideology of policy-makers, academics, and liberal-minded reformers. Ryan defined "blaming the victim" as a way of thinking about social problems that locates their origins in the purported deficits and failings of their victims rather than in the social institutions and practices that had brought about and sustained their victimization:

> The old-fashioned conservative could hold firmly to the belief that the oppressed and the victimized were born that way—"that way" being defective or inadequate in character or ability. The new ideology [of blaming the victim] attributes defect and inadequacy to the malignant nature of poverty, injustice, slum life, and racial difficulties. The stigma that marks the victim and accounts for his victimization is an acquired stigma, a stigma of social rather than genetic origin. But the stigma, the defect, the fatal difference—though derived in the past from environmental forces—is still located *within* the victim, inside his skin. With such an elegant formulation, the humanitarian can have it both ways. He can, all at the same time, concentrate his charitable interest on the defects of the victim, condemn the vague social and environmental stresses that produced the defect (some time ago), and ignore the continuing effect of victimizing social forces (right now). It is a brilliant ideology for justifying a perverse form of social action designed to change, not society, as one might expect, but rather society's victim. (Ryan, 1971, p. 7)

Ryan's critique of victim-blaming ideology had a profound impact not only on social welfare professionals but, more broadly, on the thinking of those concerned with racial injustice, social inequality, and the reform of human services. Whether victims were high school dropouts, rape victims, the homeless, public housing tenants, or unemployed workers, greater sensitivity to the structural and political aspects of victimization was displayed in the professional literature in part as a result of Ryan's critical insights.

Since the publication of *Blaming the Victim* over two decades ago, analyses of inequality involving class, race, gender, or ethnicity have had to contend with the new ways in which the dominant American social discourse succeeds in normalizing invidious distinctions. Given the changed social landscape created by movements of women, the unemployed, racial minorities, and the "new ethnic groups" to subvert their statuses as victims, Ryan's insights into this process cannot be borrowed without certain modifications. The recent challenges to inequality have cast victims in a new light, while critical theory itself has been altered by the successes and limitations of these collective struggles. Those who are blamed for their marginalization—racial minorities, women, the unemployed, the culturally "inferior"—often display resilience in the face of ideological distortions of their statuses in society. Victim-blaming does not inevitably undermine their resistance to the pernicious workings of social inequality. Paul Willis's *Learning to Labor* (1977), Patricia Hill Collins's *Black Feminist Thought* (1991), and Henry Giroux's *Border Crossings* (1992) explore this tension between the critical voice of the marginalized and its silencing within the established social order. At the same time, a growing body of critical analyses of victim-making suggests that both the institutional means for perpetuating structural inequalities and the consequences of social and economic repression are much greater than may have been envisioned by Ryan's early students.

The issue of resistance among victims is addressed in several of the contributions to this section. Ramsay Liem and Joan Huser Liem question the prevailing view in research on mental health and unemployment that displaced workers are inevitably reduced to helpless casualties in the face of large-scale economic downturns. While the tendency to blame one's self for the loss of a job is reinforced in many ways in our society, the Liems make the case that displaced workers contest both this version of victim-blaming and the threats to their economic and social welfare created by unemployment. Michelle Fine, Toni Genovese, Sarah Ingersoll, Pat Macpherson, and Rosemarie Roberts, on the other hand, note "faint signs" of institutional responsiveness to female victims of sexual violence who have been willing to challenge male abuse in spite of prevailing beliefs that women are fundamentally accountable for their mistreatment by men. At the same time these authors share more ominous views of the social mechanisms of victim-making and victim-blaming, which include institutional discourses that exclude the efficacy of the unemployed and normalize unequal relations of power between men and women.

In Ryan's work, the scope of victim blaming and victimization was restricted to minorities and the poor living in the United States. The contributions from M. Brinton Lykes and Ali Banuazizi reach beyond local borders and show how victim blaming operates in the international arena. Based on her work with Guatemalan Maya child survivors of state-sponsored violence, Lykes critiques the category of "post-traumatic stress disorder" that has been widely employed to understand and treat victims of massive human rights violations. Concerned primarily with the imprint of trauma on the individual, this biomedical syndrome fails to acknowlege the social dimensions of trauma such as collective terror, dehumanization of social relations, and, inevitably, the rupture of community. Banuazizi exposes the victim-blaming ideology underlying psychological explanations for the failure of "underdeveloped," non-Western societies to match the pace of economic and political development in the West. He analyzes social-psychological theories that embody a pernicious process of "othering," whereby "they" in the non-West are presumed to lack the requisite values, attitudes, and cognitive styles that have enabled "us" to achieve our privileged status vis-à-vis other nations.

IV

William Ryan's contributions to the critique of the "culture of inequality" addressed not only its ideological foundations but also its institutional practices. Throughout his scholarship one finds an interplay between the "savage discovery" of deficiency and deficit within the individual, on the one hand, and the systematic exclusion of the poor and minorities from access to work, education, and health care, on the other. In *Distress in the City* (1969), Ryan showed how mental health services in a major metropolitan area failed to "work" for the poor. His examination of privileged access to psychiatric care helped to spawn a new era of community-based strategies with greater accountability to their local consumers.

The health care reforms that Ryan advocated have since become another casualty of the neoconservative backlash against the more egalitarian agenda of the War on Poverty. In the arena of mental health, in particular, the resurgence of the biomedical model of mental illness, the failure to develop adequate community supports for deinstitutionalized patients, cutbacks in federal and state aid for a broad array of basic human services, and the overall decline in the U.S. economy have created a system so besieged with unmet needs for care that the issue of equity has been virtually set aside. Cost containment and the "pharmaceutical management" of those with the most intractable psychological impairment have effectively become the dominant concerns of policy-makers, practitioners, and researchers.

Nonetheless, the rising costs of health and mental health care have opened, somewhat paradoxically, a window of opportunity for reintroducing demands for equal access and more comprehensive care. As the cost of health and mental health services have escalated, the lack of health insurance for over thirty-five million people in this country, the overreliance on "high tech" treatment modalities, and the neglect of more holistic approaches to care have led to a new politics of reform among consumers. The need for health care reform and serious initiatives at the national level were among the highest priorities for voters in the 1992 presidential election. Furthermore, as David Eisenberg (1993) recently estimated, over one-third of Americans turned to unconventional therapies in 1990, seeking more humane, less mechanistic care than is typically offered by the medical and psychiatric establishments.

Four essays in this section document some of the inequalities that continue to plague the health care system, examine their causes, and contribute to the debate on how to reform a medical system run amok. Paula B. Doress-Worters, and Jean V. Hardisty and Ellen Leopold address the increasingly vocal concerns of women whose particular health needs have historically been a neglected priority of medical providers and researchers. Doress-Worters shows how gender bias in the medical system is especially detrimental to the health of middle-aged and older women, whereas Hardisty and Leopold focus on the intersections of gender, race, and class to analyze the failure of the health care system to respond to the needs of women with cancer.

The politically contentious issue of health care financing is also addressed by these contributors as well as by Elizabeth Sparks and Matthew P. Dumont. Sparks examines a promising earlier model of health care delivery for minorities and the poor advocated by the community health centers movement. One of her concerns is the declining capability of these centers to provide effective, innovative services because of their dependence on financial institutions that ignore the role of social and economic factors in the health of marginalized groups. Dumont questions the viability of the entire psychiatric service system, which he sees as overrun by privatization. He offers a radical critique of the commodification of health services in capitalist economies and advocates bold and comprehensive reform of mental health care.

V

The concluding essays of this volume address an important theme evident throughout William Ryan's work: his conviction that critical social analysis should grow out of participation in the process of social change and, in turn, inspire new strategies for implementing egalitarian reforms. Ryan's contributions to the social equality agenda are themselves insights gleaned in part from his intimate involvement in the Civil Rights movement, the establishment of programs to achieve community control of human services, and efforts to reform the mental health system. For him neither theory construction nor social policy-making are domains apart from concrete efforts to combat the assault on equality. They are integral components of the process of change itself.

Ryan's commitment to social action as a necessary counterpart of analysis and understanding has always been unequivocal:

> Let me repeat . . . my general recipe for achieving equality: collective action for collective benefit. . . . It provides at once a direct method of winning a larger share and the kind of experience that nourishes an egalitarian, Fair Shares ideology and contradicts the antiegalitarian ideology of individual internal differences. . . . Successful efforts to achieve greater equality will consist of integrating the actions of organizing, of experiencing, and of interpreting. That's the chief way we'll learn what's good for us. (Ryan, 1981, p. 205)

The model exemplified by Ryan's life and work challenges both the claims to political neutrality of social scientists and professional practitioners, and their isolation from one another. Organizing against housing code violations in New Haven, marching in the streets of Boston with African American leaders during the school boycott of 1964, and sitting in Massachusetts prisons to ensure the protection of prisoner rights contributed richly to his understanding of both systems of discrimination and liberal ideology.

Ryan's conception of "activist scholarship" may be the one facet of his work that is least resonant with the methods of critical social analysis today. The rise of neoconservativism, the demise of collective responsibility in the name of protecting individual rights, and the accompanying cynicism that social reform is neither necessary nor possible have reduced the appeal of activism in both the community and the academy. Movements for change and critical social commentary have become increasingly separated from each other and marginalized. Activist feminists, for example, frequently critique feminist scholars for the inaccessibility of their theorizing or distance from the life struggles of many women or both. Similarly, some African American scholars have noted the isolation of academic life from the day-to-day struggles in the Black community, another indication of a more systemic divorce of critical theory from practice.

The final essays in this collection present work in which thinking about social change and practicing it are considered inseparable activities for good theorizing and for the discovery of creative solutions to social problems. They emphasize the development of the individual as a social or political actor and of the community as the site of contestation and resource for change. The essays resonate with many of the points presented in earlier chapters that sought to link research with policy debates (e.g., Piven and Cloward), while placing special emphasis on the role of the activist.

Abigail J. Stewart and Sharon Gold-Steinberg discuss the development of political consciousness among a group of women who have experienced abortion. They treat abortion and women's responses to it as a paradigmatic example of how personal experiences can influence the development of an individual's political consciousness and activism. They demonstrate how a particular individual's experience can transform her into a public actor.

Shifting the focus away from the individual, the essays by Bill Berkowitz and Tom Wolff and R. Elizabeth Thomas and Julian Rappaport examine the dialectics of action and reflection within the community. Berkowitz and Wolff's paper is styled to reflect the action-reflection process *sui generis,* modeling through their writing what they are advocating in the community, whereas Thomas and Rappaport examine the dialectics of the person-in-community and change-in-action. Berkowitz and Wolff discuss models of community empowerment and community change, reflecting in their dialogue their differing hands-on efforts to build organizational coalitions in multiple settings across Massachusetts. Thomas and Rappaport argue that engagement in community arts projects provides a resource for groups typically excluded from power to interpret and create their collective identity and thereby gain access to a powerful resource for change. Their work resonates with Lykes's argument that fractured communities can "regroup," and that creativity as reflected in storytelling is a resource both for community healing and for reexamining traditional understandings of the experience of fracture.

Sumner M. Rosen provides an historical perspective that highlights the critical role of coalition building in attempts to influence public policy. He discusses three examples of how people are organizing, albeit with mixed results, to demand a more egalitarian distribution of the nation's resources and a public authority that embodies and expresses the needs and concerns of the majority population.

VI

This volume concludes with a conversation between M. Brinton Lykes and William Ryan, in which Ryan clarifies a number of his earlier ideas in light of contemporary social conditions and reflects on some of the ramifications of victim-blaming ideology and inequality for scholars and activists in the 1990s. The conversation offers a partial rereading of certain issues and ideas discussed by our contributors and reveals as well aspects of Ryan's personal style. We can imagine him pressing his analysis to its logical conclusions in an academic symposium, on the streets organizing a protest, or in testimony before Congress. Ryan's candid remarks also reveal the depth of his identi-fication with the struggle to build a more equitable society.

REFERENCES

Bradsher, K. (1995, April 17). Gap in wealth in U.S. called widest in West. *The New York Times,* pp. 1, D4.
Collins, P. H. (1991). *Black feminist thought: Knowledge, consciousness, and the politics of empowerment.* London: Routledge.
Eisenberg, D. (1993). Herbal and magical medicine: Traditional healing today. *New England Journal of Medicine, 328,* 215–216.
Giroux, H. (1992). *Border crossings: Cultural workers and the politics of education.* New York: Routledge.
Ryan, W. (Ed.). (1969). *Distress in the city: Essays on the design and administration of mental health services.* Cleveland: Press of Case Western Reserve University.
Ryan, W. (1971). *Blaming the victim.* New York: Pantheon.
Ryan, W. (1981). *Equality.* New York: Pantheon.
Willis, P. (1977). *Learning to labor: How working class kids get working class jobs.* Westmead: Saxon House.

Part II

Inequality, Poverty, and Social Policy

Chapter 1

Equality, Morality, and the Health of Democracy

•*S. M. Miller*

THIS CHAPTER EMPHASIZES THE IMPORTANCE OF VALUES IN THE DEVELOPment of a politics that would seek to reduce inequalities. While it is important to show that the American distribution of income, wealth, and services has become more unequal, this alone is not enough. Unfortunately, expanded disparities in the command over resources do not lead automatically to efforts to reduce them. The political will to counter poverties and inequalities grows when unrest, policies to promote economic growth, and moral values converge. The first two pressures for reduced inequalities are not strong at this time. Consequently, it is particularly important to offer a normative case for the reduction of inequalities, demonstrating that their effects violate core American values. Two such key normative concerns are health and democracy, and this chapter sketches the evidence that inequalities undermine both.

THE GROWTH IN ECONOMIC INEQUALITIES

The 1980s produced a "surge" of economic inequalities (Plotnick, 1992, p. 42). The process started in the late 1970s or early 1980s and continued through the Reagan-Bush years with a pronounced redistribution to the rich. As political analyst Kevin Phillips (1993, p. xxiii) tells the story, the United States developed a "top one percent economy" that spewed out benefits primarily to the small numbers at the top of the pyramid. In his earlier bestselling book, *The Politics of Rich and Poor*, Phillips (1990) used the term "centimillionaires" to refer to the new breed of exceedingly rich Americans who emerged in the 1980s, since "millionaires" did not adequately convey the income and wealth of this new breed. In his later book he termed the top quintile, who benefited significantly from the 1980s but not nearly as much as the upper 1 percent, "the fortunate fifth" (Phillips, 1993, p. 172). He declared that "economic polarization was becoming a reality in the 1990's" (Phillips, 1993, p. 192).

Using the ratio of the share of the top 20 percent to the share of the bottom 20 percent of households (adjusted for size and age), Plotnick (1992) found that "the Reagan years witnessed a sharp increase in inequality without precedent since 1920" (p. 34) and produced great hardship. In 1991 the largest number were receiving public assistance since the Depression of the 1930s and the food stamps rolls reached new highs. Plotnick (1992) concluded that "the average real income of persons in the bottom fifth of the adjusted family income distribution declined by about 2 percent between 1980 and 1988" (p. 38). Since this drop in the lowest income quintile occurred as real median income rose, inequalities expanded. Taking the bottom fifth as the poor—the standard used by most Western European nations—the real incomes of the poor actually declined during the 1980s.

This deterioration in incomes was particularly true for African Americans and single parent families, mainly headed by women. Thomas and Horton (1992, pp. 445–446) neatly summarized trends in family income as they affected African Americans: (1) race continued to have a negative effect on family income (after statistically controlling for a number of variables) in both 1968 and 1988; (2) race declined in importance in its effect on family income by a very modest amount from 1968 to 1988; (3) in both 1968 and 1988, the importance of race was stronger for higher-status African Americans than for lower-status African Americans; and (4) the negative effect of race was greater for married-couple families than for female-headed families. On this last point, it should be noted that in the shorter period between 1978 and 1987, black female-headed families fell from 59.4 percent of median white family income to 57.1 percent. (Center on Budget and Policy Priorities, 1988, p. 19).

Average weekly earnings of private-production workers (in 1982 dollars) decreased from $315 in 1975 to $264 in 1989 (Phillips, 1993, p. 21). Between 1965 and 1988, production workers' hourly wage increased four-fold (without adjustments for inflation), while chief executives' total compensation jumped seven-fold (Phillips, 1990, p. 181). The spread in wages between jobs has increased: in 1980, the highest paid 10 percent of American workers received 480 percent more than the lowest paid 10 percent; by

1989, the highest paid tenth's advantage had grown to 560 percent ("Rich Man," 1993, p. 71). The gap in earnings between higher and lower educated workers, which had declined in earlier periods, widened during the 1980s.

Wealth

In many ways, wealth (or assets) is a much better indicator of both present and future well-being and of inequalities than income, which is the flow of earned and unearned (e.g., dividends, governmental transfers) money resources within a year (Miller & Roby, 1970, pp. 67–68). Income can change dramatically from year to year, while assets tend to move less rapidly. Thus wealth is "a more stable indicator of status or position in society and represents stored-up purchasing power." It can be utilized in periods of need and provides "resources and status that can be passed on from one generation to the next" (Oliver & Shapiro, 1990, p. 131). As we shall see, wealth is even more concentrated than income.

Phillips (1993, p. 180n.) reports that the Federal Reserve Board estimated that the share of wealth held by the top one percent went from 31 percent in 1983 to 37 percent in 1989, revealing that this group garnered half of the additional wealth created in those years. He went on to make the discouraging point that young Americans are likely to "be the first generation to receive—or not receive—much of their economic opportunity from family inheritance, not personal achievement." In 1973, 56 percent of the wealth of those 35–39 years old "was given to them by their parents. "In 1986, this figure rose to 86 percent and it is likely that the percentage will continue to rise (Phillips, 1993, pp. 190–192).

The usual measure of wealth is net worth (assets minus debts). Disparities in net worth are especially discouraging for African Americans and Hispanics; they are much greater than income differences. In 1988, households headed by black householders had a median net worth of $4,169; those headed by Hispanics had a slightly higher median net worth of $5,524, while those headed by whites had a median net worth of $43,279 (U.S. Bureau of the Census, 1990; pp. 1–2). Differences in net worth are particularly acute among female-headed households: "for every dollar of (net worth) held by white female heads, black female heads average a mere two and one-half cents" (Oliver & Shapiro, 1990, p. 139).

For most Americans, their largest asset is their home, but this has limited use in generating future income and wealth. Consequently, Oliver and Shapiro (1990, pp. 136–137) also studied data on "net financial assets," which exclude home equity and vehicles but do subtract debts. The extent of concentration of net financial assets is amazing: the top quintile of U.S. households possessed nearly 90 percent of these resources in 1983! Furthermore, the concentration of assets at the top is much greater for both net worth and net financial assets than for income: the median value of the net financial assets of the top one-half of 1 percent was 237 times greater than the median of the rest of the 99 percent of households. Racial differences in net financial assets are substantial: 30 percent of white households have zero or negative assets, compared to 67 percent of African American households in a similar state (Oliver & Shapiro, 1990, p. 139).

Despite this emphasis on net financial assets, home ownership is important. Even when controlling for demographic and social influences, "blacks are significantly less likely than nonblacks to be homeowners. . . . The finding that higher status blacks had significantly lower levels of homeownership than comparable nonblacks indicates that class does not supersede race in the area of wealth accumulation. . . . A likely consequence of disproportionately low levels of homeownership for blacks is the elimination of a primary means of wealth accumulation and intergenerational mobility for most black families" (Horton, 1992, p. 488).

Phillips (1993, p. 192) concludes that "economic polarization was becoming a reality in the 1990's." His term for this development is "excessive stratification," or "the triumph of upper America" (Phillips, 1990, p. 208, xxvii). Thus the 1980s were disastrous for William Ryan's (1981) goal of "Fair Shares."

Unfortunately, there is little political pressure to improve this lopsided income distribution. True, the proposal to increase taxes on the income of the wealthy receives some support but is likely to be offset over time by low tax rates on capital gains or their indexing against rises in their value due to inflation. Tax avoidance schemes that benefit the rich are likely to increase again after many were weakened by the tax changes of 1986. The net effect of taxation changes is likely to do little to reduce and may increase inequalities in the posttax distribution of income and wealth.

Services

Money income and wealth are key but not sole elements in Fair Shares. Services are now an important component of resources and the standard of living. As Ryan (1981) pointed out, universal public service services importantly contribute to lessening inequalities, for they add more to the resources of those at lower levels of the economy than to those at higher levels. Sadly, the 1980s saw a trend in the opposite direction: an appalling decline in access to and the quality of public services. Service inequalities grew as the better-off could purchase services in the private sector as public services declined.

GAINING SUPPORT FOR CHANGE

The disturbing facts of widened income-wealth inequalities and their negative consequences will not automatically lead to efforts at rectification. A variety of actions—mostly but not exclusively at the federal level—will be necessary to make pronounced changes in income and wealth distributions. These changes include high employment policies, more progressive federal and state tax structures, industrial policies to promote economic activities that result in lessened inequalities; minimum wages; the promotion of unionization; expanded and improved public services (which are an important component of the command over resources) including health care, pensions, and schooling; and direct cash subsidies (e.g., improved Aid to Families and Dependent Children [AFDC] and earned income tax credits to low wage earners).

It will not be easy to win support for decisive reductions in economic inequalities. Some inequality-lessening programs are expensive or disliked (e.g., AFDC). Others involve more extensive regulations of or interventions in economic affairs, which are often characterized as antibusiness and therefore a drag on economic productivity and growth. In developing a model for present change, we can learn from two periods when redistributive measures were adopted: the New Deal of the 1930s and the Great Society of the 1960s.

THE NEW DEAL AND THE GREAT SOCIETY

The short first period of the Roosevelt administration (I follow here the neglected analysis of Basil Rauch [1944] rather than Arthur Schlesinger, Jr. [1960], in the division of the New Deal periods) was devoted to shoring up business by blocking price cuts and promoting profits. Key measures were the National Industrial Recovery Act (NIRA), which encouraged companies in an industry to establish common prices; the Agricultural Adjustment Act, which put a floor under agricultural prices; and the expanded Reconstruction Finance Administration, which had been established in the Hoover administration but was assigned a bigger role in the Roosevelt administration as a lender to businesses. A lesser role was played by the Public Works Administration, which sought to stimulate the private construction industry by building government structures. The NIRA was declared unconstitutional, however, and the first period measures had limited success in stimulating the economy.

The second period's actions were devoted more to directly expanding consumer demand: the Social Security Act, which dealt with pensions, unemployment insurance, and public assistance/welfare; the Works Progress Administration, which was based on direct government employment; and the Wagner Act, which promoted unionism. Unlike the innovations of the first period, these measures, now regarded as emblematic of the New Deal approach, had a redistributive bias. The incomes of the poor, the unemployed, and the factory worker were to be increased.

Why were such measures politically possible? One reason was the fear of unrest in the form of strikes and demonstrations. A second was the competition for the support of those attracted to the high pension benefit proposed in the Townsend Act. The third reason, I emphasize, was the widespread recognition that the economy desperately needed stimulation from consumer demand, which differed from the first New Deal's hope that investment spending would lead to consumer purchases. The Social Security Act in particular was regarded as an effective economic agent ("economic stabilizer" was the phrase that was used). Its expenditures for unemployment insurance and AFDC would rise when the economy was declining, thereby stimulating the economy when it needed stimulation. When the economy was growing rapidly, these outlays would decline, thus lowering the risk of inflation. The fiscal policy of deficits also promoted consumer demand by injecting more money into the economy than the federal government was taking out through taxation. (When political pressure led to the reduction of the deficit in 1937, a recession occurred.) Thus, the progressive New Deal measures and policies were acceptable—at least for a time—because they were regarded as having economic benefit.

I stress this economic backing for redistributive-type measures because the normative or value support for such actions was very clear. (I shall not discuss the limitations of the New Deal measures, particularly for blacks, which have become the focus of recent writing.) The awareness of extraordinarily high unemployment and the one-third of the nation that was ill-housed, ill-clad, and ill-fed, made visible by Franklin D. Roosevelt's eloquence, was basic to the feeling that something had to be done. People could not be left destitute, to make the best of desperate conditions, without any help from their government and fellow citizens. Unrest threatened, as marches, demonstrations, strikes, interruptions of farm sales, and other disruptive activities were widespread. In short, the New Deal's progressive period was fueled by economic and political considerations as well as by moral ones.

The Great Society of the 1960s yields a similar lesson. The flurry of civil rights, antipoverty, education, and other measures that constituted the Great Society also had an economic basis, although it too was propelled by political concerns as well. The tax cut of 1964 was intended to stimulate the economy in a less egalitarian direction by reducing tax rates on the well-to-do and corporations; the fear was that governmental revenues from the taxation of expanding incomes would increase more rapidly than governmental spending. This would result in "fiscal drag," with the federal government taking out more money from the economy through taxation than it would put in through its expenditures. Consumer demand would therefore decline, threatening continued economic growth.

The need then was to expand governmental spending to offset the increased tax revenues caused by economic growth. Antipoverty and other social programs were seen as ways of getting money to low-income consumers who would spend it, thereby sustaining demand and growth.

Such measures were morally attractive as well because of the concern about poverty and the conditions of blacks. Perhaps of equal or greater importance, measures for the poor, who were increasingly regarded as mainly black, were seen by many as reducing the likelihood of violence. (Summer job programs for youth, for example, were regarded as "riot insurance.")

These two overly synoptic accounts point to three influences on gaining support for promoting fairer shares: the promotion of economic growth, fear of unrest, and moral claims.

MORAL CLAIMS

The Need for a Moral Case

How do these three arguments shape up today? Economically, the country is looking to increases in foreign demand for products, not to increases in domestic consumption, as the key economic stimulant. Thus, it is more difficult today to convince many that increasing the incomes of those at the lower levels of the income distribution profile will have a great effect on improving general economic functioning. This is particularly true as tax aversiveness limits the possibility of raising government revenues in order to spend more on social programs and as widespread fears about the future of the American economy lead to the acceptance of declining real wages and employment quality. Thus, an economic argument for greater economic equality is not likely to be compelling under current circumstances.

Social turbulence might lead to efforts to reduce economic inequalities, but it seems to have lost much of its effectiveness. The 1992 outbreak in Watts, perhaps the most destructive one in this century, has not led to sizable improvements in the economic situation for the area. Minor adjustments, at best, seem to be the typical response to local uprisings. If there were many Watts, would the demand for reducing inequalities overcome the pressure for suppressing uprisings? A guess: the response to upheaval is more likely to be military might rather than economic change.

The inescapable conclusion is that a convincing moral case for lessening inequalities is especially important today. Even if economic pressures and social unrest were positive factors in inducing concern for reducing inequalities, normative concerns would still be important. Certainly, this is the case when disruption occurs: people can simply be angry at the unrest when they feel it has little justification. In the economic situation, it is important that those who are to benefit have what is generally regarded as a creditable claim for their gain. The tarnishing of the poor as welfare cheats and an undeserving underclass undermines their claims to improving their economic conditions (Ryan, 1981). (Reducing the taxes on the rich was not based on their moral claim but on the assertion that their greater income would lead to savings and thus to investment, with a gain in economic growth that presumably would benefit almost all. The pressure to increase the taxes on the rich occurred at the beginning of the Clinton administration not only because of the need for more tax revenues to reduce budget deficits but also from the feeling that the enormous gains of this small group may have harmed the economy over the long run.)

Many public intellectuals and media pundits resist ideas of and measures for greater equality as not only drags on the economy, but as downplaying the personal responsibilities and obligations of those at the bottom (Kaus, 1992; Mead, 1986; Murray, 1984). They see the antisocial behavior of an "undeserving poor" rewarded and unfair burdens imposed on others, as exemplified in the cry against "reverse discrimination." Arguments over moral claims cannot be avoided.

With the likely prospect of high levels of unemployment and slow if not declining rates of growth in household incomes of those who are not well-to-do, inequality is likely to increase. Only strong moral claims can offset fears about the future of the economy, for the political pressure will be for any kind of economic growth even if inequalities expand.

What are today's strong moral claims for greater economic equality? Two are offered here: the improvement of health and the realization of political democracy. The argument is that inequalities in health and political influence related to economic circumstances are incompatible with cherished ideals about this nation and therefore should be rectified.

The Moral Claim to Health

Not long ago, many politicians and physicians debated whether access to medical care was a right or a privilege. (In the early 1960s, a leader of the American Medical Association still contended that it was a privilege.) The enactment of Medicare and Medicaid in the mid-sixties ended that controversy, even if it did not provide care for all, by establishing the principle (if not always the practice) that all people deserved medical attention.

Today, a deeper national commitment goes beyond the right to access to medical care to the right to equal chances of good health and long life. Neither class nor race should affect our health prospects. It is no longer morally acceptable that economic or social differences should privilege some and disadvantage others in vital matters of life and death. Even if one believes that individual differences in merit and desert alone produce economic differences, they are repugnant if they result in disparities in longevity or infant mortality.

Although the link between class and race on one side and good health on the other is not well known, it should be. Understanding that inequalities are associated persistently with shorter and less healthy lives creates a strong claim that they should be reduced.

Overwhelming international and U.S. evidence shows that economic inequalities affect health. Raising average incomes in nations with high per capita income does not reduce disparities in health conditions and mortality (Kawachi, Levine, Miller, Lasch, & Amick, 1994). Although health indicators such as longevity or infant mortality manifest distinctive improvement over time, differences among socioeconomic classes have continued (Wilkinson, 1992, p. 1083). For some health conditions, they have even widened. Clearly, the distribution of income (or education or occupational standing) has health consequences: "individuals higher in the social hierarchy typically enjoy better health than do those below; SES [socioeconomic] differences are found for rates of mortality and morbidity for almost every disease and condition." Clearly, "social class is among the strongest known predictors of illness and health" (Adler, Boyce, Chesney, Cohen, Folkman, Kahn, & Syme, 1994, pp. 15, 22).

Do narrowed inequalities improve health prospects? Japan's rapid improvement in life expectancy is instructive, for it has been "accompanied by a narrowing in the differences in income between the richest and poorest." A comparison of Japan with Britain concludes that it is not cultural differences but widening inequalities that explain the slower improvement of life expectancy in Britain since 1965 (Marmot & Smith, 1989, p. 1551). A cross-national comparison concludes that "there is a significant tendency for mortality to be lower in countries with a more egalitarian distribution of income" (Wilkinson, 1992, p. 165). This conclusion applies to the United States: it has the lowest percentage of income received by the lowest 70 percent of house-holds, and the second lowest life expectancy of advanced industrial nations (Wilkinson, 1992, p. 166).

Health researchers emphasize "the gradient," pointing to the variety of findings that show that "the association of SES and health occurs at every level of the SES hierarchy, not simply below the threshold of poverty" (Adler et al., 1994, p. 15). As one goes down the socioeconomic ladder in the United States, rates of poor health and high mortality typically increase. Inequality differences are displayed in health outcomes.

An important study of differences in mortality rates of American so-cioeconomic groups was replicated in 1986. (The age range was from 25 to 65.) The findings are deeply disturbing. Although mortality declined overall during the twenty-six-year period, class differences did not wither. Not only did "the inverse relation between mortality and socioeconomic status (per-sist) in 1986 and was stronger than in 1960," but "the disparity in mortal-ity rates according to income and education increased for men and women, whites and blacks, and family members and unrelated persons. . . . Despite an overall decline in death rates in the United States since 1960, poor and poorly educated people still die at higher rates than those with higher in-comes or educations, and this disparity increased between 1960 and 1986" (Pappas, Queen, Hadden, & Fisher, 1993, p. 103). A survey of developed countries concluded that "social class differences in health have not nar-rowed despite growing affluence and the fall of absolute poverty" (Wilkin-son, 1992, p. 168).

Black-white differences in mortality rates also increased (Pappas et al., 1993, pp. 103, 107; Miller, 1989, pp. 505–506). Another study estimated that family income differences explain 38 percent of the excess mortality among blacks compared to whites (Otten, Teutsch, Williamson, & Marks, 1990, pp. 845–850). A third study found that when environmental and eco-nomic variables are controlled, black-white differences are reduced by 75 percent: "racial differences in mortality are therefore in large part a conse-quence of poverty, not racial genotype" (Mencik, 1991, p. 1).

In a series of charts, the important Kaiser Foundation report *Pathways to Health* depicted social class (income) differences for males in mortality from all causes, heart disease, and cancer as well as similar differences for all Americans in selected chronic diseases, lung cancer, and osteoarthritis (Bunker, Gomby & Kehrer, 1989, pp. 118–135). The results showed that economic differences make a difference in longevity.

An intensive study of Alameda County, California, over a nine-year pe-riod compared the mortality experience of Oakland residents, thirty-five years of age or older, who lived in a poverty area, with the situation of those residing in nonpoverty sections of the city. Even after a variety of adjustments for health status, race, income, access to medical care, and other influences, those in the poverty area had "higher age-, race-, and sex-adjusted mortality" (Haan, Kaplan, & Camacho, 1987, p. 989).

In a study of self-assessed quality of health, a U.S. Public Health survey found that "excellent health" was associated with class position. (Self-reported health is a widely used indicator of actual health.) Among those classified as upper-middle and upper class, 53 percent reported themselves as in excellent health; of those in the middle classes, 37 percent gave themselves this rating; and of those in the lower classes, only 28 percent regarded themselves as in excellent health. In an analysis of data from the 1991 National Opinion Research Center survey, Karen Ferroggiaro and I found similar differences by income in self-reported conditions of health.

Many other studies point in the same direction: where you stand in the American socioeconomic profile affects your mortality and health prospects. Dutton and Levine's (1989) authoritative review concludes that "one of the most striking features of the relationship between SES and health is its pervasiveness and persistence over time. This relationship is found in virtually every measure of health status: age-adjusted mortality for all causes of death as well as specific causes, the severity of acute disease and the incidence of severe infectious conditions, the prevalence and severity of nearly every chronic disease, and measures of disability and restricted activity." (p. 31; see also Levine, 1993).

Perhaps the most disturbing finding is that the United States is not only high in U.S. infant mortality rates compared to other developed nations but that socioeconomic differences in infant mortality rates are substantial. Although the general level of infant mortality has decreased in the United States, disparities in income and race remain (Gortmaker & Wise, 1994, p. 6).

Such findings are disturbing because the United States spends more per capita on health and medical care than other nations. As a consequence, Gortmaker and Wise (1994) argue that "the first priority [in dealing with infant mortality] is not more obstetricians and pediatricians or hospitals, not even more prenatal clinics or well-baby clinics, but rather to provide more social, financial and educational support to families with pregnant women and infants" (p. 2).

It is now deeply accepted in U.S. society that differences in mortality by class and race are not acceptable, and that good health and longevity should not be restricted to those who are better off. Americans suffer health-wise because of their position in the social hierarchy. In health-conscious USA, showing that inequalities are associated with shorter and less healthy lives strengthens the political impact of the moral claims for greater equality.

ECONOMIC EQUALITY AND POLITICAL DEMOCRACY

The United States has had two great assertions for supporting the contention that it is the greatest nation on earth: (1) its streets may not be paved with gold, but here many people can earn decent incomes; and (2) this is a land of democracy. Political democracy is widely cherished, at least in general sentiment if not in everyday practice. It is not only instrumental to other goals, but "is important in its own right—it is a goal in itself, not merely a means to an end" (Verba et al., 1987, p. 157). Central to democracy is political equality, which means that each person has equal influence on the political process through elections and other means.

With the lowering, although certainly not the elimination, of many of the barriers to voting that were imposed on African Americans, the deepest blemishes on American democracy now are the great disparities in voting rates and the enormous influence on legislation and its implementation of the lobbying and money of business and other organizations

Elections are key components of democracy. They shape both political cultures and governmental policies (Dunham, 1991, p. 226). "The ideal of equality. . . in relation to political influence is more firmly entrenched than is that of equality. . . in economic matters. . . . If using differential economic resources in politics subverts desirable political equality, then that ideal becomes an argument for decreased income inequality" (Verba et al., 1987, pp. 4–5). "Not only is income more unequally distributed [than in Japan and Sweden], but the economically advantaged are somewhat more likely to convert economic into political advantage" in the United States (Verba et al., 1987, p. 14).

This nation, as is now widely known, has much lower levels of voting in national elections than comparable countries (Teixeira, 1987, p. 7). Americans are taught to pride themselves on free elections. Yet, in reality only half of the voting population has a direct effect on the presidential election process. Participation in state and local levels is even lower.

Even more significant is that "the relationship between socioeconomic status and political participation is strongest in the United States among the Western democracies" (Chen, 1992, pp. 175, 183). Another study, concentrating on the United States, concludes that "relative income, or the voter's position on the income distribution, is a very important determinant of voter turnout" (Filer, Kenny, & Morton, 1993, p. 81). While turnout in presidential elections declined overall from 1960 to 1988, the decline was much greater for the lowest income quintile—from 65.2 percent to 47.4 percent—

than for the highest quintile, which ebbed slightly from 96.2 percent to 95.6 percent (Leighley & Nagler, 1992, p. 731).

The pattern is clear: voting levels are related to income (and/or other socioeconomic variables, such as education). Those with lower incomes vote less than those with higher incomes. Filer, Kenny, and Morton (1993) report that the differences in voting rates of the top and bottom income quartiles of whites increased from 18.2 percent in 1960 to 28.7 percent in 1976 (p. 72). Race disparities in voting are also significant: African Americans vote less than whites. To be of low income or marginalized in the United States impairs one's participation in the political process.

This pattern has been termed "selective demobilization" by Walter Dean Burnham, a leading analyst of trends in voting rates. This "class-based skew to political participation" was probably not the case a century ago, but after 1900, class differences in political participation expanded. New Deal programs "temporarily relieved the [socioeconomic] bias in turnout." After World War II, the differences increased, and it is likely that "the gap in turnout between upper- and lower-level people may have increased after 1960" (Bennett & Bennett, 1986, pp. 184–85). While experts argue about whether the differences between the top and bottom socioeconomic groups have widened or stabilized in recent years, the differences between SES groups remain significant. As Leighley and Naylor (1993) conclude, "stability is not necessarily good news" (p. 734).

A somewhat different way of looking at voting turnout and socioeconomic position is in terms of the impact of economic adversity. In contrast to theoretical outlooks about democracy, the fact is that the poor, the unemployed, and the financially troubled are likely to vote even less than they once had as they suffer economic reverses and are preoccupied with coping with them. Consequently, their voices and concerns are little represented and have little impact. The paradox is that as their concerns grow and their need for political response mounts, "the very problem that is foremost in their minds impedes their participation in the political process" (Rosenstone, 1982, p. 44). The disparities in voting rates by socioeconomic groups form one of the most biting indictments of the practice of American democracy.

A second infraction of democracy is the influence of the monied on political actions and inactions. As Greider (1992) and many others have stressed, "the political inequality generated by inequalities of wealth" is most disturbing. "Money is power in American politics" (Greider, 1992, pp. 50, 28). The Democratic Party, which many regard as the representative of those who suffer, is beholden to large funders, as a number of analyses show (Edsall & Edsall, 1992; Kuttner, 1987).

The importance of money in elections and policy is an affront to the ideal of democracy in which each person is regarded as having equal weight. "The decayed condition of American democracy" (Greider, 1992, p. 11) supports the moral claim for reducing inequalities. Taking money out of politics is not only an important factor in the reduction of inequalities but also a moral call to pay attention to the impact of inequalities on democracy.

Increasing the voter participation of lower socioeconomic groups might affect issues and the political responses to them in addition to overcoming the impact of big money. As Piven and Cloward (1988) conclude, "A 'New Politics'. . . requires new constituencies" that can develop from the ranks of the low voting socioeconomic groups. "[A] substantial influx of new voters can be expected, over time, to exert pressures for new leaders and progressive appeals that reflect their interests" (p. 253). Extending this analysis, new constituencies can reduce the power of money by forcing politicians to be concerned about the emergence of new voting blocs. Candidates and elected officials might then have a different stance on economic and equality issues if more people of lower socioeconomic levels were organized and voted. The data above strongly suggest that as people move up the income ladder and inequalities are reduced, they are more likely to vote.

Thus, easing the barriers to voting, as was done with the Motor Voter Law of 1993, is a big step. Nonetheless, reducing inequalities in the socioeconomic sphere will also be important in promoting the emergence of new constituencies and in realizing democracy.

BEYOND EQUALITY

When the issues of poverty and inequality gain attention, the usual response is that economic growth and enhanced productivity will eliminate or reduce them. "A rising tide lifts all ships" is the reassuring metaphor. The recurrent but surprising recognition of the persistence or reappearance of poverty and inequality overwhelms the metaphor. As Jencks (1992) argued, doubling or tripling everyone's income would not eliminate poverty, let alone inequality. Needs change. To be included in American society one now requires a telephone, a television set, and often a car. What is happening to those who are better off in society affects what happens to those in lower socioeconomic situations. If the omnipresence of automobiles has curtailed public transportation and if the dispersion of jobs requires long travel, then a car is now a necessary part of one's economic (as well as social) life (Jencks, 1992, pp. 7–8; Sen, 1992). The challenge of Fair Shares cannot be avoided.

Even if concerns about the quality of democracy and the distribution of health are not sufficiently compelling to lead to lessened inequalities, they and similar issues merit open discussion, for they question what kind of society we seek and what changes and costs would result from realizing it. Most discussions of economic reasons for equality are narrowly phrased in terms of economic growth, implying that we only want more of the same. But the issue of equality should lead to questions of value: what is the worth of what is to be better distributed? While economic equality tends to be measured in terms of dollars and cents, it should be framed in terms of what is to be achieved in daily life[1] socially and politically as well as economically. After long neglect, philosophical discourse, stimulated particularly by the writings of Rawls (1971) and Dworkin (1977), debates moral claims to justice. We similarly need to face up to the never-ending challenge of inequalities and the damages they inflict.

NOTE

1. Sen's (1992) emphasis on "equality of what?" and "capabilities" comes close to this question but fails to deal directly with the issue of competing values, except to point to the likelihood that seeking one goal blocks the achievement of others.

REFERENCES

Adler, N. E., Boyce, T., Chesney, M.A., Cohen, S., Folkman, S., Kahn, R.L., & Syme, S.L. (1994). Socioeconomic status and health: The challenge of the gradient. *American Psychologist, 49*(1), 15–24.

Bennett, S. E., & Bennett, L.L.M. (1986). Political participation. In S. Long (Ed.), *Annual review of political science* (Vol. 1, pp. 157–197). Norwood, NJ: Ablex.

Bunker, J. P., Gomby, D. S., & Kehrer, B. H. (Eds.). (1989). *Pathways to health: The role of social factors*. Menlo Park, CA: The Henry J. Kaiser Family Foundation.

Center on Budget and Policy Priorities. (1988). *Still far from the dream: Recent developments in black income, employment and poverty*. Washington, DC: Author.

Chen, K. (1992). *Political alienation and voting turnout in the United States, 1960–1988*. San Francisco: Mellon Research University Press.

Dunham, P. (1991). *Electoral behavior in the United States*. Englewood Cliffs, NJ: Prentice Hall.

Dutton, D. B., & Levine, S. (1989). Socioeconomic status and health: Overview, methodological critique, and reformulation. In J. P. Bunker, D. S. Gomby, & B. H. Kehrer (Eds.), *Pathways to health: The role of social factors* (pp. 29–69). Menlo Park, CA: The Henry J. Kaiser Family Foundation.

Dworkin, R. (1977). *Taking rights seriously*. Cambridge, MA: Harvard University Press.

Edsall, T. B., & Edsall, M. D. (1992). *Chain reaction: The impact of race, rights, and taxes on American politics.* New York: W. W. Norton.

Filer, J., Kenny, L. W., & Morton, R. B. (1993). Redistribution, income, and voting. *American Journal of Political Science, 37*(1), 63–87.

Gilbert, D., & Kahl, J. A. (1993). *The American class structure: A new synthesis* (4th ed.). Belmont, CA: Wadsworth.

Gortmaker, S. L., & Wise, P. H. (1994). *The first injustice: Socioeconomic disparities in infant mortality in the United States: Theoretical and policy perspectives* [draft]. Harvard School of Public Health and The Health Institute. Boston: New England Medical Center, Society and Health Program.

Greider, W. (1992). *Who will tell the people: The betrayal of American democracy.* New York: Simon & Schuster.

Haan, M., Kaplan, G. A., & Camacho, T. (1987). Poverty and health: Prospective evidence from the Alameda County study. *American Journal of Epidemiology, 125*(6).

Horton, H. D. (1992). Race and wealth: A demographic analysis of black home ownership. *Sociological Inquiry, 62*(4), 480–489.

Jencks, C. (1992). *Rethinking social policy: Race, poverty, and the underclass.* Cambridge, MA: Harvard University Press.

Kaus, M. (1992). *The end of equality.* New York: Basic Books.

Kawachi, I., Levine, S., Miller, S. M., Lasch, K., & Amick, B., III (1994). *Income inequality and life expectancy: Theory, research, and policy.* Working Paper Series. Harvard School of Public Health and The Heath Institute, Boston: New England Medical Center, Society and Health Program.

Keil, J. E., Sutherland, S., Knapp, R. G., Lackland, D. T., Gazes, P. C., & Tyroler, H. A. (1993). Mortality rates and risk factors for coronary disease in black as compared with white men and women. *New England Journal of Medicine, 329*(2), 29–69.

Kuttner, R. (1987). *The life of the party.* New York: Elizabeth Sifton Books–Viking.

Leighley, J. E., & Nagler, J. (1992). Socioeconomic class bias in turnout, 1964–1988: The voters remain the same. *American Political Science Review, 86*(3), 725–736.

Levine, S. (1993). *Inequality and health* [draft]. Harvard School of Public Health and The Health Institute. Boston: New England Medical Center, Society and Health Program.

Marmot, M. G., & Smith, G. D. (1989). Why are the Japanese living longer? *British Medical Journal, 299,* 1547–1551.

Mead, L. (1986). *Beyond entitlement: The social obligations of citizenship.* New York: Free Press.

Menchik, P. L. (1991, January). Poverty and mortality rates. *Insights.*

Miller, S. M. (1989). Race in the health of America. In D. P. Willis (Ed.), *Health policies and black Americans* (pp. 500–531). New Brunswick, NJ: Transaction.

Miller, S. M., & Roby, P. A. (1970). *The future of inequality.* New York: Basic Books.

Murray, C. (1984). *Losing ground: American social policy 1950–1989.* New York: Basic Books.

Oliver, M., & Shapiro, T. (1990, April). Wealth of a nation: A reassessment of asset inequality in America shows at least one third of households are asset-poor. *American Journal of Economics and Sociology,* pp. 129–150.

Otten, M. W., Jr., Teutsch, S. M., Williamson, D. F., & Marks, J. S. (1990). The effects of known risk factors on the excess mortality of black adults in the United States. *Journal of the American Medical Association, 263,* 845–850.

Pappas, G., Queen, S., Hadden, W., & Fisher, G. (1993). The increasing disparity in mortality between socioeconomic groups in the United States, 1960 and 1986. *New England Journal of Medicine, 329*(2), 103–109.

Phillips, K. (1990). *The politics of rich and poor: Wealth and the American electorate in the Reagan aftermath.* New York: Random House.

Phillips, K. (1993). *Boiling point: Republicans, Democrats, and the decline of middle-class prosperity.* New York: Random House.

Piven, F. F., & Cloward, R. (1988). *Why Americans don't vote.* New York: Pantheon.

Plotnick, R. D. (1992). Changes in property, income inequality, and the standard of living during the Reagan era. *Journal of Sociology and Social Welfare, 19*(1), 29–44. Reprinted as IRP Reprint Series No. 669, Institute for Research on Poverty, University of Wisconsin–Madison.

Rauch, B. (1944). *History of the New Deal, 1933–1938.* New York: Creative Age.

Rawls, J. (1971). *A theory of justice.* Cambridge, MA: Harvard University Press.

Rich man, poor man. (1993, July 24). *The Economist,* p. 71.

Rosenstone, S. J. (1982). Economic adversity and voter turnout. *American Journal of Political Science, 26*(1), 25–46.

Ryan, W. (1981). *Equality.* New York: Pantheon.

Schlesinger, A., Jr. (1960). *The age of Roosevelt: The politics of upheaval* (Vol. 3). Boston: Houghton Mifflin.

Sen, A. (1992). *Inequality reexamined.* Cambridge, MA: Harvard University Press.

Teixeira, R. A. (1987). *Why Americans don't vote.* Westport, CT: Greenwood.

Thomas, M. E., & Horton, H. D. (1992). Race, class, and family structure: The case of family income. *Sociological Perspectives, 35*(3), 433–450.

U.S. Bureau of the Census. (1990). *Household wealth and asset ownership: 1988* (Current Population Reports, Series P-70, No. 22). Washington, DC: U.S. Government Printing Office.

Verba, S., Kelman, S., Orren, G. R., Miyake, I., Watanuki, J., Kabashima, I., & Ferree, G. D., Jr. (1987). *Elites and the idea of equality.* Cambridge, MA: Harvard University Press.

Wilkinson, R. G. (1992). National mortality rates: The impact of inequality? *American Journal of Public Health, 82*(8), 1082–1084.

Chapter 2

Culture, Structure, and the Underclass

• *Michael Morris*

NOWHERE CAN THE CONTINUING RELEVANCE OF THE CRITIQUE OF THE blaming-the-victim process (Ryan, 1971) be more vividly seen than in discussions of the dynamics of poverty. To be sure, the labels have changed over the years. The "culture of poverty," a notion that William Ryan deconstructed with surgical precision in his book, does not appear much anymore in scholarly or public discourse. Its place has been taken, with a vengeance, by the "underclass."

Regardless of one's opinions about the desirability of the "underclass" as a term and/or a theory, its galvanizing effect on the social science community in recent years cannot be denied. Special issues of scholarly journals (e.g., See, 1991; W. J. Wilson, 1989), books (e.g., Devine & Wright, 1993; Gans, 1995; Jencks & Peterson, 1991; Katz, 1993b; Kelso, 1994; Lawson, 1992; Massey & Denton, 1993), conferences and research programs funded by the federal government and prestigious foundations (e.g., Prosser, 1991), and a host of freestanding journal articles all attest to the fact that the underclass is an idea—good, bad, or indifferent—whose time has come and not yet gone (Morris, 1989).

How can the analysis of ideology presented by Ryan in *Blaming the Victim* (1971) and *Equality* (1981) enhance our understanding of the current controversies surrounding the underclass? Indeed, to what extent can this analysis enable us to transcend the conceptual false starts and dead-ends that have plagued much of the underclass literature, especially in terms of policy implications? These are the major questions to be addressed in this chapter.

THE IDEOLOGICAL LEGACY OF THE
CULTURE OF POVERTY DEBATE

Even though the culture of poverty and the underclass are not synonymous concepts, the issues they raise concerning the existence and persistence of poverty have much in common, a reality that has been noted by numerous observers (e.g., Edari, 1991; Gans, 1991; Greenstone, 1991; Jencks, 1992; Katz, 1989; Lemann, 1986; Morris, 1989; Peterson, 1991; Stafford & Ladner, 1990; W. J. Wilson, 1987). Foremost among these issues is the long-standing debate between the "cultural determinists" and the "structuralists," to use Carole Marks's (1991) terms. When explaining poverty, theorists in the former group emphasize the poor's psychological and behavioral characteristics (i.c., motivational, subcultural, and life-style factors), while those in the latter focus on the role of society's major economic and political systems and institutions in placing subgroups of the population at risk .

Oversimplification is the inevitable by-product of dichotomizing in social science, and the culturalist-structuralist distinction is no exception. In fact, most culturalists do acknowledge that culture represents an adaptation to a surrounding environment, an environment that includes the economic and political institutions that structuralists believe are crucial (e.g., J. Q. Wilson, 1994). And few structuralists would deny that, in a labor market that cannot accommodate all those who seek well-paid employment, behaviors such as dropping out of school, taking drugs, or becoming a teenage mother can significantly impair one's chances of avoiding or escaping poverty through work. What separates culturalists and structuralists is the *relative importance* they assign to the two categories of causal factors (Ellwood, 1988).

These contrasting emphases reflect one of the fundamental dimensions that, in Ryan's (1981, 1994) view, underlie ideologies concerning economic stratification: the extent to which human behavior is believed to be internally, as opposed to externally, motivated. He hypothesizes that those who regard high levels of stratification as acceptable and even desirable (the "Fair Play" perspective) are likely to be internally oriented (i.e., culturalists), while those who advocate greater economic equality ("Fair Shares") tend to be externally oriented (i.e., structuralists).

Against this background, it should not be surprising that the cultural-structural debate concerning poverty has been waged for decades among social scientists, especially given Ryan's (1981) claim that ideological questions such as those involving internal versus external causation "can be argued about forever because they cannot be settled in any finally convincing way. A given person's answer . . . is almost surely a reflection of values, of unquestioned assumptions and beliefs that are taken for granted, and are *experienced* as the perception of facts, of *reality*" (p. 48). To the degree this is true, it is wishful thinking to expect that the empirical research of psychologists, sociologists, economists, anthropologists, and others on the ideologically laden topic of poverty dynamics will ever resolve these issues to the satisfaction of all concerned, although some light is bound to be shed on them.

It was into this conceptual mine field that Oscar Lewis (1959, 1966, 1969) wandered when he developed the notion of the culture of poverty in the 1950s and 1960s. Although, strictly speaking, Lewis's theorizing in this domain incorporated both cultural *and* structural components, the latter received relatively little attention in the maelstrom of controversy that swirled around his ideas (e.g., Leacock, 1971; Valentine, 1968; Waxman, 1977; Winter, 1971). Thus, the structural factors that Lewis (1969) believed gave rise to the culture of poverty—"a class-stratified, highly individuated, capitalistic society" (p. 188)—faded into the background as various commentators, including Lewis (1969) himself, dissected the implications of his claim that:

> The culture of poverty. . . is not only an adaptation to a set of objective conditions in the larger society. Once it comes into existence, it tends to perpetuate itself from generation to generation because of its effect on the children. By the time slum children are age six or seven, they have usually absorbed the basic values and attitudes of their subculture and are not psychologically geared to take full advantage of the changing conditions or increased opportunities that may occur in their lifetime. (p. 188)

By the time this dissection was completed, the concept of the culture of poverty had been largely discredited among social scientists (e.g., Beeghley, 1983; Hill et al., 1985; Morris & Williamson, 1982; Rigdon, 1988; Rodman, 1977). At a theoretical level, critics found serious flaws in Lewis's use of *cultural* terminology to describe the distinctive characteristics he claimed to have observed among the poor in his case-study investigations. In essence, the data he produced were not viewed as strong enough to justify the interpretative framework he applied to them, especially a framework that his discipline (anthropology) had labored so long and hard to erect. At a more mundane, but no less important, level, researchers who tested the culture-of-poverty hypothesis in a variety of settings in the United States and elsewhere found relatively little support for it (for reviews of this work see Morris & Williamson, 1982, 1986). In general, the studies indicated that the poor were not as distinctive in their values, attitudes, and aspirations as the culture-of-poverty thesis had suggested, and that, in a longitudinal sense, it was unclear how relevant these psychological variables were to economic mobility in the first place.

The demise of the culture-of-poverty perspective within the social science community represented not so much a victory for structuralists as it did a temporary setback for culturalists. The American public has a long history of regarding poverty in individualistic/cultural terms (Kluegel & Smith, 1986; Morris & Williamson, 1982), and a dispute largely confined to university professors and think-tank researchers was not about to produce a sea change in that world view. Indeed, from colonial times to the present, Americans have identified a sizable subgroup of the poor as being "undeserving" or "unworthy" (Katz, 1989). These "disreputable poor," to use David Matza's (1966) phrase, are those "who remain unemployed, or casually or irregularly employed, even during periods of full employment and prosperity" (p. 289). Inherent in the notion of disreputable poverty are internal, as opposed to external, attributions about the causes of low income (e.g., the accusation that commitment to the work ethic is lacking). Consequently, conceptions of disreputable poverty are, as a practical matter, inextricably linked to *moral* evaluations of a subgroup of the poor, and the various labels used to identify this subgroup—no matter how scientific they may sound—all "serve to isolate one group of poor people from the rest, and stigmatize them" (Katz, 1989, p. 10).

In historical terms, then, the decline and fall of culture-of-poverty terminology did little more than set the stage for the emergence of yet another linguistic device for focusing attention on the undeserving poor. With the arrival of the "underclass," this succession had indeed taken place.

THE UNDERCLASS: HOW MUCH MORE THAN DÉJÀ VU?

An examination of the way in which scholarly analysis of the underclass has evolved over the past three decades yields at least two insights having special relevance for this chapter. First, Ryan's delineation of the blaming-the-victim process has had an undeniable impact on the sensitivities that many commentators have brought to the topic. Second, ideological dynamics relevant to poverty continue to pervade the conceptualizations that are put forth, with theorists often appearing to be unaware that such an influence is occurring. In the discussion that follows, both of these issues will be highlighted.

Although a detailed review of the development of the underclass concept is beyond the scope of this chapter (for such a history, see Aponte, 1990), it is important to realize that, as originally formulated by Gunnar Myrdal (1963), the underclass represented a notion that was predominantly *structural* in nature. It referred to a "useless and miserable substratum" (Myrdal, 1963, p. 35) of the population that, because of its relatively low level of skill and education, was highly vulnerable to the chronic unemployment and underemployment generated by labor market forces in a society that was becoming increasingly credentialed. Myrdal viewed the members of this substratum as being poorly positioned to take advantage of the major routes to upward mobility offered by society and as not benefiting from the structurally oriented government policies that provided economic assistance to those above them in the class structure. Myrdal's underclass was composed of true victims, with no blame assigned to them. Although he predicted that the underclass would eventually become "disheartened and apathetic," with children living in a "home environment" ill-suited to upward mobility (Myrdal, 1963, p. 42), it is clear from Myrdal's analysis that he did not believe these factors held the key to understanding the underclass's plight.

As the popular and scholarly literature on the underclass mushroomed in the 1980s and 1990s, it was inevitable that portraits would emerge in which individualistic themes received much more attention (e.g., Auletta, 1982). In analyses that emphasize these variables, the underclass tends to be defined in terms of " 'abnormal' behavioral or cultural characteristics—in particular, present orientation, lack of a work ethic, sexual promiscuity, and illegitimacy. These characteristics prevent participation in 'normal' economic and social activities and make welfare dependency the preferred choice" (Heisler, 1991, p. 463). Ultimately, then, the underclass represents "a shorthand term for the behavioral and attitudinal problems of inner-city minorities" (Heisler, 1991, p. 464). Nowhere can this perspective be seen more starkly than in the work of political scientist Lawrence Mead (1992), for whom the underclass is, most fundamentally, "a disorganized group unable to get ahead because of a lack not so much of opportunity as of personal organization" (p. 29; see also J. Q. Wilson, 1994).

These characterizations of the underclass, typically labeled as "conservative" or "neoconservative," are what commentators have in mind when they claim that the underclass concept "represent[s] little more than the application of the late Oscar Lewis's culture-of-poverty arguments" (W. J. Wilson, 1987, p. 13), or that the culture of poverty is simply "an earlier generation's equivalent of the underclass" (Gans, 1991, p. 321). When presenting this critique of behavioral/cultural perspectives on the underclass, authors almost always invoke blaming-the-victim terminology, occasionally acknowledging Ryan explicitly, but more often not.

Is the underclass merely the culture of poverty reheated and served on a new plate? Not really. In striking contrast to the case of the culture of poverty, where structuralists made virtually no attempt to render Lewis's original concept viable by salvaging its macro-level (i.e., economic and political) components, there have been ambitious—and in some cases widely publicized—efforts to develop detailed structural models of the underclass (e.g., Katz, 1993a; Massey & Denton, 1993; W. J. Wilson, 1987). As a result, the underclass has proven to be a much more popular sobriquet than the culture of poverty ever was, embraced not only by conservatives but by many liberals as well. A number of factors have contributed to this latter group's acceptance of the term (see Heisler, 1991; Morris, 1989; Stafford & Ladner, 1990); underlying all of them, however, is the belief that it is possible to construct theoretical models of the underclass that are immune to the blaming-the-victim critique.

The work of sociologist William Julius Wilson (1987) is, by far, the best-known example of this structuralist genre, with his hypotheses concerning the underclass dominating the research agenda in recent years (Mincy, 1994). Wilson's focus is the poverty and related social problems experienced by black, inner-city populations. In his view, these problems have grown in the past several decades due to the interaction of a number of structural factors, which include the following: (1) a decreased demand for low-skilled and semiskilled labor in urban areas; (2) the resulting decline in the number of black males who represent economically attractive candidates for marriage, which in turn increases out-of-wedlock childbearing and welfare dependency among black females; (3) the exodus of upwardly mobile blacks from urban ghettos, a process that, by definition, elevates the rates of poverty and related problems in these areas; and (4) the diminishing presence, due to (3), of role models, social networks, and a general "social milieu" that could effectively link inner-city residents to patterns of upward mobility sanctioned by the larger society.

In identifying this fourth variable—"social isolation" (W. J. Wilson, 1987, p. 61)—as an important one, Wilson is acknowledging that any comprehensive analysis of the underclass must include a component that is at least partially interpretable in cultural terms. As a structuralist, however, he is emphatic in pointing out that his model of the underclass should not be confused with those that are primarily cultural: "The concept of *social isolation* . . . highlights the fact that culture is a response to social structural constraints and opportunities. From a public policy perspective, this would mean shifting the focus from changing subcultural traits (as suggested by the "culture of poverty" thesis) to changing the structure of constraints and opportunities" (W. J. Wilson, 1987, p. 61).

Recently, however, Wilson has expressed doubts concerning his (or anyone else's) ability to conceptualize the underclass in a fashion that could protect the term from the pejorative, blaming-the-victim connotations that
tainted the culture-of-poverty perspective. Indeed, in his 1990 presidential
address to the American Sociological Association, he used the phrase "ghetto
poor" rather than "underclass" in presenting his model of poverty dynamics in the inner city (W. J. Wilson, 1991: see, however, W. J. Wilson, 1992).
Whether this self-described attempt "to focus our attention less on controversy and more on research and theoretical issues" (W. J. Wilson, 1991, p.
11) will prove to be successful remains to be seen, but a certain amount of
skepticism would seem to be warranted. As Mincy (1994) observes, "there
is nothing particularly flattering about the term 'ghetto poor' " (p. 134). Over
time, this latter phrase could be expected to take on the same negative attributes as the labels that preceded it, and another chapter in the history of
word substitution concerning the disreputable poor (Matza, 1966) would
have been written. Indeed, as long as the poverty of this population is subject to ideologically based perceptions involving the internal-external dimension, there is little reason to believe that *any* phrase used to identify or
describe it could escape being employed for blaming-the-victim purposes. To
the extent that this is true, the concerns of structuralists who object to underclass terminology (e.g., Gans, 1991) are probably misplaced. Their *real*
argument is with the cultural analyses that are put forth, analyses that are
bound to arise no matter what label is used.

Of the four factors that Wilson hypothesized were involved in the
growth of the ghetto underclass, the one that has been most consistently documented is the shrinking of the low-skilled, moderate-wage labor market in
urban America (Mincy, 1994; see also Burtless, 1990; Murphy & Welch,
1993; Sugrue, 1993). Indeed, on the basis of the available evidence, it would
not be unreasonable to conclude that this shrinkage is the primary structural
change to which underclass life styles represent an adaptation.

The remaining three components in Wilson's model have received mixed
support (Mincy, 1994). Although some studies have found that the movement of economically successful blacks out of ghetto neighborhoods has
contributed to the growing poverty in those areas, others (e.g., Massey &
Denton, 1993) indicate that the persistence of residentially based *racial*
segregation is much more important than out-migration in producing the
concentrated poverty and other characteristics associated with underclass
groups. Douglas Massey and Nancy Denton (1993), for example, conclude
on the basis of their research that "residential segregation is the principal organizational feature of American society that is responsible for the creation
of the urban underclass" (p. 9).

With regard to the social isolation hypothesis, some investigations have found a quantitative relationship between levels of this variable and such behaviors as drug and alcohol use, sexual conduct, out-of-wedlock births, criminal activity, and educational attainment, while others have not. Finally, there is little quantitative evidence to support Wilson's hypothesis that the labor-market troubles of black males are responsible for declining marriage rates among the minority underclass (Mincy, 1994; see, however, Lichter, McLaughlin, Kephart, & Landry, 1992).

It is important to note that Wilson's model of underclass dynamics fares much better when viewed through the lens of *qualitative* research (Mincy, 1994). Taken as a whole, ethnographers' accounts of the lives of underclass members (e.g., Anderson, 1990, 1991; Hagedorn, 1988) tend to be consistent with all four, rather than just the first, of his hypotheses.

One's preferences for quantitative or qualitative studies notwithstanding, there is no doubt that social science knowledge concerning poverty dynamics has increased significantly as a result of research motivated by questions about the underclass. Insofar as *any* increase in knowledge is a good thing, this outcome should be applauded. An ovation may be less called for, however, than the sound of one hand clapping. A lukewarm response seems appropriate, given the results of attempts to estimate the *size* of the underclass. As with many concepts in social science, a consensus on how to define the underclass operationally has proven elusive. Consequently, the estimates that have been generated vary significantly (Mincy, 1994). Even so, the assessments that have been accorded the greatest credibility are consistent in indicating that the underclass represents, *at most,* 10 percent to 15 percent of the overall poverty population (Ellwood, 1988). Indeed, this is a smaller percentage of the poor than Lewis (1969) believed the culture of poverty represented (20 percent).

To be sure, the problems experienced by and associated with the underclass are serious and should not be minimized. Nevertheless, the fact that such a small subgroup of the poor has been the subject of so much discussion suggests that ideological concerns play a nontrivial role in the process. More specifically, one could argue that the focusing of scholarly and public attention on the underclass represents a version of what Ryan (1971) has called "Savage Discovery," in which the objective is to identify "those who 'have' the problem in question, to separate them out and define them in some way as a special group, a group that is *different* from the population in general" (p. 9).

What is noteworthy in the present context is that this process diverts attention from the *much larger* subgroup of the population that is poor even though they do *not* share the troublesome behavioral characteristics of the underclass (Marks, 1991). Under these circumstances it is extremely difficult to retain poverty as the organizing principle for analysis, and very tempting to use the behavioral characteristics instead. Thus, we have Savage Discovery "with a twist." That is, after identifying a problem that is experienced by many people (i.e., poverty), a very small and distinctive subgroup *within* that population is located. In relatively short order the distinctive characteristics of that subgroup begin to command a disproportionate amount of attention in discussion of the original problem, which includes the larger group not having those characteristics.

Contributing to this shift in focus is a tendency on the part of the nonunderclass to underestimate the similarities and exaggerate the differences between themselves and the underclass. Several processes have been hypothesized to account for this phenomenon, including the images of the underclass presented in the mass media, attributional biases (including the Fundamental Attribution Error), social comparisons involving feelings of guilt and personal responsibility for the sufferings of others, and the greater salience of intergroup differences in *behavior* when contrasted with intergroup similarities in *values and aspirations* (Cook & Curtin, 1987; Morris & Williamson, 1982; Pettigrew, 1980). All of these factors probably play a role, thereby making the perceived distinctiveness of the underclass a classic example of an overdetermined outcome.

DISTINGUISHING THE FOREST FROM THE TREES IN UNDERCLASS POLICY

In theory, the concept of the underclass can accommodate virtually any combination of culturally and structurally oriented policy recommendations, depending on where a policy advocate resides on the internal-external ideological continuum. And even a cursory review of the policy proposals that have been put forth confirm this expectation; the suggestions range all the way from training in parenting skills to guaranteed public service employment; from programs teaching values, responsibility, and bicultural competence to guaranteed medical care, community empowerment, and the venerable guaranteed annual income (Devine & Wright, 1993; Ellwood, 1988; Mincy, 1994; J. Q. Wilson, 1994).

Against this background, a theme that is increasingly encountered in discussions of the underclass is the need to move beyond the dichotomous, either/or approach to policy that has traditionally accompanied the culture-versus-structure debate concerning poverty (e.g., Corbett, 1993; Ellwood , 1988; Greenstone, 1991; Jencks, 1992; Katz, 1993a: Marks, 1991; W. J.

Wilson, 1991). Implicit in many of these analyses is the notion that the poor population is very heterogeneous and that policies designed to combat poverty must reflect the complex set of causes that contribute to low-income status. Thus, a comprehensive antipoverty strategy would include both structural and cultural components, coordinated in an innovative and effective fashion.

Thinking in terms of structure *and* culture rather than structure *or* culture certainly represents a step forward, although one might have a difficult time finding a significant number of theorists, researchers, and policy-makers who would ever admit to having engaged in the "either/or" mode of analysis. A much more important issue, however, is whether this shift represents a truly substantive change in the way in which the underclass "problem" is conceptualized. Judged according to the standards employed by Ryan in *Equality,* the answer would seem to be, "not really."

Why might the verdict be so harsh? Answering this question is perhaps best accomplished through the use of a metaphor. The image that probably captures most vividly the status of the underclass in contemporary social science discourse is that of a major league baseball team that is a perennial last-place finisher. These dismal outcomes year after year might be due to a variety of internal factors, such as poor hitting, poor pitching, and poor fielding, any or all of which could be traced to the players' lack of ability and/or desire to win. On the other hand, more externally oriented analyses might point out that the team's ownership is undercapitalized or that the franchise's geographical location is unattractive to star players who would make the club more competitive if they joined. Although both sets of observations concerning this "underclass" team may be valid, none of them call into question the fundamental desirability of a competitive system that guarantees that, every year, there will be a team that finishes last.

In the case of baseball, there are very few sportswriters who would maintain that such a question needs to be asked. It is, however, precisely the type of question that Ryan raises in *Equality* when he examines economic stratification. When discussing the underclass, the mainstream social science community has tended to follow the sports-writing model. The policy prescriptions that have been generated (or revived) typically have as their primary objective a modest ascent in the class hierarchy by the underclass, with the level of the (barely) nonpoor working class possibly being reached in the short term (Morris, in press). Justification of programs usually invokes a Fair Play ideology of equality of opportunity, either in terms of helping the underclass take advantage of existing opportunities (internal/cultural interventions) or creating new ones for them (external/structural interventions). Once the assistance is provided, the longer term expectation is that individual members of the (former) underclass will experience additional upward mobility to whatever extent is consistent with their abilities and motivation.

The *overall* high level of economic inequality within society (see Danziger & Gottschalk, 1993; Danziger & Weinberg, 1994) is not explicitly addressed by these policy initiatives, and there is no reason to believe that they would produce any major shift in the distribution of resources between classes. At the upper reaches of the class hierarchy a relatively small segment of the population would continue to control a disproportionately high percentage of these resources, and at the other end there would be a much larger group possessing a disproportionately low percentage. This latter group would include many former members of the underclass, along with others from the lower class, the working poor, and the near-poor, individuals whose life chances could not be credibly described in terms of "equality of opportunity." Although their day-to-day existence might not be as desperately deprived as that of the (presumably defunct) underclass, they would still be clearly identifiable as "last-place finishers" in the stratification game.

This outcome would seem to be inevitable as long as the policy agenda is driven by problem definitions that leave unquestioned the core premises, assumptions, and values underlying the stratification system as a whole. The fact that such an examination might be criticized as Marxist, socialist, utopian, or merely unfashionable does not deter Ryan in *Equality*. He presents a compelling case on behalf of significant resource redistribution in the United States, a redistribution in the direction of greater equality that goes far beyond anything that has been or is likely to be proposed by the major participants in the underclass debate. In the Fair Shares society he envisions, the distance between last place and first place in the economic hierarchy would be diminished to the point where such designations would carry little meaning. In social class terms, it would be a profoundly different United States than the one that exists now.

Would there still be an underclass in a Fair Shares society? Optimists—who are likely to be those with an ideological predisposition to view the world in terms of "a collectivity of similar persons behaving in response to their environmental situations" (Ryan, 1981, p. 48)—would probably say no, while pessimists—those who perceive "unique individuals acting on the basis of internal factors" (Ryan, 1981, p. 48)—would probably say yes. To be sure, predictions at this level represent, at best, an ideological Rorschach test. Nevertheless, if society's resources *were* shared to the degree that Ryan proposes, it is hard to imagine how a severely deprived, behaviorally distinct subgroup of the population could emerge. This is not to say that substance abuse, out-of-wedlock births, gang violence, dropping out of school, and other problems associated with the underclass would be reduced to negligible levels in such a society. But they probably would be reduced somewhat, perhaps by a large amount, and are likely to be distributed throughout society in a pattern that does not lend itself as easily to stereotyped perceptions of an underclass as the current pattern does.

It might be argued, of course, that the underclass problem does not require a solution as "drastic" as the Fair Shares society proposed by Ryan, and that a combination of more limited structural and cultural strategies would be equal to the task. Comprehensive reviews of the evaluation literature concerning these interventions raise serious doubts, however (Danziger, Sandefur, & Weinberg, 1994; Morris, in press; Morris & Williamson, 1986, 1987). For example, programs that straightforwardly redistribute resources (e.g., Social Security) have proven to be much more effective in reducing poverty than those that attempt to achieve this goal indirectly by increasing individuals' economic self-sufficiency (e.g., skill training). And it is the latter, equality-of-opportunity approach that has dominated the policy initiatives recommended for dealing with the underclass. Put more bluntly, it is not clear that Fair Play strategies, regardless of whether they are culturally or structurally oriented, are potent enough, even when combined, to resolve either the symptomatic or more substantive social class problems symbolized by the underclass. The available empirical evidence may not allow us to draw definitive conclusions about what *would* work in these circumstances, but it is of great value in helping us determine what we should be skeptical of.

CONCLUSION

Discussion of the underclass in the 1980s and 1990s by social scientists has been much more sophisticated and productive than it was when the topic was the culture of poverty in the 1960s and 1970s, an improvement that can be attributed in no small measure to the heightened sensitivity to structural issues generated by Ryan's delineation of the blaming-the-victim process. This process does not represent the culmination of his thinking about such matters, however. His examination in *Equality* of more fundamental ideological issues as they relate to Fair Play versus Fair Share models of society has important implications for the quality of the underclass debate, as this chapter has attempted to demonstrate. The time has come to move beyond claims, however well intentioned and justified they may be in a narrow sense, that our analyses of the underclass do not blame the victim. When such assertions are not linked to more comprehensive models of resource distribution and social class dynamics, it is difficult to avoid responding, sympathetically but with disappointment, "Saying it's so doesn't necessarily make it so."

REFERENCES

Anderson, E. (1990). *Streetwise: Race, class, and change in an urban community.* Chicago: University of Chicago Press.

Anderson, E. (1991). Neighborhood effects on teenage pregnancy. In C. Jencks & P. E. Peterson (Eds.), *The urban underclass* (pp. 375–398). Washington, DC: Brookings Institution.

Aponte, R. (1990). Definitions of the underclass: A critical analysis. In H. J. Gans (Ed.), *Sociology in America* (pp. 117–137). Newbury Park, CA: Sage.

Auletta, K. (1982). *The underclass.* New York: Random House.

Beeghley, L. (1983). *Living poorly in America.* New York: Praeger.

Burtless, G. (Ed.). (1990). *A future of lousy jobs? The changing structure of U.S. wages.* Washington, DC: Brookings Institution.

Cook, T. D., & Curtin, T. R. (1987). The mainstream and the underclass: Why are the differences so salient and the similarities so unobtrusive? In J. C. Masters & W. P. Smith (Eds.), *Social comparison, social justice, and relative deprivation: Theoretical, empirical, and policy perspectives* (pp. 217–264). Hillsdale, NJ: Lawrence Erlbaum Associates.

Corbett, T. (1993). Child poverty and welfare reform: Progress or paralysis? *Focus, 15*(1), 1–17.

Danziger, S., & Gottschalk, P. (Eds.). (1993). *Uneven tides: Rising inequality in America.* New York: Russell Sage Foundation.

Danziger, S., Sandefur, G. D., & Weinberg, D. H. (Eds.). (1994). *Confronting poverty: Prescriptions for change.* Cambridge, MA: Harvard University Press.

Danziger, S., & Weinberg, D. H. (1994). The historical record: Trends in family income, inequality, and poverty. In S. Danziger, G. D. Sandefur, & D. H. Weinberg (Eds.)., *Confronting poverty: Prescriptions for change* (pp. 18–50). Cambridge, MA: Harvard University Press.

Devine, J. A., & Wright, J. D. (1993). *The greatest of evils: Urban poverty and the American underclass.* New York: Aldine De Gruyter.

Edari, R. S. (1991). "Underclass": An inquiry into its theoretical status and ideological dimensions. *Nature, Society, and Thought, 4,* 31–56.

Ellwood, D. T. (1988). *Poor support: Poverty in the American family.* New York: Basic Books.

Gans, H. J. (1991). *People, plans, and policies: Essays on poverty, racism, and other national urban problems.* New York: Columbia University Press.

Gans, H. J. (1995). *The war against the poor: The underclass and antipoverty policy.* New York: Basic Books.

Greenstone, J. D. (1991). Culture, rationality, and the underclass. In C. Jencks & P. E. Peterson (Eds.), *The urban underclass* (pp. 399–408). Washington, DC: Brookings Institution.

Hagedorn, J. M. (1988). *People and folks: Gangs, crime, and the underclass in a rust belt city.* Chicago: Lake View Press.

Heisler, B. S. (1991). A comparative perspective on the underclass: Questions of urban poverty, race, and citizenship. *Theory and Society, 20,* 455–483.

Hill, M. S., Augustyniak, S., Duncan, G. J., Gurin, G., Gurin, P., Liker, J. K., Morgan, J. N., & Ponza, M. (1985). *Motivation and economic mobility.* Ann Arbor, MI: Institute for Social Research.

Jencks, C. (1992). *Rethinking social policy: Race, poverty, and the underclass.* Cambridge, MA: Harvard University Press.

Jencks, C., & Peterson, P. E. (Eds.). (1991). *The urban underclass.* Washington, DC: Brookings Institution.

Katz, M. B. (1989). *The undeserving poor: From the war on poverty to the war on welfare.* New York: Pantheon.

Katz, M. B. (1993a). Reframing the "underclass" debate. In M. B. Katz (Ed.), *The "underclass" debate: Views from history* (pp. 440–472). Princeton: Princeton University Press.

Katz, M. B. (Ed.). (1993b). *The "underclass" debate: Views from history.* Princeton: Princeton University Press.

Kelso, W. A. (1994). *Poverty and the underclass: Changing perceptions of the poor in America.* New York: New York University Press.

Kluegel, J. R., & Smith, E. R. (1986). *Beliefs about inequality: Americans' views of what is and what ought to be.* New York: Aldine de Gruyter.

Lawson, B. E. (Ed.). (1992). *The underclass question.* Philadelphia: Temple University Press.

Leacock, E. B. (Ed.). (1971). *The culture of poverty: A critique.* New York: Simon and Schuster.

Lemann, N. (1986, June). The origins of the underclass. *Atlantic Monthly,* 31–55.

Lewis, O. (1959). *Five families: Mexican case studies in the culture of poverty.* New York: Basic Books.

Lewis, O. (1966). *La Vida: A Puerto Rican family in the culture of poverty.* New York: Random House.

Lewis, O. (1969). The culture of poverty. In D. P. Moynihan (Ed.), *On understanding poverty: Perspectives from the social sciences* (pp. 187–200). New York: Basic Books.

Lichter, D. T., McLaughlin, D. K., Kephart, G., & Landry, D. J. (1992). Race and the retreat from marriage: A shortage of marriageable men? *American Sociological Review, 57,* 781–799.

Marks, C. (1991). The urban underclass. *Annual Review of Sociology, 17,* 445–466.

Massey, D. S., & Denton, N. A. (1993). *American apartheid: Segregation and the making of the underclass.* Cambridge, MA: Harvard University Press.

Matza, D. (1966). The disreputable poor. In R. Bendix & S. M. Lipset (Eds.), *Class, status, and power: Social stratification in comparative perspective* (2nd ed., pp. 289–302). New York: Free Press.

Mead, L. M. (1992). *The new politics of poverty: The non-working poor in America.* New York: Basic Books.

Mincy, R. B. (1994). The underclass: Concept, controversy, and evidence. In S. Danziger, G. D. Sandefur, & D. H. Weinberg (Eds.), *Confronting poverty: Prescriptions for change* (pp. 109–146). Cambridge, MA: Harvard University Press.

Morris, M. (1989). From the culture of poverty to the underclass: An analysis of a shift in public language. *The American Sociologist, 20,* 123–133.

Morris, M. (in press). Psychological perspectives on welfare reform. In C. E. Stout (Ed.), *The integration of psychological principles in policy development.* New York: Praeger Publishers.

Morris, M., & Williamson, J. B. (1982). Stereotyping and social class: A focus on poverty. In A. G. Miller (Ed.), *In the eye of the beholder: Contemporary issues in stereotyping* (pp. 411–465). New York: Praeger.

Morris, M., & Williamson, J. B. (1986). *Poverty and public policy: An analysis of federal intervention efforts.* Westport, CT: Greenwood Press.

Morris, M., & Williamson, J. B. (1987). Workfare: The poverty/dependence trade-off. *Social Policy, 18*(1), 13–16, 49–50.

Murphy, K. M., & Welch, F. (1993). Industrial change and the rising importance of skill. In S. Danziger & P. Gottschalk (Eds.), *Uneven tides: Rising inequality in America* (pp. 101–132). New York: Russell Sage Foundation.

Myrdal, G. (1963). *Challenge to affluence.* New York: Pantheon.

Peterson, P. E. (1991). The urban underclass and the poverty paradox. In C. Jencks & P. E. Peterson (Eds.), *The urban underclass* (pp. 3–27). Washington, D.C.: Brookings Institution.

Pettigrew, T. F. (1980). Social psychology's potential contributions to an understanding of poverty. In V. T. Covello (Ed.), *Poverty and public policy: An evaluation of social science research* (pp. 189–233). Cambridge, MA: Schenkman.

Prosser, W. R. (1991). The underclass: Assessing what we have learned. *Focus, 13*(2), 1–18.

Rigdon, S. E. (1988). *The culture facade: Art, science, and politics in the work of Oscar Lewis.* Urbana: University of Illinois Press.

Rodman, H. (1977). Culture of poverty: Rise and fall of a concept. *Sociological Review, 25,* 867–876.

Ryan, W. (1971). *Blaming the victim.* New York: Pantheon.

Ryan, W. (1981). *Equality.* New York: Pantheon.

Ryan, W. (1994). Many cooks, brave men, apples, and oranges: How people think about equality. *American Journal of Community Psychology, 22,* 25–35.

See, K. O. (Ed.). (1991). Special issue on the underclass in the United States. *Social Problems, 38*(4).

Stafford, W. W., & Ladner, J. (1990). Political dimensions of the underclass concept. In H. J. Gans (Ed.), *Sociology in America* (pp. 138–155). Newbury Park, CA: Sage.

Sugrue, T. J. (1993). The structures of urban poverty: The reorganization of space and work in three periods of American history. In M. B. Katz (Ed.), *The "un-*

derclass" debate: Views from history (pp. 85–117). Princeton: Princeton University Press.

Valentine, C. A. (1968). *Culture and poverty: Critique and counter-proposals.* Chicago: University of Chicago Press.

Waxman, C. I. (1977). *The stigma of poverty: A critique of poverty theories and policies.* New York: Pergamon Press.

Wilson, J. Q. (1994). Culture, incentives, and the underclass. In H. J. Aaron, T. E. Mann, & T. Taylor (Eds.), *Values and public policy* (pp. 54–80). Washington, DC: Brookings Institution.

Wilson, W. J. (1987). *The truly disadvantaged: The inner city, the underclass, and public policy.* Chicago: University of Chicago Press.

Wilson, W. J. (Ed.). (1989). The ghetto underclass: Social science perspectives. *The Annals of the American Academy of Political and Social Science, 501.*

Wilson, W. J. (1991). Studying inner-city dislocations: The challenge of public agenda research. *American Sociological Review, 56,* 1–14.

Wilson, W. J. (1992). Foreword. In B. E. Lawson (Ed.), *The underclass question* (pp. xi–xii). Philadelphia: Temple University Press.

Winter, J. A. (Ed.). (1971). *The poor: A culture of poverty or a poverty of culture?* Grand Rapids, MI: William B. Eerdmans.

Chapter 3

The Homeless Shelter and the Nineteenth-Century Poorhouse: Comparing Notes from Two Eras of "Indoor Relief"

• Dennis P. Culhane

> Miserable, poorly managed, underfinanced institutions, trapped by their own contradictions, poorhouses failed to meet any of the goals so confidently predicted by their sponsors. (Katz, 1986, p. 3)

AS PUBLIC EXPENDITURES FOR THE PROVISION OF SHELTER TO HOMELESS men, women, and children continue to grow (U.S. Department of Housing and Urban Development, 1989), so does public anxiety over the fate of these institutions and their residents (Steinfels, 1992). Expectations that shelters would reduce the visibility of homelessness and rehabilitate their clients have been replaced by concerns that shelters are ever-expanding bureaucracies lacking direction and purpose (Roberts, 1991). Governmentally prescribed needs-tests, behavioral standards, and caps on length of stay have seized the initiative from homeless advocates who have attempted to establish "open door" policies on shelter (City of Philadelphia, 1990b; Morgan, 1991b; Spolar, 1991). Indeed some cities, such as Philadelphia and Washington, D.C., have reversed earlier commitments effectively protecting an unconditional right to shelter and have reduced ("downsized") nightly shelter capacity (Culhane, 1992; Spolar, 1991). Other cities, such as New York, have likewise confronted open resistance to new shelter development (Morgan, 1991a).

The problems confronting homeless people and the officials charged with their protection are not new. They echo those from other periods in American history, when private and public welfare organizations built congregate facilities for the purpose of "poor relief." Poorhouses and almshouses as well as their descendants—prisons, asylums, and municipal lodging houses—have faced similar crises in public confidence, questions about their social utility, and concerns over their burdensome cost. Yet the impulse to institutionalize the poor has found a receptive audience throughout American history.

That history is the subject of a book by Michael Katz (1986), *In the Shadow of the Poorhouse: A Social History of Welfare in America,* in which he traces the continuing contradictions and deficiencies of the American welfare system to the early nineteenth century. According to Katz's research, poorhouses were created to deter people from seeking cash assistance from local welfare authorities, thus ostensibly balancing concern for the poor with the preservation of the work ethic. Katz argues that the current debate over welfare "dependence" and the "underclass" is a refashioning of this time-worn theme, although he concludes that this debate has always had more of a basis in politics than in the exigencies of life at the margins of the labor economy.

Such historical perspective has been lacking in contemporary discussions of homelessness and the adequacy of shelter provision. Hopper (1990) has conducted one of the few historical analyses of the current shelter system, based on the legacy of New York and Chicago lodging houses. His study links the growth and contraction of homeless shelters throughout the last century with dynamics in the labor market, the capacity of families to support unemployed members, and gaps in unemployment assistance. Hopper argues that shelters have historically perpetuated the demoralization they sought to end by ignoring the economic nature of homelessness and by favoring punitive methods both for determining "worthiness" for assistance and for rehabilitation.

Building on that work, this chapter uses the history of the nineteenth-century poorhouse, as described in the first chapter of Katz's text, to compare and contrast its historical context, functions, and structure with those of the contemporary homeless shelter.

THE HISTORICAL CONTEXTS OF POORHOUSES AND HOMELESS SHELTERS

In the poorhouse era, as in our own period, the transforming power of the economy forced a major reorganization of traditional social relations, creating new forms of poverty, and public anxiety about the impact of lost industries, lost wages, and lost ways of life. In the early nineteenth century it was the widespread introduction of waged labor that radically redefined the relationship between workers and the products of their labor. The development of manufacturing technologies eroded the position of independent artisans, displacing young and old workers alike. Economic development was uneven, characterized by significant temporal and regional variations. Katz (1986) describes the unsteady and seasonal nature of work, how workers were often forced to migrate great distances to find employment, and the vulnerability of the working class to the frequent, periodic depressions. Wages were at best inadequate. Katz cites a calculation from 1828 based on the costs of goods that revealed that a household in which two adults were employed full-time, year-round, could not meet even the "bare bones budget," the conceptual equivalent of today's "poverty level." The threat of illness haunted most families, as even a short-term affliction could send a family into destitution. Unskilled workers, many of them newly arrived immigrants, flooded urban labor markets. As Katz (1986) observes, "the availability of work for every able-bodied person who really wants a job is one of the enduring myths of American history. In fact, work was not more universally available in the early and mid-nineteenth century than it is today" (p. 6).

Whereas industrialization, urbanization, and European immigration transformed the United States in the early nineteenth century, in the latter half of the twentieth century the country experienced a very different but equally significant set of transforming forces that were near-inversions of their nineteenth-century counterparts: deindustrialization, suburbanization, and black urban migration. Important signs of these structural shifts began to emerge dramatically around World War II. Indeed, a literature has developed that explicitly links many of these postwar structural changes to the recent growth of homelessness (Burt, 1992; Hopper & Hamburg, 1986; Hopper, Susser, & Conover, 1985; Stern, 1984).

Beginning in the 1950s, the movement of manufacturing from central cities, first to the suburbs and then beyond our national borders, led to a steep decline in the absolute and relative share of manufacturing employment in urban centers. In its place arose a two-tiered service economy, with relatively stable work at high wages for the better-educated population, primarily from the suburbs, and relatively unstable, temporary and part-time work at low wages for the unskilled laborers, primarily from the cities (Harrison & Bluestone, 1988). Philadelphia, for example, had lost 18 percent of its 1950 employment base by 1980, with particularly devastating losses in the manufacturing sector (a loss of 210,590 jobs). The surrounding suburban counties, however, saw a 170 percent increase in their employment base. The relative prosperity of the Philadelphia suburbs resulted in a 23 percent higher median income, by 1980, with only 46 percent of the city's unemployment rate (Summers & Luce, 1987).

The inequities that emerged between the city and its suburbs were destined to have a racial character, as Philadelphia's African American population increased threefold, from 220,000 or 11 percent of the population in 1950 to 630,000 or 38 percent in 1980. As African Americans urbanized, job opportunities suburbanized—a pattern repeated in many cities throughout the United States. Correspondingly, the unemployement rate for young black men has grown to twice that of whites nationally, a measure that conceals the equally significant declines in labor force participation among black youth (Wilson, 1987). And as unemployment has increased among African Americans, so has the economic insecurity of the unemployed. By 1988, only 32 percent of unemployed workers received unemployment benefits, the lowest proportion since the program was initiated during the Great Depression, and less than half the rate only thirteen years earlier (75 percent in 1975) (US Employment and Training Administration, Washington, D.C., January 29, 1993). Even low-wage workers with full-time jobs are more likely to be poor, as the value of minimum wage fell from 118 percent of the poverty level for a family of three in 1967 to 68 percent of the poverty level for a similar family in 1990 (McCambridge, 1992).

As jobs and people suburbanized, urban unemployment grew, and wages and benefits declined, housing costs continued to grow. Consequently, the rent burden (defined as the percent of income devoted to rent) increased by 28.7 percent from 1970 to 1988 (Burt, 1992). Cushing Dolbeare (1991) reports that the "affordability gap" for the poorest fourth of American households (defined as the shortage of units renting at 30 percent of income) grew fivefold from 1970 to 1991. The differential impact by race of these combined pressures on housing affordability is especially dramatic. Consider that in Philadelphia, the median proportion of income spent on rent by black households rose from 22 percent in 1970 to 53 percent in 1988, while it remained relatively stable for whites, growing from 21 percent to 26 percent (Dolbeare, 1988).

The social and economic transformations of the early nineteenth and late twentieth century occurred under very different historical circumstances. Structural shifts in the economy of both eras exposed unmet needs and increased the demand for public assistance. With the emergence of new forms of poverty and with the growing demand for "poor relief" in urban centers, a debate raged in both periods about the merits of public assistance to the poor. Unfortunately, the change in historical circumstances was not accompanied by a change in the underlying attitudes about poverty and its victims. Stale arguments, failed policies, and, ultimately, an atavistic institutional form were resurrected to cope with the deepening impoverishment of American cities.

ATTACKS ON WELFARE
("OUTDOOR RELIEF")

Poor relief in the beginning of the nineteenth century primarily took the form
of cash assistance, or "outdoor relief." It was funded and distributed through
local public authorities (thus with great regional variation) only to those with
a demonstrated need—those with no family available to care for them in their
homes. Pauper children were frequently taken from their parents, and placed
with farmers and artisans agreeing to train and house them. Some of the poor
were auctioned to the lowest bidder who would care for them. As demand
for relief grew under the combined pressures of industrialization, urbanization, and immigration, so did the tax burden of paying for relief, a fact that
did not go unnoticed by taxpayers (people often received a separate tax bill
for poor relief) and politicians. Searching for an explanation to the growing
"poor rates," Katz (1986) explains that commentators cited the obvious
forces of urbanization and immigration, but "even more, they stressed the
role of intemperance . . . the real villains were existing public poor relief practice and the indiscriminate generosity of private charity" (p. 16).

The attack against outdoor relief was based on the premise that it encouraged idleness and undermined the work ethic. It interfered with the cal-
culus of wages based strictly on the supply of labor and was proof to the
working class that one could live a comfortable life without hard work. According to some observers, outdoor relief was an invitation to the able-bodied poor to become beggars. Critics furthermore claimed that it destroyed
character and weakened its beneficiaries. They lamented the impersonality of
outdoor relief and the class antagonism it promoted. Katz (1986) notes, however, that amidst all their commentary, critics were not concerned with ending poverty, only with determining how to save the "truly needy" from starvation, while keeping the "fake needy" lined up for work: "Indeed it is only
a slight exaggeration to say that the core of most welfare reform in America
since the early nineteenth century has been a war on the able-bodied poor:
an attempt to define, locate, and purge them from the roles of relief" (p. 18)

Reformers set about trying to define behavioral categories of the poor so
that poor relief could be distributed more discriminately (and cheaply). They
tried labels such as the "impotent" versus the "able" and the "permanent
poor" versus the "temporary poor." As markers for these attributes proved
elusive, they turned increasingly to moral categories, such as the "worthy"
versus the "unworthy" poor, and made a distinction between poverty and
pauperism (poverty results from "misfortune," pauperism from "shameful
indolence").

The debate over poverty has not fundamentally changed since the 1820s, and neither have many relief practices. Poor relief in the United States is still administered by local authorities, with great variation from state to state, and is dispensed only to those with demonstrated need (means-tested). Welfare recipients are scrupulously monitored for compliance with arcane and bureaucratic regulations, frequently intended to compel people to work at low wages (Piven & Cloward, 1971, 1982), and are portrayed by critics as morally corrupt persons with little desire for work or for financial independence (Mead, 1986, 1992; Murray, 1984). Attacks on welfare, such as those launched under the Reagan administration, reduced eligibility for cash assistance among single-parent households, the disabled and the working poor (Katz, 1989; Piven & Cloward, 1982; Zinn & Sarri, 1984). States have participated in this assault by allowing the median purchasing power of welfare benefits to deteriorate against inflation 43 percent from 1970 to 1992 (Center on Budget and Policy Priorities, 1992); by allowing Supplemental Security Income (SSI) for the disabled to decline nearly 50 percent against inflation from 1975 to 1989 (Burt, 1992); and, furthermore, by eliminating some programs altogether. Most significantly, many states have either stopped, reduced the monthly allotment for, or severely restricted eligibility for general assistance (GA), the welfare program most likely to benefit single homeless persons and others not covered by federal unemployment insurance or Aid to Families with Dependent Children (AFDC). Burt (1992) reports that in 1987 seventeen states offered *no* general assistance of any kind, that in nine states it was provided only in large urban counties, that in fourteen states it was available only to "unemployables," and that in only seven states was it available statewide, even to "employables." Where GA is available, its value has, like AFDC, lost ground to inflation, forcing people to "choose between necessities" (Burt, 1992, p. 105).

Consider the case of Pennsylvania. In 1982, legislation was introduced and passed by Governor Richard Thornburgh categorically excluding "employables" from receiving GA for nine months out of the year (Act 75). Despite its low value (GA beneficiaries received $96 every two weeks in 1988), GA was perceived as a deterrent to work. Thus Act 75 required the Pennsylvania Department of Public Welfare to determine who among GA applicants were "transitionally needy" (i.e., employable) and to restrict them from receiving cash benefits for most of the year. Cash grants were subsequently restricted for 68,000 Pennsylvania residents deemed unworthy under the law. A study of the law's impact found that 81 percent of those cut from GA had no income from employment at the time of follow-up; that the post-Act 75 reemployment rate for GA recipients was no different from the pre-Act 75 reemployment rate; that the number of beneficiaries who experienced losses of their homes, utilities, cars, and/or furniture due to the inability to pay bills and debts went from a projected 9,044 prior to Act 75 to 17,612 after implementation; that 42 percent reported having to use emergency shelters, food, and clothing programs; that 45 percent were living with relatives or friends and were unable to contribute to household expenses; that 33.2 percent were in "indentured relationships," receiving food and shelter only in exchange for working for the provider of that food and shelter; and that fully 25 percent experienced worse health after the implementation of welfare "reforms" (Advocacy Committee for Emergency Services [ACES], 1984). The period following GA reforms saw the capacity of the Philadelphia shelter system increase by more than 2,000 percent (Culhane, 1992), with demand for shelter being highest among single adults under the age of thirty-five who constituted nearly half of all shelter residents in 1988 (Ryan, Bartelt, & Goldstein, 1988).[1] The link to homelessness would appear obvious. As Katz (1986) has observed for the nineteenth century:

> The years when public officials and charity reformers complained most about an increase in tramps coincided with the general cutback in outdoor relief throughout the country. Most tramps, in fact, were men in their twenties and thirties who had been on the road a relatively short time looking for work. (p. 51)

THE ASSUMPTIONS OF "INDOOR RELIEF"

Disconcerted by the rising costs of outdoor relief and its administration, nineteenth-century reformers advocated replacing cash assistance with the poorhouse, believing it to be a cheaper alternative and a deterrent to outdoor relief. Katz (1986) cites the case of New Bedford, Massachusetts, where "with the opening of the poorhouse, 'their applications' [for outdoor relief] had 'almost entirely ceased.' Once people knew 'that every Pauper must be removed to the Poor House, many causes combined to prevent their application for assistance' " (p. 23).

Poorhouses were expected to be more than cost-efficient deterrents to cash assistance. Developing as part of a more widely held belief among nineteenth-century reformers that new institutions could improve society through their impact on individual personalities, "poorhouses shared in this rehabilitative vision; they would suppress intemperance, the primary cause of pauperism, and inculcate the habit of steady work" (Katz, 1986, p. 11). Sponsored by a combination of public and private interests, poorhouses reflected the imperatives of the new wage economy for a disciplined work force, capable of "steady, punctual, and predictable labor" (Katz, 1986, p.

12). They could presumably transform behavior and character, converting people from idleness to industry through make-work, forced labor, and discipline. Even pauper children were believed to benefit from poorhouses, where they too could be more adequately prepared for a life of labor.

However, as Katz (1986) notes, the poorhouse was "stamped" with irreconcilable contradictions:

> The almshouse was to be at once a refuge for the helpless and a deterrent to the able-bodied; it was supposed to care for the poor humanely and to discourage them from applying for relief. . . . The almshouse was to be both a voluntary institution, entered with no more coercion than the threat of starvation, and, in some cases, a penal institution for vagrants and beggars. . . . If the almshouses worked, the aged and infirm would be held hostage to the war on able-bodied paupers. . . . In the end, one of these poles would have to prevail. . . . In essence, social policy advocated shutting up the old and sick away from their friends and relatives to deter the working class from seeking poor relief. (p. 25)

The able-bodied poor were a persistent problem for poorhouse officials, and their ranks swelled with economic downturns. However, rather than attending to the structural nature of the poverty driving poorhouse utilization, relief reformers believed that better classification was the key to improving poorhouse efficiency. But the dynamic reality of working-class life and the lack of clear criteria by which to separate categories of the poor thwarted reform efforts: "Working class experience was a continuum; no clear line separated the respectable poor from paupers. This is why all attempts to divide the poor into classes and all policies based on those divisions ultimately failed. In no instance was the failure more spectacular than in the history of the poorhouse" (Katz, 1986, p. 10).

In contrast to the nineteenth-century experience, the expansion of the shelter system in the 1980s was not always as explicitly tied to welfare "reforms," although some states (Michigan, Connecticut, and Pennsylvania) did trade increases in shelter expenditures for cuts in general assistance benefits. Nevertheless, the growth of this system and its design reveal a set of assumptions that is similar to those of the poorhouse. Organizationally, the mixture of public and private support for shelter has resulted in a range of local approaches to shelter financing and management. Not-for-profit voluntary associations, many of them religious charities, were among the first to respond to the growing visibility of the homeless problem in the early 1980s. However, as data from the U.S. Department of Housing and Urban

Development ([HUD] 1989) indicate, public sector revenue accounted for 65 percent of the dollars spent on shelter in the United States by 1988. In many cities, such as in Philadelphia, New York, and Boston, most voluntary shelter organizations eventually became contract entities of city and state governments.

Again, consider the case of Philadelphia. In 1982, Philadelphia had a small, loosely organized system of private shelters with an estimated total capacity of 250 beds. By 1988, the system had grown to 5,600 beds, with nearly all administered and funded through a centralized public shelter authority, and reimbursed, like hospitals on a per diem basis (Culhane, 1993). Until 1988, shelter contracts were literally "put out for bid," or awarded to the lowest bidder (as in the poorhouse era) often with little regard for the adequacy of the facilities or services rendered. A centralized shelter referral system allowed the City of Philadelphia to subcontract shelter for the disabled and elderly population in smaller facilities, particularly in boarding homes. However, as demand for shelter among families and young, "able-bodied" men increased in the mid-1980s, the city government was forced to respond quickly, opening six large congregate shelters with capacities exceeding 200 beds each.

By their program design (or lack thereof), most shelters are no more than temporary resting places, focused primarily on the immediate material needs of their clients and providing little in the way of social services. The City of Philadelphia reports that fewer than half of its shelters provide any on-site social services (City of Philadelphia, 1990a). Shelters require residents to leave in the early hours of the morning (around 6 A.M.), typically justified by the argument that shelters should not promote "dependence" and should encourage "work-seeking" behavior. Many shelters likewise have limited lengths of stay, such as two weeks or one month, also to discourage "dependence." As in the poorhouse era, however, the goals of reducing dependence (deterrence) and promoting rehabilitation have often been in conflict. For example, a study of a large congregate shelter for men in New York found that the official shelter policy of "discouraging settling in" severely limited the effectiveness of mental health and substance abuse programs that required a stable client base for their success (Gounis & Susser, 1990).

While professing a goal of self-sufficiency for their clients, few shelters have the resources to enable a person to gain stable employment. None of the more than fifteen facilities visited by this author between 1986 and 1989 in Boston or Philadelphia had established procedures for assessing individuals' capacity for work or need for employment assistance. Although there is often a suspect affinity between shelters and some temporary labor agencies, most shelters have no employment programs.[2] Activists from the Union of the Homeless in Philadelphia waged a campaign early in their organizing effort simply to persuade shelter administrators that clients *wanted* to work. In a 1987 interview one of the activists, Ronald Darnaby, described that some shelter providers had a contradictory attitude that insulated them from such challenges: "Shelters justify doing as little as possible for clients by believing that, on the one hand, we are helpless, and on other hand, that we should be able to help ourselves. We lose either way."

Shelter reformers are more recently promoting shelters' rehabilitative functions. Like poorhouse reformers, shelter reformers have had to embrace the hope of better classification by promoting specialization for subsegments of the population, such as the mentally ill or substance abusers (Culhane, 1992). But while a rehabilitative vision continues to guide shelter reformers, the potentially higher cost of a rehabilitative system could leave a deterrence orientation in place. Ironically, it may also force some recognition that providing rehabilitation services, while helpful to the currently homeless, is likely to do little to reduce the future demand for shelter.

THE FAILURE OF POORHOUSES AND THE
SHELTER SYSTEM

Eventually, the optimism of nineteenth-century reformers with institutional responses to social problems waned: "Mental hospitals did not cure; prisons and reform schools did not rehabilitate; public schools did not educate very well; and poorhouses did not check the growth of outdoor relief or promote industry and temperance. A preoccupation with order, routine, and cost replaced the founders' concern with the transformation of character and social reform" (Katz, 1986, p. 25). The conditions of the poorhouses—poorly constructed, crowded, noisy, filthy, and foul smelling—were evidence that little of worth could be accomplished within. Katz (1986) cites one observer who noted that within poorhouses, good health was an "impossibility." Management problems with poorhouses proved formidable. Administrators and suppliers conspired to inflate orders and overcharge. The trials of management drove even well-intentioned overseers to brutality, as the typical "keeper" "was sent 'a miscellaneous assortment of the diseased, defective and incapable,' and told to care for them without 'the proper facilities'. . . . 'He becomes brutal unconsciously, and almost in self-defense. After a few years, he does, without question, things that would have seemed absolutely awful to him when he first entered his duties' " (p. 27). Overseers of the poor were often recruited from the class just "slightly superior" to the inmates. However, over time, they attempted to forge a professional identity, with their own "organizations, journals and training procedures" (Katz, 1986, p. 27).

Within poorhouses, inmates did the most of the work to sustain them, virtually running the larger facilities. Katz (1986) reports that in Philadelphia's poorhouses, inmates even formed their own organizations, and ethnic tensions would often erupt between competing groups; inmates peddled small goods to one another while the guards sold "drugs, fruits and candy" (p. 28). Even liquor was "easily available," whether doctors prescribed it as medicine, inmates stole it from the physicians' supplies, or the staff smuggled it in. At one facility Katz (1986) writes that the purchase of an average of one-half gallon of liquor per admission was authorized. "This easy availability of liquor, of course, defeated attempts to curb the intemperance thought to be the major immediate cause of pauperism" (p. 29).

An observer of poorhouse procedures in the nineteenth century lamented that there was a "laxness" in discharge policies, and that "the door swings outward or inward with the greatest of ease." Accordingly, poorhouses did less to churn out reformed persons than to become a "temporary refuge for the degenerate poor" (Katz, 1986, p. 29). Critics even feared the creation of a class of almshouse "recidivists." Apologists for the poorhouse, on the other hand, attributed its failure to the helpless, long-term dependents who occupied it. But Katz (1986) notes that they "knew perfectly well that poorhouses were full of able-bodied men" (p. 87). Indeed, two patterns of poorhouse utilization were documented: the first and dominant pattern, consisting of younger, able-bodied people who used the poorhouse for less than six weeks, accounted for approximately three-fifths of poorhouse admissions, while the second pattern, consisting of the "helpless and elderly" who stayed for a year or more, was characteristic of between one-fifth and one-quarter of poorhouse admissions (see Katz, 1986, p. 90). Thus, for most, the poorhouse functioned as a temporary refuge in times of crisis and was not a permanent residence.

Once again, much of the poorhouse's problems were blamed on poor classification, with one commentator calling it a "dumping ground" (Katz, 1986, p. 29). Criminals, the insane, children, the elderly, and those whose only offense was being poor were all lumped together in the same institutions. Observers were especially disturbed by the conditions for the mentally ill, found nude in their cells, covered with "the long accumulated filth of their occupants" (Katz, 1986, p. 30). Children too were cause for concern, as their improper care was likely to create a new generation of poorhouse dependents. However, the separation of the poor into different facilities was rarely attempted, primarily because of the increased cost associated with the replication of facilities and administration.

Even the goal of converting the poor with disciplined labor was eventually abandoned, as administrators discovered that finding or creating enough work for inmates cost more than the labor was worth. Nevertheless, some poorhouses continued to require senseless labor on treadmills and farms because work had moral value and, more importantly, deterred people from staying in poorhouses. Discipline in poorhouses developed a penal character, with inmates convicted of minor offenses forbidden to speak to one another, denied meals, or forced to labor. Poor relief policy in general confounded crime and poverty, given that "extreme poverty among able-bodied men itself was a crime that justified their detention" (Katz, 1986, p. 31).

The rehabilitative goals of poorhouses were ultimately sacrificed because they were supposed to *reduce,* not increase, expenditures on poor relief. In the end, deterrence "won," because offering rehabilitation, work programs, and medical care would have driven up costs considerably. But this was a qualified victory, as deterrence only prevailed in becoming the guiding *principle* of poorhouse practice. In fact, poorhouses did not succeed in deterring applicants for outdoor relief nor in reducing overall expenditures on poor relief. Contrary to the predictions of poorhouse advocates, it cost more to support a person in a poorhouse than on outdoor relief: "trapped by their contradictory purposes, undercut by poor management and inadequate funds, poorhouses never could find useful work for their inmates or offer the old, sick, and helpless, not to mention the able-bodied unemployed, much more than a roof and escape from death by starvation. Nor did they reduce pauperism or cut the cost of poor relief. In fact, despite the diffusion of poorhouses, the volume of outdoor relief continued to grow" (Katz, 1986, p. 35)

Shelters have not fared much better, becoming crowded, and in many cases, deteriorating facilities, long since abandoned for other purposes, where the poor are herded into one line after another for small cups of juice, a squeeze of toothpaste, and a ritual delousing in a congregate shower room. As with poorhouses, shelter managers have been accused of corrupt and exploitative practices. Investigative journalists in Philadelphia (Maryniak & Gerhart, 1987) discovered that one of the city's largest shelter contractors (with contracts equal to $1.4 million a year) had formerly been in prison for Medicaid fraud associated with his operation of a nursing home. The nursing home, closed by the Board of Health, was later reopened as a homeless shelter, and continued to operate with numerous violations of health and safety regulations noted on official inspection records. Maryniak and Gerhart (1987) found that inspection reports cited substandard living conditions throughout the shelter system: "immobile client being kept in room";

"roaches, mice and rats"; "electrical wires hanging"; "strong urine smell throughout building"; "unclean food equipment and contaminated food"; "too many beds in one room"; "excessively hot water"; "patients deprived of medication"; "17 hours between breakfast and supper"; "unrefrigerated insulin"; "no doors or other privacy"; "no locks on bathroom doors"; "feces on bathroom floor." Two boarding homes "lost state personal care home licenses because residents allegedly were physically abused by other staff members or live-in relatives of staff members" (p. 4). Four facilities were cited for crowding too many people into rooms. Owners accused of overcrowding complained that they were only trying to serve all of the people sent to them by city officials, who, they argued, were well aware of their capacity. Human service officials of Philadelphia acknowledged that because of the desperate need for beds, contracts with shelters were canceled only when conditions were found "life-threatening" (Maryniak & Gerhart, 1987).

Homeless people in Philadelphia have accused shelter managers of abdicating management of the facility to insensitive "counselors" ("guards," according to the clients) (Culhane, 1990). Experienced as the "overseers of the poor," these guards typically have much more direct contact with residents than do shelter managers. In Philadelphia, most are young men, often drawn from the neighborhoods around the shelters, from which many of the shelter residents come as well. Indeed, guards are often recruited from among shelter residents. It is not uncommon for guards and clients to know one another or one another's families. This common background, combined with the desperate impulses of a large, poor client population, combine to increase the likelihood of underhanded collaboration between staff and clients. Thus, some staff are accused of dealing drugs in the shelters, of turning a blind eye to drug dealing and loan-sharking, and of letting client groups control the facility "from inside." Similar observations have been made by Kostas Gounis and Ezra Susser (1990) regarding the conditions in a New York City shelter. The authors describe a "marginal affinity" between guards and clients; a perceived path of "upward mobility" from client to guard in the shelter hierarchy; and relatively "autonomous territories" within the shelter for guards, client-workers, drug dealers, and prostitutes.

Given that most work in shelters is done by shelter residents, typically for small rewards such as an extra sandwich, a cigarette, or juice, favoritism and "power cliques" can develop among clients and guards regarding work and the rewards of work. In some shelters, clients are even asked to work for little or no compensation under the banner of a work readiness program. Gounis and Susser (1990) reported on one such work program in a shelter for homeless men in New York, where resident workers received $12.50 per week, a wage viewed by some as "slave labor" (p. 238). Some shelters even provide explicit noncash privileges to client-workers, such as a bed in a room with fewer people or even a private room. Privacy is thus used as a form of reimbursement.

Although the living and working conditions surrounding shelter life suggest that shelters are not rehabilitative environments, it is difficult to evaluate them on this basis alone. Unlike poorhouses, shelters do not have the explicit mandate to deter people from outdoor relief. Nor have they been charged with a great rehabilitative purpose, although some reformers and advocates are increasingly likely to make such a claim about their potential. However, with a fair amount of consistency, a goal of shelter policy does appear to be aimed at reducing both the length of stay and "dependence" (see Culhane, 1992). And, superficially, they may be successful.

Consider that in Philadelphia in 1990, 16,350 people (including 4,743 children) were admitted into the public shelter system, although its average daily capacity was 2,699 beds.[3] Based on these and other data, I have calculated (Culhane, 1993) that the annual rate of turnover in Philadelphia's shelter system was 6 persons per bed in 1990, and that the average length of stay was 60 nights per person per year (cumulatively, with not necessarily continuous stays). Given that the city's housing relocation assistance funds were limited to assisting 1,200 households that year, most people apparently left the shelters without receiving any formal housing assistance. Preliminary analyses of shelter utilization data in Philadelphia suggest that, as with poorhouses, there are two primary patterns of shelter use, the dominant being short-term stays of forty-five days or less (more than half of all admissions annually), with a small but visible minority with stays of six months or more (10%–15% of all admissions annually). However, evidence that people use shelters episodically over the course of the year and that as many as one-third of shelter residents have had prior homelessness episodes suggests that shelter exits are not always toward improved living circumstances. And, as in the poorhouse era, this recidivism has concerned some shelter managers, who feel that the frequent exits demonstrate that many homeless people have alternatives in the community, or that they are simply using the shelter system to avoid rent and to support drug habits. Regardless, these data and those reported elsewhere (Culhane, Dejowski, Ibanez, Needham, & Macchia, 1994; Sosin, Piliavin, & Westerfelt, 1990) support an emerging picture of "homelessness" as the periodic use of shelters to supplement unstable residential resources in the community. While shelter conditions may deter long and continuous stays, they probably do not deter people from applying for shelter, because a poverty of choices, not shelter availability, is driving shelter utilization.

Like poorhouses, shelters have not proven to be cheap alternatives to welfare. It has bewildered some that a shelter system like that in New York City spends as much as $53,000 annually to shelter a homeless family and $18,000 annually to shelter a single adult (Mayoral Commission on Homelessness, 1992). One could cover the annual rent for five or six families for every one family kept in shelter for a year. Yet, system managers recognize that if homeless families and individuals were automatically given rent subsidies instead of shelter, the shelters would be emptied one day only to be filled again soon after. Recall that the high turnover rate found in Philadelphia's shelter system suggests that the population of "near homeless" is at least five times that of the nightly census in just one year's time. Thus, the line of people who would similarly request housing assistance, and who could show that their existing housing was substandard or unaffordable, could grow quite long. For this reason, deterrence, not rehabilitation, has been and is likely to remain the guiding principle of shelter policy.

Although some shelters may be providing more and improved social services, it remains the norm that public shelters provide minimal assistance, and that shelter systems are more committed to *not* fostering dependence (thus to deterrence) than to promoting independence. There are of course exceptions, dedicated to the dignity and independence of their clients, but as Katz (1986) notes with regard to the poorhouse era, "whether some poorhouses chose compassion over deterrence in the mid-nineteenth century . . . is not the main point. Most poorhouses offered few comforts or attractions. By the close of the century, dread of the poorhouse was virtually universal" (p. 34).

WHAT HISTORY, WHAT FUTURE?

Poorhouses proved to be expensive failures at deterring applicants for relief. Observers could not help but recognize that they accomplished so little at such great expense (Katz, 1986). So reformers set out to transform the poorhouse by siphoning off segments of the population to other institutions and leaving the poorhouse with the care of the aged and infirm. New state facilities for the "chronically insane" were constructed, and while county poorhouse officials were reluctant to have their power over the poorhouse population usurped by the state, eventually the mentally ill, along with many "aged senile persons," were transferred to the care of state hospitals. Children, including those who had parents willing to care for them, were sent to state reform schools and orphanages as part of a policy of family break-up, intended to end the intergenerational transmission of poverty. Even children with parents who were not in poorhouses but who felt that they could not adequately care for them were sent to orphanages and reform schools.

The presence of the able-bodied in poorhouses inspired fierce attacks on their eligibility for aid. Just as their receipt of outdoor relief was viewed as undercutting their incentive to work and rewarding their idleness, so was their inclusion in poorhouses with more deserving categories of the poor—the aged and infirm—seen as an irresponsible endorsement of their derelict life style. Proposals were offered to create a separate system of "industrial almshouses," leaving the poorhouses for the sick, aged, and otherwise helpless. However, county superintendents took more cost-efficient routes to weeding out the able-bodied by relying on medical knowledge to distinguish categories of eligibility, by applying a strict work test, or simply by having able-bodied "tramps" arrested. Ejected from the poorhouse, the able-bodied were forced to resort to begging and living on the streets. Police stations were eventually opened to the new "homeless," allowing them to sleep in cells or on the floor. "By the 1890s, thousands of homeless men (called 'lodgers') slept in police stations every night" (Katz, 1986, p. 94). In Columbus, Ohio, more people slept in police stations than in poorhouses. Observers noted that sleeping conditions were wretched. By the end of the nineteenth century, reformers had mounted a campaign to end police station lodging. It was to be replaced by lodging houses and flophouses, designed explicitly for the purpose of offering cheap lodging to the "wayfaring" population. Public, or "municipal," lodging houses as well as those run by private charities were also erected. According to Katz (1986), "all of them inherited the mixed goals of the poorhouse: shelter, punishment, deterrence" (p. 96) And, generally, they inherited the unsanitary, crowded, and filthy conditions of their predecessor.

As children, the mentally ill, and the able-bodied poor were removed or excluded from poorhouses and placed in separate institutions, the poorhouse was slowly converted into a home for the elderly and infirm. Reformers were successful in stimulating the expansion of new, more specialized institutions, further reducing the need for poorhouses over time. The transfer and exclusion of demographic groups from poorhouses were never complete, but the era of indiscriminate congregate care for the entire class of paupers appeared over. "In the end, however, [reformers] did not solve the real problems they had identified; they simply displaced them" (Katz, 1986, p. 91), transferring to other institutions both the residents of poorhouses and their legacy of neglect.

What future awaits the shelter system? Recent reform strategies seem similarly inclined to create subsystems of care for various populations among the homeless. Two reform proposals, *The Way Home,* by the Mayoral Commission on Homelessness in New York City (1992), and *The DC Initiative,* by a collaborative of HUD and the District of Columbia (1993), share the vision of replacing the indiscriminate care of shelters with specialized "transitional housing" targeted to troubled families, the mentally disabled, substance abusers and people with employment and training needs. While this policy would likely improve services for the currently homeless, it is limited by failing to account for the dynamic nature of the homelessness problem and to address its underlying causes.

As noted, recent research suggests that most homeless people use the shelter system on a short-term or intermittent basis, and that the population who uses shelters is far larger than identified previously. More than 3 percent of New York City's and Philadelphia's populations have used shelters in the last five years (Culhane et al., 1994). In contrast, the assumption of the transitional housing, or enhanced shelter models is that the homeless population consists of a fairly stable set of persons over time. Rather than emphasizing a reduction in the incidence of homelessness, this approach aims to alleviate the problem primarily by moving people who are currently homeless through a system of specialized housing programs. Unfortunately, this could to lead to a significant *increase* in the daily size of the emergency housing system, while doing nothing to reduce the rate at which people become homeless.

By expecting homeless (and nearly homeless) people to enter transitional housing programs in order to access housing assistance and social services, and by requiring people to stay in shelters for specified periods before they are eligible for such assistance, reformers could create a system with perverse incentives for long shelter stays and for the "dumping" of clients into shelters by other social welfare and mental health agencies. It risks creating a secondary public health, welfare, and housing system, with potentially lower standards of care, while failing to address the deficits of the existing health, welfare, and housing systems that drive the utilization of shelters. Increases in shelter admissions and shelter stays will by necessity require increases in the capacity of the emergency housing system. Judging from history, the resulting increase in costs and utilization would likely lead shelter system managers to restrict eligibility for shelter or to discourage people from entering shelters. This could further the dominance of a deterrence over a rehabilitation orientation in the structure of emergency services and undermine the whole reform effort.

To avoid the contradictions inherent in this approach, an alternate set of assumptions and a corresponding set of strategies would need to be considered, some of which were outlined in the Clinton administration's federal homelessness plan (Interagency Council on the Homeless, 1994). Recognizing the structural and dynamic nature of homelessness, the fundamental problem for policy-makers is not how to improve the efficiency and quality of shelters, but how to prevent people from needing them. This requires a better understanding of the social contexts in which homelessness is produced, including the neighborhoods and households from which homeless people come. Unfortunately, while the vulnerabilities and characteristics of homeless people have been well documented, much less is known about the places that have failed to remain "home" for them, and future research should seek to understand the specific factors associated with that ecology. However, it can be reasonably assumed that poorer neighborhoods, with substandard housing, inadequate services, and concentrations of unemployment and crime, are likely to have a greater incidence of homelessness than other neighborhoods. If this is the case, a strategy designed to assist people in avoiding shelters and living more satisfactory lives in the community would, most fundamentally, require a broadening of access to resources in those communities.

Rather than attaching more services to shelters alone, resources might be better targeted by improving the quality and accessibility of housing, jobs, and services in distressed neighborhoods, not only for people who find themselves homeless but also for people who are struggling to avoid it. This would include short-term interventions designed to alleviate the impact of temporary economic and domestic crises, and long-term interventions designed to strengthen the capacity of communities to house, employ, and serve their members adequately. The provision of crisis and respite services for people with mental illness and their families, residential treatment for people with mental illness and/or substance abuse disorders, and in-home support and advocacy services for people with disabilities would greatly help with reducing the risk for homelessness among vulnerable adults who otherwise face the continuous threat of a housing emergency. Similarly, improved services for families with domestic or financial crises, including bridge loans, relocation assistance, and support services, would help many families with emergencies avoid the disruptions of homelessness. However, without a long-term revitalization strategy that includes jobs and housing assistance, short-term interventions alone are unlikely to achieve a sustained reduction in the frequency of housing emergencies in poor communities.

CONCLUSION

In conclusion, reformers of the shelter system should heed the lessons of history. Like the poorhouse, the shelter system will likely defy attempts at reform. Subpopulations may be displaced, once again, from one miserly institution to another, but the underlying structural problems, unless addressed directly, will remain and will continue to generate demand for emergency housing. Inhumane conditions in shelters may make shelter reform compelling, but because shelters and shelter conditions do not cause homelessness, reformers should not make the mistake of assuming that by fixing shelters, they are going to remedy the problem. Reform efforts should not ignore the lack of housing, employment, income, health care, and social services for poor people with *homes,* for it is only by improving the quality of life and availability of resources and services for people with homes that the flow of people into shelters can be reversed. Failing this, we are consigned to repeat the shameful legacy of poorhouses.

ACKNOWLEDGMENTS

The author wishes to acknowledge the generosity of Michael Katz for permitting the quotation of his work here, and of Kim Hopper, who along with Mr. Katz reviewed earlier versions of this manuscript and offered helpful suggestions for its revision.

NOTES

1. The Pennsylvania legislature and Governor Robert Casey passed another round of GA cuts in 1994, reducing eligibility for cash grants for the "transitionally needy" from 3 months every year to 2 months every 2 years (for a total of approximately $420 every 2 years), and to extend the presumption of "transitionally needy" status to adults *over the age of 45.*
2. Most of the large shelters for single men in Philadelphia and Boston either have a day labor agency a short distance from the shelter, or a day labor agency hires vans that come directly to the shelter to pick up recruits. Recruiters will typically look the crowd over, picking the most visibly "able" people first. The jobs usually involve covering for absenteeism in cafeterias and small manufacturing settings. Other work is of a short-term, even high-risk nature. For example, day laborers are hired for demolition jobs, dock work, or temporary industrial tasks that would take other employees off their routine jobs. In most cases, agency policy mandates turnover in job assignments to discourage recruits from becoming permanently hired. Such practices by one day labor agency in Philadelphia, Arrow Employment, led the Philadelphia Union of the Homeless to wage a strike against the agency. Another source of work for homeless people in Philadelphia is farm labor. In the summer and fall, three buses leave from a specified location not far from one of the large shelters for men and take people to New Jersey farms, where they are employed to pick fruits and vegetables. Another employment agency in Philadelphia sends people from the shelters to work for the summer in hotels and resorts in the Poconos.

3. The Philadelphia shelter system had its bed capacity cut from 5,400 beds in 1988 to 2,700 in 1990 because of the city's fiscal crisis. Shelter administrators instituted new requirements on clients and providers, details of which are explained elsewhere (Culhane, 1992).

REFERENCES

Advocacy Committee for Emergency Services. (1984). *Act 75: The hidden impact.* Philadelphia: Author.

Barlett, D. L., & Steele, J. B. (1992). *America: What went wrong?* Kansas City, MO: Andrews & McMeel.

Blau, J. (1992). *The visible poor: Homelessness in the United States.* New York: Oxford University Press.

Bluestone, B., & Harrison, B. (1982). *The deindustrialization of America: Plant closings, community abandonment, and the dismantling of basic industry.* New York: Basic Books.

Burt, M. (1992). *Over the edge: The growth of homelessness in the 1980s.* New York: Russell Sage Foundation/Urban Institute Press.

Center on Budget and Policy Priorities. (1992). *Selected background material on welfare programs.* Washington, DC: Author.

City of Philadelphia. (1990a). *Comprehensive homeless assistance plan.* Philadelphia: Office of Services to the Homeless and Adults.

City of Philadelphia. (1990b). *Protocol: Services for and expectations of persons in temporary and permanent housing.* Philadelphia: Office of Services to the Homeless and Adults.

Culhane, D. P. (1990). *On becoming homeless: The structural and experiential dynamics of residential instability.* Unpublished doctoral dissertation, Boston College.

Culhane, D. P. (1992). The quandaries of shelter reform: An appraisal of efforts to "manage" homelessness. *Social Service Review, 66*(3), 428–440.

Culhane, D. P. (1993). The organization and utilization of the shelter system in Philadelphia: Estimating average length of stay and annual rate of turnover. *Journal of Health and Social Policy, 4*(2), 55–78.

Culhane, D. P., Dejowski, E., Ibanez, J., Needham, E., & Macchia, I. (1994). Public shelter admission rates in Philadelphia and New York City. *Housing Policy Debate, 5*(2), 107–140.

Dolbeare, C. (1988). *Housing in Philadelphia: A report for the Public Interest Law Center of Philadelphia.* Philadelphia: Public Interest Law Center of Philadelphia.

Dolbeare, C. (1991). *Out of reach: Why everyday people can't find affordable housing.* Washington, DC: Low Income Housing Information Services.

Dugger, C. (1991, September 4). Benefits of system luring more families to shelters. *The New York Times,* p. A1.

Gounis, K., & Susser, E. (1990). Shelterization and its implications for mental health services. In N. L. Cohen (Ed.), *Psychiatry takes to the streets: Outreach and crisis intervention for the mentally ill.* (pp. 231–255). New York: Guilford Press.

Grunberg, J., & Eagle, P. F. (1990). Shelterization: How the homeless adapt to shelter living. *Hospital and Community Psychiatry, 41*(5), 521–525.

Harrison, B., & Bluestone, H. (1988). *The great U-turn: Corporate restructuring and the polarizing of America.* New York: Basic Books.

Hopper, K. (1990). Public shelter as a "hybrid institution": Homeless men in historical perspective. *Journal of Social Issues, 46*(4), 13–30.

Hopper, K., & Hamburg, J. (1986). The making of America's homeless: From skid row to new poor, 1945–1984. In R. G. Bratt, C. Hartman, & A. Meyerson (Eds.), *Critical perspectives on housing* (pp. 12–39). Philadelphia: Temple University Press.

Hopper, K., Susser, E. & Conover, S. (1985). Economies of makeshift: Deindustrialization and homelessness in New York City. *Urban Anthropology and Studies of Cultural Systems and World Economic Development, 14,* 183–236.

Interagency Council on the Homeless. (1994). *Priority home! The federal plan to break the cycle of homelessness.* Washington, DC: Author.

Johnson, K. (1992, February 6). Weiker proposes big spending cuts: Connecticut would join move to cut back welfare. *The New York Times,* pp. A1, B6.

Katz, M. (1986). *In the shadow of the poorhouse: A social history of welfare in America.* New York: Basic Books.

Katz, M. (1989). *The undeserving poor: From the war on poverty to the war on welfare.* New York: Pantheon.

Kondratas, A. (1991). Ending homelessness: Policy challenges. *American Psychologist, 46*(11), 1226–1231.

Maryniak, P., & Gerhart, A. (1987, February 17–19). Bed, board and big bucks: Who's profiting from the homeless. *Philadelphia Daily News.*

Mayoral Commission on Homelessness. (1992). *The way home: A new direction in social policy.* New York: Office of the Mayor.

McCambridge, R. (1992). *Giving to end homelessness: A study of national philanthropic responses to homelessness.* Boston: The Boston Foundation.

Mead, L. (1986). *Beyond entitlement: The social obligations of citizenship.* New York: Free Press.

Mead, L. (1992). *The new politics of poverty: The non-working poor in America.* New York: Basic Books.

Morgan, T. (1991a, October 2). New York planning homeless shelters across city. *The New York Times,* p. A1.

Morgan, T. (1991b, September 27). Shift in view on housing all the homeless. *The New York Times,* pp. B1, B2.

Murray, C. (1984). *Losing ground: American social policy 1950–1980.* New York: Basic Books.

Piven, F. F., & Cloward, R. (1971). *Regulating the poor: The functions of public welfare.* New York: Pantheon.

Piven, F. F., & Cloward, R. (1982). *The new class war: Reagan's attack on the welfare state and its consequences.* New York: Pantheon.

Roberts, S. (1991, October 28). Crackdown on homeless and what led to shift. *The New York Times,* pp. B1, B4.

Ropers, R. (1988). *The invisible homeless: A new urban ecology.* New York: Human Sciences Press.

Rossi, P. (1990). *Down and out in America: The origins of homelessness.* Chicago: University of Chicago Press.

Ryan, P., Bartelt, D., & Goldstein, I. (1988). *Homelessness in Pennsylvania: How can this be?* Philadelphia: Institute for Public Policy Studies, Temple University.

Sosin, M., Piliavin, I., & Westerfelt, H. (1990). Toward a longitudinal analysis of homelessness. *Journal of Social Issues, 46*(4), 157–174.

Spolar, C. (1991, August 12). Two shelters for homeless close in DC. *Washington Post,* pp. D1, D4.

Steinfels, P. (1992, January 20). Apathy is seen toward agony of the homeless. *The New York Times,* pp. A1, B7.

Stern, M. (1984). The emergence of the homeless as a public problem. *Social Service Review, 58,* 291–301.

Summers, A. A., & Luce, T. F. (1987). *Economic development within the Philadelphia metropolitan area.* Philadelphia: University of Pennsylvania Press.

U.S. Department of Housing and Urban Development. (1989). *A report on the 1988 national survey of shelters for the homeless.* Washington, DC: Author.

U.S. Department of Housing and Urban Development and the District of Columbia. (1993). *The DC initiative: Working together to solve homelessness.* Washington, DC: Office of Community Planning and Development.

Wilson, W. J. (1987). *The truly disadvantaged: The inner city, the underclass, and public policy.* Chicago: University of Chicago Press.

Zinn, D. K., & Sarri, R. C. (1984). Turning back the clock on public welfare. *Signs, 10*(2), 355–370.

Chapter 4

Welfare Reform and the New Class War

• *Frances Fox Piven and Richard A. Cloward*

THE PROGRAM WE CALL WELFARE PROVIDES A BARE SUBSISTENCE INCOME TO more than four million women raising children. It costs $22 billion dollars, less than 1 percent of the federal budget, and only 2 or 3 percent of most state budgets. Yet this small program has become the target of big guns, both intellectual and political. Liberals and conservatives agree that welfare is the nation's major problem, bad for the country, and bad for the poor. Presumably, it drains public budgets and reduces work effort. And, by allowing poor mothers to opt out of paid work, it saps their initiative, and nourishes cultural and psychological disabilities. As a result, welfare is said to worsen poverty, not to speak of its ostensible role in fostering crime, illegitimacy, and the growth of an "underclass." The proposed remedies vary, but they usually involve cutting benefits and pushing mothers into the labor market.

These themes have been developed in an enlarging stream of conservative literature: Glazer's "The Limits of Social Policy" (1971) and Anderson's *Welfare* (1978) were among the opening salvos. Gilder's *Wealth and Poverty* (1981), Auletta's *The Underclass* (1982), and Murray's *Losing Ground* (1984) expanded the attack. For the conservative assault on welfare, 1992 was a banner year, what with the publication of Mead's *The New Politics of Poverty*, Moynihan's "How the Great Society 'Destroyed the American Family,'" by which he means the black family, and Kaus's *The End of Equality*. As for liberals, they rallied around Elwood's *Poor Support* (1988), which differed from conservative proposals mainly in placing greater emphasis on education and training before expelling mothers from the rolls.

To cope with these new issues, critics of welfare urge putting women to work. Their claims for this reform are as unreal as their depiction of the problem. Near-miraculous social and cultural transformations are predicted once welfare mothers are removed to the labor market: cohesion will be restored to family and community, crime and other aberrant behaviors will disappear, and poverty will decline. Kaus (1992), who advocates replacing welfare with a WPA-type jobs programs, invokes a grand historical parallel: "Underclass culture can't survive the end of welfare any more than feudal culture could survive the advent of capitalism" (p. 129).

Not unexpectedly, the 1992 presidential campaign featured welfare reform. Bill Clinton promised to "end welfare as we know it." Polls showed that this was his most popular campaign issue (and it still is, as of this writing in early 1994). There have since been various studies and commissions, and the recommendations are all of a piece: provide some training, develop more workfare programs coupled with new sanctions, and place a two-year lifetime limit on welfare.

WORK AND THE NEW CLASS WAR

There is no economically and politically practical way to replace welfare with work, given the contemporary conditions of the labor market. After the great post–World War II boom, which lasted until the early 1970s, the American economy went into decline. For a quarter of a century after the war, the American economy enjoyed unparalleled expansion, and economists could write books with titles like *The Affluent Society* (Galbraith, 1958). But wages peaked in 1973 and then turned down, a response in part to intensified competition first from Europe and Japan, and later from newly industrializing countries, which devastated the automobile, steel, textiles, electronics, and machine tool industries in the United States, reducing manufacturing employment from 30 percent of the work force in 1960 to less than 20 percent in 1990. Meanwhile, the service sector grew, with its low wages and meager benefits, and economists wrote books with titles like *The Deindustrialization of America* (Bluestone & Harrison, 1982), and *A Future of Lousy Jobs* (Burtless, 1990), and *The Age of Diminished Expectations* (Krugman, 1990).

In response to these global changes that threatened profitability, American business declared "class war." They pillaged the economy. They shored up profits by closing plants and moving capital out of the old high-wage industrial regions and into low-wage regions here and abroad. They turned to speculation—in real estate and in the financial markets, including mergers and leveraged buyouts of industrial assets. They looted the multibillion-dollar defense contracting sector and the savings and loan industry. Following

Ronald Reagan's election in 1980, business taxes were cut, depriving the federal treasury of $2 trillion by 1992 (Sasser, 1993).

Most importantly, business abandoned its postwar policy of accommodation with labor, using the threat of plant closings accompanied by capital flight to strike fear in the hearts of workers. Capital's power over labor was enlarged all the more by other changes. One was the end of the Cold War and with it the gradual shrinking of defense employment. Another was the shedding of workers by corporations seeking to reduce costs. And still another was the flooding of the labor market by women, who entered the market in great numbers to try to shore up family income, as well as by the millions of immigrants from Asia, Mexico, and other Latin American countries. Unemployment averaged 4.4 percent in the 1950s, 4.7 percent in the 1960s, 6.1 percent in the 1970s, and 7.2 percent in the 1980s, and job prospects look little better in the 1990s. Consequently, every measure of labor's power fell. Overall, the percentage of unionized workers in the private sector fell from 29.1 percent in 1970 to 12 percent in 1990 (Brody, 1992, p. 33).

With labor cowed, business could make enormous cuts in its permanent work force, hire temporary and part-time workers instead, and slash wages and benefits. By the 1990s, 30 million people—over a quarter of the U.S. labor force—were working in jobs outside the regular full-time work force. Nonsupervisory personnel (who make up 81 percent of the work force) suffered a real hourly wage decline of 15 percent between 1973 and 1992.[1]

The spoils reaped by business in the war against labor were large enough to cause an historic shift in the distribution of income and well-being in American society. Overall, the simultaneous growth of poverty and wealth was unprecedented in the twentieth century (Krugman, 1990, p. 20). This was partly a simple and direct consequence of lowered taxes for the rich and social program cuts for poorer groups. Between 1977 and 1992, according to the Congressional Budget Office, the poorest tenth lost 20.3 percent of its posttax income, whereas the top tenth gained 40.9 percent, the top 5 percent gained 59.7 percent, and the top 1 percent gained 135.7 percent (Table 4.1).

And poverty increased. By the official measure, poverty had fallen from 22.4 percent in 1959 (39.5 million people) to a low of 11.6 percent in 1977 (24.7 million people). But then it rose to 14.2 percent in 1991 (35.7 million people), the highest level in a quarter of a century. Moreover, the official poverty measure greatly underestimated poverty. When the poverty line was first calculated in the 1960s, the average family spent one-third of its income on food, and the poverty line was set at three times food costs, adjusted for family size. But by 1990, food costs had dropped to one-sixth of the average family budget because other components—such as housing—had inflated at

TABLE 4.1
CHANGES IN POSTTAX FAMILY INCOME, 1977–92

Decile Rank	Changes in Income (%)
Poorest tenth	−20.3
Second	−11.2
Third	−10.9
Fourth	−9.8
Fifth	−10.5
Sixth	−4.7
Seventh	−1.0
Eighth	3.8
Ninth	8.4
Richest tenth	40.9
Top 5%	59.7
Top 1%	135.7
All deciles	−9.1

Note: In constant 1992 dollars. From the U.S. Congressional Budget Office.

far higher rates. If the 1990 official poverty line of $13,360 for a family of four had been recalculated to reflect changes in the real costs of these components, it would have been about 155 percent of the official rate, or $21,700. By that measure, poverty soared. From the same 22.4 percent in 1959 (39.5 million people), it fell to a low of 17.3 percent in 1972 (35.6 million people), and then rose to 25.6 percent in 1989 (62.8 million people)—or to almost twice the numbers shown by the official indicator. (Schwarz & Volgy, 1992, p. 42 and Table 6.62).

The most dramatic measure of the reordered class structure was wealth accumulation—aggregate household assets, whether homes and other real estate, stock, bonds, paintings, jewelry, or yachts. Studies by the Federal Reserve show that between 1983 and 1989—the core Reagan years—the richest 1 percent of families increased their share of net private wealth from 31 percent to 37 percent, and they did so at the expense of all other social strata. The share of next richest 9 percent fell from 35 percent to 31 percent, and the bottom 90 percent lost 1 percent, from 33 percent to 32 percent.[2] In a characteristically opaque statement, Alan Greenspan, chair of the Federal Reserve, remarked of this finding that material distribution has become "more dispersed"; Claudia Goldin, the economic historian, put the data in perspective when she said that "inequality is at its highest since the great leveling of wages and wealth during the New Deal and World War II" (*New York Times*, April 2, 1981, p. 1). Plainly, business had won the war against workers.

WELFARE AND THE NEW CLASS WAR

Even as this degradation of the lot of workers worsened, all eyes turned toward welfare, and one heard a growing chorus of antiwelfare rhetoric about the "cycle of dependency." Thus Moynihan grandiosely proclaimed in the press that "just as unemployment was the defining issue of industrialism, dependency is becoming the defining issue of post-industrial society" (*New York Times*, December 9, 1991, p. A3). Mead (1992) bemoaned the way that "dependency" signals "the end of the western tradition" (p. 237). The national press announced that "dependency" has reached "epidemic proportions." By these accounts, rising unemployment, declining wage levels, and disappearing fringe benefits need not concern anyone. "The old issues were economic and structural," according to Mead (1992), and "the new ones are social and personal" (p. 221).

What is not understood is that this attack on welfare and, relatedly, on other income programs, is an extremely significant part of the new class war. To see this connection, it is useful to remember an old Marxist idea: that the unemployed constitute a reserve army of labor to be used by capitalists to weaken and divide the proletariat. Desperation pits the unemployed against the still-employed, thus weakening labor's bargaining power. But income security programs reduce unemployment and temper desperation. They remove millions of people from the labor market and protect millions of others from the ravages of unemployment. The consequence is to tighten labor markets and reduce fear among those still in the market and thus to strengthen workers in bargaining with employers over wages and working conditions.

Not surprisingly, programs with such potentially large effects generate conflict. They also, from time to time, spur a good deal of high-blown and usually unilluminating commentary by the experts of the day. A main theme, in the past as now, is that public income programs do more harm than good by leading to indolence and demoralization among the poor. Reams of such criticism accompanied the passage of the English poor law reform in the 1830s, which eliminated "outdoor relief" in favor of the workhouse. Writing more than a century later, and in a far more compassionate spirit than is typical, Polanyi (1957) nevertheless reiterated the same arguments in his analysis of the 1795 "relief-in-aid-of-wages" plan inaugurated in Speenhamland, England, by the landed nobility in response to the rising civil disorder among the peasantry, who had been displaced from their traditional agricultural occupations during the latter half of the eighteenth century. Under this system, the poor were required to work for whatever wages they could get, with relief authorities supplementing their incomes. Polanyi concluded that this allowance system produced massive destitution and immiseration because its main effect was to depress wages below the subsistence level. With this conclusion, he left the impression that it was the giving of relief that had depressed wages and produced immiseration.

What Polanyi failed to see was that the debilitating consequences of the Speenhamland system were the result not of income guarantees but of the use of relief to flood the labor market with surplus workers, thus empowering employers in bargaining over wages. By contrast, a relief system that takes surplus workers out of the labor market empowers those still working in bargaining with employers.

In the current period, business advisers seem to understand this, even if the left does not. Concern about the impact of public income programs on wages became evident in the 1970s. Policy-makers were troubled: unemployment rose in the late 1960s and early 1970s, but wages did not fall. This contradicted the common wisdom among economists that unemployment and wage levels vary inversely—a relationship embodied not only in the reserve army thesis, but also in the neoclassical formula known as the "Phillips Curve" (Phillips, 1958).[3] Post-World War II government macroeconomic policies were designed with this relationship in mind. Fiscal and monetary policies, by expanding or contracting aggregate demand and by raising or lowering the price of money, enabled the government to control wage demands by manipulating levels of unemployment.[4]

For two decades following World War II, the unemployment-wages trade-off varied to order. Cyclical increases in unemployment were matched by the expected fall-off in the rate of wage increases. In the late 1960s, however, wages spiraled upward despite a 6 percent unemployment level. Barry Bosworth (1980), who later headed Jimmy Carter's Council on Wage and Price Stability, reported that "wage rate increases had actually accelerated slightly despite the high unemployment" (pp. 60–61). The problem persisted in the early 1970s: unemployment rose to the highest levels since the 1930s, but wages still did not fall. Wage levels appeared to be immune to rising unemployment. Something had happened to disrupt the traditional relationship between unemployment and wage levels, between the supply of labor and the power of labor. In another idiom, the reserve army of labor was no longer performing its historic function.

A good number of economic analysts concluded that the expansion of income maintenance programs in the late 1960s and early 1970s had insulated wages from the effects of rising unemployment. The extension of Social Security coverage, together with higher benefits, sharply reduced work force participation among older people. At any one time, three million women were on the Aid to Families with Dependent Children (AFDC) rolls in the early 1970s, and few of them were then required to participate in welfare-supplemented work. The expansion of the disability programs from less than one million recipients in 1960 to more than four million in 1975 also produced a sizable drop in labor force participation, since many of these people were of prime working age.

Unemployment benefits also shrank the numbers looking for work. In the decades since 1935, coverage was extended to more workers, and benefits were liberalized, most importantly by congressional action extending the duration of coverage during periods of high unemployment. In the recession of 1973–74, when unemployment rose above 10 percent, the basic twenty-six-week period of coverage was extended to sixty-five weeks (and many workers displaced from jobs by foreign competition also received benefits under the Trade Adjustment Assistance Act). As a result, two out of every three of the twelve million unemployed received benefits during the 1973–74 downturn. Almost all studies concluded that the availability of unemployment benefits increases the length of unemployment spells (Danziger, Haveman, & Plotnick, 1981). The unemployed could now "prolong [their] job search . . . [and] refuse to accept work except at higher offered wages or cease active labor market participation" (Haveman, 1978, p. 46) for months, thus tightening the labor market. Looking at the labor-market effects of all of the social programs taken together, the total hours worked by *all* workers were reduced by between 4.8 percent and 7 percent.[5] It is little wonder that economists concluded that "a change has taken place" in the unemployment-wages trade-off (Fiedler, 1975, p. 117).

In sum, mainstream analysts (regardless of the fact that they couched their conclusions in the idiom of the Phillips Curve rather than of the reserve army) began to recognize that income maintenance programs had weakened capital's ability to depress wages by the traditional means of intensifying economic insecurity. Unemployment had thus lost some of its terrors, both for the unemployed and for those still working. In effect, social programs had altered the terms of struggle between capital and labor.

What followed, of course, was an effort to restore labor discipline by slashing the income support programs. This was no easy matter, given the nearly universal public support for programs like Social Security. In the drawn-out contest that ensued, the Reagan administration sometimes backed off or turned to administrative subterfuge to achieve the cuts it wanted. For some programs, such as Social Security, the result was something of a stand-off. Still, other programs, especially those that reach more vulnerable groups,

were badly damaged. Unemployment insurance coverage was severely restricted, for example, through a series of little-understood changes in the law,
so that only one in three receive benefits. Nearly a half a million people were
removed from the disability rolls (although the courts subsequently ruled
that many had been removed illegally). In other programs, new and confusing bureaucratic obstacles were introduced to deter utilization. Their significance is suggested by a series of studies of the food stamp program—by the
Urban Institute, the Congressional Budget Office, and the General Accounting Office—that found that only one-third to one-half of all eligible persons
were receiving food stamp benefits. And an Urban Institute study reported
that one-third of those eligible for Medicaid, a health insurance program
specifically for the poor, were not receiving benefits.

Welfare grant levels fell sharply (in lockstep, we should add, with the
drop in the minimum wage).[6] AFDC grant levels began to fall when riots and
protests by the welfare rights movement subsided at the close of the 1960s,
as state legislatures generally stopped raising AFDC payments, or even ad-
justing them for inflation. The result was that benefits lost 42 percent of their
purchasing power between 1970 and 1990. By 1990, the maximum benefit
was less than half the poverty level in a majority of the states and less than a
third of that level in a quarter of the states; for a family of three, the daily
per capita benefit in the median payment state was $4 (Table 4.2). (And as
the nation entered recession in 1990, the pace of AFDC cuts actually accelerated. [Center on Budget and Policy Priorities, 1992, 1993]).

However, since food stamp benefits were made uniform nationally and
indexed for inflation by Congress beginning in 1972, they maintained their
purchasing power and partly offset AFDC losses. In constant 1990 dollars,
average monthly food stamp payments per person rose from $43.50 in 1972

TABLE 4.2
MEDIAN STATE MONTHLY AFDC BENEFIT, 1970–90

Year	Payment ($)	Constant (1990 $)
1970	221	739
1975	264	635
1980	350	552
1985	399	483
1990	432	432
1970–90 (% change)	+ 195%	− 42%

Note: For a family of four with no other income.

to $61.50 in 1990. (U.S. House of Representatives, 1992, p. 1639, Table 12). Combining payments from AFDC and food stamps, the purchasing power of AFDC families was reduced by about 27 percent between 1972 and 1990.

Throughout this contest, however, and continuing today, the main focus of discussion by politicians and policy intellectuals was less on the range of major social programs that were at issue and more on the welfare program. It is easy to see why. Welfare, with its ancient connotations of pauperism and its contemporary association with blacks, could easily be made to symbolize the error of the very idea of income support programs. And welfare recipients—most of whom are single mothers, many of whom are minorities, and all of whom are desperately poor—could easily be made to symbolize the failures of character of those who drop out of wage work.

Welfare clients have always suffered the insult of extremely low benefit levels, and have always been degraded by the overbearing and punitive procedures of welfare agencies. Now, as public furor over welfare builds, meager benefits are cut, and degrading procedures multiply. The moral for Americans who are working more and earning less is clear: there is an even worse fate, an even lower status, than hard and unrewarding work.

Because most AFDC mothers are unskilled, they can only command the lowest wages, a problem that is worsening as wages decline. According to the U.S. Bureau of the Census (1992), there were 14.4 million (or 18 percent) of year-round, full-time workers sixteen years of age or older who had annual earnings below the poverty level in 1990, up from 10.3 million (14.6 percent) in 1984, and from 6.6 million (12.3 percent) in 1974. (The Bush administration tried to suppress these findings [see Mahar, 1992].) There is no reason to think that most AFDC mothers can become "self-sufficient" when growing millions of workers cannot. In a study of the finances of welfare families, Jencks and Edin (1990) find that "single mothers do not turn to welfare because they are pathologically dependent on hand-outs or unusually reluctant to work— they do so because they cannot get jobs that pay better than welfare" (p. 204).

Research on work programs bears this out. Block and Noakes (1988) conclude that recipients typically cannot find jobs that pay more than welfare. A review of research conducted by the Center on Budget and Policy Priorities (Porter, 1990) shows that work programs—highly publicized stories of individual successes notwithstanding—do not result in more than a handful of recipients achieving "a stable source of employment that provides enough income for a decent standard of living (at least above the poverty line) and job-related benefits that adequately cover medical needs" (p. 5). Still another general review, this time sponsored by the Brookings Institution (Burtless, 1989), reports that none of the programs succeed in raising the earnings of welfare mothers by more than $2,000. And Schwarz and Volgy

(1992) conclude that "no matter how much we may wish it otherwise, work-fare cannot be an effective solution" because "low-wage employment riddles the economy": in 1989, one in seven year-round, full-time jobs, or eleven mil-lion jobs, paid less than $11,500 for the year, which was roughly $2,000 be-low the official poverty line for a family of four (pp. 81, 106).

Another reason to be skeptical about welfare-to-work programs is that, although they are promoted as economy measures, they would in fact be very expensive, if anyone actually intended to implement them widely. Adminis-trative costs alone would overshadow any savings from successful job place-ments. And to this must be added the much larger costs of government-sub-sidized child care and health care, especially since the private market is offering fewer benefits to newly hired workers. For example, Medoff (1992) estimates that the proportion of new hires who get health benefits dropped from 23 percent to 15 percent during the last decade. Jencks (1992) estimates that AFDC mothers working at the minimum wage would have to be given free medical care and at least $5,000 worth of resources to supplement their wages, at a cost in excess of $50 billion, a quixotic sum that he agreed was unlikely to be appropriated by Congress. Kaus (1992) offers a similar dollar estimate for his recommendation for a mandatory jobs program for the poor. The Congress is certainly not unmindful of these costs, as it shows by its end-less squabbling over whether health and day care benefits to working recip-ients should be funded at all, or for only four months, or nine months, or twelve months, or whatever.

Given these constraints, the results of existing work program are pre-dictable enough. Studies show that a substantial proportion of former recip-ients end up reapplying for welfare because they cannot survive on their earn-ings, even with welfare supplements, and because temporary child care and Medicaid supports run out, or because of periodic crises such as a job layoff or an illness in the family. During the 1992 presidential campaign, Clinton claimed that 17,000 Arkansas residents had been successfully moved off the AFDC and food stamps rolls under a state jobs program between 1989 and 1992. But the administrator of the program subsequently acknowledged that many people had returned to welfare during that period. And so the charade goes on, as experts and politicians promise to put an end to welfare "depen-dency." None of it seems to make pragmatic sense.

Other professed goals of the work programs, such as the unsubstanti-ated assertions that work would transform family structure, community life, and the so-called culture of poverty, are equally irrational if taken at face value. Kaus (1992) insists that "replacing welfare with work can be expected to transform the entire culture of poverty," including family patterns, be-cause "it's doubtful" that working women would "be willing to share their hard-earned paychecks with non-working men the way they might have been willing to share their welfare checks," so that "the natural incentives toward the formation of two-parent families will reassert themselves" (p. 129). However, Kaus presents no data to support the view that the source of a woman's income influences marriage rates. In our judgment, marriage rates might indeed increase were jobs with adequate wages and benefits available to men, as well as to women on welfare who choose to work, but that seems entirely unlikely in view of current economic trends.

It is also doubtful that putting poor women to work would improve the care and socialization of children. Kaus (1992) claims that "if a mother has to set her alarm clock, she's likely to teach her children to set their alarm clocks as well" (p. 129), thus trivializing the real activities of most of these women. Many AFDC mothers with younger children get their children up every morning and, because of the danger in the streets, walk them to school, walk them home, and keep them locked up in their apartments until morning. Forcing these overburdened women to work would mean adding the market job to the exhausting job of maintaining a home without funds or services, all the while surrounded by dangerous and disorganized neighborhoods.

Work is also advertised as the way to reverse the deterioration of community life. This is hardly a new idea. The minutes of a meeting of academics, intellectuals, and administrators held in New York City after Nixon's election in 1968 reported a general consensus that the rising welfare rolls accompanied by spreading urban riots and other manifestations of civil disorder proved that "the social fabric . . . is coming to pieces. It isn't just 'strained' and it isn't just 'frayed'; but like a sheet of rotten canvas, it is starting to rip" (cited in Moynihan, 1973, p. 76). Converting AFDC to a work system was the remedy; work would restore the social fabric.

Removing women from their homes and neighborhoods would more likely shred the social fabric more. Putting mothers to work would deprive the poor community of its most stable element—of the women, for example, who have mounted campaigns to drive drug dealers from their housing projects and neighborhoods. Sally Hernandez-Pinero, the chair of the New York City Housing Authority, commented on the social roles played by the 75,000 women living and raising children alone in the city's projects: "anyone with even a nodding acquaintance with these women knows them for what they are, the sanity of the poor community, resourceful survivors of abandonment, slander and brutality. . . . In many poor communities, they are the only signatures on the social contract, the glue that keeps our communities from spinning out of control."[7]

None of the critics explains convincingly why these women would contribute more to their communities by taking jobs flipping hamburgers. Nor do they explain why it would not be the better part of public policy to shore up income supports (as we noted, the real value of AFDC benefits has fallen by 43 percent since the early 1970s, and by 27 percent if food stamps are counted), and social supports for women who are struggling to care for children under the junglelike conditions of urban poverty. Instead, the family and community work performed by these women—like the family and community work of women more generally—is consistently ignored or devalued.

Many welfare mothers do of course want to work, and they should have the chance, together with training and supportive benefits, such as day care and health care, as well as wage income and supplemental welfare payments that would enable their families to survive in the market. Under such conditions, many would take jobs, and coercion would be unnecessary. As a realistic matter, however, such opportunities are not on the reform agenda. It is the charade of work that is on the agenda.

Despite the record of work fare failures, an aura of optimism continues to permeate the literature on welfare reform. Most experts are convinced that most welfare mothers can achieve self-sufficiency through work, and that benign consequences for family and community will ensue. The key to eventual success is to find the proper mix of programs targeted to those who can best benefit from them. As theories and policies proliferate—none of them gaining ascendance for long, since none of them succeeds in practice—the search goes on and on for new strategies, or a mix of strategies, that will produce the desired outcomes. And this is so, Schram (1992) points out, even though the research data that reformers invoke to justify work fare legislation show that there will be few if any effects, leading him to conclude that these initiatives represent "symbols at the expense of substance."

REINFORCING WORK NORMS AND THE
NEW CLASS WAR

However, the charade is in fact the point. Welfare bashing is an easy political strategy. Politicians are rushing to divert voter discontent by focusing on welfare mothers, a majority of whom are black and Hispanic, and easy scapegoats. Moreover, this sort of appeal draws strength from an inherited political culture, from nineteenth-century ideas about the low morals of the poor and from nineteenth-century schemes to make the poor shape up by disciplining them.

In other words, politicians are pandering to the currents of race and class hatred in American culture. The reasons are obvious. Political leaders have nothing to say about jobs, about widening economic inequality, about pervasive economic insecurity, or about the broad social demoralization these economic conditions bring in their wake. The public is anxious, but political leaders have neither the ideas nor the courage to speak to that anxiety. Instead, they point the finger of blame at poor women. Politicians have discovered that AFDC moms make good scapegoats.

Not only are people encouraged to blame the poor for their own troubles, but the rituals that degrade welfare recipients reaffirm the imperative of work at a time when wages are down, working conditions worse, and jobs less secure. Kaus (1992) writes that while we cannot promise the poor who work that "they'll be rich, or even comfortably well-off" (and, he might have added, we cannot even promise them a living wage), "we can promise them respect" because they "would have the tangible honor society reserves for workers" (pp. 138–39). The charade of work enforcement reform should thus be understood as a symbolic crusade directed to the working poor rather than to those on relief, and the moral conveyed is the shame of the dole and the virtue of labor, no matter the job and no matter the pay.

NOTES

1. Data supplied by D. Henwood, editor of the *Left Business Review* in New York.
2. Relevant studies of wealth redistribution are summarized in *Dollars and Sense,* October 1992, p. 32.
3. This formula included prices as well as wages.
4. Unionization and minimum wage laws modify but do not eliminate these effects.
5. See Danziger, Haveman, & Plotnick (1981, p. 996) for the lower estimate, and Lampman (1979) for the higher one.
6. Even the *New York Times* noted the coincidence, reporting that the 27% drop in the real value of welfare and food stamp benefits over the past 2 decades roughly matched the 23% drop in the value of the minimum wage.
7. From an unpublished speech at Columbia University in 1992. With thanks to Val Coleman.

REFERENCES

Anderson, M. (1978). *Welfare: The political economy of welfare reform in the United States.* Stanford, CA: Hoover Institution.
Auletta, K. (1982). *The underclass.* New York: Random House.
Block, F., & Noakes, J. (1988). The politics of new-style workfare. *Socialist Review, 18.*
Bluestone, B., & Harrison, B. (1982). *The deindustrialization of America.* New York: Basic Books.

Bosworth, B. (1980). Re-establishing an economic consensus: An impossible agenda? *Daedalus, 109*, 3.

Brody, D. (1992, Winter). The breakdown of labor's social contract. *Dissent.*

Burtless, G. (1989). The effect of reform on employment, earnings and income. In P. Cottingham & D. Ellwood (Eds.), *Welfare policy for the 1990s.* Cambridge, MA: Harvard University Press.

Burtless, G. (1990). *A future of lousy jobs: The changing structure of U.S. wages.* Washington, DC: Brookings Institution.

Center on Budget and Policy Priorities. (1992, September 8). *Number in poverty hits 20-year high.* Washington, DC: Author.

Center on Budget and Policy Priorities. (1993, February). *The states and the poor: Budget decisions hurt low income people in 1992.* Washington, DC: Author.

Danziger, S., Haveman, R., & Plotnick, R. (1981). How income transfer programs affect work, savings, and the income distribution: A critical review. *Journal of Economic Literature, 19*, 00–00.

Elwood, D. (1988). *Poor support.* New York: Basic Books.

Fiedler, E. R. (1975). Economic policies to control stagflation. In C. Lowell-Harris (Ed.), Inflation: Long-term problems, *Proceedings of the Academy of Political Science, 31*, 4.

Galbraith, J. K. (1958). *The affluent society.* Boston: Houghton Mifflin.

Gilder, G. (1981). *Wealth and poverty.* New York: Basic Books.

Glazer, N. (1971). The limits of social policy. *Commentary 52*, 3.

Haveman, R. H. (1978). Unenployment in Western Europe and the United States: A problem of demand, structure, or measurement. *American Economic Review. 68*, 2.

Jencks, C. (1992) *Rethinking social policy: Race, poverty, and the underclass.* Cambridge, MA: Harvard University Press.

Jencks, C., & Edin, K. (1990, Spring). The real welfare problem. *The American Prospect* No. 1.

Kaus, M. (1992). *The end of equality.* New York: Basic Books.

Krugman, P. (1990). *The age of diminished expectations: U.S. economy policy in the 1990s.* Cambridge, MA: MIT Press.

Lampman, R. (1979). *Focus 4,* 1. Madison: University of Wisconsin, Institute for Research on Poverty.

Mahar, M. (1992, May 18) Numbers game: A census bureau wage report takes five months to surface. *Barrons.*

Mead, L. (1992). *The new politics of inequality: The nonworking poor in America.* New York: Basic Books.

Medoff, J. (1992, April). *The new unemployment.* Testimony prepared for Senator Lloyd Bentsen, Chairman, Subcommittee on Economic Growth, Trade, and Taxes, Joint Economic Committee, U.S. Congress (revised December 4, 1992).

Moynihan, D. P. (1973). *The politics of a guaranteed income: The Nixon administration and the Family Assistance Plan.* New York: Random House.

Moynihan, D. P. (1992). How the Great Society "destroyed the American family." *The Public Interest.*

Murray, C. (1984). *Losing ground.* New York: Basic Books.

Phillips, A. W. (1958). The relation between unemployment and the rate of change of money wage rates in the United Kingdom, 1861–1957. *Economica, 25.*

Polanyi, K. (1957). *The great transformation.* Boston: Beacon Press.

Porter, K. H. (1990, March) *Making JOBS work: What research says about effective employment programs for AFDC recipients.* Washington, DC: Center on Budget and Policy Priorities.

Sasser, J. (1993, February 2). *The New York Times,* Op-Ed. page.

Schram, S. F. (1992). Post-positivistic policy analysis and the family support act of 1988: Symbols at the expense of substance. *Polity, 24,* 4.

Schwartz, J. E., & Volgy, T. J. (1992). *Forgotten Americans.* New York: W. W. Norton.

U.S. Bureau of the Census. (1992, March). *Workers with low earnings: 1964 to 1990.* Washington, DC: U.S. Government Printing Office.

U.S. House of Representatives, Committee on Ways and Means. (1992, May 15). *1992 Green Book: Overview of Entitlement Programs.* Washington, DC: U.S. Government Printing Office.

Chapter 5

The So-Called Underclass and the Future of Antipoverty Policy

•*Herbert J. Gans*

DURING THE 1980s, A NUMBER OF JOURNALISTS AND POVERTY RESEARCHERS defined into existence an "underclass," a set of poor people whom they saw as behaviorally, and thus morally, inferior to other poor Americans. The actions that set them apart were, among other things, participating in street crime, being an unmarried welfare mother, leaving high school without graduating, failing to hold a job, and being homeless. Other poor people, especially those currently working and married, were assumed to be morally superior rather than just better able to survive in a declining economy.

To friends, colleagues, and readers of Bill Ryan, all this must have sounded very familiar, for the notion of a behaviorally defined underclass is really just a new way of, and term for, blaming the various victims of poverty. Consequently, what Ryan wrote in *Blaming the Victim* in 1971 about the victim can be applied verbatim to the underclass: the term "attributes defect and inadequacy to the malignant nature of poverty, injustice, slum life and racial difficulties. The stigma that marks the victim and accounts for his victimization is an acquired stigma, a stigma of social rather than genetic, origin. But the stigma, the defect, the fatal difference—though derived in the past from environmental forces—is still located *within* the victim, inside his skin" (p. 7 [italics in original]).

Nonetheless, a semantic escalation has also taken place, because what Ryan described so eloquently twenty-plus years ago was largely about stigmatization. While the poor *were* being blamed, they could also still be characterized as victims. Today, however, the poor are increasingly being treated as *victimizers*.

To be sure, journalists point out that they use the term "underclass" not because they want to accuse the poor, but because they think it "grabs" their audience, while researchers generally explain that they use it either because the media have emphasized it or because it grabs *their* audience, including those funding research. (Politically hopeful liberals in both occupations add that the term helps them call attention to the plight of the poor.)

Undoubtedly, "underclass" *has* grabbed the audience. Even so, because the term lumps everyone from drug dealers and street criminals to unemployed young people and unmarried mothers, any possible distinction between victimizers and victims is lost. What is also lost is the essential fact that all of the people who are assigned to the underclass, including those participating in illegal activities, are victims of a declining economy—and if they are blacks or other minorities, of various degrees of racism. Even so, once the people labeled as the underclass are seen as victimizers, they are also seen as people who do not deserve help from society. In short, "underclass" has become the newest word for—and symbol of—the undeserving poor (Gans, 1991).[1]

Since few elected officials can afford to be seen as helping people viewed as undeserving, the underclass label has also become the latest political obstacle to a revival of antipoverty policy. Even so, the term's rise to popularity can be used for understanding public attitudes toward poverty in the United States as well as for thinking once more about how to attack it. That is the main purpose of this paper.

THE RISE OF THE UNDERCLASS IDEA

The term "underclass" itself was introduced by the late Swedish economist Gunnar Myrdal.[2] In his little book about the American economy, *Challenge to Affluence* (1962), the Swedish scholar borrowed an obsolete Swedish word for "lower class" to warn of American workers being made unemployed and unemployable by the coming of what we now call the postindustrial economy. Myrdal said nothing about their race or their behavior; for him, the underclass was an *economic* concept to describe some victims of a changing economy.

Myrdal's concept was virtually ignored by other scholars until the 1980s, when it began to appear in scholarly writing, either as he had defined it, or more often in a sociological adaptation first proposed by William Julius Wilson (1978). Both definitions, and further variations on them, are still used by scholars today, although Wilson (1991) has since disavowed the term.

The popular media followed roughly the same time schedule but quickly moved toward the behavioral version of the term. *The Public Interest* carried an article about a "dangerous" underclass in 1973 (Moore, Livermore, and Salland, 1973), but no one noticed, and even a *Time* magazine cover on the underclass four years later (Russell, 1977), which made the same point in more graphic detail, evoked little attention. Only at the start of the 1980s, when the journalist Ken Auletta (1981) used "underclass" in a series of *New Yorker* articles and then as the title of a best-selling book about ex-convicts, ex-addicts, welfare recipients, and delinquent and other school dropouts in a sheltered workshop program, did the term begin to develop its current popularity. By then, it had become a very different concept from the one first used by Myrdal.

As a term for poor people who have participated in illegal or disapproved of behavior, underclass is hardly new, however, for as Katz (1989), Matza (1966), and others have pointed out, over the last five hundred years at least a variety of such terms have come and gone, with pauper, beggar, vagrant, and vagabond being among the oldest. During the 1960s, the allegedly undeserving poor were called "culturally disadvantaged," "hard core," and "members of a culture of poverty," among other things—and it was these terms, as well as all of the other stigmatizing language and ideology accompanying them, that set the stage for Ryan's *Blaming the Victim.*

The list of behaviors associated with being undeserving has changed little since the fifteenth century; only the words are different. "Welfare dependency" has replaced "pauperism"; "mugging," "banditry"; and "not working," "idling." Now as then, the pejorative has often evolved from describing a single behavior pattern to diagnosing a general personality failure; thus paupers, like today's welfare recipients, were believed to breed criminals, idlers—and more paupers. Moreover, pauperism and similar conditions were often thought to be irremediable and hereditary, and thus it should not be surprising that references to a permanent and "biological" underclass have appeared in the news media.

New terms, or renewed concern with old terms, for the poor thought undeserving do not appear randomly. They seem to develop at times of increased social and economic stress, notably when new and culturally or racially different populations arrive during periods of economic difficulty. Also, fear of the newcomer and the stranger rarely ebbs, which helps to explain why the list of behavior patterns associated with undeservingness has changed so little over the centuries. Thus, "culturally disadvantaged" and "hard core" became popular in the 1960s in response to the increasing joblessness among blacks and Hispanics who had come to the cities after World War II, the first glimmer of the soon-to-come urban "fiscal crisis" and ghetto uprisings.

Perhaps underclass or some term like it would have become popular in the mid-1980s even if Auletta had not written his book and his term had not been spread by others. It was a time when the children of the Hispanic and black newcomers to the city entered adulthood and an ever more depressed urban labor market.[3]

Nonetheless, new pejorative terminology for the poor does not emerge by itself; it is created by specific people. Most often these are professionals dealing with the poor; conservative reformers bent on moral uplift and economic efficiency (some of whom are called "policy analysts" today); scholars—some with the same reform impulses; and writers whose job it is to grab an audience. The term "feeble-minded," which was used to label the immigrant poor early in the twentieth century, was first applied to the poor by psychologists working in asylums and prisons; and a correctional psychologist in Chicago was the senior author of the first article, nearly a one hundred years later, about the "dangerous underclass" (Moore et al. 1973)

The diffusion of the idea of a behavioral underclass has been mainly the work of journalists and other writers. However, conservative social scientists and economists unfamiliar with the lives of the poor but ready to label them with pejorative terms have supplied the journalists with conceptual legitimacy and in some cases the "scientific" legitimacy attached to numerical data, especially about the size of the underclass, for news stories.

FEELINGS ABOUT THE UNDERCLASS

In effect, "underclass" and terms like it emerge to describe people others in the society would like to see disappear with verbal magic since they cannot be disposed of physically. The desire for their elimination is fundamentally based on a mixture of fear and anger. In the United States, the fear reflects above all feelings of *personal* threats, some justified, some imagined, which are connected to the fact that some poor people commit street crimes, including violent ones. The *political* threats, which made Europeans think of the poor as a dangerous class, have been virtually absent in the United States; instead, better-off Americans also fear the poor as an *economic* threat. Despite the fact that the total national expenditures for welfare recipients are inconsequential, recipients are feared because they are "dependent" on the taxpayers and imagined to be able to bankrupt the economy.

There is, however, another threat—a *moral* one. Some poor people are thought to subvert traditional familial, sexual, educational, work ethic, and other values by their behavior, thus setting bad examples to others in the society, especially young people. Like most moral threats, however, this one also involves a threat to the larger social order. When school children disrupt classrooms, adolescents join violent gangs, and young adults refuse dead-end jobs, some people worry that their own moral and social order may not continue.

OBSTACLES TO ANTIPOVERTY POLICY

Perhaps precisely because the feelings about the poor are based in part on fear and anger, those judged or imagined to be undeserving represent cultural-political obstacles to a revival of antipoverty policy. No politician who has to run for election wants to be accused of favoring public expenditures for people not thought to deserve them. The same constituents who have apparently been tolerant of huge Pentagon cost overruns, immense bank scandal bailouts, and "corporate welfare" believe that their taxes could be significantly reduced if "welfare cheats" were only eliminated from the welfare rolls.

A less visible obstacle is the correlative inability, or unwillingness, of better-off Americans to empathize with the situation of the poor and thus to understand the extent to which the behavior they blame on moral failure is in fact poverty-related. However, the tendency of any group in the United States to empathize with any other is limited, even if people tend to be more respectful of others of higher status.

Another obstacle, which is partly a result of the social distance that helps to discourage empathy, is the hyperbolic quality of the feelings about the poor. Once fear of and anger toward the poor take over, those who harbor such feelings tend to exaggerate both the frequency and seriousness of the offending behavior. Since hyperbole is largely based on impulse and is thus blind to empirical fact, persuading people that they have their facts wrong is extremely difficult and in fact often useless.

Hyperbole also creates, or adds to, a stereotype of the undeserving poor and justifies it at the same time. This then leads to a vicious circle, for once the stereotype is established, those who use it are apt to exaggerate further, which in turn establishes the stereotype even more firmly. The term "underclass" and the imagery behind it is one form of that stereotype.

There is, however, also a very different kind of obstacle, which has more to do with the lives of the nonpoor than with the shortcomings of the poor. The poor may be scapegoats who absorb worries the more fortunate have about themselves and their children. For example, the adolescent poor may be thought undeserving for their active sex lives in part because of the rising amount of adolescent sex among nonpoor youngsters.

Likewise, the better-off may worry about an alleged decline of the work ethic among the poor because they are concerned about the occupational future of their own youngsters. This becomes particularly salient as young people encounter difficulties in finding work and become downwardly mobile in larger numbers as the age of affluence ends. However, the scapegoat hypothesis is hard to document empirically. In addition, it can be questioned by the historical fact that contemporary American moral objections to the poor were invented in England hundreds of years ago and have remained stable (on both sides of the ocean) ever since, dramatic changes in both societies notwithstanding.

SOME USES OF THE UNDERCLASS

Despite their hostility toward the poor, better-off Americans also have some uses for them—even if they are not often aware of these.[4] To begin with, by being either in need of help or under threat of punishment or both, the poor who have been judged undeserving can be required to live by the values that the better-off preach—or can be punished for not doing so—even as those who set the requirements or punishments practice them less and less.

The poor are in effect offered an unspoken deal: they will be helped materially—as well as praised as deserving—if they finish school, work hard at dirty, dead-end jobs, remain publicly chaste until they are properly married, and prove by their other actions (for example, properly deferential attitudes toward caseworkers) that the traditional values remain valid. Thus, they will be given a chance to escape poverty in exchange for maintaining the legitimacy of some currently fragile moral standards. Unfortunately, however, the chance has strings, for those who legislate about and offer jobs and monies to the poor insist that the poor must uphold the standards *before* they will get economic help, although they generally need the help first, before they can afford to uphold some of the standards, either financially or socially.

Whether the rest of society really wants to help is, however, open to question, for having poor people around who can be described as undeserving also has some other uses for the members of that society. In an era of labor surpluses, the old function of the undeserving poor as a reserve army of labor may have declined sharply, but those labeled "undeserving" still provide clients for what might be called the salvation occupations, altruistic and respected callings in both American religion and social work. The poor also make possible and justify the creation of professional and nonprofessional jobs in a variety of institutions that exist to decide which poor are undeserving and then to help protect the rest of society from them. Social work, the police, the courts, the prison system, and even social science research on the underclass—as well as on poverty—would be smaller without them.

Elected officials at all levels likewise use the undeserving poor, for the unwillingness to look for nonexistent jobs that makes some poor people undeserving in the eyes of the better-off also allows the government to stop treating them as part of the labor force. As a result, they are not counted as jobless, and the *official* unemployment rate is lower than it would otherwise be.

These same politicians should also be pleased that more Americans are angered by beggars and the homeless than by the economic and political systems that help to produce the joblessness and the shortage of affordable housing. And every taxpayer benefits from the idea of the undeserving poor, for if they are not deserving of help, some taxes can remain lower than they would otherwise be.

Some of the other "users" of the idea of the undeserving poor are less noticeable and also more dispensable. One set, for example, includes the devotees of "action" films, for since the end of the cold war, such undeserving poor people as drug sellers and gang leaders have supplied the villains that enable movie or television heroes to be heroic. Last but not least, rightwing ideologists could not survive without the poor they consider undeserving, for their attacks on welfare, antipoverty policy, and the welfare state are partly justified by the ways in which they allegedly "coddle" the poor people who are automatically assumed to be undeserving.

POLICIES AGAINST UNDESERVINGNESS

Given the current political climate, antipoverty policy cannot be put on a solid footing without reducing the cultural and therefore political potency of undeservingness. This is a long-term and exceedingly difficult venture, which will at best succeed only partially, but I believe that it must be tried.

Probably the *first* policy against the idea of undeservingness requires taking up, and taking on, the conventional belief that those poor people who turn to crime or to other behavior repugnant to mainstream norms do so as a result of moral failure or weakness. The argument that such behavior is one response to the stresses of poverty may only become persuasive if the nonpoor can understand how much stress is associated with poverty, what stress does to hopes and ideals as well as personal values, and what would happen to their own moral strength if faced with such stress.

A part of this policy would seek to persuade the nonpoor to replace *moral* analysis with *causal* analysis, and to emphasize the extent to which offending behavior is what I earlier called poverty-related. The nonpoor should be able to understand why the middle class does not mug, or for that matter, drop out of school, or produce men of marriageable age who will never be able to function as proper breadwinners. Since these activities are and have historically been associated with poverty, lack of work and income must play a major causal role.

Perhaps most important task is to supply information about the scarcity of work, thereby debunking the old American myth that there are always more jobs than workers and that those without jobs are therefore lazy. Not coincidentally, free-market economists also hold to this myth, but as a result, very little research has been done to compare the number of available jobs with the number of people who are seeking or who have become discouraged from seeking work.

A related version of this myth holds that joblessness would disappear if the jobless began to behave like immigrants by reducing their wage and other demands to those available to immigrants. In effect, the myth demands that people whose ancestors have been in the United States for centuries nevertheless still need to prove their moral worth, and one way to do so is to go back once again to the end of the employment line.

A *second* policy is to delegitimize the notion of the underclass and of the undeserving poor in a variety of ways, both for the general public and for those social scientists who unfortunately must still learn to be more reflexive about the concepts they use.

Perhaps one good way to go about this is to draw on the long experience in fighting racial and religious prejudice, to attack the underclass idea as a form of class prejudice, to document the extensive practice of class discrimination, and to show how much "classism" results in invidious treatment of the poor. For example, only the poor live under constant moral judgment— from moralists as well as researchers. Bankers and stockbrokers may be watched periodically by the law, but unlike the poor, they are able to defend themselves in court or in the halls of Congress, and are not guilty until they are so proven. Poor people can be labeled undeserving without evidence or the right to confront their labelers. However, they lack access to politicians, lobbyists, or the media to make their case, while social scientists who make that case are often dismissed as "knee-jerk liberals."

A *third* policy is to attack the stereotypical nature of undeservingness, exploiting the general, if not necessarily deeply felt, consensus that stereotypes and stereotyping are bad, and to educate people about the labeling process by which stereotyping and assignment to the underclass take place. Part of this approach would be to demonstrate the immediate damages that labeling and stereotyping cause in the lives of the poor. For example, boys from poor single-parent families are often labeled as delinquents even before they have done anything wrong, simply because of the stereotype that they grow up without paternal or other male supervision. More generally, once poor people are labeled as undeserving, public officials providing them with services feel justified in not being helpful, but without realizing that their lack of help may push some people further down the road to homelessness or street crime. Thus labeling can create a population that virtually has no choice but to act out the expectations built into the label.

Attacks on stereotypes and on prejudice have limited effectiveness, but they do something to reduce the respectability of prejudice and at least question the social acceptability of labeling others as undeserving.

A *fourth* policy for attacking undeservingness is to question its effectiveness and efficiency. Although people do not realize it, describing the poor as undeserving or assigning them to an underclass does not end or otherwise affect the behavior that is judged undeserving. Such judgments are only a form of name calling, and do not attack the causes of street crime or the need to go on welfare. Blaming the victim can be criticized instrumentally as well; its main accomplishment is to make the blamer feel better temporarily for having expressed himself or herself.

A *fifth* and related policy is to identify and call attention to the difference between behavior among the poor that is socially *dangerous* and behavior that is situationally or culturally *divergent* but not dangerous. For example, it should be possible to demonstrate, especially in this day and age, that for poor people to live together without formal marriage is not harmful to anyone or anything—other than their own dreams that they could afford to be married. The poor have lived in common-law and other unions as well as in single-parent families in many societies for a long time (e.g., Collman, 1988; Finan & Henderson, 1988; Smith, 1988). Attempts should be made to persuade policy-makers as well as the general public to worry less about the "brokenness" of poor families, or even the official number of parents in them, and more about their poverty.

Moreover, single-parent families may not be as problematic as often thought, and because they are often found in economies that have insufficient decent jobs for men, they are a good example of situational divergence, even if poor people would be the first to argue for the virtue of the two-parent family. Single parenthood is hard to begin with, and poverty makes it even harder, but some studies suggest poor two-parent families in which the parents fight constantly may be much worse for the children (e.g., Peterson & Zill, 1986; Raschke & Raschke, 1979).

A *sixth* policy requires an ideological and empirical attack on the conservative scholarship about the poor to debunk, with data, its notions that poverty is caused by not looking for work or by being on welfare. A second attack needs to be launched in the social sciences generally against focusing virtually all research on the poor and not on the processes, institutions, and actors involved in their becoming and staying poor. The social science tendency to focus on victims is perhaps most evident in the endless studies of the homeless and the lack of research on the employers, landlords, housing industry, government agencies, relatives, and others who help drive them into the street. Even the studies of homelessness and mental illness always assume that being mentally ill causes homelessness, while minimal attention is being paid to how homelessness itself leads to mental illness.

Finding supportive constituencies and media audiences for these policies requires recruiting journalists, intellectuals, and researchers who have incentives to provide the needed information and carry out the needed studies. Mobilizing them and the institutions in which they function to swim against the contemporary ideological tide is difficult, as proven by the speed with which the steam went out of the liberal antipoverty research and writing of the 1960s after the decline of the Great Society. Neutral or liberal researchers and writers are usually in adequate supply, but the funding organizations to support the researchers and the publishers and editors to print the writers are not, especially if there is no ready-made audience eager to pay attention and conservatives are on the warpath against them.

ANTIPOVERTY POLICY

The final chapter of Bill Ryan's *Blaming the Victim* bears the title, "In Praise of Money and Clout," but this is still what the poor and their advocates lack most. They also lack an escape hatch from the Catch-22 that now haunts us: that undeservingness is best eliminated by an *effective* antipoverty policy that integrates as many of the poor into the mainstream economy as quickly as possible, but that such a policy is unlikely to come about as long the obstacles of undeservingness remain, and the poor neither vote nor mobilize.

In fact, the likelihood of an effective antipoverty policy is further reduced the less the nonworking poor are needed in the economy. Nonetheless, some possible programs toward an effective antipoverty policy deserve mentioning once more.

First, since the effect of political appeals is ultimately impossible to predict, and since the high moral ground is always the best start, morally based appeals for antipoverty policy must be given further trial. The likelihood of such appeals working, at least by themselves, seems small these days, but they cannot be ignored.

Second, on the assumption that moral appeals alone will not work, antipoverty policy must be designed from the start in a hard-headed fashion: a combination of what is most effective for helping the poor and what is most feasible for getting political approval. Today, any antipoverty program that begins by helping poor people who can be labeled undeserving seems sure to fail; conversely, any policy that begins with effective anticrime programs might have a chance of success.

Third, programs to help the poor will most likely work only if other, politically more influential people are helped first or concurrently. This means "universalistic" policy programs such as those suggested by Schorr (1986), Skocpol (1991), Wilson (1987), and others, although Greenstein (1991) is right to insist that some programs that are targeted solely on the poor remain politically viable. Moreover, labor-intensive helping services that are designed for poor clients are still more expert at dealing with their specific problems than universal services.

Fourth, with every new year, the conventional universalistic programs that hark back to the New Deal seem less relevant, for what is needed is more drastic: a job-centered *economic security* program for all Americans in occupational and related economic difficulties, which is oriented to job preservation and job creation, and emphasizes jobs, job quality, and job security.

We are currently living in the first stages of what might be called *worker-shedding capitalism,* in which firms survive and profit by employing labor-saving computers and other machinery, and employing the fewest number of people possible, especially on permanent basis. A downsizing trend that began with manufacturing has now spread to many services, and no end to the trend, or the economic reasons for it, seems in sight.

Unfortunately, the political consequences of this trend are not in sight either. Currently, most Americans still have faith in the ability of private enterprise to create jobs and an equally strong lack of faith in what government, or any other economic arrangement, might do instead. As always, the already jobless often become depressed and lose whatever interest in political protest they might otherwise have.[5] Eventually, however, economic disaster must have politically disastrous consequences.

At that point, government and private enterprise will clearly have to act, but the general economic policy, capitalistic, socialistic or utopian, that would revive the economy and restore labor-intensive economic growth— and make a real economic security program feasible—has not yet been invented.

Fifth, most antipoverty programs need to be merged into the larger economic security program, but the latter needs to be targeted in one respect. Jobs for the poor, as for the unskilled and poorly educated people still in the

working class, need to be accessible to them in terms of social and skill requirements—and in firms as well as public agencies that are willing to hire
low-status and dark-skinned workers. As long as classism exists, poor people will not automatically be welcome in middle-class workplaces. Still, the
jobs must be good enough to get as many women off welfare and men out
of drug sales and other criminal parts of the informal economy as possible.

One obvious targeting solution is public works, which now means badly
needed public construction and reconstruction jobs as well as the establishment of new social programs, public data bases, and the like. In other words,
this would be a modernized New Deal work policy, for men and women
both, perhaps under the supervision of skilled workers, including professionals, who are also jobless.

Public works is largely a short-term solution, however, not only because
the tasks are eventually accomplished but because taxpayer protest is apt to
make itself felt. As a result, it is only a way station toward the general—and
as yet uninvented—economic policy mentioned above.

Sixth, welfare, like unemployment insurance, is really only a temporary
and often punitive pension system for victims of the economy's labor surplus,
classism, and racism. It deserves to be incorporated into mainstream pension
systems, and its clients treated like other pensioners, but with one difference:
the pension should be designed so as to save the children from having to repeat the parental experience if at all possible. The system should also be designed with the possibility that worker-shedding capitalism may become
more permanent and will affect large numbers of the middle classes.[6]

Seventh, in the longer run, the economy may run out of full-time jobs for
everyone. In order to avoid the creation of a society in which some work full-
time, others become involuntary part-timers, and the rest are permanently
jobless, the list of solutions—above and beyond the previously mentioned
general economic policy—will surely have to include work sharing: the reduction of work weeks or years to create new jobs, so that everyone who
wants work has a chance to get it (Best 1988; Cross, 1988). By then, full-
time may mean thirty hours a week or less, with a two-breadwinner household supporting itself on sixty hours a week or less (Gans 1990). Because this
will mean a reduction in national standards of living, there is also need for a
universal basic income grant—or an extension of the pension system discussed above—to make up as much as possible of what people will lose in
wages and salaries when their work hours decline. In the long run, then, people may demand the egalitarian solution that Bill Ryan called "Fair Shares,"
since that is one way to help counteract worker-shedding capitalism and
work sharing.

CONCLUDING CAVEATS

Even the less-than-expert reader will surely have realized by this point that the general economic policy I have mentioned above is a *deus ex machina* and that the proposed resort to "Fair Shares" is utopian. However, much darker scenarios can also be suggested.

Thus, the present process of driving people out of the labor force, turning them into a labor surplus, and then labeling them as lazy and otherwise morally deficient and undeserving of jobs or other entitlements is making worker-shedding capitalism operate very efficiently—and without viable political opposition. To be sure, this process has so far not touched many whites, for its victims have been largely black, Hispanic, and in some places Asian. Whites, especially suburban working- and middle-class ones, may not let themselves be forced into an undeserving underclass all that easily.

Conversely, rosier scenarios need to mentioned as well. Fears of worker-shedding capitalism are not new, and there may have been Luddites in ancient Babylon already. Thus, it is possible that new raw materials, technologies, human needs and wishes, other economic opportunities, and even yet unimaginable organizationalisms will appear once more, as they seem to have appeared in the past to revitalize the economy and to put people back to work.

In that case, much of what I have written here is irrelevant, although despite all the new technologies, opportunities, and isms, the poor have remained with us throughout—ever since the end of hunter-gatherer societies. A brief and not entirely perfect exception could be found in some of the Western European welfare states, which had almost eliminated poverty between about 1960 and 1980, but they only make the case once more for Ryan's Fair Shares.

NOTES

1. I should note sociologists are not expected to be moral judges of their fellow humans. If they were, I would have to introduce this analysis by suggesting that some of the poor *are* undeserving and *do* victimize, first and foremost other poor people. Still, I would add that such people are concurrently victims, even if not innocent ones.
2. For a history of the usage of "underclass" in the United States, see Aponte (1990).
3. The immigrants that followed the black and Hispanic newcomers after 1965 have generally been spared the underclass stigma, in part because most appear to be employed, but also because they are less visible—and less angry.

4. This section on "uses" is based on a conceptual framework that I applied to the poor generally in an earlier article (Gans, 1972) and to the allegedly undeserving ones in more recent one (Gans, 1994).
5. I doubt that the Republicans would have borrowed the term "empowerment" from the left if they had any thought that the poor would obtain and use political power for themselves.
6. The system must also make room for a number of the so-called discouraged workers who may be so discouraged that they are no longer employable. Some may have to be offered drug treatment, prison rehabilitation, and social support programs to help them become employable again.

REFERENCES

Aponte, R. (1990). Definitions of the underclass: A critical analysis. In H.J. Gans (Ed.), *Sociology in America* (pp. 117–137). Newbury Park, CA: Sage.
Auletta, K. (1982). *The underclass.* New York: Random House.
Best, F. (1988). *Reducing workweeks to prevent layoffs: The economic and social impacts of unemployment insurance–supported work sharing.* Philadelphia: Temple University Press.
Collman, J. (1988). *Fringe-dwellers and welfare: The aboriginal response to bureaucracy.* St. Lucia, Australia: University of Queensland Press.
Cross, G. (Ed.). (1988). *Worktime and industrialization: An international history.* Philadelphia: Temple University Press.
Finan, T. J., & Henderson, H. K. (1988). The logic of Cape Verdean female-headed households: Social response to economic scarcity. *Urban Anthropology, 17,* 87–103.
Gans, H. J. (1972). The positive functions of poverty. *American Journal of Sociology, 78,* 275–289.
Gans, H. J. (1990). Planning for work sharing: The promise and problems of egalitarian work time reduction. In K. Erikson & S. P. Vallis (Eds.), *The nature of work: Sociological perspectives* (pp. 258–276). New Haven: Yale University Press.
Gans, H. J. (1991). *People, plans, and policies: Essays on poverty, racism, and other national urban problems.* New York: Columbia University Press.
Gans, H. J. (1994). Positive functions of the undeserving poor: Uses of the underclass in America. *Politics and Society 22,* 269–283.
Greenstein, R. (1991). Universal and targeted approaches to relieving poverty. In C. Jencks & P. E. Peterson (Eds.), *The urban underclass* (pp. 437–460). Washington, DC: Brookings.
Katz, M. B. (1989). *The undeserving poor: From the war on poverty to the war on welfare.* New York: Pantheon.
Matza, D. (1966). Poverty and disrepute. In R. K. Merton & R. A. Nisbet (Eds.), *Contemporary social problems* (2nd ed., pp. 619–669). New York: Harcourt Brace & World.

Moore, W., Livermore, C., & Salland, G. (1973). Woodlawn: The zone of destruction. *Public Interest, 30,* 41–59.

Myrdal, G. (1962). *Challenge to affluence.* New York: Pantheon.

Peterson, J., & Zill, N. (1986). Marital disruption, parent-child relationships, and behavior problems in children. *Journal of Marriage and the Family, 48,* 295–307.

Raschke, H. J., & Raschke, V. J. (1979). Family conflict and children's self-concepts: A comparison of intact and single-parent families. *Journal of Marriage and the Family, 41,* 367–374.

Russell, G. (1987, August 28). The American underclass. *Time,* pp. 14–27.

Ryan, W. (1971). *Blaming the victim.* New York: Pantheon.

Schorr, A. L. (1986). *Common decencies: Domestic policies after Reagan.* New Haven: Yale University Press.

Skocpol, T. (1991). Targeting within universalism: Politically viable policies to combat poverty in the United States. In C. Jencks & P.E. Peterson (Eds.), *The urban underclass* (pp. 411–436). Washington, DC: Brookings.

Smith, R. T. (1988). *Kinship and class in the West Indies: A genealogical study of Jamaica and Guyana.* Cambridge: Cambridge University Press.

Wilson, W. J. (1978). *The declining significance of race: Blacks and changing American institutions.* Chicago: University of Chicago Press.

Wilson, W. J. (1987). *The truly disadvantaged: The inner city, the underclass, and public policy.* Chicago: University of Chicago Press.

Wilson, W. J. (1991). Studying inner-city social dislocations: The challenge of public agenda research (1990 presidential address). *American Sociological Review, 56,* 1–14.

Part III

Beyond Victim-Blaming: The Emergence of New Voices

Chapter 6

Mental Health and Unemployment: The Making and Unmaking of Psychological Casualties

•*Ramsay Liem and Joan Huser Liem*

> Unemployment is a two-edged sword. For worse, it's meant financial loss . . . . You go along and have successes for a number of years and then this. It's a shock . . . . At the same time it can enhance other kinds of feelings; the desire to strike out in a new direction, a moment to pause in your life, to reflect, and reorganize things, and move in other directions . . . . But I'm not as positive as I was before. I worry more . . . . Certain basic assumptions are no longer what they seemed to be." (Unemployed worker participating in the Work and Unemployment Project)

SINCE 1970 DOZENS OF ARTICLES AND BOOKS HAVE ADDRESSED THE PSY-chological consequences of unemployment, with a large proportion devoted to the mental health of unemployed workers. Using a variety of methods—epidemiological assessment of macroeconomic and mental health indicators (Brenner, 1973; Catalano, Dooley, & Jackson, 1981; Dooley & Catalano, 1986), population surveys (Kessler, Turner, & House, 1988), quasi-experimental designs (Gore, 1978; Kasl & Cobb, 1979, Liem & Liem, 1988a), and in-depth case studies and ethnographies (Buss & Redburn, 1980)—this body of writing makes a compelling case that emotional well-being is linked to the health of the economy through workers' employment status.

Although the influence of economic recession and unemployment on mental health seems obvious, labor force participation has only recently been considered to be an important risk factor for emotional disorder by mental health professionals. Most clinicians typically view employment status as a by-product rather than a determinant of emotional health. Acute or chronic psychiatric disability is an impediment to employability according to this stance, necessitating institutional practices such as vocational rehabilitation, sheltered workshops, and transitional community homes to facilitate the reentry of previously disabled persons into the work force. In their regional study of displaced aerospace workers, Paula Rayman and Barry Bluestone

(1982) were unable to locate a single psychiatric facility using intake procedures that assessed employment status as a potential factor contributing to mental illness.

Given the dominance of the biomedical perspective in American psychiatry and clinical psychology, we welcome the affirmation of the interdependence of emotional well-being and the state of the economy. It challenges the artificial boundary between the domains of intrapsychic and social dynamics, and redresses what William Ryan and others have described as the complicity of the mental health professions in victim blaming through neglect of the structural roots of psychological distress. "We must learn that the emotionally disturbed individual is not an unusual abnormal unexpectable 'case,' but is rather a usual, highly predictable index of the distortion and injustice that pervades our society" (Ryan, 1971b, p. 645). From a policy angle, the economy–mental health connection reframes emotional disorder as a public health rather than solely a private concern. Sclar (1982), for example, contends that unemployed workers are as entitled to compensation for lost health as they are for lost wages.

This perspective motivated the Work and Unemployment Project, which we designed primarily to explore the mental health of displaced men and their spouses. It was also largely confirmed by our findings (Liem & Liem, 1979, 1988a). Neither the men we interviewed over the twelve months following unemployment nor their spouses exhibited clinical levels of disturbance. Still, as a group, they displayed marked increases in a broad range of psychological symptoms in comparison to demographically similar but employed workers and their wives. Because we conducted multiple interviews with each couple, we were able to establish that emotional distress occurred in response to the loss of work and abated sharply upon reemployment. What other investigators largely inferred from global indicators of the economy and mental health, or from cross-sectional data, we examined directly.

VICTIMIZING THE VICTIM

We chose a social structural approach to this work influenced heavily by Ryan's critique of victim-blaming (Ryan, 1971a). In time, however, a related but different issue began to emerge as we listened to the families we met describe their efforts to cope with hard times, and reflected on the strong emphasis we had placed on structural unemployment as the determining factor in their lives.

Many of the people we spoke to were indeed greatly stressed by the loss of their jobs. On the other hand, while their anxiety and depression were initially triggered by threats to the material and social foundations of their personal and family lives, over time their distress also appeared to signify active, if frustrated, attempts to put order back into their lives and to continue to pursue long-term personal and family goals. We began to feel that we had inadvertently neglected the resilience and resistance of these workers and their families by focusing our attention on the recessionary economy as the driving force in their emotional lives. In the shift from victim-blaming—which saw unemployment as a result of idleness or moral defect, lowered productivity, or mental illness—to institution blaming, we lost sight of these workers as engaged and purposeful people, struggling to control the disorder in their circumstances. Our initial model, on the contrary, suggested demoralization and helplessness in the face of a declining economy. Freed of the burden of blame for being out of work, workers were conferred the status of helpless casualty in our structural analysis.

This point was driven home by a journalist who interpreted our research along with the findings of others as signaling the capitulation of labor to the interests of capital. Recession restricts workers' options and undermines the value of labor. The unemployed, forced out of work, become anxious and depressed, and vent their anger on family members. What he envisioned was workers internalizing the stress of unemployment, displacing their anger and frustration, and losing the will to resist or fight back.

This scenario, however, did not fit the workers we interviewed, even those who suffered the greatest emotional toll following their loss of work. We began to suspect that the combination of the adoption a structural model of the impact of the economy on workers and the widespread currency of the victim metaphor played major roles in this perception of the unemployed as defeated. More importantly, we were compelled to consider how our own reading of these workers' experiences might have been guided by an unreflective, "victim-making" stance, surely not the resolution envisioned in Ryan's critique of victim-blaming.

Part of the explanation for this unanticipated shift in stance toward the unemployed resides in the institutional posture of medicine and psychiatry. Mental health professionals do not contest economic policy; they treat emotionally disordered people. Regardless of social circumstance, the troubled person is the focal concern. Those distraught by widespread recession are seen as economic casualties and focusing on their psychological distress enhances the severity of the perceived damage done to them. Liberal academics and policy analysts, therefore, may protest layoffs and plant shutdowns, but casualties, particularly emotional casualties, are expected to have lost their voices. Without overstating the case for the unemployed as a political force, it is clear to us that even the most genuine concern for the psychological pain created by job loss risks an ideological representation of the unemployed as helpless. To understand better how a structural approach to unemployment that seeks to counter victim-blaming can result in victim-making requires an examination not only of the individualistic bias in modern mental health practice but also the social meaning of unemployment as it has evolved historically.

THE "DISCOVERY" OF UNEMPLOYMENT

In his studies of unemployment preceding and following the Great Depression, Alex Keyssar (1987) concludes that by and large unemployment has been "an intractable and resilient problem in the United States for more than a century" (p. 221). In spite of several notable exceptions, the Great Depression and the post–World War II period from 1947 to 1974, long-term trends in the incidence and duration of unemployment are unremarkable, reflecting year-to-year fluctuations between 3 percent and 11 percent. With respect to the economic hardships of job loss, "the impact of unemployment remains [today]—in critical ways—very similar to what it was a century ago" (p. 206), in spite of relatively recent public programs of economic compensation. "Family strategies for coping with unemployment resemble those that were common fifty or a hundred years ago; families draw on their savings, cut down on their expenditures, and, if possible, send an additional household member into the labor force" (p. 206).

Given these broad contours of the sociological dimensions of unemployment, it appears that joblessness has been endemic to the capitalist United States throughout the twentieth century. In all likelihood its mental health consequences have also remained unchanged. There is considerable evidence, although much of it is indirect or anecdotal, that jobless men and women and their families throughout the century have experienced the anxiety, self-doubt, and disorganization of family life associated with economic insecurity. Following their review of over one hundred studies, David Fryer and Roy Payne (1986) conclude that "in all cases, the evidence suggests that groups of the unemployed have higher mean levels of experienced strain and negative feelings, and lower levels of happiness, present life satisfaction, experience of pleasure and positive feelings than comparable employed people" (p. 247).

A related but separate issue, however, involves the social definition of unemployment as a human event and the extent to which the psychological consequences of losing a job are *perceived* to be integral to this experience. Regardless of the *actual* psychological effects of joblessness occurring at different historical moments, has there been a corresponding continuity in the salience attached to the mental health of displaced workers, particularly as inferred from historical, social science, and media accounts of hard times?

Part of the answer to this question lies in the origins of the social category of unemployment itself. Common wisdom suggests that unemployment as involuntary separation from wage labor is a timeless burden shared by all working people. Keyssar (1986) offers a counterview, however, in his study of nineteenth- and twentieth-century unemployment in Massachusetts. He proposes that the very existence of unemployment as we conceive of it today is predicated on the transformation of preindustrial, agrarian economies into modern, urban capitalist modes of production. Prior to the industrial revolution of the nineteenth century, labor was dependent on access to land, and the ability to farm for use or exchange purposes dictated the capacity to meet one's basic material needs. Being out of work was not so much a question of job loss but of land dispossession, seasonal disruptions of agricultural production, or one's proclivity to idleness. Even with the advent of early home and crafts industries, workers who were unable to compete in the new marketplace often maintained their ties to the land, to which they could return during hard times.

The rise of industrial capitalism and a monied economy in the New England states radically altered the relation of labor to the means of production, creating an impersonal marketplace defined and controlled by a new class of capital-holding entrepreneurs. As the industrial economy gained hegemony over the labor market, workers faced a new form of economic dependency, becoming increasingly beholden to the interests of capital for employment. Although Keyssar (1986) does not dispute inequities in access to land in the preindustrial agrarian economy, he argues that the new capitalist economy radically expanded the percentage of laborers dependent on an externally controlled labor market for their livelihood: "by 1875, more than 85 percent of the people [of Massachusetts] who worked in 'manufactures and mechanical industries' were employees" (p. 16). Unemployment took on a new meaning, applicable to the vast majority of workers, in which the threat to subsistence shifted from the whims of nature to the interests of capital. As further evidence of the periodicity of modern unemployment, it was not until 1878 that the Massachusetts Bureau of Statistics of Labor attempted to measure systematically the incidence of "involuntary idleness" among wage earners, the first effort of its kind in the United States (Keyssar, 1986).

As an integral by-product of a newly emerging form of industrial production in the United States, unemployment became a pivotal indicator of the economy's capacity to provide for the needs of the population. Major periods of unemployment—the recessions of 1873, 1893, and 1913, and the

Great Depression of 1929—witnessed intensifying political debate over the legitimacy of unfettered capitalist development given the growing concentrations of power and expanding dependencies it spawned. Owners and, to a degree, the government sought to represent the new industrial order as serving the interests of labor and capital alike. Workers, on the other hand, were skeptical and struggled for a share of control over capital through the formation of workers associations and unions (Folsom, 1991).

This struggle reached its apex during the Great Depression, when some sectors of the labor movement challenged the viability of an economic system unable to control rampant unemployment. Unemployment became the focal point of an ideological struggle that threatened the stability of the social order at its foundations. "Nevertheless, the dramatic Soviet boast that unemployment had been abolished had a large impact on the capitalist world, especially during the depression-ridden decade of the 1930's" (Garrity, 1978, p. 153).

By the time of the Great Depression unemployment had become a refined economic category thoroughly integrated into the popular discourse and imbued with political meaning. It signified not only great personal suffering and hardship but also impending social instability that, in the extreme, could invite either fascism or communism (Lipset, 1959). A product of the Industrial Revolution and the intensification of competing class interests, this particular construction of unemployment dominated the American landscape during the 1930s.

SOCIAL AND PSYCHOLOGICAL RESEARCH
DURING THE GREAT DEPRESSION

The intense political debate over the ramifications of unemployment also defined the context in which over one hundred studies of the social and psychological impacts of unemployment were conducted during the 1930s. It formed the subtext of this work, influencing the kinds of questions deemed worthy of investigation as well as the interpretation of findings.

Most contemporary reviews of this literature assume that it addressed essentially the same issues that motivate current research on the psychological effects of losing a job—the variety of stresses that unemployment provokes, the strategies workers use to cope with these stresses, and the conditions under which stress leads to the breakdown of mental health. Many of the classic studies—Marie Jahoda, Paul Lazarsfeld, and Harold Zeisel's (1933/1972) ethnography of a small town facing imminent economic collapse, E.W. Bakke's (1933, 1940) extensive interviews of English and American workers, and Mira Komarovsky's (1940) exploration of the family life of unemployed men—offer insights into the mental health of the unemployed. However, the emotional health of the unemployed was only one of a variety of psychological issues addressed by these and other investigators during this period, and it was not necessarily a primary concern.

For example, in their 1938 review of research on the psychological effects of unemployment, Philip Eisenberg and Paul Lazarsfeld discuss the mental health of dislocated workers as one topic in a section on "Personality Traits." Other sections review sociopolitical attitudes, the distribution of attitudes by employment experience, and the effects of unemployment on children. They describe lowered self-confidence as a common reaction to unemployment generally preceding anxiety and depression but also suggestibility. The concept of suggestibility, however, as taken from the work of Harry Cantril (1934), is referred to as "susceptibility to advertising, money schemes, fortune tellers, or leaders" (p. 364). The political subtext is then expressed directly: "the political implications may be very important, since the unemployed might follow any political group or leader who appealed directly to their needs" (p. 364).

To contemporary readers, Eisenberg and Lazarsfeld may appear to have been reviewing the mental health consequences of unemployment. It is evident, however, that they were just as concerned with the potential instability in the society created by the extensive dislocation of workers during the Depression. The psychology of social unrest is a theme consistent with the broader political climate that infused the social meaning of unemployment with an element of class conflict: "People who have never been out of work are more frequently conservative, and identify more frequently with the upper and middle classes. Radicalism increases . . . , proportionately as the time that people have been out of work is lengthened, or at least it does so among manual workers" (Centers, 1949, pp. 177–179).

Eisenberg and Lazarsfeld's review also covers an abundance of psychological research devoted to sociopolitical attitudes regarding morality, religion, and politics. A prominent concern in the domain of morality involved the family and its ability to maintain traditional lines of patriarchal authority in the face of the economic assault of unemployment. Komarovsky's classic work, *The Unemployed Man and His Family* (1940), illustrates this point. Her research examined the marital relationship of unemployed men and their status in the eyes of their children. The work is usually cited as evidence that the quality of the marriage prior to unemployment influences the family's psychological adjustment to the loss of work. A closer look at Komarovsky's discussion of adjustment, however, reveals an implicit assumption that the preservation of the authority of the father/husband is the key to maintaining

the stability of the family. By implication the underlying threat of unemployment appears to have been its impact on the man's ability to maintain
his role as disciplinarian and decision-maker in the home.

Family instability and worker's susceptibility to undesirable social and
political influences are related to a more general theme in the work conducted
during the Great Depression—fear of the collapse of the larger social and
economic order. Bakke's research (1933, 1940) is a case in point. Best known
as a proponent of a stage model of physical and mental exhaustion among
displaced workers, Bakke actually devoted much of his research to investigating the level of political consciousness and activism among the hard-core
unemployed. A scant ten pages in his first three hundred-page volume, *The
Unemployed Man* (1934), cover the mental effects of unemployment. Although he found little evidence that the unemployed were likely candidates
for insurrection, it was clearly the anticipation of the politicizing effects of
unemployment that motivated much of Bakke's inquiry.

In a recent commentary on this body of work, Gordon O'Brien (1986)
claims that Bakke attributed the despair he found among some workers not
to the hopelessness of their status as unemployed but to the alienating conditions of the work these men had experienced before losing their jobs.
O'Brien argues that the Bakke studies actually contained an indictment of the
condition of working people under industrial capitalism rather than simply
the assurance that the Depression did not engender revolutionary sympa-
thies. Bakke's social science appears to have lined up on labor's side of the
political struggle engendered by the Depression.

This reading of three major publications from the era of the Great Depression suggests that social and psychological research during this period
was heavily influenced by the wider political discourse on the state of the
economy and its implications for the health of the society. Rampant unemployment fueled labor's challenge to the new industrial order, provoking
questions about the effects of job loss on workers' political leanings. Mental
health outcomes, while important to early investigators, appear to have been
"discovered" as *the* central concern in early research by contemporary re-
viewers for whom the emotional cost of unemployment has become the
salient issue.

The secondary concern for the mental health consequences of unemployment in psychological research from the Great Depression is also evident
in early epidemiological studies devoted to exploring the social distribution
of psychiatric disorders. Several of the classic studies in psychiatric epidemiology were conducted during the Depression years. The work of Robert Faris
and Warren Dunham, published in 1939, examined admissions to state psychiatric hospitals in the Chicago metropolitan area according to patients' res-

idential locations. The findings are well known and describe high concentrations of psychiatric admissions from geographic areas closest to the center of the city containing the most socially disorganized and transient neighborhoods. Faris and Dunham's report of this pattern provoked some of the earliest debates about the relationship of social class to mental illness and the role of class-linked stresses in precipitating psychiatric disorder.

It is striking that there is virtually no reference to the Depression in this major investigation, although the data were drawn from 1922 to 1936. Only a two-line comment in the book's introduction, written by Ernest Burgess, mentions that "financial depression beginning in 1929 was accompanied by little or no increase in mental disorders" (p. xii). What is odd about this sweeping disclaimer is that nowhere in the detailed account of this work is there any indication that a systematic effort was made to examine the influence of unemployment on the social patterning of hospitalizations. The evidence for this conclusion cannot be found in the research report.

The omission of the Depression is startling in a study explicitly designed to examine the social contexts of mental illness. Surely the unprecedented economic displacement of workers during this period was a dominating feature of the social landscape. Yet, in reading the Faris and Dunham study one encounters no hint that the society was in deep recession and that rates of unemployment in center city neighborhoods were as high as 50 percent. One is left with the impression that this omission reflects the constraints of prevailing mental health theory and the broader political discourse on unemployment rather than the personal biases of these particular investigators. For those whose point of departure was the problem of unemployment, mental health was only one of many concerns, and for others focusing on psychiatric disorder, the depressed economy was at best marginally significant. The absence of a link between unemployment and mental illness in Faris and Dunham's work thus adds to our suspicion that emotional health was not a salient parameter of the problem of unemployment during the 1930s.

REPRESENTATION OF UNEMPLOYMENT
AND MENTAL HEALTH IN THE MEDIA

The absence of an integral connection between psychiatric well-being and unemployment suggested by this review of Depression research is also reflected in more public accounts of joblessness during the same period. We conducted a content analysis of a small number (40) of randomly selected articles on unemployment published in the *Boston Globe* and the *New York*

Times in the years 1929–36 and 1980–84. The latter period coincides with the most severe recession in the United States since the Great Depression and also the years during which we conducted our research on the mental health consequences of unemployment.

Articles published during the Depression portray a vast, undifferentiated population of unemployed facing severe economic hardships linked to national and international economic conditions. They focus more on the macroeconomy than on individual workers, and describe numerous proposals for local relief programs and federal legislation. Rarely is mention made of the day-to-day emotional strain of unemployment either for workers or their families. Articles written during the 1980s also examine the aggregate economic picture, often presenting detailed statistics of unemployment rates in various labor market sectors. However, they also tell the story of the recession through the lives of individual workers and the particular circumstances faced by different groups of the unemployed, such as youth, auto workers, and professionals. Although the mental health of workers is given no special attention in the latter accounts, there is much more detailed coverage of the "human costs" of unemployment during this period than one finds in reporting during the 1930s. A significant portion of the recent articles speak of the discouragement and disillusionment of the unemployed, the threat of family conflict and divorce, and the prospects of emotional exhaustion in the face of continuing economic hardship.

What most distinguishes the coverage from each period is the emphasis during the Depression on macroeconomics and the programs and policies needed to restore the health of the economy in contrast to a focus in recent articles on the experience of individual workers. This difference is consistent with the concern for the stability of the social order evident in the subtext of research conducted during the Depression and the heightened interest in unemployment as a risk factor for emotional disorder among contemporary investigators. The analysis of journalistic reporting also reveals the pervasiveness of unemployment sentiment during both periods and the potential influence of the wider public discourse on social science practice.

UNEMPLOYMENT: FROM CONTEST
TO COMPENSATION

We have proposed that the kinds of psychological concerns addressed in research conducted during the Great Depression were compatible with the prevailing social climate of political debate provoked by massive economic dislocations. For workers, widespread unemployment was contested as an unacceptable burden of industrial capitalism. To industrialists and their supporters, the greatest danger lay in the escalation of worker unrest and skepticism about the viability of the capitalist economic order. The fundamental structure of the society was placed in question in the political drama of the Great Depression. Psychological research on workers' attitudes toward the economy, religion, and politics and the effects of unemployment on the patriarchal structure of the American family reflected this uncertainty.

According to labor historians, government intervention in the form of New Deal programs significantly transformed the terms of the debate regarding unemployment and the economy (Garrity, 1978). Rather than a focus of contention over the viability of the urban industrial economy, unemployment was reenvisioned as a necessary factor of capitalist production to be regulated and managed through a new partnership among government, private industrialists, and representatives of labor. The Social Security Act of 1935 symbolized this new consensus and affirmed the institutionalization of unemployment as an undesirable but tolerable fact of economic life.

In her writing about full employment policies over the past four decades, Margaret Weir (1987) describes a gradual process, beginning in the post-Depression period, through which unemployment was transformed from a political into a technocratic problem. Over time the demand for a full-employment economy was marginalized by a new economic discourse in which Keynesian theory, the emergence of inflation as a competing evil, organized labors' shift from the protection of jobs to job seniority, and the rise of the welfare state formed the basis of a new social contract.

The ideological legacy of the Great Depression was the social construction of unemployment as a necessary, predictable factor of what was otherwise to be considered a fundamentally sound industrial economy. What made this formulation of the problem of unemployment palatable to labor was the promise that the rate of joblessness could be controlled and that its economic costs would be a shared burden of industry, government, and labor. According to Keyssar (1986), to be out of work became "involuntary idleness routinized and institutionalized, absorbed into the familiar and accepted fabric of American life . . . . The very word 'unemployment' came to refer not to the condition of being out of work but to the benefits they [workers] received from a government agency" (p. 298). In the official discourse, joblessness no longer signified an economic system to be contested. Rather, it became a fact of working life to be managed by experts like any other periodic wrinkle in an otherwise healthy economic system.

The social redefinition of unemployment as a problem for technical management rather than political debate is an integral component of the context in which contemporary psychological studies of job loss are conducted. Related public policy issues that also contribute to this climate are concerned with voluntary versus involuntary unemployment, "covered" versus "uncovered" unemployment, and the social and economic costs of job loss entitled to compensation. What constitutes an adequate social safety net for dislocated workers? For what costs of losing a job is there a public responsibility, and at what levels should unemployed workers be compensated for them? These are the kinds of questions that are now provoked by recession, plant closings, and layoffs. Unemployment itself has been replaced as a subject of contention by its material and social consequences and the resources needed to handle them.

Psychological studies of unemployment reflect the influence of this public discourse today much as they were shaped by the social construction of joblessness during the Depression. The problems that current studies address conform in broad outline to the new social consensus, which holds that what is important about losing a job are its negative consequences, against which workers are entitled to protection. Mental health and illness represent the newest claim for expanded coverage for the unemployed.

MENTAL HEALTH AND UNEMPLOYMENT

The incorporation of mental health into the discourse on unemployment was the product of more than a new consensus on the inevitability of economic downturns. Mental health theory and practice needed the appropriate conceptual tools to envision a social event like unemployment as a serious factor in the etiology of emotional disorder. Several trends in psychiatry and clinical psychology contributed to this readiness. Briefly, they include more holistic approaches to physical and mental health; wider recognition of the social distribution of mental disorders according to social class, marital status, ethnicity, and the like; and the prominence of stress and trauma theory in research on psychological disorders (Pearlin, Lieberman, Menaghan, & Mullin, 1981). These developments represent an orientation to mental health and illness as social as well as biological facts and enable the mental health professions to entertain economic recession as a factor relevant to their mission.

These changes within both the mental health fields and the wider discourse on unemployment have led to the prominence of research questions regarding the emotional rather than political implications of losing a job. This seemingly enlightened concern for the psychological consequences of unemployment, however, should be regarded cautiously. On the one hand, common sense suggests that in a society where labor force participation is essential to material subsistence for most people and where work is idealized as self-actualizing, forced displacement would logically be a serious blow to mental health. Hence, these costs should be figured into the formula for a just and adequate social safety net for those predictable bust cycles in the economy.

What is less evident is that emphasizing what job loss does to the mental health of workers is particularly effective in reinforcing the new politics of unemployment as a technocratic rather than a contestable problem. Focusing on emotional distress lends itself to an ideology of problem management that emphasizes strengthening the coping resources of the individual rather than eliminating the problem (Jahoda, 1988). The promotion of healthy adjustment and accommodation to one's circumstances are deemed realistic goals *particularly* in view of the structural origins of unemployment.

Paradoxically, what may appear to be a progressive stance within the mental health professions—the recognition of the structural determinants of emotional health and a sensitivity to victim-blaming—actually serves to reinforce the ideological rendering of unemployment as a normative fact of working life. It emphasizes outcomes versus causes, juxtaposes the relative powerlessness of the individual in relation to the scale of the macroeconomy, and is laden with the person-centered tradition of American psychiatry and clinical psychology. The mental health stance foregrounds the displaced worker to the neglect of the economy and affirms the intractability of economic forces that drive unemployment. How potent a force for structural change can individual workers be, particularly emotionally distraught workers?

The association of mental disorder with job loss is both beholden to and affirming of the depoliticization of unemployment. Its most insidious effect is to transform the meaning of "victim," as employed by William Ryan to focus attention on structural inequalities, into a status of helplessness. In spite of benign intentions that motivate a concern for the emotional casualties wrought by a capital-serving economy, structural models of the economy and mental health border on victim-making. Labeling the unemployed as victims and casualties may elicit sympathy and support from others, but it does so at the cost of negating the ability of workers to act on their economic, political, and private interests. Such an approach authorizes liberal academics and policy analysts to "rescue" the unemployed.

UNEMPLOYED CASUALTIES AS IDEOLOGY

This analysis of the inadvertent victim-making stance of research on unemployment and mental health required an examination of the historical precedents for a new discourse on joblessness. It helped us to understand how our own research questions were circumscribed by a particular social definition of unemployment as a technocratic problem warranting compensatory action rather than structural change. In this context adding emotional impairment to the costs of job loss is vulnerable to creating the impression that the unemployed are incapable of contesting their own status or asserting their own interests. However, mindful of the psychological stresses engendered by job loss, we contend that this characterization of the unemployed is also an ideological construction that distorts the experience of many who are involuntarily displaced.

The work of Michael Frisch and Dorothy Watts (1980) is based on extensive oral histories of unemployed workers in Buffalo, New York, during the mid-1970s, when the heartland of American industry was entering an extended period of structural decline. Frisch and Watts were interested not only in the economic, social, and psychological setbacks experienced by workers but also in how the unemployed understood the recession and integrated it into their personal autobiographies. They approached their respondents as *informed* observers of a deteriorating economic scene that dominated the lives of working people in the Buffalo community.

What is most relevant for our thesis can be found in an article describing the editorial process accompanying the preparation of a story on the Buffalo unemployed commissioned by the *New York Times Magazine* (Frisch & Watts, 1980). It reconstructs an emerging tension between the authors and the editors of the *Magazine* as the writing progressed and reveals a striking contrast in images of the unemployed as victims of an industrial collapse. These contrasting perceptions are illustrated by the following example of the editorial process as applied to an interview with a domestic worker. The portions selected by the *Times* editors are in roman type; the fuller text suggested by Frisch and Watts (1980) includes this material as well as the statements highlighted in italics:

. . . about the people. They got the wrong type of people for the wrong type jobs to make Buffalo come up. Buffalo could be number one, it could be done. If they put the right type people in, they'd see how Buffalo would bloom. *You have to spend to make, that's all there is to it. In Buffalo, it seems like they don't want to put out money, they just want to hold money, and they're just killing it. If we could put our money in something good, why we could get something out of it. But we got to put it in first. They're going to have to do something, people can only go hungry for so long. I don't know what the cause is, but it's something to think about. I'm telling you.* It looks like people, we pull against each other so much now. We're not like we used to be; more together. We're divided, and it looks like all we care for is: if I live. I don't care what becomes of you. *But we can't be like that. Until we get together we're gonna be this way, and farther apart, in worser shape. That's true in Buffalo. You could come out of that, though, but you're not going to bloom overnight; when you're into something so deep, you got to gradually work your way out of it.* (p. 105)

Frisch and Watts note that the passage as edited by the *Times* is emotive, exclamatory, ungrounded, and seemingly arbitrary, whereas the more complete text provides some of the context and reveals the worker's thoughtful reflection. In this woman's view, the local economy needs people who are "right" not in some abstract sense but in terms of a willingness and ability to commit financial resources and to make sound investment decisions. In the complete text she also expresses a commitment to collective solutions as essential to solving personal problems, in contrast to apparent feelings of competitiveness and divisiveness among workers that one might attribute to her on the basis of the edited text alone.

A similar difference in perspective can be found in the following versions of a passage from a union representative:

But then Litton came in, in 1965. They loaded the plant with salaried workers; these out of towners would be walking around here and we couldn't even find out what their jobs were . . . . Most people know that Litton is a holding company. They get in, they make a buck, they get out. *I don't think it's fair. I don't think it's right to the community. You're not only talking 750 jobs. Add their families, their warehouses, and other interests all over the country. There's truckers involved, there's railroads involved, people getting cut back all over. Now, when you're talking 750 jobs, you might be talking 10,000 people before you're done.* (p. 104)

The *Times* version expresses this man's contempt for absentee management and its proxies but excludes his succinct analysis of how the decisions of disinterested parties can undermine an entire community through the ripple effects of a major layoff. Without the complete text this worker appears simply to be venting his emotions rather than expressing his frustrations toward an industry at odds with the interests of rank-and-file workers.

When allowed to speak, the workers interviewed by Frisch and Watts reveal themselves to be thoughtful individuals reacting to their economic circumstances in critical and incisive ways. They are angry and frustrated, but they are also proscriptive, even didactic. Their feelings resonate with their understanding of the conditions that have produced the crisis of unemployment and about which they have judgments and opinions. Removing the emotional content of these interviews from this context of thoughtful reflection creates the impression that these workers are emotive casualties of the recession, victims who suffer but are incapable of critical action or thought. They elicit sympathy and provoke the *reader* to contemplate the state of the economy. The elite readership of the *New York Times* is invited to appropriate the subjectivity of these workers.

The essence of the disagreement was made clear in the final dispute concerning this article, its title. Frisch and Watts proposed "America Not Working," a commentary on the state of workers *and* the industrial economy. The *Times* opted for "Down and Out in America," underscoring its vision of the unemployed as defeated.

The editorial exchange that Frisch and Watts report illustrates the making of social victims as an interpretive act. Given the prestige of the *New York Times,* it also offers insight into how the public discourse on unemployment is shaped. What occurred is a second order of victimization. Having first been displaced by recessionary labor market forces, the unemployed are subjected to a selective telling of their experiences in which they are absent as active, critical voices. They are denied intentionality, thoughtful reflection, and action in service of their personal and class interests.

In spite of the emphasis on mental health outcomes in our study of unemployed men and their families, we too found evidence of resilience even among those suffering the greatest distress. The following excerpts were provided by an older, middle-aged couple who experienced a very difficult adjustment to the husband's unemployment. Ultimately, the couple separated, and the husband experienced a brief psychiatric hospitalization. The wife developed agoraphobia for a short period following the separation. First, a flavor of the negative side of their experience:

HUSBAND: I've been getting depressed and that isn't really dealing with it. Just worrying about the future while I try to improve on it at the same time which isn't quite that easy to do especially when you're in job interviews. You're just not at your psychological best when you know that you don't have any income and you need a job and you want a job. You come across, I come across, as somewhat desperate, which is what I am and it just about kills your chances for getting a job.

WIFE: I'm giving 400 percent of myself to him and my daughter to maintain normalcy and I'm tired, very tired. I find myself jealous of my friends because they are now where we would have been financially and it hurts.

HUSBAND, IN RESPONSE TO A QUESTION ABOUT FINANCIAL PROBLEMS:

Fuel, foreclosure on my house, foreclosure on my car, foreclosure on my life (mumbles). I've created a mess.

HUSBAND, REGARDING THE MEANING OF UNEMPLOYMENT: It means being without power to control the things you normally like to have control over in you life like happiness, for me, anyway. I lost confidence . . . . I'm actually scared to go on a job interview. (Liem & Liem, 1988b, p. 143)

These remarks poignantly convey the burden of unemployment. By themselves, they suggest the helplessness of casualties of the economic system. There is another side, however:

HUSBAND, REGARDING THINGS THAT ARE BETTER OR WORSE SINCE HIS UNEMPLOYMENT: . . . Doesn't mean anything for the better. For worse, poverty and the possibility of lower paying jobs for doing the hardest work. Those who move paper get big money and those who sweat are exploited. . . . People in positions to help me have not come forward; blue-collar workers have offered more help and given me more leads. The white-collar professionals never offered me anything, except sympathy which I didn't want.

WIFE, ALSO REGARDING POSITIVE AND NEGATIVE ASPECTS OF UNEMPLOYMENT: It's better in a sense because I've become much more politically aware, doing a lot of reading about the system of government. I've become interested in socialism . . . opening up my eyes to corporate and government corruption.

HUSBAND, REGARDING SUPPORT FOR THE JOB HUNT: Help wasn't available because in my opinion the corporate system from government on down is not really concerned with the plight of the unemployed person, be they white or blue collar.

HUSBAND, COMMENTING ON WHAT HE WANTS IN A JOB: I have been trying to resolve whether or not I should take a job at which I would be unhappy; make a week's pay or continue to go for the American dream of an executive position which is what I understand I am qualified to do but no one else understands it. (Liem & Liem, 1988b, p. 144)

What is striking about these two sets of responses is that even in the midst of the virtual collapse of this family, the husband and wife have not completely internalized their difficulties. There is a clear sense of the inequities in the system and an emerging identification with blue-collar workers in a man whose job history includes both white-collar public relations work and unskilled manual labor. Similarly, in spite of the intense fear associated with her agoraphobia, this woman is hardly complacent having begun to develop a political awareness that questions the validity of basic social institutions.

Like the Buffalo unemployed, the workers we interviewed had much to say about the circumstances behind their unemployment and were not hesitant to indict corporate and managerial initiatives.

ASSEMBLY-LINE WORKER: Polaroid goofed a lot of things. They overpro-
duced and overspeculated. Some guy making $100,000 a year made a film
cartridge for $27 (a piece). They had to sell it by government standards for
$10 and also the chemicals leaked into the camera. Suddenly, making of that
camera ceased and the people making that camera were higher than us [in
seniority]; so they had to get rid of the excess and we were the excess bag-
gage. Those people got our jobs.

HOSPITAL MAINTENANCE WORKER: Hospital said they could save money
by bringing in an outside firm. Two months after I started, the shop signed
cards to have a union come in for elections; everybody in the shop was in
court except for two guys. Hospital went to court, spent $30,000 to keep the
union out. The union won, and the hospital fired the whole crew and brought
in an outside firm which offered you a job, cut in pay, and less benefits, and
I would have to cross a picket line.

RETAIL WORKER: There's a change in the nature of the business such that
they don't hire trained people in my job; because of the economy, they're firing instead of hiring and using less-qualified people.

These brief remarks cover deskilling, union busting, and failures in product planning. Another remark offers a recommendation for handling an economic slowdown more equitably:

WIFE OF A HOSPITAL WORKER SHORTLY BEFORE HER OWN LAYOFF FROM
A CLERICAL POSITION: We could have been receiving a full pay check; would
make it a lot easier to deal with unemployment. Everything takes money. In
my employment, I don't know if they could do it, but cut hours rather than
lay people off. If we could work three days a week all year it would be a lot
better, but they let you go for an undetermined amount of time. (Liem &
Liem, 1988b, p. 147)

Finally, there are occasions when inaction can signify resistance. No single burden occupies an unemployed person as much as the job hunt. It is a
transaction that exposes one's sense of value and worth to the judgment of
others, often under conditions where workers have much at stake yet little
control. Holding fast to one's sense of entitlement when jobs are scarce is
thus an expression of resistance, albeit one that can cost workers financial
resources in the short run:

ELECTRICIAN: In my profession, marine electrician, there's nothing available. I've gone to companies to train as an apprentice electrician, commercial, and they're only paying $3–4 an hour. I was making $8.50. You can't
take that!

ASSEMBLY-LINE WORKER: I haven't been offered a job that is acceptable
to what I want, we need. Something that would pay better and have medical
benefits, retirement.

ELECTRICAL WORKER: I could get any amount of jobs as an electrician's helper or minor maintenance man changing light bulbs, when in fact I'm more qualified to design the systems they're changing the parts in. If I wanted to cut my income by two-thirds, I could go to work tomorrow. (Liem & Liem, 1988b, p. 145)

The claim to self-worth implicit in these comments can easily be missed by those who see "holding out" for a better job as extravagant, self-defeating, or even irrational. What it does suggest, however, is that even the most direct victims of economic downturns are not automatically reduced to the ranks of a docile reserve army of labor mindlessly prepared to take their places in a new labor market of deskilled, low-paying jobs. Furthermore, refusing to cede control over one's employment objectives is what makes the job hunt so stressful and discouraging. Much of the anxiety and depression that workers exhibit during this phase of their unemployment is a product of active striving in the face of a shrinking job market, a point noted a half-century earlier by Bakke (1933): "it would be closer to truth to describe it as physical and mental exhaustion from the doing of work [searching for a job] which is unaccompanied by any reward or hope of reward" (p. 71).

Our emphasis on the weariness of such struggles as the source of emotional strain for unemployed workers is not a trivial matter. As discussed below, mental health theories, even newer social psychological perspectives, focus on internal deficits in psychologically troubled individuals. Consequently, they shift attention away from external conditions even as they may acknowledge the role of environmental factors in precipitating a breakdown. They also call into question the ability of the individual to act effectively on his or her own behalf. Applied to the condition of displaced workers, person-centered approaches reinforce a particular ideological construction of unemployment; one in which the problem is the damage it creates and for which the technical skills of the clinician are needed to repair. By neglecting the ways that workers contest their loss of work even as they suffer emotional pain and disorganization, the problem of unemployment is further depoliticized, and distraught workers are represented as casualties rather than actors.

RETHINKING UNEMPLOYMENT AND MENTAL HEALTH

As we have suggested, however, there is another side to the unemployment experience. Workers enter into unemployment not only as victims of material, social, and psychological deprivation but as self-conscious, purposeful actors with interests cultivated through their experiences on the job as well as outside the domain of work. The frustration of these desires creates the stress of losing a job, but personal, family, and class interests also determine how workers view the economy, understand their compromised status, and decide to act in light of their eviction from the workplace. The emotional life of displaced workers is, therefore, the product of a constant but dynamic balance between the threats to one's agenda and the effectiveness of cognitive and behavioral strategies employed to overcome them.

From this perspective, symptoms of psychological distress signify the frustration of positive efforts to surmount external barriers, rather than the incipient process of deterioration and breakdown proposed by traditional models of emotional disorder. This view does not foreclose on such an outcome, but it emphasizes active striving over psychological or constitutional deficits. The latter play a prominent role in most stage models of the unemployment experience, which envision a downward spiral of apathy, despair, and hopelessness.

Even psychological theories of abnormal behavior that incorporate social factors in the etiology of disorder often adopt the deficit view of "symptoms," because they identify the root causes of mental disturbance as defects in motivation, cognition, early acquired patterns of maladaptive coping, or biological structures (Mishler, 1981). Social factors or stressors merely enhance the risk that these dispositions will undermine mental health by threatening a satisfactory but tenuous adjustment prior to the occurrence of pronounced, external threats. The distress one experiences in the face of stressful challenges, therefore, is seen as an indication of a breakdown in coping rather than a persistent and difficult struggle to achieve one's ends in the face of externally imposed obstacles.

Our view of the mental health of unemployed workers has become increasingly more sympathetic to the latter view, in which competent, healthy individuals are seen as being challenged by the task of making good on their dreams and aspirations in the face of significant hardships created by the loss of work. The stress of unemployment is thus seen as the product of opposition between the willful striving of workers and their families and externally imposed threats to social relatedness and psychological integrity. The manifestation of this stress in anxiety, depression, or even demoralization is no less intense or "real" than were it the result of a fundamental breakdown in basic psychological processes. What differs is that the emotional response to losing a job is embedded within a dialectical tension between striving to subject social reality to one's purposes and needs, and accommodating to the compromising demands of external events and structures. Emotional distress is thus a sign of willful action in the face of limiting economic and social conditions.

This is not a perspective that fits comfortably with a definition of unemployment as a technocratic problem to be consigned to the tinkering of
experts. It requires taking into account the unemployed as social actors engaged on different levels in contesting their economic status and the hardships it imposes. While it acknowledges the structural roots of unemployment and the psychological distress created by the loss of work, it does not
envision workers as passive casualties of the economic order. We believe
that this approach to the mental health consequences of unemployment is
consistent with William Ryan's broader analysis of the victims of inequality.
In his trenchant critique, Ryan names the victims of structural inequality but
also joins with them to urge collective action for social change. In his view
also, victims are not helpless casualties. This is the insight that we have
tried to incorporate into our approach to the mental health of unemployed
workers:

> A vast welfare structure has grown up as a kind of buffer state, pro-
> tecting the possessors from the dispossessed. It is one of my purposes
> . . . to look at the origins of this structure in relation to the recurring
> chant, "We Demand!" (Folsom, 1991, p. 2)

ACKNOWLEDGMENTS

This research was supported in part by National Institute of Mental Health
Grant No. MH 31316. The authors would like to acknowledge the major contributions of Thomas Atkinson, Stephen McElfresh, and Joseph Schipani to this project.

REFERENCES

Bakke, E. W. (1933). *The unemployed man.* New Haven: Nisbet.
Bakke, E. W. (1940). *Citizens without work.* New Haven: Yale University Press.
Brenner, M. H. (1973). *Mental illness and the economy.* Cambridge, MA: Harvard
    University Press.
Buss, T. F., & Redburn, F. S. (1980). *Shutdown: Public policy for mass unemploy-
    ment.* (Research Rep.) Youngstown, OH: Youngstown State University, Center
    for Urban Studies.
Cantril, H. (1934). The social psychology of everyday life. *Psychological Bulletin, 31,*
    297–330.
Catalano, R., Dooley, D., & Jackson, R. (1981). Economic predictors of admissions
    to mental health facilities in a nonmetropolitan community. *Journal of Health
    and Social Behavior, 22,* 284–297.

Centers, R. (1949). *The psychology of social classes.* Princeton: Princeton University Press.

Dooley, D., & Catalano, R. (1986). Do economic variables generate psychological problems? Different methods, different answers. In A. J. MacFadyen & H. W. MacFadyen (Eds.), *Economic psychology: Intersections in theory and application* (pp. 503–546). Amsterdam: North-Holland.

Eisenberg, P., & Lazarsfeld, P. (1938). The psychological effects of unemployment. *Psychological Bulletin, 35,* 359–391.

Faris, R., & Dunham, H. W. (1939). *Mental disorders in urban areas.* Chicago: University of Chicago Press.

Folsom, F. (1991). *Impatient armies of the poor.* Niwot: University Press of Colorado.

Frisch, M., & Watts, D. (1980). Oral history and the presentation of class consciousness: *The New York Times* vs. the Buffalo unemployed. *Oral History, 1,* 89–110.

Fryer, D., & Payne, R. (1986). Being unemployed: A review of the literature on the psychological experience of unemployment. In C. L. Cooper, & I. Robertson (Eds.), *International review of industrial and organizational psychology, 1986* (pp. 235–278). New York: John Wiley & Sons.

Garrity, J. A. (1978). *Unemployment in history.* New York: Harper & Row.

Gore, S. (1978). The effects of social support in moderating the health consequences of unemployment. *Journal of Health and Social Behavior, 19,* 157–165.

Jahoda, M. (1988). Economic recession and mental health: Some conceptual issues. *Journal of Social Issues, 44,* 13–25.

Jahoda, M., Lazarsfeld, P., & Zeisel, H. (1972). *Marienthal: The sociography of an unemployed community.* New York: Aldine-Atherton. (Original work published 1933.)

Kasl, S., & Cobb, S. (1979). Some mental health consequences of plant closings. In L. Ferman & J. Gordus (Eds.), *Mental health and the economy* (pp. 255–300). Kalamazoo, MI: The Upjohn Institute.

Kessler, R. C., Turner, J. B., & House, J. S. (1988). Effects of unemployment on health in a community survey: Main, modifying, and mediating effects. *Journal of Social Issues, 44,* 69–87.

Keyssar, A. (1986). *Out of work: The first century of unemployment in Massachusetts.* London: Cambridge University Press.

Keyssar, A. (1987). Unemployment before the Great Depression. *Social Research, 54,* 201–221.

Komarovsky, M. (1940). *The unemployed man and his family.* New York: Dryden.

Liem, R., & Liem, J. H. (1979). Social support and stress: Some general issues and their application to the problem of unemployment. In L. Ferman & J. Gordus (Eds.), *Mental health and the economy* (pp. 347–378). Kalamazoo, MI: The Upjohn Institute.

Liem, R., & Liem, J. H. (1988a). Psychological effects of unemployment on workers and their families. *Journal of Social Issues, 44,* 87–107.

Liem, R., & Liem, J. H. (1988b). Unemployed workers and their families: social victims or social critics? In P. Voydanoff & L. Majka (Eds.), *Families and economic distress* (pp. 135–151). Newbury Park, CA: Sage Publications, Inc.

Lipset, S. M. (1959). *Political man.* Garden City, NY: Doubleday.

Mishler, E. (1981). Viewpoint: Critical perspectives on the biomedical model. In E. Mishler, L. AmaraSingham, S. Hauser, R. Liem, S. Osherson, & N. Waxler (Eds.), *Social contexts of health, illness, and patient care* (pp. 1–23). London: Cambridge University Press.

O'Brien, G. E. (1986). *Psychology of work and unemployment.* New York: John Wiley & Sons.

Pearlin, L. I., Lieberman, M. A., Menaghan, E. S., & Mullen, J. T. (1981). The stress process. *Journal of Health and Social Behavior, 22,* 337–356.

Rayman, P., & Bluestone, B. (1982). *The private and social response to job loss: A metropolitan study.* Rockville, MD: National Institute of Mental Health.

Ryan, W. (1971a). *Blaming the victim.* New York: Vintage Books.

Ryan, W. (1971b). Emotional disorder as a social problem: Implications for mental health programs. *American Journal of Orthopsychiatry, 41,* 638–645.

Sclar, E. D. (1982). Social-cost minimization: A national-policy approach to the problems of distressed economic regions. In F. S. Stevens & T. F. Buss (Eds.), *Public policies for distressed communities* (pp. 15–26). Lexington, MA: D. C. Heath & Company.

Weir, M. (1987). Full employment as a political issue in the United States. *Social Research, 54,* 377–402.

7

Insisting on Innocence: Accounts of Accountability by Abusive Men

• *Michelle Fine, Toni Genovese, Sarah Ingersoll,*
Pat Macpherson, and Rosemarie Roberts

IF YOU LISTEN CLOSELY, YOU CAN HEAR WOMEN WHISPERING, GOSSIPING, and contesting the borders of male heterosexuality. Having arrived on playgrounds where men once played unchallenged, women of all colors are arguing that men cannot play with them without their "consent." The slippery constructions of consent and coercion are being challenged through the feminist lens of gender, class, race, and power.

A vibrant critical consciousness is being voiced by young women whose biographies constitute twenty years of second-wave feminism and twelve years of Reagan-Bush individualism. In their lifetimes, notions of date and marital rape, incest, woman battering, and sexual and racial harassment were "invented." Feeling entitled to their bodies and sexualities, these girls/women question the "rights" of male violence. Experimenting with the sexual sovereignty of their passions, they are refusing the passive position of sexual victim (see Alcoff & Gray, 1993; American Association of University Women, 1993). Expecting fairness, they are astonished by the response to their grievances from institutions of "justice."

In this chapter, we pry open those institutions of justice that are designed to offer remedy to young women who call foul on male sexual violence. Propelled by experience and provoked by theory, we seek to understand how such institutions fail to hear these women and how they even more consistently refuse to deploy a discourse of male accountability.

We are interested in cases involving white men in particular in order to understand the relationship between their central place in such institutions and the systematic institutional refusal to *hear* the claims of girls/women. We found that the concept of male accountability barely showed up in court; instead we saw the grievance go on trial. Consider a *New York Times* article written about one of our scenes—the Glen Ridge, New Jersey, rape trial:

> Just two weeks after the start of the Glen Ridge sex assault case, the mildly retarded young woman at its center has hardly any privacy left . . . . Supporters of both sides in the case say the tactic is turning a trial that once appeared to be about one thing—teenage suburban boys accused of taking advantage of a helpless girl—into a case of something else entirely: Can women lodge sex-assault and rape charges without taking the chance that they will, in effect, be placed on trial? (Hanley, 1992c, p. B26)

In William Ryan's intellectual legacy, we probe not *if* these women will be placed on trial, but *how*. In this chapter we try to understand how acts of sexual assault are subtly and yet explicitly reconstituted within the interactions and discourses of three major social institutions—courts, schools, and families. Interactional analysis allows us to examine the institutional alignment of resources and supports for accused men and against accusing women (Goffman, 1963). Discourse analysis allows us to examine the relations of power underlying the words and representations of men, women, and institutions. Borrowing from Michel Foucault (1978), we understand that discourses carry and construct power, and that silences can be part of subjugation, challenge, or resistance: "Discourse transmits and produces power; it reinforces it, but also undermines and exposes it, renders it fragile and makes it possible to thwart it. In like manner, silence and secrecy are a shelter of power, anchoring its prohibitions; but they also loosen its hold and provide for relatively obscure areas of tolerance" (p. 101).

In this essay we are trying to weave an argument through both structural and discourse analysis. While these two have typically run a parallel course, here we braid them in order to display how institutions of social justice operate, both materially and discursively, to appear neutral with respect to race and gender, while surrounding the claims of white elite men with institutional regard and purging the claims of women as though they had violated institutional integrity.

We are attempting, therefore, two feats, one methodological and one conceptual. Our methodological feat is to attach discourse analysis to structural analysis to make visible how resources, status, language, and silences are deployed by social institutions, including courts, schools, and families, to validate primarily the claims of white boys/men and to trivialize in order to efface the grievances of girls/women. Our conceptual feat is to shift attention, within the heated terrain of violence against women, away from both the women and the men, and onto those institutions within which grievances and counter claims are being voiced and contested.

Our analyses draw from three scenes of male violence we have been studying in depth as observers, participants, and/or qualitative analysts. Each scene involves girls/women, of varied ages, who have been raped, harassed, or incested at the hands of an older, once trusted, usually white man, maybe a father, uncle, brother, teacher, childhood friend, or boy in the neighborhood.[1] While we recognize that our "scenes" of rape, incest, and sexual harassment are not comparable in their origins, experiences, or consequences for the girls/women, we believe, nevertheless, that across these "scenes," *institutions of justice* have responded in an astonishingly similar way—flight, denial, and protection of the men. It is this response that we seek to understand. We move to snapshots of our scenes.

SCENE I: GANG RAPE IN A MIDDLE-CLASS NEIGHBORHOOD

Sarah Ingersoll observed the Glen Ridge rape trial in a Newark courtroom for its duration.[2] In the early 1990s, a group of white elite boys are accused of sexually assaulting a young, mildly retarded woman. The woman, Pam, is responding to the defense attorney:

PAM: There were fifteen boys. [She ticks off their names.] I was standing alone.

DEFENSE: So why'd you take your clothes off?

PAM: Somebody asked me, so I did . . . . They asked me to finger myself.

DEFENSE: Did you?

PAM: They asked me to.

DEFENSE: Did you say, "I don't want to do it?"

PAM: No . . .

DEFENSE: But you don't always do what you're asked to do, do you? When you were giving a blow job to Kyle, you stopped before he ejaculated. Why? ·

PAM: But his hand was there. [She puts her hand on her head.]

DEFENSE: Was anyone stopping you from raising your head up?

PAM: They were saying, "Go further, go further" . . .

DEFENSE: But no one was holding you or threatening you, right?

PAM: That's a hard question.

DEFENSE: No one was holding you?

PAM: When he stopped with this? [She pushes her hand on the top of her head.]

DEFENSE: You were able to leave?

PAM: Yup.

DEFENSE: But you made no attempt to leave.

PAM: Yup . . . . I had to take my underwear off. . .

DEFENSE: Nobody grabbed your legs, did they?

PAM: They told me to spread my legs. They started putting stuff [Vaseline] on the broom.

DEFENSE: How were they holding it? You take the broom and show me how they were holding it.

[She holds it horizontally. The defense attorney takes back the broom and points it at her, tipping it into the witness stand where she sits.]

DEFENSE: When it was inserted did it go straight in? How far was it inserted?

PAM: Pretty far.

DEFENSE: How far?

JUDGE: [Interceding] She said, "pretty far . . . "

DEFENSE: Did you leave?

PAM: No.

DEFENSE: You didn't want to leave?

PAM: No.

DEFENSE: You wouldn't have said, "No"?

PAM: No.

DEFENSE: But you can say, "No"?

PAM: No.

DEFENSE: You've never said anything to anyone if you didn't want them to do something.

PAM: No . . . .

DEFENSE: But you wouldn't let anyone try to burn you?

PAM: No.

DEFENSE: Or stick you with a pin?

PAM: No.

DEFENSE: They wouldn't be your friend, would they? [Silence] Did anything bother you the next day?

PAM: Yeah. . . .

DEFENSE: But yesterday when you said, "Nothing," was that true?

PAM: It was confusing to me.

DEFENSE: You weren't lying . . . ?

PAM: No.

DEFENSE: But you had no marks or bleeding?

PAM: No marks.

DEFENSE: And no bleeding.

[Pam looks down and does not answer.]

Later, when describing the incident to a psychologist, Pam said she wanted to stop giving [one of the boys,] Bryant Grober, the blow job, but, "I didn't want to put him down. It would be putting him down not to do it." When asked, "Why did you allow it [the entire event] to happen?" Pam answered, "The way they looked at me, like I was supposed to do it—like a movie" (Hanley, 1992b).

SCENE II: SEXUAL HARASSMENT IN A PRIVATE SCHOOL—THAT "CREEPY FEELING"

We cannot report an actual case of sexual harassment in the context of the power relations of an actual school, because we could be sued for defamation of character and breach of confidentiality. Allegory, a symbolic story and set of characters, makes possible a translation from the dangers of facts to the safety of fiction—but at the expense of much authority and analysis of the complexities of real human relations. Our allegory begins in a way that will sound familiar, with a male gym teacher at an elite private school, where confidentiality and "privacy" are privileged. He touches female students in a way that makes them uncomfortable. His behavior becomes a class joke, part of an informal network of gossip, about his preference for the pretty girls when he is demonstrating a hold or step. Eventually several girls complain to other teachers about particular examples of his behavior. The girls who complain are feminist, and so are the female teachers to whom they bring their stories. The girls trust the women to carry the feminist complaint to the halls of justice and release them from further involvement. In a discussion of the handling of the case, the male head of the school and board members receive information and input from female administrators responsible for student affairs (deans and counselors) and for faculty supervision (principals and department heads). Already a hierarchy becomes apparent when input is received from women, but their inclusion in the final decision is either unclear or explicitly cut off. The decision is made to suspend the teacher and require him to receive counseling if he wants to reapply for his job. Later, after counseling, the teacher is rehired.

SCENE III: STORIES OF INCEST AND ITS SILENCING

Our third scene draws from a series of narratives collected by Toni Genovese from adult women who have survived incest. Their stories tell not the details of incest nor the violence of family life as much as their experiences, as children and adults, of trying to tell, trying to let someone know their pain, and of being silenced and being silent. While no story is typical, we offer you an image from the waiting room in family court, as Genovese interviewed Patti in the midst of criminal proceedings she has lodged against her father:

> Patti whispers, in secret, that when no one is around she plays with the stuffed animals here in the Victim Assault Unit in the courthouse. Patti sits on the floor, gently moving the arms and legs of the animals to make them dance. She colors a picture and does a puzzle. They wait together for the verdict. She is afraid, unsure, and confused about her decision to go through with this trial, re-creating a childhood before her family went on trial. Her father is on trial for childhood sexual abuse. She thinks she made the right decision. During the trial her boyfriend and her counselor have been in the courtroom, and she has been waiting alone. She is a twenty-year-old survivor of sexual abuse long ostracized from her family for telling them and the police.

THE SET: THE INSTITUTION PROTECTS ITSELF

Whether we eavesdrop on the courtroom in which the Glen Ridge case is being heard, the private elite school, or the incested families of interviewed women, we hear features of a common set: courts, schools, and families are ideologically "safe spaces," sites for moral reasoning, contexts for debate in which all are entitled to get a hearing. William Ryan, in analyzing contexts of victim-blaming, might consider these to be settings that promise, but don't deliver, a "Fair Shares" perspective.

The Fair Shares perspective, as compared with Ryan's Fair Play idea, concerns itself much more with equality of rights and access, particularly the implicit rights to a reasonable share of society's resources, sufficient to sustain life at a decent standard of humanity and to preserve liberty and freedom from compulsion. Rather than focusing on the individual's pursuit of personal happiness, the advocate of Fair Shares is more committed to the principle that all members of the society obtain a reasonable portion of the goods that society produces. From this vantage point, the overzealous pursuit of private goals by some individuals might even have to be bridled. From this it follows, too, that the proponent of Fair Shares has a different view of what constitutes fairness and justice, namely, an appropriate distribution throughout society of sufficient means for sustaining life and preserving liberty.

These are the very settings to which women bring their claims of abuse. And these are the very settings structured by the "liberal humanism" that Rachel Hare-Mustin (1991) has described:

> The liberal/humanist tradition of our epoch assumes that the meanings of our lives reflect individual experience and individual subjectivity. This tradition has idealized individual identity and self-fulfillment and shows a lack of concern about power. Liberalism masks male privilege and dominance by holding that every individual is free. The individual has been regarded as responsible for his or her fate and the basic social order has been regarded as equitable. Liberal humanism implies free choice when individuals are not free of coercion by the social order. (p. 65)

Across sets, we watch a girl/woman come forward, or be brought forward, to reveal the abuse. We hear alarm that becomes suspicion, disbelief. And we hear inquiry become concern for the accused man. We notice evidence of institutional retreat and sometimes cover-up. We watch the girl/woman wither as she sees her story be denied, denigrated, reconstituted, or respectfully discarded. After the telling, the institution reasserts it coherence, seals its borders, and struggles to insure its sense of integrity. The girl/woman has dared to fragment its encasement. Local interests scurry to collaborate on repair. Her demands for male accountability, once voiced, are considered shrill, partial, and vengeful if repeated. Official discourses normalize what has happened, burying the woman's words. Sooner or later we realize: because the accused man somehow embodies the neutral (white) institution, there is a collective investment, a wish, for his survival "in place." If he "falls," the institution "falls." If "justice" is defined as granting everyone a chance to speak, these cases can be officially dispatched without the case for male accountability ever being heard.

Most significant to our analysis, we argue three points:

1. Social institutions are splintered not by acts of abuse, but by women's acts of telling about the abuse.
2. Institutions of justice, in the name of Fair Play, rely upon discourses that legitimate the stories of abusers and disintegrate the stories of survivors who tell.
3. Despite much marbled evidence of a fragmented discourse of male accountability, narrated by girls/women who have been assaulted, by concerned and feminist teachers, therapists, or mothers, or by lawyers for the plaintiffs, contemporary institutions of social justice are without the discursive resources to hear these fragments, integrate them, or grant them institutional currency. That is, despite the screams, whispers, or threats of "angry" women, of which there is much growing and encouraging evidence, institutions of "justice" are still without a legitimate discourse of male accountability in which to carry these women's demands.

To illustrate, we turn to Glen Ridge, New Jersey, where the defense maintains that the boys indicted for sexual assault were just innocent "kids" playing:

> The boys were merely "pranksters" and "fool-arounds." [They] were simply responding to "basic boyish human needs . . . When the trigger goes off, when the feeling goes off, if you have got a lady friend, you do it." (Hauppert, 1992, p. 11)

> The defendants are all over the Glen Ridge High School yearbook. Kevin Scherzer, holding a baseball bat, is posed as best male athlete. . . . Mr. Quigly was voted "best looking," as well as being singled out for having the "best body" . . . . Mr. Gruber was noted for having the nicest eyes. (Nieves, 1992, p. B1)

Pam, on the other hand, touted by defense attorneys as the "suburban Lolita,"[3] became identified as the source of the neighborhood problem. One of the defense lawyers suggested that when her breasts had developed, men were uncontrollably attracted to her: "Boys were magnetized to her," he says (Hanley, 1993a). "She thrived for affection . . . . But she also thrived for the kissing, she craved the caressing, she craved the embracing, she craved the euphoria because her brain functioned that way" (Hanley, 1992a).

The prosecution was not allowed to mention that one of the boys who was in the basement where and when Pam was assaulted had once beaten his girlfriend so badly she ended up in the hospital. This evidence of his agency and violence was buried as "past history." The defense, on the other hand, was allowed to explore Pam's history, *her* agency: her use of birth control pills, her grades, her ability to travel in town, even her sister's past, her mother's judgment, and the like. The boys' "normalcy" was always evoked but never questioned. Their mothers were never called to the witness stand. Pam's "normalcy" was destroyed by her own attorneys, who "defended" her as a helpless, retarded "victim" who could not give legal consent. To support this defense, her mother was on the stand for over three days.

Once the violence within the community was announced by Pam's simple question to a counselor, "If the boys do it again, can I say, 'No'?" the citizenry rallied around an image of *the town's* innocence or "lost":

> "We'd always thought of this as a town with very decent people and that we cared about what our children did . . . but something went wrong," says one resident. "It was Norman Rockwell land . . . . It was small-town America, football and mom" . . . . "You should've seen the place for the annual Thanksgiving Day game. Kids in convertibles honking their cars through the streets and everyone waving like it was the greatest thing. It's like 1955 here" . . . . "This genteel suburb is still mourning its lost innocence . . . ," said the wife of a police officer. "We're not supposed to talk . . . . The hope is the whole thing will go away and everything *will be like it was*" [Italics added]. (Nieves, 1992, p. B1)

Through an inversion of blame, the town was now described as a "virgin" violated by Pam. Her telling, not the boys' abuse, ripped open the community. To return everything back to "normal," the community sealed up and laminated the wound inflicted by the tentative cry of a girl with mental retardation. The mothers, aunts, and girlfriends, the church, the school, the police, and the press came out in full force to assure the community (identified with the boys) both coherence and innocence. In a conversation with Ingersoll during a break in the trial, the great-aunt of one of the boys articulated *her identification with the boys:* "They're such clean-cut boys . . . it's such a shame . . . . I'm a mother. I have such compassion for what they're going through" . . . . [Sarah: "What about Pam's mom?"] . . . "For her too." But she quickly returned to identify with the boys:

There's such a thin line between good and bad. Even if they are found innocent, this will have affected their lives terribly. They have lost their scholarships, and they weren't able to participate in the graduation ceremonies despite the petition. They've been shown as criminals on the Geraldo show. They're not criminals. *Everybody* does these things. Even my husband. He told me things he used to do as a boy.

This feat of institutional coherence, despite a recognized transgression, was accomplished easily in a town where the twins involved in the incident were former captains of the school football and baseball teams; where the Glen Ridge chief police detective, who led the initial investigation, was the father of one of the boys; and where two of the churches in town supported the defense financially and socially through their courtroom presence. Indeed, the pastor of the Glen Ridge First Christ Episcopal Church, William Ganon, snapped at the women from the National Organization of Women (NOW): "Why are you hassling these boys? God has forgiven them for their sins." The boys' abuse was normalized and redeemed. The community and its institutions were saved. Pam and her family were pathologized, the girl's deviance causing the mother's resentment: "During his two-hour and 20-minute summation [defense lawyer Alan] Zegas . . . hypothesized [that] the alleged victim's mother resented her because when the girl was adopted the family was told she had a correctable problem but later found that was not true . . . . The attorney maintained the alleged victim 'might have picked up on some resentment in the mother' " (Family blamed, 1993, p. 19).

Indeed, while voices of outrage and demands for male accountability were carried by the women from NOW, the police officer and counselor who defended Pam, the psychologist who interviewed her, Ingersoll and other women witnessing the trial, the institutional and legal support for Pam displayed and caricatured her retardation. As Pam's attorney explained to the court: " 'What she got was spread-eagled in a cramped little basement and raped with sticks wrapped in garbage bags and smeared with Vaseline,' Mr. Goldberg told the jury. 'It was not an act of love. It was not even an act of sex. If it was performed on a helpless creature it would be considered inexcusable cruelty' " (Defense denounced, 1993).

The only legal strategy for holding the boys accountable was to prove, in excess, Pam's "incompetence," her inability to consent. This was the one thing she and her mother had tried all her lives *not* to do—using "helplessness" and "handicapped" as defining terms for Pam.

THE PLOT: SHIFTING THE BLAME

Across the scenes, about the time when the institutions began to protect the men, we heard a surprising but consistent *shift* in the plots. In the beginning, across the scenes, a young, assaulted woman tells another woman—teacher, counselor, therapist, mother—about abuse at the hands of a respected, white, elite boy/man. The woman who hears the story may decide to do nothing, to deny or bury the story, to protect the man. Or the teacher, counselor, therapist, or mother may decide to carry the story to a "legitimate" institutional audience. The carrier expects a sympathetic hearing. She is shocked to find little sympathy and not much of a hearing.

Soon thereafter the institution discovers a local storyteller who narrates a now revised text. Enter the *shift*. The shift comes in two forms, either a shift in blame or a shift in tragic consequence. If it is a shift in blame, it sounds like, "He's not to blame—she is." We may hear about biological urges, seduction, or miscommunication (Hollway, 1984). She provoked, consented, or misconstrued. As Ryan (1971) has written: "The stigma that marks the victim and accounts for his [*sic*] victimization is an acquired stigma, a stigma of social rather than genetic origin. But the stigma, the defect, the fatal difference—though derived in the past from environmental forces—is still located *within* the victim, inside his [*sic*] skin" (p. 7). Often within working- or middle-class institutions, the focus of *blame* shifts early in the plot, from him to her.

Among elites, the structural shift occurs not through *blame* but *tragedy*. This shift moves, much more subtly and politely, a little later from her to him. A simple changing of the subject maneuvers the focus onto the man. Sad tragedy, but he needs his job. What about his reputation? What about his wife and children? What about his health? What about all the good he's done? The consequences to the girl/woman, with the accountability of the male, are gently escorted off-stage.

Watching this three-card Monty game played with blame and tragedy, the feminist teacher, therapist, counselor, or mother is shocked at the institution's refusal to believe. She is confused by the impenetrable discursive barricades. She feels trapped by her professional and personal investments—to be legitimate, professional, in control. The girl/woman watches another sinking failure of second-wave feminism. She asks the woman to drop the case. It is too "embarrassing." Consent and coercion begin to get muddled. Agency slips, as does responsibility.

Across our plots, as narrated by the women and confirmed by the men, these boys/men all admitted they *were* involved with "subordinates"—children and students—using hands, pinches, bats, or brooms. Amazingly, across our cases, not one of the accused men denied his involvement. However, all fathers, teachers, and neighbors understood that there was consent, *because they heard no "No."* Women's consent was assumed. We are reminded of the writings of Rousseau from *Emile* (1911) and *Politics and Arts* (1968).

> Why do they consult their words, when it is not their mouths that speak? . . . The lips always say "No," and rightly so; but the tone is not always the same, and that cannot lie . . . . Must her modesty condemn her to misery? Does she not require a means of indicating her "inclinations" without open expression? (1911, p. 348)

> To win this silent consent is to make use of all the violence permitted in love. To read it in the eyes, to see it in the ways in spite of the mouth's denial . . . . If he then completes his happiness, he is not brutal, he is decent. He does not insult chasteness; he respects it; he serves it. He leaves it the honor of still defending what it would have perhaps abandoned. (1968, p. 85)

The men in these cases represent their behavior as natural, common, a joke or an honest mistake. *Her* behavior in going along becomes "the problem," if she finds *his* behavior objectionable. By not stopping the man, her consent is "given" (Sanday, 1990).

In a powerful critique of consent theory, Carole Pateman (1988) stated, "Only if women are seen as 'free and equal individuals' is their consent relevant at all." But our analyses today suggest something even more terrifying. Women, adult and sexual, may be assumed to be "free and equal," and therefore may be held accountable for provoking and then allowing male heteroviolence. Are women being punished for entering the playground of male heterosexuality? Is our consent assumed upon entry?

When female consent or provocation is assumed *by virtue of her sexual involvement,* male accountability evaporates. Thus, the Glen Ridge defense lawyers argued that Pam provoked the young men:

> You can't tell the heat of a woman by the way she looks. You have to touch her, and then she might be cold even if she is pretty. There are flirtatious women, aggressive women, devious women. Some girls are Lolitas; they like to entice and attract. Some girls are flirtatious. Some crave kissing, caressing . . . . Some feel a tingle . . . and like to see the joy on a boy's face when he ejaculates. (Hanley, 1992a)

Pam, he continued, "thrives for kissing" and craves "the caressing . . . her genitals' signals—are greater than normal."

Across these scenes of male hetero-violence, women and men search for evidence of girls'/women's consent. A fixed gaze lands on the woman, taking the form of a *fundamental attribution error* (Jones & Nisbet, 1972). To investigate empirically this troubling question of gaze on women versus male accountability, Rosemarie Roberts (1994) conducted a clever study of young adults' perceptions of sexual harassment. The twenty-nine subjects, age twenty to fifty-two, 72 percent female and 24 percent male (7 percent unknown), 21 percent white, 10 percent African American, 35 percent Latino, three percent Asian, and thirty-one percent other, were given a hypothetical sexual harassment case, and invited to generate three questions for the hypothetical "victim" and three questions for the hypothetical "accused." Striking differences were found between the kinds of questions asked of the woman/victim and man/accused.

Of the eighty-four questions posed to the woman/victim, 76 percent focused on *her* behavior: what did you wear? Why did you visit his office? Have you filed a complaint before? Why didn't you push him away? In contrast, only 47 percent focused on the *man's* behavior.

Of the eighty-four questions asked of the man/accused, 28 percent focused on *his* social status and broader context of his life: are you married? How long have you taught? Do you work well with students? Do you have children? Were you abused as a child? Only 5 percent focused on *her* social status. Further, 20 percent asked questions of both about "prior offenses" and "rumor/informal networks" (e.g., "If not accused, is it common knowledge around campus about his attempts at harassment?" "Was he ever accused before?"). And last, 8 percent inquired about the nature of the relationship between "victim" and "accused" (e.g., "Were you and the offender known to each other and for how long?" " . . . sometimes teachers and students are more than that . . . "); such comments accounted for six percent of the women's questions, but 15 percent of the men's questions.

In this sample of twenty-nine, we see a fixed gaze seeking evidence of consent or even invitation in the victim's behavior, and a roving eye "balancing" any momentary male accountability against his "broader life," commitments, and responsibilities (see also Brodkey & Fine, 1988). In this hypothetical situation, respondents had no investments in a real institution— unlike Glen Ridge, the private school, or the incesting families. Yet even here Roberts documents more excusability than accountability for men and a search for how the woman was "implicated." What did *she do?* What does *he* have to *lose?* Even in the abstract, a cognitive and discursive hole opens where male accountability might reside.

Back in context, these complex dynamics of victim-fixation and accused-redemption play out clearly in the private school story, just after the girls complained. In this case, as in Roberts's study, we witness how under the weight of accumulated questions and ongoing indecision the girls come to be held accountable for causing "the problem." Thus the girls can resolve it "fairly" by accepting the institutional solution—therapy for the teacher and complete silence about the whole affair.

A female administrator explains this shift to the feminist teacher, insisting that the girls' complaints, not the teacher's behavior, "jeopardized the teacher's career." This is why, she explains, she has devoted so much care to "protecting the girls' confidentiality" and "protecting them from the consequences" of a teacher being fired *because of their complaints*. This administrator's line of reasoning identifies the girls' complaints as the catalyst for administrative action, granting agency not to the man but to the girls. The "innocence" of the girls is used to protect "their" confidentiality, and conveniently, to conceal the episode. The administrative solution to the problem the girls have "caused" is to refuse the punishment demanded (firing) as an unfair victimization of the teacher ("ruining his career and his marriage"). Here the "innocence" of the victim is used to bury their stories, and the "guilt" of the victims (for demanding retribution) is used to justify *not* punishing the teacher. *Once we realize that, across the scenes, the telling (and not the abuse) is the crime, and the telling (and not the abuse) divides these institutions, then it makes sense that girls/women are blamed and that men are protected.* She violates her (nice) nature by telling. He submits to his nature, and she calls foul. She is the victimizer. He is the victim. She threatens the institution. He must be protected if the institution is to survive. We ask: why aren't victims assumed to speak for the institution? And who silences them?

PLAYERS: SPLIT LOYALTIES WITHIN AND AMONG WOMEN

> Splitting is a dynamic which only becomes apparent when it is interrupted, because when it is working successfully its effect is that of the unitary subject. (Hollway, 1984, p. 72)

Within public cases of gang rape, sexual harassment, and incest, we can typically find a man, if white, standing "wrongly" accused; an ambiguous, not quite believable, and easily shaken girl/woman who has "allegedly" been assaulted; and a "feminist" teacher, therapist, counselor, mother, or other

A COCK & BULL STORY

advocate "painting" the girl's/woman's "obvious innocence" and the boy's/man's "predator behavior *motives*." And then there are the "Other Women," defending the men. In the beginning of these scenes, the sets are always crowded with players. By mid-performance, the dialogue, the big fights, are typically being held among the women. The men involved will not have to speak much. They will not deny the abuse, and they will not be alone. The institution will offer up its discursive capital and material resources. The institutional morality, the victim-blaming, and the male tragedy may all be narrated by Other Women. In a corner, quietly, the young girl/woman eventually stands alone or with a few advocates. She is a lightning rod for violence against women—too hot. She will have to defend her story, her history, and her right to speak these accusations.

Women split. Some women rally round the woman. Those who care, listen, or support abused girls/women may be transformed ideologically into "hysterical feminists" who "always wear black," as was said about the women from NOW; therapists who propagate "antifamily false memories" about incest, as is argued by false memory syndrome advocates; "feminist" teachers who have an ax to grind; mothers who are raising unruly or vengeful daughters; counselors looking for fame, revenge, or promotion. But many more rally round the man. In each of our scenes there were these Other Women, defending the moral virtue of the accused men (Walkerdine, 1986).

Most boldly voiced within the narratives of adult incest survivors, Other Women appear to identify with the man, constructing family "loyalty" through layers of resistance, collusion, confusion, and struggle. In the six incest narratives collected by Toni Genovese, these Other Women deny the abuse and protect the men. One woman explained to Toni:

> I told my mother. I have memories of telling my mother as a very young child; like two years old or something. Coming to her bleeding and her putting me in the bathtub; and I have memory of watching the blood go down the drain and mixing with the water and her telling me, "No, no, no. This is wrong . . . it's not what you're saying. It's not that." So from very early on I doubted what I saw. I doubted what I heard. I trusted no one. And my voice was buried. My voice had no sound . . . . I did not doubt my mother. I doubted myself.

Jill told her mother about the abuse a year after it had ended. At the time she was fourteen years old:

> After I told her I regretted it so much. She yelled and screamed at me. She told me that *I* had ruined *her* life. I remember telling her that

[my stepfather] was weird. And she looked at me and . . . it was almost a cross-examination in her pinning me down. I didn't say it directly . . . . I wanted it out, but it was a very scary thing to actually
get it out. She told me that I ruined her life. Then she sent me to the
store for something. I remember literally walking to the store and
. . . wishing a car would hit me and that it would be over . . . . It was
just the longest walk to the store and coming back. And I remember
being really, really embarrassed because she had told her best friend
. . . when I came back home her best friend was there and . . . had
red eyes and [she was] patting my mother and holding my mother
so I knew she had told. (Interview with T. Genovese, 1993)

In these external splits, Other Women serve as the moral guardians of a
civic order built on gendered violence and inequity (Walkerdine, 1986). Focus and blame scamper onto the assaulted females. At these fragile, critical
moments of gender socialization, young women learn that *they* are expected
to change, accommodate, or accept.

When she was a child, Patti, the daughter of a white American father and
a Vietnamese mother, told her mother that her father was "bothering her"
sexually. Her mother made her show what he did. She was told to remove
her clothing and demonstrate to the whole family what her father had done.
After this, her mother continued to leave her alone with her father. Patti became a surrogate mother/wife—taking care of her siblings and her father's
emotional and sexual needs. Her mother kept telling her, insisting, that her
father would never touch her again. Publicly, the mother denied the abuse.
Even when Patti brought her father to court, in her mid-twenties, her mother
said she "made it up." Her sister, when pressed by the prosecution about her
father's abuse of her, explained, "It's not abuse, if you consent."

Patti's father was found guilty. That evening, in 1993, Patti explained,
"I won . . . . Yes, I guess so. I watched my father taken out in handcuffs. My
mother said I was hallucinating and my sister testified to consent. They
kicked me out of the family." She could remain a family member only insofar as she denied the abuse. She won the case and lost her family. Girls who
have survived incest are split between their loyalties to themselves and their
loyalties to their families. Even in those cases where someone is willing to
hear, the costs of telling are high.

In the courtroom transcripts for both Patti and Pam, we hear glimmers
of a discourse of male accountability. There may be some insights here. Institutions may hold white males accountable *if* the "victim" is a child or can
be determined to be "incompetent." But if the "victim" is a woman, much
less a sexual agent, then white male accountability more readily evaporates

and arguments over female responsibility divide women amongst themselves.

Splitting happens not just among women but also within individual women. Sitting at the bottom of the sex/gender system (Miller, 1976; Rubin, 1984), women listen, study, embody, and can mimic voices of domination and subordination (Collins, 1990). As able "students from below," women can ventriloquize multiple and even contradictory perspectives on male violence. They can deliver the scripts for most of the characters in these scenes. While women "victims" are notorious for their ability to explain compassionately why *everyone* did what everyone did (Blackman, 1994; Brodkey & Fine, 1988), least compelling, usually, is the woman's defense of herself. When a woman splits inside, is the "victim" the first to lose her own advocacy? Consider the testimony of Pam on cross-examination: "When prosecutor, Robert D. Laurino, asked if it was difficult testifying with the four defendants sitting about 25 feet away, the young woman [Pam] hesitated and stammered, to some extent, finally saying that she was confused. Mr. Laurino asked why. [She said] because here's one side and here's the other side . . . . It's hard to choose between one side or the other" (Hanley, 1992d, p. B1).

The multiple voices and the split selves that self-consciously float through the mind and body of Pam are theorized in poststructural theory. As Chantal Mouffe (1991) writes:

> It is [therefore] impossible to speak of the social agent is if we were dealing with a unified, homogeneous entity. We have rather to approach it as a plurality, dependent on the various subject positions through which it is constituted within various discursive formations. And to recognize that there is no, a priori, necessary relation between the discourses that construct its different subject positions. But, for the reasons pointed out earlier, this plurality does not involve the coexistence, one by one, of a plurality of subject positions but rather the constant subversion and over determination of one by the others, which make possible the generation of totalizing effects within a field characterized by open and indeterminate frontiers. (p. 371)

Yet Pam, the girls who have been harassed, and the interviewed incest survivors, all of whom speak through split consciousness and multiple loyalties, do not celebrate these cerebral pluralities. They feel tortured, compelled to choose "sides." What makes incest, for instance, so complicated is that children are betrayed not only by their (father) perpetrators and by the (mother) "listeners" to their stories, but sometimes also by their own bodies. Perpetrators impose physical violence/stimulation on children, and yet we know that girls/women who are raped may experience "physical pleasure." Whether or not children want that stimulation, it may provoke bodily responses that children are expected to control, and then consent may be imputed by Others or by Self. As Shannon offered in her interview with Toni:

> I guess it's hard to say that I loved him [her uncle] in any sort of way
> but I suppose I did . . . but I also think he's a pathetic creature . . . .
> I was just somehow ready to say more than just I hate you I
> have these total mixture of feelings where sometimes I hate his guts
> other times I think I really want to . . . be a good aunt to [my]
> nephew . . . or should I be calling the department of children services
> and warning them . . . horrible mixture of feelings.

While white men stand in court, school, and family silent, coherent, and identified with and protected by the institution, a public telling of a woman's split selves breeds pity, contempt, disbelief, or confusion.

DECONSTRUCTING SCRIPTS: EXTRACTING THE DISCOURSES OF INSTITUTIONAL MORALITY

> In our view, law, in general and the courtroom, in particular, are
> arenas where narratives are contested, and the power of interpreta-
> tion exercised. In that sense, the legal realm is a political realm. But
> it would be a mistake to see narratives simply as some after-the-fact
> story about events, concocted after the *real* power has already been
> exercised: the story lines developed in law "mediate" power in the
> sense that they both "translate" power as non-power (the beating of
> [Rodney] King becomes the "reasonable exercise of force necessary
> to restrain a prisoner"); and they also *constitute* power, in the sense
> that the narrative lines shape what and how events are perceived in
> the first place. Understanding these relationships between law,
> power, and ideology is necessary to comprehending that, in many
> ways, the King verdict was *typical*, not extraordinary. (Crenshaw &
> Peller, 1993, pp. 59–60).

We shift now from a structural analysis of setting, blame, and players to a discourse analysis of institutional talk. We find two primary discourses that enable institutions of "justice" to flee white male accountability: the "Family as Safe Haven" and the "Fair Play" discourses emerge as institutional white lies that disallow talk of male accountability or gendered power.

The "Family as Safe Haven" Discourse

The "Family as Safe Haven" (FSH) discourse supports and is supported by the economic realities of gender inequality and holds that for women and children, the (idealized) family seems to be the safest place. Supported mainly by a man's wages, especially in white working- and middle-class homes, women with children do not have to look far to witness how untenable life is for those outside this unit. In the face of plenty of evidence of the danger or undependability of men within the family, many women remain loyal to their material interests and defend male providers against the accusations of daughters and other dependents' claims of abuse.

Ranging far beyond the private family, into communities, churches, and courts, the FSH discourse rests on two ideological assumptions about provision within American families: men are *naturally* providers for and protectors of women, and good women are *naturally* wives and mothers. Gender here is primary, and nature produces this most basic "difference" affecting all social organization. "Nature" (whether "human nature," male hormones, maternal instinct, or the animal kingdom), then, gets evoked as the root cause of (*always gendered*) behaviors within the FSH. The power of this discourse lies in its apparently "natural" origins and "universal" applications.

Feminism has deconstructed all three parts of the white lie within the FSH: the "nature" of women to nurture; the "nature" of men to provide and protect; and the assumption that women's only protection and value lies in the family. Yet feminism's cries of "wolf" are a poor substitute for the promised protections of FSH. The FSH remains a widely proliferated discourse because it evokes the safety and fairness of gendered family relationships across social context and institutions.

The FSH can be seen dominating both the incest narratives and the Glen Ridge rape case. As a defense strategy, first the "safe space" is defended. When a crime has been acknowledged within it, the defense shifts to the basic integrity and normalcy of the perpetrators. The "fault" lies somewhere hidden in the victim. The women and men in our cases deflected claims of abuse by protecting the man and his image as innocent, or at worst, indiscreet, misguided, perhaps alcoholic. The FSH discourse *cannot* admit male abuse is possible (much less typical) within normal families, because men are naturally protectors (not exploiters) of their dependents, and women are naturally nurturers and defenders of their offspring against all harm. We see this discourse most powerfully in the incest narratives. To acknowledge that all men have the opportunity and some men have the inclination to coerce, exploit, and abuse women under their care, with white men having very little chance of discovery, conviction, or punishment, and that women will go along with or remain silent about such abuse, would overturn the assumptions about the "nature" of females and males, and reveal that the (patriarchal) family's privacy and dependency on men (the very tenets of "safety" for the family) make abuse more than possible (Weis, 1993).

The Glen Ridge trial on gang rape clearly exposes this white lie of male protectiveness. How then do those within the FSH discourse defend the boys' abusive acts? The boys' lawyers defended the naturalness of all boys' male sexual drive and the consent implicit in a sexually active female's interest in male attention. "Boys will be boys" evokes FSH's gendered nature. One of the boys' lawyers explained how "nature" initiates male action: "When the trigger goes off, when the feeling goes off, if you have got a lady friend, you do it" (Hauppert, 1992, p. 11). In this account, the FSH's role in protecting and providing the male's decision-making accountability is overridden by the more basic "nature"—the (testosterone) trigger. The defense lawyers called the accused "not criminals, but teenage boys who were swayed by their hormones and a young woman's sexual aggression," again submerging male accountability into nature, while shifting the initiative and blame to female sexual aggression.

Shifting the blame to the bad woman reassigns initiative and clarifies who is deservedly outside the FSH. Formerly, the defense lawyers argued that only bad ("loose") girls ventured outside the FSH to receive boys' initiatives: "all the good girls" (as Tom Petty sings), "stayed home with broken hearts." Girls' badness was proven by their sexual interest and availability, and their punishment was provided by boys being boys. Querques, a lawyer for the boys, reminded the jury of this once "natural" and unquestioned norm by assuming that the male jurors themselves had experienced preying on loose girls: "You bring them up that way, and when they do it you call them criminals? You people are going to forget about the girls you knew in high school who were loose and the boys who took? Are men going to forget, hey, I got a girl who is loose, do you want to join me? . . . The fact is that's the way these children were raised" (Hauppert, 1992, p. 11).

Girls got sorted into good and bad by "boys will be boys" behavior: the effect stigmatizes sexual girls irreversibly, placing them outside the boundaries of the FSH for women. By not staying within the family as potential wife and mother material, such girls forsook the protections of family and their place and nice "nature" in FSH, and instead became sexual objects "outside" the FSH. The borders of the sexual playground are constituted by such cases as Glen Ridge when communities and courts decide who deserves protection within the FSH and who deserves punishment for having violated the FSH. Was it the girl or the boys who violated the FSH? Much of the defense of the Glen Ridge boys was aimed at proving how available the bad girl was to all comers, how far from her gendered "nature" her unnaturally strong "sexual aggression" had driven her. The prosecution, on the other hand, argued that her mild retardation made her incapable of consent, a helpless innocent (female victim) especially deserving of the protections of the FSH:

> Just how wrong and unnatural was the sexual agency of the girl in the Glen Ridge case? Querques, one of the boys' lawyers, seemed to be coding this girl *as a boy* [Italics added], subject to a "nature" that makes her sound like their own description of "boys will be boys." She had an aggression . . . an aggressive attitude toward sex . . . . She had her feelings for sex, her drive, if you like, for sex. Her brain and her stomach and her genital signals are greater than normal. Obsession. One word. Obsession. (Hauppert, 1992, p. 11)

By saying that her body (nature) signals (instincts) "are greater than normal," Querques gestures toward the "unnatural" propensities of appetite in abnormal (retarded or mentally ill) people, and asks us to imagine how grotesque such sexual aggression and obsession are in a female. With such an image of girl-become-boy following her genitals' triggered signals, all female-consent issues disappear with the disappearance of the yielding/submitting female object. If she wants to *initiate* play like a boy, she cannot later claim the protection of female objecthood back in the family.

While expelling the bad girl from the FSH, the defense lawyers had to show how the defendants—deservingly—remained *within* the FSH. The first line of defense insisted on identifying them as boys, not men, more like children in behavior and motive; however sexual they may be, they were still always "playing." The second line of defense admitted to momentary mistakes while never acknowledging intention, active agency, or lasting consequences. The last possibility was that the boys were just sowing their wild oats. Defense lawyer Zegas suggested they were "learning from indiscretion": "Male hormones are at their peak levels. It can be, for adolescents, a time of exploration . . . experimentation . . . mistakes and indiscretions are made, and there is learning from indiscretion" (Enda, 1993). If boys make their mistakes within the FSH, the unspoken understanding has been that they will not be punished outside it; justice is enacted "in house."

The "Fair Play" Discourse

If the Family as Safe Haven discourse operates to validate the relations of gender inequality in many heterosexual families and communities, the Fair Play (FP) discourse operates to assure relations of gender equality in those institutions that promise to deliver equal access to resources, especially education and the workplace. Schools and professional-class businesses and professions have been most challenged by feminism to assure women's equal access and fair treatment, and professional-class women (in their families and jobs) are most likely to evoke and insist on this FP discourse.

Gender is the absolute and natural difference defining the places within (and around) the Family as Safe Haven discourse. In contrast, the Fair Play discourse insists that *genderlessness* is the most basic human nature. Gender and race are customized add-ons to a "basic human nature" people. "Fairness," then, involves ignoring the inessentials (race, gender, class) and evaluating the essentials (individual merits) in the case. The FP discourse assumes that gender is transcended and inoperative in the "fair" workplace and in court. The FP discourse assumes a level playing field where suited team players, selected by merit, are refereed impartially as they play by fair rules; they are promoted or demoted on their own achievements. The seductive promise of the discourse is that *white men's entitlements will be extended to white women if they measure up*. The white lie, exposed in our cases, is that gender is inoperative.

As in the FSH, within Fair Play there are some truths: white women's gains in the professional workplace in the last twenty years, and the achievements and rewards for women who identify as (and with) white men (rather than as and with women, nonwhites, or others who are "different"). In a perverse twist, by seeing gender and race as unfair factors in determining merit or hearing legal accusations, the gender and race of newcomers to the professional playing field have officially been "whited out." As long as they are suited up and prepared to play with the old boys by the old rules, newcomers are welcome (see Guinier et al., 1994). But should they drag their partialities (race, class, gender factors) in the workplace or into court, they disqualify themselves for the game, and must either sit it out or relearn the rules and rejoin when they are ready to play by them. The Fair Play discourse rests on a particular legal model of justice:

> a view of law and society in which the social and political realm is
> distinct from, and subordinate to, the legal. This view of the primacy
> of the legal order creates the illusion that law is a source of power
> and authority disconnected from other power structures in society.

> Thus, legality has its origins in the pathology of social relations; con-
> flicts, such as racial discontent, are seen as aberrational incidents
> that occur when the social structure breaks down, and the intro-
> duction of the law maintains order . . . . The deep logic of law does
> not reflect the complex social reality of discrimination in society, but
> rather confines legal resolution to social problems appropriate for
> litigation. (Bumiller, 1987, p. 10)

Professions such as law and medicine now have enough women in them
to insist on this legal model of workplace fairness; private schools and colleges have students paying for equal access to the professional class, who insist that institutions play officially by the FP rules. The administration of such
schools must be likened to the legal system, "a source of power and authority disconnected from other power structures in society," above the social
and political concerns of constituents and therefore impartially prepared to
adjudicate. Essential to the white lies of the FP discourse are the assumptions
that "*the law*," whether lawyers, judges, juries, or administrators, is "disconnected from other power structures" and that conflicts are caused only
"when the social structure breaks down"—when someone lets in the unfairness of racism and sexism, and when raced or gendered players charge onto
the playing field and disrupt the game. By confining these problems to
pathologies and repairing the break in the fences, the game is allowed to re-
sume. With the introduction of law, order is presumably maintained. Ob-
scured are the extent to which these "problems" constitute (rather than interrupt) social structure and the law (Minow, 1993).

The sexual harassment case at the private school shows how these white
lies are necessary to preserve morale and morality within the institutional
boundaries of the Fair Play discourse. The teacher's harassment of students,
in the first place, suggests that discontent and unfairness *constitute* the official playing field. Likewise, the school's process of decision-making, relying
upon the legal model of individual rights, reveals the limits of "fairness"
within the Fair Play discourse: "Rights analysis sees the individual in social
isolation. The risks inherent in human interaction are pretended away by the
formal processes of allocating entitlements and drawing lines to settle conflicts . . . . Rights theory conceptualizes a society composed of self-interested
individuals whose conflicting interests are mediated by the state" (Olson,
1991, p. 310).

"Sexual harassment" not only challenges basic tenets of Fair Play, it also
violently confronts them. It is first of all "unstable" in ungendered terms,
and harassment or abuse are almost inconceivable on a level playing field.
Pressed to conceptualize, in an administrative meeting, where and how the

"wrong" occurred between a "well-intentioned teacher" and "innocent students," the administrators can name *no risks* on the level playing field: players, rules, referees, crowd of onlookers, all selected for fairness. Administrators decide on and among rights defined as individual entitlements. The students are "entitled" to complain about (perceived) unfairness, and the teacher is "entitled" to his job if no (damaging enough) wrongs against him are proven. Without too much work on anyone's part, the Fair Play discourse can *translate* girls' complaints of abuse into correctable instances of unfairness, and can judge a teacher to be entitled to his job if he agrees to therapy to address his individual problem. His "problem" will then be named and known only by his therapist, and all specifics of the problem and treatment and recovery will be kept confidential. This solution marks the problem as individual, not systemic. He is presumably fixed, via the care of another "professional." The institution survives intact, as does the Fair Play discourse.

Ironically, the girls' complaints too can be seen as an appeal to rather than a challenge to the Fair Play discourse: "Hey! We're not being treated fairly! We're not being treated as genderless team players!" (see Fox-Genovese, 1991). Once they have been given a "fair hearing" and warned of the "fairness" of full confidentiality for all, what further action would be "fair"? When the school decides to keep the teacher, thanks the girls for their unwritten complaints, and sends them back to class, the girls' voices have been buried beneath institutional interests. In retrospect, we realize that we too may have framed our advocacy and their grievances within the discourse of Fair Play. Does all our feminist outrage operate from within the Fair Play discourse that we, as two generations of feminists, have tried so hard to establish in our institutions? If so, these cases show how easily FP buries or simply ignores women. We need alternative discourses that articulate and advocate our concerns as central institutional issues.

FEMINIST INTERRUPTIONS: THE FAINT
DISCOURSE OF MALE ACCOUNTABILITY

> There is no single locus of great Refusal, no soul of revolt, source of all rebellions or pure law of the revolutionary. Instead, there is a plurality of resistances .... More often one is dealing with mobile and transitory points of resistance, producing cleavages in a society that shifts about, fracturing unities and affecting regroupings, furrowing across individuals themselves, cutting them up and remodeling them, making irreducible regions in them, in their bodies and minds. (Foucault, 1979, p. 95)

Across these cases we were sufficiently misled by the depth of our own outrage so as to be "naïve," that is, taken by surprise, at the institutional absence of a discourse of male sexual accountability. While in each research site we heard encouraging whispers, narrated by agents of resistance within each plot, we only gradually came to see the massive amount of change necessary before women's "complaints" can effectively be registered institutionally, with accountability assigned. The close identification of these institutions with the accused individual men has two key effects, much like a white corpuscle response to a wound.

Much of the response of men and women invested in these institutions is "instinctively" rallied toward defending the institution from the harm brought by the wound of public exposure of alleged wrongdoing. To defend the good name, basic integrity, and safety of the family, school, or neighborhood, participants minimize the assault and its effects (keeping the inside "good") and maximize the effects of the negative publicity unfairly given the case, whether it comes from in-house feminists "making a federal case" out of a private consensual exchange, or "the media coming in" to scapegoat a group to further an activist agenda (making the outsiders biased and unfair to those inside) (Brodkey, 1994). Parents must believe their children are safe from sexual assault (and derogation) in their schools, neighborhoods, and families. Cases such as these described reveal not only how unsafe some places are, but also that many people responsible for children's safety will rush to cover up or explain away stories of assault.

The "white corpuscle response" seeks to defend the good name and basic integrity and safeness of the insider, whether by denying that "our boys" are capable of violence against a girl in the neighborhood; by redefining a teacher's conduct as immature rather than illegal; or by assigning responsibility for incest to victims or provocative therapists.

We end, however, not dismally fatalistic, but eager for evidence that there is a growing chorus of voices, institutional and individual, calling for male sexual accountability. We think we find such evidence in two very recent developments in the law that suggest what may be an emergent interruption in the nonconscious identification of institutions with white men, and the attendant exclusion of considerations of gender and racial differences as inherently unequal and unfair.

One development is marked in the "reasonable *woman*" legal standard that now defines the nature of sexual harassment in the workplace. Such a standard inserts gender explicitly into the case—in this case, being a *woman* rather than a legally ungendered "person." Supreme Court Justice Ruth Bader Ginsburg, in hearing a sexual harassment case in November 1993 before the Supreme Court, clarified the difference that the "reasonable woman" standard makes to understanding the nature of the offense against her:

> Justice Ginsburg asked why sexual harassment should not be defined simply as conduct that on the basis of an employee's sex makes it more difficult for one person than another to perform the job. "How about just saying that?" she said. "Is it really more complex? The terms and conditions of employment are not equal if one person is being called names and the other isn't. Sexual harassment could be found if one sex has to put up with something that the other sex doesn't have to put up with," she said at another point. (Savage, 1993)

A juror in the Glen Ridge case, after the conviction of three of the four boys for sexual assault, in explaining his reasoning in finding the boys guilty, seemed to be using a makeshift "reasonable *woman*" standard of fairness and also referring to the unfair practice of "blaming the victim" that William Ryan identified: "That's a good defense, to blame the victim. But I don't think the jury felt it was the woman's fault. I felt the jury thought there was not a woman alive who would want that done to her." By including Pam, rather than excluding her as a deviant or defective, in "womanhood," the juror then applied a standard of reasonable treatment of *her* (gendered female). We begin to hear a discourse of male accountability.[4]

The second encouraging sign can be read in a recent sexual harassment decision made by the New Jersey Supreme Court (*Lehman v. Toys R' Us*, 1993). The court, in finding Toys R' Us, the employer, guilty, defined the nature of the harm done to include *harm to the State*. This marks a crucial identification of the State with the interests of the victim. The "hostile work environment for women is the legally recognized harm" (p. 610), the judgment states. The problem then becomes "the conditions of hostility and discrimination," and the legal solution is "designed . . . to change existing standards of conduct . . . to remediate conditions of hostility and discrimination" (p. 612). The judgment assigns accountability to "the harasser's conduct, not the plaintiff's injury, that must be severe or pervasive" (p. 610). And the State assigns itself and employers the responsibility for remediating those conditions.

Further, a sexual harassment policy put in place after the case in the private school suggests that the school came to see its institutional interests as identified with the protection of "future girls" from unwanted sexual attention. Whether or not the school was too vulnerable without such a written policy if it had fired the teacher, and whether or not the school continues to define its interests based on fear of legal suits, the result in this case—perhaps because of the notoriety of the Anita Hill–Clarence Thomas case and the new legal developments in sexual harassment case law—ended formally with an institutional identification with any victims (rather than perpetrators) of sexual harassment. In keeping with its Fair Play discourse, the policy never named females or gender, only unfairness to any *person* through unwanted sexual attention.

As we hear a chorus of fragmented demands for male sexual accountability, we recognize that changing the discourses, policy, and practices of institutions to name male accountability for mistreatment of women is going to take a lot more work than can be done by an outraged individual girl or her embattled feminist sponsors. Katha Pollitt (1994) calls for women to "change the game, and add a few rules of their own" in challenging men on their sexual rights and responsibilities. We would conclude that institutions of presumed justice, whose gendered and raced (and classed) interests must be made visible, need to be challenged and transformed, in order "to act as though there are two people in bed and two sexes in the classroom and workplace" (p. 166) We have tried to begin this work by casting a critical gaze off of women and onto these institutions of (in)justice.

NOTES

1. We are producing an analysis of institutional demands for accountability for white elite men—although 2 of the men accused in our scenes are nonwhite. While we make no claim that white males are disproportionately violent or abusive, we do find that social institutions established to grant a hearing seeming fail to hold these men accountable, despite evidence of and often admission of their involvement in criminal violence against women. It is this curiosity we examine.

2. This interchange is based on her personal notes and therefore is not 100 percent verbatim.

3. Lolita is the multiply raped child whose story is told through the eyes of her patho-

logical rapist in Vladimir Nabokov's novel with her name. Despite the fact that a woman from NOW explained this many times to the news reporters covering the Glen Ridge case and even gave the novel to one of them, they never once printed the distorted inversion of the label and rather insisted on using "Lolita" in its recently derived misogynist meaning.

4. For a more recent review of the "reasonable women" standard see Gutek and O'Connor (1995).

REFERENCES

Alcoff, L., & Gray, L. (1993). Survivor discourse: Transgression or recuperation? *Signs, 18*(2), 260–290.

American Association of University Women. (1993). *Hostile hallways.* Washington, DC: Author.

Blackman, J. (1994). At the frontier: In pursuit of justice for women. In G. Vanden-Boff & B. Sales (Eds.), *Psychology in litigation and legislation* (pp. 137–173). Washington, DC: American Psychological Association.

Bourdieu, P. (1984). Rites of institution. In P. Bourdieu, *Language and symbolic power.* Cambridge, MA: Harvard University Press.

Brodkey, L. (1994). Making a federal case of difference: The politics of pedagogy, publicity, and postponement. In V. Clifford & V. Schilb (Eds.), *Writing theory and critical theory* (pp. 236–261). New York: Modern Language Association.

Brodkey, L., & Fine, M. (1988). Presence of body/absence of mind. *Journal of Education, 170*(3), 84–89.

Bumiller, K. (1987). *Violence and intimacy: The social construction of rape.* Baltimore: Johns Hopkins University.

Bumiller, K. (1988). *The civil rights society: The social construction of victims.* Baltimore: Johns Hopkins University.

Collins, P.H. (1990). Black feminist thought. New York: Routledge.

Crenshaw, K., & Peller, G. (1993). Reel time/Real justice. In R. Gooding–Williams (Ed.), *Reading Rodney King, Reading urban uprising* (pp. 56–70). New York: Routledge.

Defense denounced in sex assault trial (1993, March 3). *The New York Times,* p. B8.

D'Erasmo. (1993, January 12). The three faces of Amy. *Village Voice.*

Enda, V. (1993, February 11). Defense lawyer in rape case describes 'moral indiscretion' *Philadelphia Inquirer.*

Family blamed in Glen Ridge. (1993, February 12). *New Jersey Star Ledger,* p. 19.

Foucault, M. (1978). *The history of sexuality* (Vol. 1). New York: Vintage Books.

Foucault, M. (1979). *Discipline and punish: The birth of the prison.* New York: Vintage Books.

Fox-Genovese, E. (1991). *Feminism without illusions.* Chapel Hill: University of North Carolina Press.

Gates, D. (1993, March 29). White male paranoia: Are they the newest victims—or just bad sports? *Newsweek,* p. 48–53.

Genovese, T. (1993, March). *Incest narratives: Confessionals, silencing, and survivor discourse.* Paper presented at the Ethnography and Education Forum, Philadelphia.

Gillers, S. (1993, March 29). The Senate is also on trial. The Packwood case: *The Nation,* pp. 404–406.

Ginsberg, F. (1989). *Contested lives.* Berkeley: University of California Press.

Goffman, E. (1963). *Stigma: Notes on the management of a spoiled identity.* Englewood Cliffs: Prentice Hall.

Gross, J. (1993, March 29). Where boys will be boys, and adults are befuddled on spur posse. *The New York Times,* p. A7.

Guinier, L., Fine, M., Balin, J., Bartow, A., & Sachel, D.L. (1994). Becoming gentlemen: Women's experiences at one Ivy League law school. *University of Pennsylvania Law Review, 143,* 1–110.

Gutek, B. A., & O'Connor, M. (1995). The empirical basis for the reasonable woman standard. *Journal of Social Issues, 51*(1), 151–166.

Hanley, R. (1992a, October 17). Defense layers in Glen Ridge abuse case say woman was aggressor. *The New York Times,* p. A31.

Hanley, R. (1992b, October 29). Witness in abuse trial calls accuser vulnerable: Says her behavior was governed by fear. *The New York Times,* p. B8.

Hanley, R. (1992c, November 5). Accuser's past at issue in assault case; Lawyer suggests Glen Ridge woman was sexually experienced, p. B26.

Hanley, R. (1992d, December 17). In sex case, witness talks of confusion: Woman central to trial says she lied on stand. *The New York Times,* p. B1.

Hanley, R. (1993a, January 6). Young woman was aggressive toward boys, psychiatrist says. *The New York Times,* p. B5.

Hanley, R. (1993b, January 7). Glen Ridge witness says woman asked for help. *The New York Times,* p. B8.

Hare-Mustin, R., (1991). Sex, liess, and headaches: The problem is power. In T.J. Goodrich (Ed.), *Women and power: Perspectives for therapy* (pp. 63–85). New York: Norton.

Hauppert, K. (1992, November 10). Boystown: Glen Ridge circles the wagons. *Village Voice,* p. 11.

Hollway, W. (1984). Gender difference and the production of subjectivity. In J. Henriques, W. Hollway, C. Urwin, C. Venn, & V. Walkerdine (Eds.), *Changing the subject: Psychology, social regulation and subjectivity* (pp. 26–59). London: Methuen.

Hooks, B. (1990). *Yearning.* Boston: South End Press.

Ingersoll, S. (1993, March). *Whiteness and gang rape.* Paper presented at the Ethnography and Education Forum, Philadelphia.

Jones, E.E., & Nisbett, R.E. (1972). *The actor and observer: Divergent perceptions of the causes of behavior.* In E.E. Jones, et al. (Eds.), *Attribution: Perceiving the causes of behavior* (pp. 79–94). Morristown, NJ: General Learning Press.

Lehman v. Toys R' Us. 132 N.J., 587 (1993).

Miller, J. B. (1976). *Toward a new psychology of women.* Boston: Beacon Press.

Minow, M. (1993). *Family matters.* New York: New Press.

Mouffe, C. (1988). Hegemony and new political subjects: Toward a new concept of democracy. In C. Nelson & L. Grossberg (Eds.), *Marxism and the interpretation of culture,* (pp. 89–104). Urbana: University of Illinois Press.

Mydans, S. (1993, March 24). Eight of nine teenagers freed in sex case: One is charged in California as part of a competition re. spur posse. *The New York Times,* p. A14.

Nieves, E. (1992, December 15). Loyalties in Glen Ridge are divided by sex-attack trial. *The New York Times,* p. B1.

Olsen, F. (1991). Statutory rape: A feminist critique of rights analysis. In K.T. Bartlett & R. Kennedy (Eds.), *Feminist legal theory: Readings in law and gender,* (pp. 305–317). Boulder: Westview Press.

Pateman, C. (1988). *The sexual contract.* Stanford University Press.

Pollitt, K. (1994). *Reasonable Creatures: Essays on Women and feminism.* New York: Vintage.

Roberts, R. (1994, August). Sexual harassment in a college setting: Attributions by and about women and men. Paper presented at the meeting of the American Psychological Association, Los Angeles.

Roberts, S. (1993, March 29). As Wachtler awaits fate, A tortured tale emerges. *The New York Times,* p. B3.

Rousseau, J.-J. (1911). *Emile.* London: Dent.

Rousseau, J.-J. (1968). *Politics and the arts.* Ithaca: Cornell University Press.

Rubin, G. (1984). Thinking sex: Notes for a radical theory of the politics of sexuality. In C.S. Vance (Ed.), *Pleasure and danger:* Exploring female sexuality (pp. 267–319). Boston: Routledge, Kegan and Paul.

Ryan, W. (1971). *Blaming the victim.* New York: Pantheon Books.

Ryan, W. (1981) *Equality.* New York: Pantheon Books.

Sanday, P. (1990). *Fraternity gang rape.* New York: New York University Press.

Savage, D. (1993, October 14). Defining sex harassment splits justices. *Los Angeles Times,* p. A1.

Waff, D. (1994). Girl talk. In M. Fine (Ed.), *Chartering urban reform.* New York: Teachers College Press.

Walkerdine, V. (1986). Poststructuralist theory and everyday social practices: Family and school. In S. Wilkinson (Ed.), *Feminist social psychology* (pp. 57–76). London: Open University Press.

Weis, L. (1993). White male working-class youths. In L. Weiss & M. Fine (Eds.), *Beyond silenced voices* (pp. 237–258). Albany: SUNY.

Chapter 8

Meaning Making in a Context of Genocide and Silencing

•*M. Brinton Lykes*

SINCE 1983 I HAVE ACCOMPANIED GUATEMALANS IN A SERIES OF RESEARCH projects, community interventions, mental health projects, and political actions in their country and in Mexico. Through each of these experiences I have deepened my knowledge of Guatemala and the struggles of her people. I have also experienced some of the personal effects of living within a deeply traumatized society. Yet, as a white, female, educated citizen of the United States, whose government sponsored the overthrow of the democratically elected government of Guatemala in 1954, I am aware of my situated "otherness." Feminist scholars, critical anthropologists, and postmodern theorists have written about the multiple ways in which the researcher's subjectivity is shaped by and shapes the subject of her study.[1] Although not always in agreement, these theorists begin with an assumption of *difference,* not similarity, in analyzing contemporary social reality. Similarly, my position of situated otherness and difference within a praxis of solidarity and collective struggle informs my criticisms of dominant theoretical models for conceptualizing the effects of war on children (e.g., *post*-traumatic stress disorder, (or PTSD). This chapter summarizes my thinking about the symbolic or the non-functional aspects of terror and the multiple meanings I have made of my experiences accompanying child survivors of war and their caretakers.[2]

Most contemporary Central American wars have been understood in terms of class conflicts over unequal distribution of resources, as constrained and/or shaped by the Doctrine of National Security. Although these remain critical forces in any context of modern revolutionary struggle, the world events of the past several years suggest that ethnicity and culture are critical determinants of conflict and efforts to resolve it. Guatemala's five hundred years of Mayan struggle demand such consideration and both constrain and facilitate my reflections. This chapter reflects, therefore, my efforts to "think culturally" (Rosaldo, 1989) about war and its effects, about terror, silence, and voice.

THE CONTEXT

In Guatemala there are twenty-four different languages,[3] and the majority of the approximately nine million inhabitants are Maya and live in rural communities (see, for example, Barry, 1992, for a brief introduction to Guatemala today). Strategies of terror and silencing remain central to the Guatemalan government's counterinsurgency project. They include the razing of more than two hundred rural villages, the disappearance of more than forty thousand people, and the assassination of more than one hundred thousand. Although these figures span ten years, the worst of these violations occurred during a very brief period in the early 1980s. They have been followed by the installation of systems of military and paramilitary control that persist in Guatemala today despite a so-called return to democracy. The unsuccessful presidentially initiated coup on May 25, 1993, reflects both the weakness of "democratic institutions" and the growing investment of multiple sectors within Guatemalan society to build alternatives to continued military force, as well as the devastating effects of neoliberal economic policies that are increasingly impoverishing Central America.

STUDYING THE CONSEQUENCES
OF TERROR

Psychological and Psychiatric Meaning Systems

Psychologists and mental health workers offer one set of responses to child survivors of the type of horror experienced in Guatemala. Typically they focus on the *effects* of war on civilian populations, describing psychological symptoms and behaviors observed in children. Peter Jensen and Jon Shaw (1993) recently reviewed this research and concluded that advances have been made in correcting earlier methodological flaws (e.g., lack of adequate controls; problems with self-report and retrospective data), thus facilitating greater understanding of the complex range of responses of children and youth in situations of war. They recommend extending the individual focus on children and youth to include family and community and, further, shifting from a predominant interest in the psychopathological consequences of war (dominant in much of the literature) to a study of war's effects on children's attitudes, values, and development. Through their review they widen the lenses typically used to examine children in war. However, their strategy for knowing, applied in many parts of the world to children and adults in situations of organized violence, remains embedded in traditional Anglo-Saxon medical conceptions of illness, where selected symptoms and behavioral indexes provide evidence of PTSD or other "diseases."

Judith Herman (1992) analyzed the emergence of this model of meaning making within the context of two U.S. social movements, popular resistance to the Vietnam War and the contemporary women's movements, particularly the movements against violence against women. Her historical contextualization of this theory's origins clarifies the important contribution the construct PTSD made to traditional psychiatric theories that failed to acknowledge the environmental sources of extreme trauma. Herman extends current thinking by emphasizing the continuing and chronic dimensions of trauma in some contexts, for example, ongoing war. However, she supports a medicalized model for making meaning of trauma and its effects and thereby fails to capture trauma's community and social dimensions that remain exogenous variables within her model.

Chalsa Loo (1993) contributes importantly to a recently emerging discussion of the continuities between the stress and trauma literatures within U.S. psychological and psychiatric theorizing, cautioning clinicians and researchers about the seeming ease with which we "diagnose" PTSD. In a similar vein Raija-Leen Punamaki's (1989) introduction to a three-volume special issue of the *International Journal of Mental Health* identified several severe limitations of traditional psychological and psychiatric theories of stress and trauma. She suggested that traditional (i.e., Anglo-Saxon) theories "portray . . . the *essence* of being a *victim* of politically induced violence and repression" (p. 4; italics added). The theories' "implicit concept of the human being, . . . assumption of the universality of psychological responses, and . . . inability to describe accurately the interaction between social-political and psychological developments and to catch both the collective and the individualistic dimensions of the human psyche" (p. 5) limit their usefulness in understanding war and its effects. The inability to describe what Punamaki calls the "collective dimension of the human psyche" is particularly costly for theorizing the meaning of terror and voice in Guatemala.

162 M. Brinton Lykes

Alternative Images

These models focus on terror's functions and immediate effects, often over-looking the symbolic, ideological, and expressive objectives of state-sponsored violence. Anthropological and historical works offer important images that have informed the thinking and practice of a small but growing number of psychologists who seek alternative models for conceptualizing the lived experiences of terror. For example, in his analysis of the Guatemalan counterinsurgency, Shelton Davis (1988) describes terror's "objectives"—"to generate an attitude of terror and fear—a 'culture of fear'—in the Indian population, ensuring that never again would it support or ally itself with a Marxist guerrilla movement" (p. 24). Robert Carmack (1988) elucidates the symbolic importance of terror in one Guatemalan town, Santa Cruz del Quiché, (Saint Cross of the Ki'ché), by identifying parallels between the Spanish victory in the 1500s and Guatemala in the 1980s. The Spanish achievement through superior weaponry, the massacre of many Maya, and the chaining of others as slaves is echoed in the Guatemalan army's campaign of 1981–83 in which well-armed soldiers ruthlessly tortured and killed Indians and burned their communities to the ground without real resistance.

Richard N. Adams (1988, 1989) described the functioning of the "culture of fear" that permeates life in contemporary Guatemala as a part of the dynamics of Ladino-Maya relations that have been intentionally manipulated by the army. Its genesis lies, according to Adams, in the conquest that sought not only to conquer but to ensure the survival of native labor.

Ricardo Falla (1984) referred to similar experiences of terror as a "partial genocide." This term suggests both the military's intention to destroy and sow fear, thereby controlling an entire population, *and* to maintain a cheap labor force to support a repressive, inegalitarian economic system in the country. The army's "guns and beans" program of the 1980s—intense repression and benevolent assistance—exemplifies these dual objectives (see, for example, An America's Watch Report, 1982), and for many Maya not only signifies contemporary counterinsurgent strategies but resymbolizes earlier repressive relations between the Spaniards and their ancestors. Further, a "conquest that fails to exterminate or assimilate the conquered inevitably leaves a population of divided identities" (Adams, 1988, p. 284). Subordinated Maya retain their pre-Conquest cultural memory, and Ladino populations, who have controlled the Maya through force, fear their potential rebellion. Adams echoes Michael Taussig's (1986–87, 1989) analysis of the symbolic functioning of fear, while introducing an important dimension heretofore absent, Mayan "cultural memory."

In her discussion of torture, one of the most extreme forms of state-sponsored violence, Elaine Scarry (1985) analyzes another face of silence and the rupture of relationships experienced in situations of terror. In the interrogation process that accompanies torture, silence appears to be a form of resistance, as the person being tortured refuses to reveal information about him- or herself or his or her *compañeros* to the torturer. Scarry offers another view of this response/nonresponse. While the verbal act of question-and-answer represents the destruction of voice, the infliction of physical pain reflects the destruction of body. The intense physical pain reduces the person to utterances, causing the disintegration of one's world and of the self. The combination of the infliction of pain and interrogation serves to "unmake" the world of the person being tortured. Voice is deconstructed and thus identity, self, is destroyed. World, self, and voice are "lost, or nearly lost, through the intense pain of torture" (Scarry, 1985, p. 35).

The counterinsurgency campaign of the Guatemalan army is a form of collective torture. One cannot understand the role of war in Guatemalan children's lives without approximating an understanding of its symbolic meanings as they resonate through time where past and future converge, that is, in the seemingly never-ending present. Terror, thus, creates a situation of "normal abnormality" (Martín-Baró, 1989; Taussig, 1986–87) or "terror as usual"—where "one moves in bursts between somehow accepting the situation as normal, only to be thrown into a panic or shocked into disorientation by an event, a rumor . . . something said or not said" (Taussig, 1986–87, p. 8). The state thus silences the population through terror, exploiting fear in a particular way.

State-imposed silencing is often met by the silence of the people (Lykes & Liem, 1990). As a response to a counterinsurgency situation, silence is often an adaptive strategy for survival. However, at the same time, it exacerbates people's feelings of isolation. It also interferes with Mayan communities' traditional forms of organizing and structures of authority, thus undermining the role of the elderly, making it difficult to develop and sustain social ties, or to develop a collective response. A deep lack of trust is evident in the individual, in the family, in the community, and in the state. The self-silencing within the population complements and reinforces the government's "official story," making it nearly impossible to recognize what is happening.

The reality of war and the symbolic meanings of terror suggest a reconceptualization of trauma. Ignacio Martín-Baró, the Salvadoran social psychologist and Jesuit who was assassinated on November 16, 1989, offered one alternative. He shifted the focus from the individual to what he called the psychosocial traumatic process, that is, the "concrete crystallization . . . of dehumanizing social relations . . . of exploitation and oppression"

(Martín-Baró, 1994, p. 125). According to Martín-Baró, psychosocial trauma is not an unusual event in the context of war but rather an everyday part of life. The slaughter of individuals, the disappearance of loved ones, the inability to distinguish what is one's own experience from what others say it is, the militarization of institutions, and the extreme polarization of social life have, despite their clear abnormality, come to be accepted as normal. Articulation of the particular expressions of psychosocial traumatic processes as experienced individually and collectively by Guatemalan and other children is one of the challenges left to us by Martín-Baró.

MAKING MEANING FROM MEANINGLESSNESS

Breaking Out of an Encircling Silencing

Research, grounded in positivist assumptions and a medical model, hypothesizes a separate subject (the child) who experiences an object (terror) in timeless space, and creates meaning from the atrocities and terrors through descriptions of effects at the level of the individual. Although important, particularly in identifying extreme cases that need individual attention, this research fails to capture both the collective nature of each child's particular experience and the fact that what is destroyed are not only individual material bodies but also cultural symbols. Meaning making itself is thereby at risk. The method fits the multiple and varied experiences of terror and the child's particular responses to it into preestablished categories that comfort the researcher more than they respond to the child and his or her community. Further, when these categories are applied back to the community, they are experienced, not surprisingly, as outside the culture and as impositions.

   Symptom checklists or even structured interviews fall far short of capturing that reality. They are frequently impossible to administer in contexts of ongoing war and may be perceived by the interviewee as intrusions designed by "the enemy" to further the war's objectives. In contrast, by accompanying a child and hearing testimony into speech (see, Morton, 1985, for reference to the expression "hearing into speech"), one enters into a relationship, and what emerges is co-constructed dialogically in time. That construction then becomes a part of a shared story that constrains and facilitates future storytelling. Relationships constructed between the researcher and the subject in time constitute sources of data that approximate more adequate bases for knowing than data gathered with more traditional research instruments. As importantly, the relationship between the researcher and the survivor creates a context in which some of the latter's multiple versions of survival are constructed and/or enacted. The remainder of this chapter will explore how my relationship as researcher-activist in a community with survivors has contributed to alternative forms of making meaning.

Traditional social science methodologists recommend longitudinal, controlled studies with representative samples for testing hypotheses derived from my field experiences. Given the political, economic, and ethical realities of war and the criticisms described above of the medical model and positivist social science methods, I would, in contrast, propose "activist participatory research" or "passionate scholarship," (see DuBois, 1983; Lykes, 1989). Most simply, this is a process through which the researcher accompanies the participant or subject over time, participating and observing while providing resources to the participant and his or her community, who, in turn, "inform" the researcher. It reflects a willingness to risk entering another's life and allowing him or her to enter one's own. Understanding, and one's possibilities for continuing engagement, are thus shaped by an experience of shared subjectivity.

CIRCLING BACK TO BEGIN AGAIN

My access to Mayan meaning making is both constrained and facilitated by many years of knowing child survivors and their adult caretakers who are themselves survivors. Those relationships have deeply shaped my experiences of Guatemala, both contributing to my understanding about life within a context of war and reminding me of the limits of my knowledge. In this phase of knowledge-seeking I have turned frequently to Carlos,[4] an educator, health promoter, displaced Maya, and father of eight children, for a deeper reading of the violence in Guatemala. He has served as a key informant clarifying Mayan conceptions of the effects of terror and has been a collaborator in the development of strategies for accompanying children. One afternoon he summarized his understanding of "the violence" in the following way:

> We can describe many problems which are perhaps not new problems but are problems that have intensified. Beginning in 1980 there were many changes in people's conduct and behavior. . . . Before, there was unity; now, there is none. . . .
> Many have spoken of confusion among the people of their communities, saying that there is lots of confusion, that people don't know what to do, that people don't have anything to believe in. . . .

> Before the [Mayan people] preached that life was worth a lot;
> the Christian religion also taught that one should respect and ap-
> preciate life. During the violence there were many violations of life
> . . . many contradictions . . .
>
> The traditional [Mayan] religion not only valued human lives
> but life in general, the life of the plants, of the animals and they
> taught a lot about life through stories and fables, about how to value
> life of the plants and of the animals, including the lives of the small-
> est of animals, like the ants, . . . the bees, all of these things were
> deeply respected.
>
> In addition to the lives of domestic animals that are commonly
> or obviously respected because they help humans, they also respect
> plants deeply. Plants are medicinal, nourish one; and also the trees,
> not only fruit trees but also trees with leaves, that give shade.
>
> If all of this is appreciated, how much more the life of a human
> being!
>
> But in the violence that began and intensified in the 1980s there
> was much violation of this respect, so the people began to doubt
> their traditional beliefs and to question why all of this was happen-
> ing if what they had learned was not this.
>
> . . . I think that [within this context] the situation of the children
> is a catastrophe, it is deplorable because they are not going to have
> an identity, even more so when they have no one to orient them, they
> will not even know where their parents come from, they will lose
> their history, their culture. . . . Perhaps others will not know whether
> or not they are Indians, and therefore they will not have an identity.
> We find this among many of the groups with whom we work; they
> don't have a sense of identity, because they don't have a piece of
> land, or a house, or a property, or even a place. Because they walk
> from one town to another . . . the house where they live is not their
> own, and they live with people who do not come from their same
> cultural group. This is an intense blow that provokes many prob-
> lems. . . . And it will be even more problematic for children in the
> future.

Meaning made of the terror of the 1980s by one Maya reverberates
backward and forward in time. Confusion dominates, because Maya have
been displaced from their homes, their land, the earth. The earth, nature, is
constitutive of who they are *and* of how they experience and name who they
are. The trees have been cut, symbolizing that their lives have been cut short.

Where there is no longer confusion, it has been replaced by a set of behaviors that depart significantly from traditional Mayan values.

Previous researchers have found that the psychological effects identified in Guatemalan child survivors do not differ significantly from those identified in survivors from other countries (see Lykes, 1994, for a summary of these findings). Yet listing symptoms barely scratches the surface. What does it mean for a Maya child to lose her land, to watch her home and crops and traditional dress burn, to see her animals killed? This is not simply the cumulative effect of traumatic experience. The Maya collective body has been deeply wounded—a body that is constituted in its deepest particularity in the individual lives of survivors—a body that is profoundly communal. It is that collective body—the ants, the trees, the corn, the domestic animals, the human beings gathered across generations—that has been ripped from its roots and wanders the earth—an earth that has been burned and scarred, an earth that both reflects and constructs the communities' scars. The burning of crops reflects not only the destruction of subsistence or physical survival but also an attack on a symbol that most fully represents the people of corn, that is, Mayan social subjectivity. Thus what has been destroyed is not only broader in scope (i.e., collective and cultural) than the notions of individual and internal trauma, captured most typically by the diagnosis PTSD. Psychosocial trauma is, as importantly, extended in time. The destruction of cultural archetypes and metaphors annihilates or deeply limits the next generation's possibility of affirming aspects of their cultural life. Only a deeper reading of Mayan life and traditions can yield more adequate theories for work with these child survivors.

SUBJECTS AS OBJECTS AS SUBJECTS: MEANING MAKING WITHIN SHARED SPACE

Creative Workshops for Children constitute the core of a program developed with Guatemalan health promoters, child care workers, and educators to accompany child survivors and develop a firmer base from which to make meaning of these experiences. The model emerged from several years of exchange with Argentines experienced in creative techniques for work with child survivors of disappeared parents and Guatemalan community leaders experienced in traditional and preventive health strategies.

The workshops (see Lykes, 1994, for a fuller description) were designed in part to facilitate communication and to help break silence. We began with a commitment to create a bounded space in which children could integrate theater, body movement and expressivity, the plastic arts, music, and words as resources for recovering their natural capacity to play (Winnicott, 1982). We sought to create a context where participants could project themselves, and share thoughts, feelings, and fears or anxieties. The group is a context in which these techniques can be appropriated as a means of communication. They enable one to take advantage of one's own resources and of "the other" as a resource. In this co-created space of the group, creativity is a resource for developing the possibility of modifying one's relations, reestablishing previously destroyed social ties, recovering or reconstructing one's story, searching for one's truth, and symbolizing one's experiences of the terror that one has lived (Lapierre & Aucouturier, 1977; Pavlovsky, Martínez Bouquet, & Moccio, 1985).

The group context enables the participant to move from individual personal tragedy toward a shared experience with the other, toward a sense of truth in the face of the effects of an organized violence that seeks to annul individual and collective identity. The group also enabled me as a situated other to be in a relationship with survivors in this social space of Mayan collectivity.

Inventing collective stories was one experience we shared in the workshop context. According to Gianni Rodari (1987), inventing stories through word games strengthens the child's sense of security, capacity to create, and pleasure of knowing. Through their stories we encounter children's conflicts, their experiences, their memories, their ideology. Rodari argues that we can use fantasy to establish an active relationship with reality. He suggests that through stories we enter reality through the window, which is, according to him, both more useful and more fun than entering through the door. The stories, created collectively by children's caretakers who were participants in our training workshops, provide equally important windows into the reality of Mayan survivors. Two of their stories that have contributed significantly to my understanding of Mayan survival are transcribed and briefly analyzed here.[5]

Nicho and Chefina (1988)

Stanza 1: Presentation of Nicho
Nicho, the white donkey,/
lives in the country./
Each hour he brays to show that he lives happily./
In the early hour he gathers grass for his nourishment./

Stanza 2: Nicho's diet
His favorite food is alfalfa/

so he doesn't have to wear glasses in the future,/
because alfalfa is good for vision./

Stanza 3: Nicho Meets a Dove
One fine day the donkey Nicho went out happily to look for herbs,/
when he met a dove./
The dove was inside a patch of alfalfa./

Stanza 4: Nicho's Encounter with the Dove
The donkey was surprised at the beauty of the dove,/
with bright, white feathers, almost like cotton./
The donkey wanted to greet the dove,/
but he realized he couldn't open his mouth because it was so cold./

Stanza 5: The Dove Initiates; Nicho, Speechless, Responds Nonverbally.
Then the dove greeted the donkey/
and he could only answer by shaking his head./

Stanza 6: The Dove Chefina—Who She is, Where She Lives
The dove Chefina, as she was called,/
lives in an oak tree where she has her nest,/
lulling to sleep together with the rustling of the leaves caused by the wind./

Stanza 7: Nicho's Appreciation of the Dove's Skill
The donkey, listening to the sweet trill of the dove in the foliage of the oak,/
decided to build his life under the same tree where the dove lives./

Stanza 8: Denouement—Division of Tasks
When the donkey wants to send messages to the town,/
the dove does it,/
and if the dove wants to transport heavy cargo,/
the donkey carries it,/

Stanza 9: Ending of the Tale—the Moral
and this is how they live together in complete cooperation./

Our multiple readings of this and other similar stories reveal a number of important themes. The pattern of reciprocity, for example, appears frequently and is sometimes patterned with that of romantic affection. In this story the development of a relationship between the donkey and the dove is represented. Although the donkey is introduced as happy where he lives, his decision to move to the dove's home or community suggests a search for companionship. The transformation of their relationship into one of reciprocity, where both participants are respected and recognized as equal contributors to the well-being of the other, suggests that they are more than companions. Relations are cemented through affection, which facilitates co-operation. The material context is also frequently stressed, suggesting that survival is accomplished through reciprocity.

In other stories, such as the following, participants represent their country's counterinsurgency war:

The Affectionate Duck and the Crafty Duck (1991)

Stanza 1: Group of Ducks: Introduction
There was a group of ducks in a lake./

Stanza 2: Affectionate Duck: Personality
Among them/
there was one who was very affectionate with all of his companions./
He conversed with them/
and everyone he found he would share with./

Stanza 3: Affectionate Duck: Social Role
He tried to defend the little ones from danger/
and at the same time/
called to all the ducks to organize themselves/

Stanza 4: Group of Ducks: Defense
and in this way they were able to defend themselves from their enemies/
who always wanted to finish off the ducks' race./

Stanza 5: Crafty One: Personality
Among them there was one dressed in leather pants, leather boots, silk shirt, cap and tie,/
who was proud, *oreja*, mocking and at the same time crafty./

Stanza 6: Crafty One: Social Role
He was always after the destruction of his fellow ducks./
He moved away from the whole organization/
and was capable of anything with which to get something for himself/
without sharing it./

Stanza 7: Crafty One Meets Affectionate Duck
One occasion he met the affectionate duck/
and started a discussion of the reason the rest of the ducks sought out his company/
and kept themselves organized/
when all could live like him, without sharing any of their possessions./

Stanza 8: Crafty One Kills Affectionate Duck with View to Destroying Ducks—The Moral
He became quite furious,/ so he flung himself at the affectionate duck/ and killed him/ to take his leadership and finish off the ducks' organization,/ which was his main objective./

The story of the ducks describes some of the ways in which the counterinsurgency has succeeded through infiltrators, or *orejas,* people who frequently come from one's own community and report its activities to the authorities in the service of destroying the community, and, according to these storytellers, the entire race. This is an ever-present theme in Mayan communities that are politically organized and is increasingly acknowledged among those who are neither Maya nor organized. This story introduces us to terror characteristic of "the violence" in Guatemala today. It ends with the destruction of an organization, suggesting the "partial genocide" described by Ricardo Falla (1984) and leaving open the threat of the entire population's destruction. The story unself-consciously introduces the listener to the group's symbolization of relations of individuality and collectivity. More specifically, we are first introduced to a group of ducks and to their children, and then, two particular ducks (i.e., two individuals) are presented. Although described in some detail, they are always positioned in relation to the group. The focus of this story is on destroying the organization (i.e., the collectivity). The death of the individual leader, although portrayed, is less important to the story than the destruction of the organization. The *oreja,* the crafty duck, kills the affectionate leader, which signals the destruction of the organization, that is, the community. As importantly, the story is a vehicle through which those who have been silenced can speak through metaphors and stories about their deepest fears and/or memories.

Nature is a central focus of these stories and of others that I have gathered. It is the source of life—sometimes representing an idyllic place to live happily; othertimes, a practical resource in preventive health care or the context in which personal and political violence erupts. As importantly, the animal kingdom, inanimate objects, and the flora all participate actively in Mayan culture. Objects, animals, and human beings are represented as having a "common language." Stories in the *Pop Wuj,* the sacred document of the Ki'ché Maya, reveal, for example, the participation of trees, jars, pots, and the like in such activities as the eradication of evil from the earth (see, for example, Chavez, 1979, pp. 8a–9a). The stories represented here thus evidence certain continuities with ancient storytelling.

Although significantly different in thematic content, the diverse stories

172

reveal cultural understandings of reciprocity, relationship, individuality, and collectivity within a natural setting. The ducks' story elaborates the threat to cultural survival, clarifying how the enemy is both "other" than the community but also within the community, that is, one of us. Situated otherness in this story is represented by the *oreja*. The stories provide vehicles for elaborating what is common knowledge within these communities but remains silenced by counterinsurgency and fear. Taken as a unit they reflect the importance of reciprocity, the meaning of collectivity, and how fear and the trauma of genocide are represented by this group of Maya. These stories and others were created and then re-created through dramatization and drawings, providing an entry point, however limited, for working in the group with some of the factors that impede a larger process of re-creating and reconstructing community. They also mobilize creativity, a resource for such work.

As importantly, these creative productions are texts that serve as resources for the group itself, its coordinators, and me, the situated other, the participant researcher. The group and its participants live the unspeakable in their storytelling, their drawings, and their dramatizations. The group's coordinators read these texts and develop multiple understandings of the affective and cognitive lives of the participants and of themselves. For example, as someone positioned as an outsider, or other, I learned more about the meaning of "being other" as it is expressed symbolically by rural Maya through their representations of the *oreja*.

Experiencing and constructing relationships that facilitate the forms of knowing described above take time. Those who organize resistance within political, social, and religious groups are known through their actions. Traditional social psychological or clinical research with structured interviews and assessment instruments provides another layer of meaning making—one grounded in positivist scientific assumptions and closely allied to the medical model—that imposes linear cause-effect models where there may be none. The work described here involves accompanying wounded individuals who seek to break the silence that enshrouds the children of their communities. Activist participatory research thus yields different versions of survival. Further, the workshops themselves are texts that reflect Guatemalan stories of survival. Unlike other versions wherein voice is achieved through the language of reason that very frequently serves as a tool for mastering experience by distancing oneself from the direct experience and/or unformulated emotion and thereby in some ways perpetuating silencing, the methods used here in a group context embrace multiple levels of the self-in-context through which embodied voices break silence.

THERE IS NO SIMPLE MAKING OF MEANING

Atrocity and Versions of Survival

The experience of building relationships with child and adult survivors over ten years has yielded different forms of knowing. To be in a relationship over time with Maya who value all of life yet daily face the threat of death, destruction, the possible annihilation of themselves and their culture, raises serious challenges for an outsider who seeks understanding as a prerequisite for action. Each of the research strategies described above—the medical model, positivist science, and activist participatory research—moves us closer to the lived story of survival silenced by the state, the traumatized social and institutional structure, and the multiple layers psychically structured that protect each of us from nothingness. I have argued here that the third model, as enacted through Creative Workshops in Guatemala, enabled me to get closer to the embodied voices of survivors while actively accompanying them in a process. Further, through the relationship of accompaniment, new meaning making was possible. This work, for example, has helped me to "think culturally" about Mayan experiences of terror and survival. Through that process I have identified two theoretical contributions to conceptualizing trauma and recovery. First, by shifting the traditional Western psychological focus on individual identity, Mayan "selfhood" is voiced and enacted through storytelling and in relationships as inherently social. To speak of "who I am" invokes family, community, the animal kingdom, one's traditions and language, and the earth. Subjectivity is collectively constituted, and the experiences summarized here suggest that the Mayan "self" might more accurately be characterized as "social subjectivity." There is, of course, a growing critique of traditional Western theories of self that, although extensive (see, for example, Gergen, 1991; Hermans & Kempen, 1993; Markus & Kitayama, 1991; Sampson, 1993), has not significantly influenced psychological theories of trauma and its effects. My work with Maya in Guatemala suggest a connection.

Secondly, in addition to the common functions of terror identified by human rights activists and scholars, consideration of terror's symbolic dimensions clarifies terror's threat to culture and to social subjectivity. This work extends both the spatial and the temporal dimensions along which we conceptualize terror. Terror's destructive forces affect community and culture, not only internal individual well-being. Further, terror not only destroys the present and forces a rethinking of the past, but it deeply threatens the future through its destructive effects on the next generation's capacity to affirm aspects of their cultural life.

My work in Guatemala contributes to an ongoing dialogue between Bill Ryan and me (see "A Conversation between William Ryan and M. Brinton Lykes," pp. 351–367) about the relative importance of similarities and differences in understanding social problems and struggles for social change (see also Ryan, 1981). Westerners (business executives, developers, religious workers, activists, social scientists, etc.) who not only assume but seek to impose their ideological assumptions of similarity on the indigenous populations of Guatemala have more frequently destroyed than created possibilities for collaboration and change. Psychologists who see similarity across diverse populations of trauma survivors are more likely to be those who seek to identify internal individual effects of trauma, diagnosing PTSD, than those, such as Ignacio Martín-Baró, who urge us to rethink trauma in terms of the community and the social context. Bill reserves comment about the implications of his thinking for international and/or multicultural work out of an admitted lack of experience in these areas. He has, however, always urged us to get at the primary problem in whatever context in which we struggle, seeking to identify the underlying contradictions. The work presented here suggests that presumed similarity in the effects of state-sponsored violence and war on children across cultures fails to consider the import and longstanding impact of a more primary problem. Those who study trauma and its wake from this perspective ignore the dynamic Ladino-Maya relationship described above and the impact of the various repressive forces (the Spanish, the United States, and the Guatemalan army) that have sought and seek to destroy Mayan culture and identity.

Elaine Scarry (1985), Michael Taussig (1986–87; 1989), and Marcelo Suárez-Orozco (1990, 1991), among others, suggest that linear models of thinking and analysis will not easily yield understanding of or responses to the reality of torture and terror. Lawrence Langer's (1991) writing demonstrates the limitations of thought and analysis for penetrating horror and atrocity. My work with children and their caretakers in Guatemala confirms that although traditional models of knowing yield some information about the effects of torture and trauma, they fall far short of either understanding the phenomena under investigation or developing responses. Alternative texts, constructed through relationship with a small number of survivors in the setting of creative workshops, offer another form and context for knowledge construction. They do not, however, transcend the limits of human meaning making or knowledge construction. As Langer (1991) suggests reading meaning where there may be none may be one way to heal our own pain, to quiet our own rage.

Through this work in Guatemala I have begun to understand dimensions of subjectivity, of terror, and of survival that are frequently neglected in psychological and psychiatric research with children in war. Thinking culturally within lived experiences of Mayan reality reveals alternative understandings of subjectivity, of terror, and of survival. Simultaneously, I understand how the multiple stories of survivors and the silence of the dead challenge all meaning making. Despite this, moving creatively with children and their caretakers, who seek collectively to resist what individually often debilitates, creates a context wherein the "positioned other" can authentically be among survivors and their multiple versions of terror and survival.

ACKNOWLEDGMENTS

A version of this paper was presented as an invited address at the XXIV Congress of the InterAmerican Psychological Association, Santiago, Chile, July 4–9, 1993. Much of the work described here was undertaken collaboratively with colleagues in Guatemala and Argentina. I mention briefly the Asociación de Servicios Comunitarios de Salud in Guatemala and the Movimiento Solidario de Salud Mental in Argentina, with whom I have worked for many years. The project has been supported by regional funding from UNICEF, in-kind contributions from participating organizations, and a fellowship from the Jesuit Institute, Boston College, where I served as a Visiting Scholar in 1992–93.

My theorizing and my commitment to persist have been deeply influenced by Ignacio Martín-Baró, with whom I had the good fortune to work for a number of years before his murder. However, I take responsibility for the ideas expressed here. Others may not agree with the ways in which I have come to make meaning of our shared experiences and surely should not be held responsible for them.

NOTES

1. See, for example, the work of Jerome Bruner (1990), Michelle Fine (1992), Henry A. Giroux (1992), Trinh T. Minh-ha (1991), and Renato Rosaldo (1989), and edited volumes by James Clifford and George E. Marcus (1986), Carol E. Franz and Abigail J. Stewart (1994), Sherna Berger Gluck and Daphne Patai (1991), Joyce McCarl Nielsen (1990), and The Personal Narratives Group (1989).
2. Several cautionary words. I have spoken and written of many examples of Guatemalans engaged in activist-based resistance—organized in labor unions, Mayan and peasant organizations, church groups, the Communities of Populations in Resistance in the Guatemalan Highlands, etc. Further, the communities described here by me and by Carlos are among those most directly affected by the war and by institutionalized violence in the Guatemalan Highlands. The ideas presented

here in no way negate my deep respect and admiration for the witness of those courageous people who break silence through overt resistance and/or rebellion, or for those Mayan communities (for example, some Ki'ché towns, including Nahualá) that were not as directly affected by war and that responded through greater unity. In this paper I seek, rather, to explore a more silent underside of terror and *other* versions of survival, silence, and voice.

3. In Guatemala there are 21 Mayan languages plus Spanish, the official language, and Xinca and Caribe. See Cojti (1988).

4. The names of Guatemalans are pseudonyms, as their identification might jeopardize their safety given the ongoing violence within their country.

5. Drawing on work by the sociolinguist James Gee (1989, 1991) and the narrative analyst Elliot Mishler (1986), I am currently developing a system for analyzing and interpreting these stories that will enable me to understand the multiple meanings communicated through each story and its reenactments, and approximate an analysis of shared patterns of meanings across multiple stories. The stanzas and lines, as delineated by bars (/), reflect the initial stages of this coding system. Each stanza represents a unit of meaning, constituted by the phrases grouped between bars. The original stories were developed orally in groups and then written down on newsprint by workshop participants.

REFERENCES

Adams, R. N. (1988). Conclusions: What can we know about the harvest of violence. In R. M. Carmack (Ed.), *Harvest of violence: The Maya Indians and the Guatemalan crisis* (pp. 274–291).Oklahoma: University of Oklahoma Press.

Adams, R. N. (1989). *The reproduction of state terrorism in Central America* (Paper No. 89–01). Austin: University of Texas at Austin.

An America's Watch Report (1982). *Human rights in Guatemala: No neutrals allowed*. New York: America's Watch Committee.

Barry, T. (1992). *Inside Guatemala*. Albuquerque, NM: The Inter-Hemispheric Education Resource Center.

Bruner, J. (1990). *Acts of meaning*. Cambridge, MA: Harvard University Press.

Carmack, R. M. (1988). The story of Santa Cruz Quiché. In R. M Carmack (Ed.), *Harvest of violence: The Maya Indians and the Guatemalan crisis* (pp. 39–69). Oklahoma: University of Oklahoma Press.

Chavez, A. I. (1979). *Pop Wuj*. Tlalpan, Mexico: Ediciones de la Casa Chata.

Clifford, J., & Marcus, G. E. (Eds.). (1986). *Writing culture: The poetics and politics of ethnography*. Berkeley: University of California Press.

Cojti, N. (1988). *Map, proyecto linguistico "Francisco Marroquin."* Texts by Lopez Raquec. Guatemala: Editorial Piedra Santa.

Davis, S. H. (1988). Introduction: Sowing the seeds of violence. In R. M. Carmack, (Ed.), *Harvest of violence: The Maya Indians and the Guatemalan crisis* (pp. 3–36). Oklahoma: University of Oklahoma Press.

DuBois, B. (1983). Passionate scholarship: Notes on values, knowing, and method in feminist social science. In G. Bowles & R. Klein (Eds.), *Theories of women's studies* (pp. 105–116). Boston: Routledge.

Falla, R. (1984). We charge genocide. In S. Jonas, E. McCaughan, & E. S. Martínez (Eds. and trans.), *Guatemala: Tyranny on trial—Testimony of the Permanent People's Tribunal* (pp. 112–119). San Francisco: Publicaciones Sinthesis.

Fine, M. (1992). *Disruptive voices: The possibilities of feminist research.* Ann Arbor: University of Michigan Press.

Franz, C. E., & Stewart, A. J. (Eds.) (1994). *Women creating lives: Identities, resilience, and resistance.* Boulder, CO: Westview Press.

Gee, J. P. (1989). Two styles of narrative construction and their linguistic and educational implications. *Journal of Education, 171*(1), 97–115.

Gee, J. P. (1991). Memory and myth: A perspective on narrative. In A. McCabe & C. Petersen (Eds.), *Developing narrative structures.* (pp. 1–25). Hillsdale, NJ: Lawrence Erlbaum.

Gergen, K. J. (1991). *The saturated self: Dilemmas of identity in contemporary life.* New York: Basic Books.

Giroux, H. A. (1992). *Border crossings: Cultural workers and the politics of education.* New York: Routledge.

Gluck, S. B., & Patai, D. (Eds.). (1991). *Women's words: The feminist practice of oral history.* New York: Routledge.

Herman, J. (1992). *Trauma and recovery.* New York: Basic Books.

Hermans, H., & Kempen, J. G. (1993). *The dialogical self: Meaning as movement.* San Diego, CA: Academic Press.

Jensen, P. S., & Shaw, J. (1993). Children as victims of war: Current knowledge and future research needs. *Journal of American Academy of Child Adolescent Psychiatry, 32*(4), 697–708.

Langer, L. L. (1991). *Holocaust testimonies: The ruins of memory.* New Haven: Yale University Press.

Lapierre, A. & Aucouturier, B. (1977). *Simbologia del movimiento* [Symbolism of movement]. Barcelona, Spain: Editorial Científico Médica.

Loo, C. M. (1993). An integrative-sequential treatment model for post-traumatic stress disorder: A case study of the Japanese American internment and redress. *Clinical Psychology Review, 13,* 89–117.

Lykes, M. B. (1989). Dialogue with Guatemalan Indian women: Critical perspectives on constructing collaborative research. In R. Unger (Ed.), *Representations: Social constructions of gender* (pp. 167–185). Amityville, NY: Baywood.

Lykes, M. B. (1994). Terror, silencing, and children: International multidisciplinary collaboration with Guatemalan Maya communities. *Social Science and Medicine, 38*(4), 543–552.

Lykes, M. B., & Liem, R. (1990). Human rights and mental health in the United States: Lessons from Latin America. *Journal of Social Issues, 46*(3), 151–165.

Martín-Baró, I. (1989, June–July). *La institucionalización de la guerra* [Institutionalization of war]. Paper presented at the annual meeting of the InterAmerican Psychological Association, Buenos Aires.

Martín-Baró, I. (1990, March 23). Reparations: Attention must be paid. Healing the body politic in Latin America. *Commonweal,* pp. 184,186.

Martín-Baró, I. (1994). *Writings for a liberation psychology.* Edited by A. Aron & S. Corne. Cambridge, MA: Harvard University Press.

Melville, M. B., & Lykes, M. B. (1992). Guatemalan Indian children and the sociocultural effects of government-sponsored terrorism. *Social Science and Medicine, 34*(5), 533–548.

Minh-ha, T. T. (1991). *When the moon waxes red: Representation, gender, and cultural politics.* New York: Routledge.

Mishler, E. G. (1986). *Research interviewing: Context and narrative.* Cambridge, MA: Harvard University Press.

Morton, N. (1985). *The journey is home.* Boston: Beacon Press.

Nielsen, J. McC. (Ed.). (1990). *Feminist research methods: Exemplary readings in the social sciences.* Boulder, CO: Westview Press.

Pavlovsky, E., Martínez Bouquet, C., & Moccio, F. (1985). *Psicodrama: Cuando y por que dramatizar* [Psychodrama: When and why to dramatize]. Buenos Aires: Ediciones Busqueda.

The Personal Narratives Group. (Eds.). (1989). *Interpreting women's lives: Feminist theory and personal narratives.* Bloomington: Indiana University Press.

Punamaki, R.-L. (1989). Special issues. *International Journal of Mental Health, 17*(4)–*18*(1–2).

Rodari, G. (1987). *La gramática de la fantasía: Introducción al arte de inventar historias* [The grammar of fantasy: Introduction to the art of inventing stories]. México: Ediciones Comamex.

Rosaldo, R. (1989). *Culture and truth: The remaking of social analysis.* Boston: Beacon Press.

Ryan, W. (1981). *Equality.* New York: Pantheon.

Sampson, E. E. (1993). *Celebrating the other: A dialogic account of human nature.* Boulder, CO: Westview Press.

Scarry, E. (1985). *The body in pain: The making and unmaking of the world.* Oxford: Oxford University Press.

Suárez-Orozco, M. M. (1990). Speaking of the unspeakable: Toward a psychosocial understanding of responses to terror. *Ethos, 18*(3), 353–383.

Suárez-Orozco, M. M. (1991). The heritage of enduring a "dirty war": Psychosocial aspects of terror in Argentina, 1976–1988. *The Journal of Psychohistory, 18*(4), 469–505.

Taussig, M. (1986–87). *Shamanism, colonialism, and the wild man: A study in terror and healing.* Chicago: University of Chicago Press.

Taussig, M. (1989, Fall–Winter). Terror as usual: Walter Benjamin's theory of history as a state of siege. *Sociological Text,* pp. 3–20.

Winnicott, D. W. (1982). *Playing and reality.* London: Tavistock.

Chapter 9

Psychology, the Distant Other, and the Dialectics of Change in Non-Western Societies

•*Ali Banuazizi*

THE "NON-WESTERN MAN" HAS LONG SERVED AS A DISTANT "OTHER" IN the intellectual discourse on the nature of the Western mind and character. Depending on the moral and intellectual mood of the times, he has been portrayed as a heathen, the "noble savage," the "direct heir and representative of the primitive man," sly and inscrutable, exotic, tradition-bound, impulsive, prelogical, fanatic, fatalist, collectivist, and the like.[1] As a "serviceable other," to borrow Edward Sampson's (1993, p. 4) apt phrase, he has been summoned regularly as a convenient object of contrast whenever his Western counterparts needed to distinguish themselves from the rest of hu mankind. For centuries, the choice of the underlying dimensions of such contrasts and all else that helped to fashion his image were part of a self-perpetuating monologue *about* him. He too, of course, carried his own monologue about the West and the ways and manners of its peoples, one that, until recently, was less audible and articulate but no less distorted than that of his Western counterparts (see Dussel, 1995; Gordon, 1989; Shayegan, 1992).

In the past few decades, a vast array of economic and political changes at the global level, combined with an unprecedented expansion in the reach and coverage of the mass media, international travel, emigration, and intellectual exchanges of all sorts, has begun to transform the centuries-old monologue about the non-Western man into a more inclusive discourse in which his voice, and, significantly, that of his sisters, are increasingly heard. The tremendous diversity of these voices—at times in harmony with those from within Western societies that had been similarly silent, muffled, or marginalized—has helped to unpack the bogus category of the "non-Western world" and to develop a more variegated and accurate view of the predicaments of those who inhabit its many worlds.

One of the contexts in which particularly invidious distinctions between the Western and non-Western peoples have been drawn is the literature on the subjective dimensions of social change and development in Third World societies.[2] Perhaps not surprisingly, many of the mental traits and cultural orientations that have been attributed to non-Western peoples in these studies bear a close resemblance to the stereotypic qualities that have been attributed to women, the poor, and disadvantaged minorities in the West itself. Such attributions and comparisons are particularly pernicious when the cultural or psychological characteristics in question are proffered as ready-made explanations for the persistent economic and political woes that beset the poorer non-Western societies.[3] This mode of thinking is similar to the "victim-blaming" ideology that William Ryan (1971) described in his analysis of American social problems some two-and-a-half decades ago.[4]

In what follows, I shall review a number of earlier, psychologically oriented studies of social change in non-Western societies in an attempt to show how certain ideological and ethnocentric biases distorted their understanding of the dynamics of social change, and, more specifically of the dialectical relationship between "traditional" and "modern" modes of thinking, values, and practices in these societies. Further, I shall briefly describe several emerging approaches to the problem of change in developing countries that are distinguished by their more critical and culturally sensitive orie.itations within the discipline of psychology.

INTELLECTUAL BACKGROUND

The study of the psychological aspects of social change in non-Western societies has a relatively short history. Its origins in studies by North American social scientists may be traced to the confluence of several intellectual trends and pragmatic concerns in the years following the Second World War. The first of these was the "culture-and-personality" school, which from the late 1930s to the mid-1950s represented an influential, if not the dominant, viewpoint on the relationship between child-rearing practices and personality development, on the one hand, and cultural norms and practices, on the other, in the primarily nonindustrial societies. Guided by the psychoanalytic theory, the major premise of this approach was that commonly shared childhood experiences in a society generate a "basic" or "modal" personality structure in its adult members, which, in turn, helps to shape and functionally integrate that society's cultural practices and symbolic systems such as religion, folklore, rituals, and the like (Bock, 1988, esp. chaps. 3–5; Kardiner, 1945; Kardiner & Linton, 1949; LeVine, 1982, esp. chaps. 1–3; Manson, 1988). Although the culture-and-personality approach came under severe criticism and suffered a rapid demise after the mid-1950s as a scholarly pursuit (e.g., Shweder, 1991), its leitmotif and basic premises continued to influence studies of the relationship between culture and psychological processes for years to come.

Academic (social) psychology's contributions to the study of social change, particularly in non-Western contexts, were quite limited for several reasons. In the first place, the study of behavior at the collective level and in real-world contexts, which had been the central concern of the pioneers of the discipline in the early decades of this century, had gradually given way to a focus on the dynamics of social interaction among *individuals,* in face-to-face dyads or in small groups, within the artificial confines of the psychological laboratory. Second, the concept of attitude, described by Gordon Allport (1968) as "the most distinctive and indispensable concept in contemporary [mid-twentieth-century] American social psychology" (p. 59), had become the equivalent of "the royal road" to the understanding of social behavior. The combination of these two developments effectively reduced the scope of social-psychological analysis of social change to studies of the impact of artificially induced interventions, in laboratory or field experiments, on the attitudes and behavior of individual subjects. And finally, in their quest to discover *universal* laws of social behavior, social psychologists tended to ignore, or at best "control for," differences among their subjects that could be attributed to their cultural or socioeconomic backgrounds (Pepitone, 1989; Tajfel, 1972). This made any attempt at cross-cultural validation of their theories or empirical findings seemingly superfluous or, at best, someone else's problem. In spite of these limitations, many quantitative research methods (especially in the areas of attitude measurement and scaling) and numerous social-psychological constructs found their way into the analytic framework of those, mostly from neighboring social-science disciplines, who were interested in studying the processes of change and development in the years following the Second World War.

Another impetus to research and theorizing in this area came from the pragmatic concerns of policy-makers and development specialists in the early post-war period. In the conservative and ideologically charged cold-war atmosphere of the 1950s, development theorists tended to be deeply suspicious of mass movements to effect social change from the bottom, preferring instead to think of development as a gradual, cumulative process that can be steered successfully by the incumbent elites from the top. Furthermore, many shared the view that, regardless of differences in points of departure and rates of development, all societies—or at least those choosing the path of modernization—are likely to go through similar stages of economic growth as did the West in its own evolution. Mindful of the limitations of institutional approaches, some development theorists turned to cultural anthropology and psychology for insights into the "people side" of development. This shift from the external, social-structural constraints to the endogenous, subjective obstacles to growth brought a new set of issues into development studies. It implied that, at least in part, underdevelopment and poverty among nations can be explained in terms of the values, attitudes, character traits, and cultural orientations of their inhabitants themselves. Hence, the identification of cultural and social-psychological impediments to socioeconomic or political development became the goal of a new genre of psychologically oriented studies of social change in developing countries (for critical reviews of this literature, see Gendzier, 1985; Nash, 1984; So, 1990).

THE POSTWAR STUDIES OF CHANGE IN NON-WESTERN SOCIETIES

Compared to the earlier writings, particularly in the culture-and-personality tradition, the postwar, psychologically oriented studies of change tended to be more empirically based, relying on first-hand observations and systematic gathering of data in the developing countries rather than on the impressionistic, "culture-at-a-distance" methods of the prewar period.

Daniel Lerner's (1958/1964) pioneering study of modernization in the Middle East set the tone for the new wave of studies. Lerner identified "empathy" (the ability to place oneself mentally in others' roles and to imagine what life is like outside one's own restrictive surround) as the crucial psychological trait that enables newly mobile ("transitional") individuals to adapt to the changing circumstances of a modernizing society. The initial thrust toward social change, he argued, may come from changes in the opportunity structure or in socioeconomic institutions. Psychological factors play a key role in subsequent phases of modernization, however, mediating between the initial structural changes on the one hand and the psychological (re-)orientations that are required for sustained economic development on the other. What is needed for a successful transition from "backwardness" to "modernity," Lerner argued, is a psychological propensity on the part of individuals to respond effectively to newly created opportunities or the demands of a changing environment. The direction of change, or rather its desired end-state in the Middle East (and, by implication, elsewhere) seemed all too clear to him: "What America is—to condense a rule more powerful than its numerous exceptions—the modernizing Middle East seeks to become" (p. 79).

David McClelland's (1961) theory of economic growth as a function of achievement motivation, which is acquired by the individual through independence training in early childhood years (for the application of the theory to developing countries, see McClelland & Winter, 1969; see also Tirandis, 1984); Lucian Pye's (1962) study of the Burmese "sense of insecurity" and weak identity as impediments to building a modern nation-state; and Everett Hagen's (1962, 1963) explanation of the dynamic of social change in terms of "innovational" personality and individual attitudes toward manual-technical labor are among the early examples of these studies.

MODERNITY AND THE "PSYCHIC UNITY OF MANKIND"

In terms of methodological rigor and theoretical sophistication, the research on "psychological modernity," initiated in the late 1950s and early 1960s, was the culmination of the postwar studies linking psychological factors to socioeconomic change in developing societies. Defined as a set of individual dispositions (attitudes, values, cognitive styles, motives, etc.), psychological modernity was considered to be the product of such structural changes as urban residence, schooling, greater exposure to mass media, and employment in modern enterprises, which in turn facilitated further modernization of a society (e.g., Dawson, 1967; Doob, 1960; Kahl, 1968).

Compared with the earlier attempts to link individual and societal levels of analysis, psychological modernity offered several distinct advantages. In the first place, it was relatively free from many of the ethnocentric biases that had characterized the earlier works on the subject. By focusing on the impact of social-structural conditions on individuals *within* the same society, it avoided invidious and facile explanations of the different levels of development achieved by differences societies in terms of their ethnic, religious, or national-cultural characteristics. Second, modernizing influences were not assumed to be limited to those of early socialization, but included life experiences well beyond childhood and early adolescent years. Third, as a continuous variable rather than a distinct personality type, psychological modernity could be assessed along a continuum rather than in an all-or-none fashion. Finally, the successful development of scales for measuring psychological modernity made it possible to estimate and compare the effects of social background and other experiential factors on a person's or group's level of modernity, and, in turn, to explore the impact of different levels of psychological modernity on the subsequent course of a society's development.

In the most systematic and extensive study of psychological modernity, Alex Inkeles and David Smith (1974) proposed that a small set of interrelated individual values, attitudes, and behaviors, comprising what they called a "syndrome of modernity," can be shown to distinguish modern individuals from those with a traditional outlook and modes of behavior across a wide range of societies. As empirical support for this hypothesis, they presented the result of a massive six-nation study in which individual modernity was measured by a theoretically anchored scale of Overall Modernity (OM). In what was one of the largest comparative social science projects ever undertaken, this scale was administered to a sample of over 5,500 men between the ages of eighteen and thirty-two in six developing countries—Argentina, Chile, East Pakistan (now Bangladesh), India, Israel (focusing on the "Oriental" Jews), and Nigeria. The study's main finding was that in all six societies studied, the same combination of values, attitudes, and behaviors coalesced around the same individual modernity factor.[5]

The "modern man," as he emerged from this massive mound of data, could be characterized in terms of a set of distinctive qualities—or a "psychosocial syndrome" as the authors called them—that were relatively consistent across the six societies under study. The central elements of this syndrome were later summarized by Inkeles (1983) as follows:

(1) Openness to new experience, both with people and with new ways of doing things such as attempting to control births; (2) the assertion of increasing independence from the authority of traditional figures, such as parents and priests, and a shift of allegiance to leaders of government, public affairs, trade unions, cooperatives and like; (3) belief in the efficacy of science and medicine, and a general abandonment of passivity and fatalism in the face of life's difficulties; and (4) ambition for oneself and one's children to achieve high occupational and educational goals. Men who manifest these characteristics (5) like people to be on time and show an interest in carefully planning their affairs in advance. It is also part of this syndrome (6) to show strong interest and take an active part in civic and community affairs and local politics; and (7) to strive energetically to keep up with the news and within this effort to prefer news of national and international import over items dealing with sports, religion, or purely local affairs. (p. 101)

To demonstrate the predictive power of their Overall Modernity construct, Inkeles and Smith made statistically controlled comparisons among several "criterion groups" that, on the basis of a set of independent criteria, could be identified as more or less modern in each of the six societies. In ascending order of their presumed modernity, these included: (1) peasants living in traditional rural communities; (2) urban nonindustrial workers; (3) recent migrants from the rural areas who had not yet been integrated into industrial work; and (4) former rural dwellers with three or more years of experience in an urban factory. The authors found that the greater a group's exposure to such modernizing experiences as formal education, mass media consumption, and work in an urban industrial factory, the higher its score on the OM. Thus, for example, among the men "fully exposed to the institutions which our theory designated as modernizing, some 76 percent scored as modern, whereas among those least under the influence of such institutions only about 2 percent achieved modern scores on our scales" (Inkeles & Smith, 1974, p. 7).

More generally, the above findings led Inkeles (1983) to the conclusion that the combination of cognitive styles, values, attitudes, and behaviors, which he and his associates had labeled "individual modernity," was indicative of the "psychic unity of mankind" (pp. 102–103). Hence, individual modernity, the psychological hallmark of the advanced industrialized societies of the West, pointed the way to the shape of things to come as people in all societies, regardless of their local traditions, are exposed to modernizing experiences such as urbanism, formal schooling, factory work, and the mass media. The enlightenment vision of human progress was not only being realized inexorably by "men everywhere" in the achievement of structural and psychological modernity, but now the social sciences had finally devised a single yardstick for measuring the extent of this achievement by individuals and groups in widely different cultural settings. This all-purpose tool—the Overall Modernity scale—Inkeles claimed (1983), was not merely "a test of what is usually learned in school, such as geography or arithmetic, but is rather a test of attitudes and values touching on basic aspects of a man's orientation to nature, to time, to fate, to politics, to women, and to God" (p. 103).

THE RESILIENCE OF TRADITION

While the term "modern" evokes an idealized image of the contemporary Western, industrialized, and liberal-democratic society, its opposite, "traditional," has been defined in mostly residual or negative terms, using charactertistics that could not be counted to be modern or attributes that are the presumed opposite of modern traits. The belief that traditional institutions, customs, and modes of thought were giving way to, and would be eventually supplanted by, their modern counterparts turned tradition into an esoteric subject, one of interest to the antiquarian or the ethnographer. For those interested in the dynamics of social and political change, it was not tradition, but modernity, that, as heir to the idea of progress, held genuine intellectual appeal. At the psychological level, too, traditional orientations were described in stereotypic and, for the most part, negative terms as irrational, dependent, mentally rigid, and authoritarian—qualities that were expected to impede a person's effective functioning in a modern society. Moreover, whereas considerable empirical attention was focused on the delineation of the various dimensions and correlates of psychological modernity, traditionalism would rarely be subjected to any systematic empirical investigation in its own right. The following description (or caricature) of the "traditional man" by Inkeles and Smith (1974), two investigators who worked so painstakingly to develop an empirically based portrait of his modern counterpart, is an example of this tendency:

> Passive acceptance of fate and general lack of efficacy; fear of innovation and distrust of the new; isolation from the outside world and lack of interest in what goes on in it; dependence on traditional authority and the received wisdom of elders and religious and customary leaders; preoccupation with personal and family affairs to the exclusion of community concerns; exclusive identification with purely local and parochial primary groups, coupled to feelings of isolation from and fear of larger regional and national entities; the shaping and damping of ambition to fit narrow goals, and the cultivation of humble sentiments of gratitude for what little one has; rigid, hierarchical relations with subordinates and others of low social status; and undervaluing of education, learning, research, and other concerns not obviously related to the practical business of earning one's daily bread. (p. 315)

The above reflexive counterposing of tradition and modernity had been criticized severely by several influential authors as creating a misplaced and unnecessary polarity in the late 1960s (e.g., Bendix, 1967; Gusfield, 1967; Huntington, 1971; Kothari, 1968; Tipps, 1973). Others were critical of the highly static and monolithic views of the role of traditional institutions and practices in the course of development (e.g., Rudolph & Rudolph, 1967). In fact by the early 1980s, Edward Shils (1981) could already claim that a "slight turn in moral sentiment and in the intellectual credit of the past is perceptible. There is a little less unease in the presence of the idea of 'tradition,' but its long exile from the substance of intellectual discourse has left its meaning hidden in obscurity" (p. 2). No longer viewed as teetering on the verge of obsolescence, traditional institutions, norms, and symbols were increasingly recognized for their considerable resilience and plasticity, thus capable of providing much more powerful ideological bases for political mobilization, legitimization, and integration than their modern counterparts (Calhoun, 1983).

Today, some three decades after the peak of the tradition-versus-modernity debate, the pendulum seems to have swung even further toward the side of tradition in many Third World countries. The myriad "traditionalist" loyalties and ideologies, expressed in religious, ethnonationalist, or other forms of communal identities, are now the principal challenges to the status quo in most Third World countries (see Juergensmeyer, 1993). And, ironically, even in the successor states to the former Soviet Union and in Eastern and Central Europe, where, for over two generations, the eradication of such loyalties and sentiments was the declared ideology of the state, the same trends are clearly visible. In short, what we are witnessing in many parts of the world, both in the East and the West, is a process of "re-traditionalization," one which involves a self-conscious embrace of indigenous beliefs, values, and symbolic structures as a quest for cultural authenticity and collective identity. And, contrary to the expectations of the theorists of psychological modernity, advocates of these traditionalist ideologies do not seem handicapped by passivity, fatalism, lack of personal efficacy, and a sense of isolation. Indeed, in terms of their personal backgrounds or psychological orientations, they do not seem to be significantly different from the modern, secular activists of a generation ago, with no less enthusiasm for change, although clearly in a different direction.

TOWARD A CRITICAL PSYCHOLOGY OF SOCIAL CHANGE

What, then, are psychology's potential contributions to our understanding of social change in less developed, non-Western societies? And why, compared to other social science disciplines, has psychology been the least engaged with the problem of social change and development in these societies?[6] These are not, of course, new questions. However, given the considerable broadening in recent years of the definition and goals of "national development" to include a wide array of quality of life and human development concerns, and considering the increasing emphasis that is placed on culture and context in contemporary psychological theory, such questions warrant further scrutiny.

One of the first attempts at the international level to examine the potential role of psychology in the study and promotion of social change was a conference at the University of Ibadan (Nigeria) from December 29, 1966, to January 5, 1967. With representatives from twenty-five nations, the conference tried to assess the potential contributions of social psychology to solving the problems of developing countries (see the special issue of *Journal of Social Issues*, edited by DeLamater, Hefner, & Clignet, 1968, for the key paper presented at the conference). While acknowledging social psychology's marginal status, compared to other social science disciplines, in addressing the problems of developing countries, the organizers underscored the field's potentially unique contribution to the analysis of development by virtue of its use of concepts and methods that deal with *both* the social system (groups, institutions, and organizations) and the individual (Hefner & DeLamater, 1968, p. 2). In his agenda-setting statement to the conference, one of the conference's principal organizers, Herbert Kelman (1968), summarized the key issues for a psychology of social change as follows:

> What can be done to meet the challenge posed by this world-wide revolution of human rights—to facilitate social change and to increase the likelihood that it will move in constructive directions? What kinds of institutional arrangements can be fashioned that would improve the conditions of the masses of the population, that would be consistent with their fundamental human needs for security and dignity, and that would bring ever wider segments of the population into full participation in their societies, polities, and economies? What institutions and values might increase, within the population of a developing country, the sense of the legitimacy of its political regime, the feeling of national identity, the readiness for involvement in citizenship responsibilities, in economic enterprises, in population control programs, in other forms of social planning? What technique of change can be developed that would minimize the use of violence, the brutalization of the active and passive participants in change process, and the predisposition to govern by coercion and repression? How can change be introduced without destroying the existing culture patterns and values that provide meaning and stability to a people, while at the same time helping to build the new patterns and values that an urbanizing, industrializing, and ever-changing society requires if it is to remain human? (p. 15)

To deal effectively with such problems, the planners of the Ibadan conference acknowledged, social psychology must develop "new ideas and new data—often, in fact, of entirely new perspectives and ways of thinking" (Kelman, 1968, pp. 15–16)—and ensure the involvement of psychologists from the developing countries as colleagues in all stages of research. However, the conference did not go very far in addressing such fundamental issues as how a discipline whose definition of the "social" rarely went beyond the interpersonal, face-to-face interactions of subjects in contrived laboratory situations could theorize about the social-structural obstacles to social change and societal development. How could psychology, with its narrow emphasis on the individual as the only appropriate unit of analysis, investigate social change phenomena that are, in their very nature, primarily collective and extrapersonal? And, under the highly repressive or exploitative circumstances that prevailed in many Third World countries in the late 1960s (and continue to exist in many parts of the Third World today), was it possible to study and/or facilitate social change without taking sides with those victimized by such conditions?

In the nearly three decades since the Ibadan conference, the above issues have been the subject of much discussion and debate among psychologists at numerous international gatherings, symposia, and special sessions of professional association meetings, as well as in several edited volumes (e.g., Blackler, 1983; Blowers & Turtle, 1987; Paranjpe, Ho, & Rieber, 1988) and special issues of professional journals (e.g., *International Journal of Psychology*, 1984, vol. 19, nos. 1–2; Sloan & Montero, 1990; Wilpert, 1991). A significant forum for the discussion of such issues has been *Psychology and Developing Societies*, a journal based editorially in India and published regularly since 1989.

Several factors may help explain the modest increase in the involvement of psychologists with the problems of non-Western societies in recent years, including: (1) a substantial growth in the number of psychologists in Third World countries with a vital interest in the pressing problems of their own societies; (2) the increasing number of African American, Latino, Asian American, and other "Third World" psychologists in the West itself; (3) increasing international communications through academic/professional media, travel, conferences, and collaborative endeavors; and (4) the establishment of several international professional associations that link psychology to other social sciences with a greater concern with the cultural, social, political, and economic aspects of change in non-Western societies.[7] The outcome has been the development of several relatively distinct psychological approaches to the study and promotion of social change that I shall try to sketch out briefly in the balance of this chapter.

Theoretical, pragmatic, and ideological orientations are the key dimensions that help define and differentiate the emerging psychological approaches to social change in non-Western societies. The first and by far the most common is what may be described as the "psychology-in-the-aid-of-development" approach. Its involves psychologists working in principal or auxiliary roles in the design, implementation, and evaluation of programs in such areas as literacy, health care, population control, community development, and the like (e.g., Bloom, 1992; Pareek, 1990; Zaman & Zaman, 1994; Segall, 1993). The success of such efforts is limited by the rather small number of native or expatriate psychologists who are currently involved with this work, insufficient economic resources at their disposal, and various political and bureaucratic obstacles. Some, in frustration, have argued that, given the fundamentally political and economic nature of the problems faced by the developing countries, there is little that psychology can offer to them (e.g., Mehryar, 1984).

Second, a relatively small group of psychologists have applied principles and techniques of negotiation and conflict resolution in situations of international or subnational conflict (e.g., Kelman & Cohen, 1976; Rouhana, 1995). Given the preponderance of ethnic, religious, and communal conflicts in nearly all parts of the Third World, such unofficial, third-party strategies for conflict management and resolution may well become one of psychology's more significant contributions to reducing the level of international tensions and violence.

Third, concern with the psychological consequences of state-sponsored or intercommunal violence, political repression, and human rights violations (particularly against minorities and indigenous peoples) has been the impetus for the work of yet another group of psychologists. Their efforts have been directed for the most part toward exposing the extent of such violations, developing programs to ameliorate their shattering psychological consequences (particularly for women and children), and, when possible, working with the victimized communities in an attempt to help them cope and to bolster their resistance (Aron, 1992; Becker, Lira, Castillo, Gómez, & Kovalskys, 1990; Lykes, 1994; Melville & Lykes, 1992).

Fourth, there are those who envisage a more radical and transformative role for psychology, one whose chief objectives are community empowerment, liberation, and structural change through close involvement with the struggles of the poor and disenfranchised communities. They view an integration of theory and practice (praxis) as the hallmark of their "liberation psychology" approach (see, e.g., Enriquez, 1992). This approach is best exemplified in the life—and ultimately the tragic death—of the Central American Jesuit psychologist Ignacio Martín-Baró, at the hands of the Salvadoran government's death squads in 1989. Building on Paulo Freire's (1971) concept of the awakening of critical consciousness (*concientización*) and the Latin American tradition of liberation theology, Martín-Baró (1994) defined the goals of a "liberation psychology" in the following terms:

> If we want psychology to make a significant contribution to the history of our peoples—if, as psychologists, we wish to contribute to the social development of the countries of Latin America—we have to redesign our theoretical and practical tools but to redesign them from the standpoint of the lives of our own people; from their sufferings, their aspirations, and their struggles. If I may be permitted to formulate this proposal in Latin American terms, we must affirm that any effort at developing a psychology that will contribute to the liberation of our people has to mean the creation of a liberation psychology; but to create a liberation psychology is not simply a theoretical task; first and fundamentally it is a practical task. (p. 25)

Finally, an increasing number of Third World psychologists, skeptical of imported theories and models from the West, have promoted a strategy of "indigenization" for psychology and its societal applications (see, e. g., Enriquez, 1990; Ho, 1988; Marin, 1983; Moghaddam, 1990; Moghni, 1987; Sinha, 1986, 1989; Turtle, 1989).[8] They maintain that it is only through the development of "indigenous psychologies"—distinctive theories and methods originating from or appropriate to particular cultural contexts—that the discipline can overcome its hitherto tenuous and marginal relationship to the lives of ordinary people and their needs and aspirations. While indigenous psychologies can draw the attention of theorists and researchers to the culturally unique or unusual features of different societies and their alternative constructions of reality, they present a danger of becoming too ethnocentric or even xenophobic. By essentializing cultural traditions, values, and practices, the proponents of this approach at times tend to overstate the extent to which putatively unique cultural characteristics hold across rural-urban, socioeconomic, educational, and gender lines.

The above approaches do not of course offer a coherent social-psychological framework for understanding or effecting social change in non-Western societies. But, collectively, they represent significant strides taken by an increasing number of psychologists to break away from the intellectual isolation and parochialism that has characterized the discipline for so long. Given the enormity of the economic, political, ecological, and demographic problems that the Third World faces today, it is doubtful that any one academic discipline—and certainly a latecomer such as psychology—could

make an appreciable difference. Nonetheless, the potential role of a culturally sensitive psychology within an interdisciplinary approach to problems of
development in the Third World can be quite significant, if not unique. Furthermore, the dialogues and collaborative efforts between Western psychologists and their Third World counterparts in recent years cannot help but
broaden the horizons of both groups. For Western psychologists, the fresh
insights gained in studying the cultures, values, aspirations, sufferings, and
resistances of these distant Others may lead as well to a better understanding of the current cultural tensions in their own increasingly diverse societies.

NOTES

1. For critical reviews of the relevant aspects of the vast literature on Western images of non-Western peoples, see E.H.P. Baudet (1965), Enrique Dussel (1995),
   V.G. Kiernan (1986), Adam Kuper (1988), Ignacy Sachs (1976), Edward W. Said
   (1978), and Marianna Torgovnick (1990).
2. Especially since the collapse of the Soviet Union, the label "Third World" no
   longer refers (if it ever did) to a meaningful grouping of nations on the basis of
   such things as geopolitics, ideological orientation ("nonalignment"), or "manifest destiny." However, until such designations as "South" (versus "North") find
   wider acceptance, "Third World" is still a convenient term in referring to those
   countries in Africa, Asia, and Latin America in which the majority of the population lives and dies under conditions of economic deprivation or abject poverty.
   I shall use the label interchangeably with "developing," "poor," "nonindustrial,"
   etc., in the present chapter. For North-South comparisons in various quality-of-
   life indexes, the persistence of poverty and its human consequences, and the
   widening gap between the rich and the poor nations, see the annual series *Human Development Report* (1990–), published for the United Nations Development Programme by Oxford University Press.
3. See, for example, Lawrence E. Harrison (1985, 1992). After spending many years
   in Central America as an official of the U.S. Agency for International Development, the author concluded that "more than any other of the numerous factors
   that influence the development of countries, it is culture that principally explains,
   in most cases, why some countries develop more rapidly and equitably than others. By 'culture' I mean the values and attitudes a society inculcates in its people
   through various socializing mechanisms, e.g., the home, the school, the church."
   (1985, p. xvi).
4. Ryan himself alluded to this parallelism in his *Blaming the Victim* (1971) as follows: "It would be possible for me to venture into other areas—one finds a perfect example in literature about the underdeveloped countries of the Third
   World, in which the lack of prosperity and technological progress is attributed
   to some aspect of the national character of the people, such as lack of 'achieve-

ment motivation'—but I plan to stay within the confines of my own personal and professional experience, which is, generally, with racial injustice, social welfare, and human services in the city" (p. 6).

5. While Inkeles and Smith felt justified in combining the various subdimensions of modernity into a single global score of Overall Modernity on the basis of this finding, other investigators, using the same or similar scales of modernity, have found the evidence in support of a unidimensional modernity construct to be much less compelling (e.g., Jones, 1977, p. 216).

6. As late as 1990, the co-editor of a special issue of the *Journal of Social Issues* on "Psychology for the Third World" (a theme to which the journal was returning some 22 years after its previous Ibadan Conference issue), portrayed the situation quite accurately as follows: "Pick up any introductory psychology or sociology textbook. Flip through its pages. Where is the Third World, the other half [in fact closer to three-quarters] of the world's population? No sign of it? Perhaps it is just not there explicitly. . . . Perhaps we will find it hiding under such topics as the psychology of poverty, immigration, exile, malnutrition, crowding, unemployment, exploitation? Not a chance. True, you will increasingly find glimpses of Third World life in brief sections on cross-cultural comparisons of psychopathology, perceptual processes, or child-rearing practices—but in these treatments we are often still dealing with Others (the mentally ill, traditional cultures)" (Sloan, 1990, p. 3).

7. These include the Society for Cross-Cultural Research (founded 1971), International Association for Cross-Cultural Psychology (founded 1972), and the International Society of Political Psychology (founded 1978).

8. Although such a stance is now associated with Third World psychologists, a similar position was adopted by a number of prominent European psychologists in the early 1970s in their attempt to fashion a critical "European perspective" on social psychology. The following statement by the French social psychologist, Serge Moscovici (1972), is a cogent example:

> As we read them [American social psychologists] and try to understand and assimilate the principles that guide them we must often conclude that they are strangers to us, that our experience does not tally with theirs, that our views of man, of reality and of history are different. . . .
>
> It must not be forgotten that the real advance made by American social psychology was not so much in its empirical methods or in its theory construction as in the fact that it took for its theme of research and for the contents of its theories the issues of *its own* society. . . . Thus, if all that we do is to assimilate the literature which is transmitted to us—be it only for comparative purposes—we do no more than adopt the preoccupations and traditions of another society; we work in the abstract, to solve the problems of American society. And thus we must resign ourselves to be a small part of a science which is made elsewhere and to be isolated in a society—our own—in which we have shown no interest. We can achieve in this way scientific recognition as methodologists or experimenters—but never as social psychologists. (pp. 18–19, emphasis in the original)

REFERENCES

Allport, G. W. (1968). The historical background of modern social psychology. In G. Lindzey & E. Aronson (Eds.), *The handbook of social psychology* (2nd ed., vol. 1, pp. 1–80.) Reading, MA: Addison-Wesley.

Aron, A. (1992). Testimonio: A bridge between psychotherapy and sociotherapy. In E. Cole, O. Espín, & E. D. Rothblum (Eds.), *Refugee women and their mental health: Shattered societies, shattered lives* (pp. 173–189). New York: Haworth Press.

Baudet, E. H. P. (1965). *Paradise on earth: Some thoughts on European images of non-European man* (E. Wentholt, Trans.). New Haven: Yale University Press.

Becker, D., Lira, E., Castillo, M. I., Gómez, E., & Kovalskys, J. (1990). Therapy with victims of political repression in Chile: The challenge of social reparation. *Journal of Social Issues, 46,* 133–149.

Bendix, R. (1967). Tradition and modernity reconsidered. *Comparative Studies in Society and History, 9,* 292–346.

Blackler, F. (Ed.). (1983). *Social psychology and developing countries.* Chichester, England: John Wiley.

Bloom, L. (1992). Toward a relevant psychology. In R. E. Gali (Ed.), *Rethinking the Third World development: Contributions toward a new conceptualization* (pp. 153–188). New York: Crane Russak.

Blowers, G. H., & Turtle, A. M. (Eds.). (1987). *Psychology moving East: The status of Western psychology in Asia and Oceania.* Boulder, CO: Westview Press.

Bock, P. K. (1988). *Rethinking psychological anthropology.* New York: W. H. Freeman.

Calhoun, C. J. (1983). The radicalism of tradition: Community strength or venerable disguise and borrowed language? *American Journal of Sociology, 88,* 886–914.

Dawson, J. L. M. (1967). Traditional versus Western attitudes in West Africa: The construction, validation, and application of a measuring device. *British Journal of Social and Clinical Psychology, 6,* 81–96.

DeLamater, J., Hefner, R., & Clignet, R. (Eds.). (1968). Social psychological research in developing countries [Special issue] *Journal of Social Issues, 24*(2).

Doob, L. W. (1960). *Becoming more civilized: A psychological exploration.* New Haven: Yale University Press.

Dussel, E. (1995). *The invention of the Americas: Eclipse of "the other" and the myth of modernity.* New York: Continuum.

Enriquez, V. G. (Ed.). (1990). *Indigenous psychologies: A book of readings.* Quezon City, Philippines: New Horizons Press.

Enriquez, V. G. (1992). *From colonial to liberation psychology: The Philippine experience.* Quezon City: University of the Philippines Press.

Freire, P. (1970). *Pedagogy of the oppressed.* Translated by M. Bergman Ramos. New York: Herder & Herder.

Freire, P. (1978). *Education for a critical consciousness.* New York: Seabury Press.

Gendzier, I. L. (1985). *Managing political change: Social scientists and the Third World.* Boulder, CO: Westview Press.

Gordon, D. C. (1989). *Images of the West: Third World perspectives*. Totowa, NJ: Rowman & Littlefield.

Gusfield, J. R. (1967). Tradition and modernity: Misplaced polarities in the study of social change. *American Journal of Sociology, 72*, 351–362.

Hagen, E. E. (1962). *On the theory of social change: How economic growth begins*. Homewood, IL: Dorsey Press.

Hagen, E. E. (1963). How economic growth begins: A theory of social change. *Journal of Social Issues, 19*, 20–34.

Harrison, L. E. (1985). *Underdevelopment is a state of mind: The Latin American case*. Lanham, MD: University Press of America.

Harrison, L. E. (1992). *Who prospers? How cultural values shape economic and political success*. New York: Basic Books.

Ho, D. Y. F. (1988). Asian psychology: A dialogue on indigenization and beyond. In A. C. Paranjpe, D. Y. F. Ho, & R.W. Rieber (Eds.). *Asian contributions to psychology* (pp. 53–77). New York: Praeger.

Huntington, S. P. (1971). The change to change: Modernization, development, and politics. *Comparative Politics, 3*, 283–322.

Inkeles, A. (1983). *Exploring individual modernity*. New York: Columbia University Press.

Inkeles, A., & Smith, D. H. (1974). *Becoming modern: Individual change in six developing countries*. Cambridge, MA: Harvard University Press.

Jones, P. A. (1977). The validity of traditional-modern attitude measures. *Journal of Cross-Cultural Psychology, 8*, 207–239.

Juergensmeyer, M. (1993). *The new cold war? religious nationalism confronts the secular state*. Berkeley: University of California Press.

Kahl, J. A. (1968). *The measurement of modernism: A study of values in Brazil and Mexico*. Austin: University of Texas Press.

Kardiner, A. (1945). *The psychological frontiers of society*. New York: Columbia University Press.

Kardiner, A., & Linton, R. (1949). *The individual and his society*. New York: Columbia University Press.

Kelman, H. C. (1968). Social psychology and national development: Background to the Ibadan conference. *Journal of Social Issues, 24*, 9–20.

Kelman, H. C., & Cohen, S. P. (1976). The problem-solving workshop: A social-psychological contribution to the resolution of international conflicts. *Journal of Peace Research, 13*, 79–90.

Kiernan, V. G. (1986). *The lords of human kind: Black man, yellow man, and white man in an age of empire*. New York: Columbia University Press.

Kothari, R. (1968). Tradition and modernity reconsidered. *Government and Opposition, 3*, 273–293.

Kuper, A. (1988). *The invention of primitive society*. London: Routlege.

Lerner, D. (1964). *The passing of traditional society: Modernizing the Middle East*. New York: Free Press. (Originally published in 1958).

LeVine, R. A. (1982). *Culture, behavior, and personality* (2nd ed.). Hawthorne, NY: Aldine.

Lykes, M. B. (1994). Terror, silencing, and children: International multidisciplinary collaboration with Guatemalan Maya communities. *Social Science and Medicine, 38,* 543–552.

Manson, W. C. (1988). *The psychodynamics of culture: Abram Kardiner and Neo-Freudian anthropology.* New York: Greenwood Press.

Marin, G. (1983). The Latin American experience in applying social psychology to community change. In F. Blackler (Ed.), *Social psychology and developing countries* (pp. 229–243). Chichester, England: John Wiley.

Martín-Baró, I. (1994). *Writings for a liberation psychology* (A. Aron & S. Corne, Trans.). Cambridge, MA: Harvard University Press.

McClelland, D. C. (1961). *The achieving society.* Princeton: Van Nostrand.

McClelland, D. C., & Winter, D. G. (1969). *Motivating economic development.* New York: Free Press.

Mehryar, A. H. (1984). The role of psychology in national development: Wishful thinking and reality. *International Journal of Psychology, 19,* 159–167.

Melville, M. B., & Lykes, M. B. (1992). Guatemalan Indian children and the sociocultural effects of government-sponsored terrorism. *Social Science and Medicine, 34,* 533–548.

Moghaddam, F. M. (1990). Modulative and generative orientations in psychology: Implications for psychology in three worlds. *Journal of Social Issues, 46,* 21–41.

Moghni, S. M. (1987). Development of modern psychology in Pakistan. In G. H. Blowers & A. M. Turtle (Eds.), *Psychology moving East: The status of Western psychology in Asia and Oceania* (pp. 23–38). Boulder, CO: Westview Press.

Moscovici, S. (1972). Society and history in social psychology. In J. Israel & H. Tajfel (Eds.), *The context of social psychology: A critical assessment* (pp. 17–68). London & New York: Academic Press.

Nash, M. (1984). *Unfinished agenda: The dynamics of modernization in developing nations.* Boulder, CO: Westview Press.

Paranjpe, A. C., Ho, D. Y. F., & Rieber, R. W. (Eds.) (1988). *Asian contributions to psychology.* New York: Praeger.

Pareek, U. (1990). Culture-relevant and culture-modifying action research for development. *Journal of Social Issues, 46,* 119–131.

Pepitone, A. (1989). Toward a cultural social psychology. *Psychology and Developing Societies, 1,* 5–20.

Pye, L. W. (1962). *Politics, personality, and nation-building: Burma's search for identity.* New Haven: Yale University Press.

Rouhana, N. N. (1995). The dynamics of joint thinking between adversaries in international conflict: Phases of the continuing problem-solving workshop. *Political Psychology, 16,* 321–345.

Rudolph, L. I., & Rudoph, S. H. (1967). *The modernity of tradition: Political development in India.* Chicago: University of Chicago Press.

Ryan, W. (1971). *Blaming the victim.* New York: Pantheon Books.

Sachs, I. (1976). *The discovery of the Third World.* Cambridge, MA: MIT Press.

Said, E. W. (1978). *Orientalism.* New York: Pantheon Books.

Sampson, E. E. (1993). *Celebrating the other: A dialogic account of human nature.* Boulder, CO: Westview Press.

Segall, M. H. (1983). Social-psychological research pointing towards localized development projects. In F. Blackler (Ed.), *Social psychology and developing countries* (pp. 105–129). Chichester, England: John Wiley.

Shayegan, D. (1992). *Cultural schizophrenia: Islamic societies confront the West* (J. Howe, Trans.). London: Saqi Books.

Shils, E. (1981). *Tradition.* Chicago: University of Chicago Press.

Shweder, R. A. (1991). Rethinking culture and personality theory. In *Thinking through cultures: Expeditions in cultural psychology* (pp. 269–312). Cambridge, MA: Harvard University Press.

Sinha, D. (1986). *Psychology in a Third World country: The Indian experience.* New Delhi: Sage.

Sinha, D. (1989). Research in psychology in the developing world. *Psychology and Developing Societies, 1,* 105–126.

Sloan, T. S. (1990). Psychology for the Third World? *Journal of Social Issues, 46,* 1–20.

Sloan, T. S., & Montero, M. (Eds.). (1990). Psychology for the Third World [Special issue]. *Journal of Social Issues, 46*(3).

So, A. Y. (1990). *Social change and development: Modernization, dependency, and world-system theories.* Newbury Park, CA: Sage.

Tajfel, H. (1972). Experiments in a vacuum. In J. Israel & H. Tajfel (Eds.), *The context of social psychology: A critical assessment* (pp. 69–122). New York: Academic Press.

Tipps, D. C. (1973). Modernization theory and the comparative study of societies: A critical perspective. *Comparative Studies in Society and History, 15,* 199–226.

Torgovnick, M. (1990). *Gone primitive: Savage intellects, modern lives.* Chicago: University of Chicago Press.

Triandis, H. C. (1984). Toward a psychological theory of economic growth. *International Journal of Psychology, 19,* 79–95.

Turtle, A. M. (1989). Psychologising Asia or Asianising psychology: A new prescription for Dr. Watson? *Psychology and Developing Societies, 1,* 65–90.

Wilpert, B. (Ed.). (1991). Latin America [Special issue]. *Applied Psychology: An International Review, 40,* 111–236.

Zaman, A., & Zaman, R. M. (1994). Psychology and development: A conceptual itinerary. *Psychology and Developing Societies, 6,* 1–19.

Part IV

Revisiting the Crisis in Health and Mental Health

Chapter 10

Choices and Chances: How a Profit-Driven Health Care System Discriminates against Middle-Aged Women

•*Paula B. Doress-Worters*

MIDDLE-AGED WOMEN HAVE LIMITED CHOICES ABOUT THEIR MEDICAL CARE. Sex and age discrimination throughout their lives circumscribe their employment options. Too often their chances of obtaining appropriate medical care are shaped by their gender, their age, their reproductive status, and their social and economic status, all of which influence their access to insurance coverage. In their older years, their lack of preventive care when they were young and middle-aged women increases their numbers in long-term care institutions.

The differences in care received by the affluent, insured middle-aged woman compared to the low-income, uninsured middle-aged woman provides a stark illustration of the workings of a profit-driven medical care system.

Health and medical care policies are devised for two distinct groups of women: women of childbearing age and the elderly (usually viewed as gender neutral), while the needs of middle-aged women are overlooked. When middle-aged women are considered at all, they are seen as providers of care rather than as persons who may need care.

WOMEN'S LABOR SUPPORTS THE HEALTH CARE SYSTEM

The medical system depends heavily on women's labor. Women give their unpaid labor as 72 percent of at-home family caregivers (Stone, Cafferata, & Sangl, 1987), and their low-paid labor in health care institutions, where they comprise 75 percent of all medical workers and 85 percent of hospital workers (Boston Women's Health Book Collective, 1992). Women are central to both formal and informal caregiving, yet they are disadvantaged in access to care for themselves (Swenson with editors, 1994) and then blamed for their disadvantage, for which they are stigmatized as "dependent."

This labeling of older women as dependent goes beyond blaming the victim (Ryan, 1976) and turns a social contribution into a liability. Ironically, women become "dependent" because they care for others. As caregivers of vulnerable persons who are marginalized, they acquire the marginal status of those they care for (Miller, 1976).

Women's role in health care is unique. Women contribute substantial amounts of time, energy, and money to the health care needs of others, providing transportation to health care facilities, communication with health care practitioners, and care at home when required. Women advocate for family members and friends, and function as unpaid administrators, arranging for their care, payment for their care, and reimbursement from cumbersome and unresponsive third-party payers (Swenson et al., 1994).

Women have little choice about taking on family caregiving roles. The combination of social and familial expectations and the lack of viable community care alternatives require them to step in and care for family members who are vulnerable and unable to manage without help. Yet the caregiver role has serious effects on women's ability to attain and advance in employment. Many women forgo promotions or new job opportunities in order to maintain employment that is compatible in time and geography with raising children or caring for a family member who is ill, disabled, or a frail elder. This scenario is commonplace because of society's anachronistic assumption that women are the dependents of wage earners. It is especially hard on those women who are single heads of households. For some caregivers, the combined working hours of employment, housekeeping, and elder care amount to the equivalent of three full-time jobs (Gibeau, 1989). About 25 percent of employed caregivers take time off without pay, 23 percent are forced to reduce their working hours, 12 percent are forced to quit their jobs, and another 15 percent choose early retirement because of caregiving demands (Stone et al., 1987). Nationally, the value of time spent providing care to elderly parents has been estimated at $7 billion annually (Spalter-Roth & Hartmann, 1988).

When women care for disabled elders, they diminish their present and future economic security, and face diminished opportunities if they try to return to the work force at more advanced ages. Those who care for disabled young adults face these stresses and more. Caregivers of children with disabilities may be prevented from ever entering the work force. Some find that as they age they are still parenting young adults who are mentally ill, mentally retarded, or for other reasons need care. Disabled children will almost certainly outlive their caregiving parents, who grow old with anxiety about the future of their dependent children after they die.

Thus, women find themselves caught by a system that holds them to a morality of responsiveness and interdependency, rather than to the more general societal norm of exchange or reciprocity (Waithe, 1989). Women are not compensated fairly according to either ethical model: neither the ethic of responsiveness, which would require that women's own care needs must be met, nor the ethic of reciprocity, which would require that women receive some form of compensation for their labor. Theirs is instead an ethic of sacrifice; women are penalized rather than compensated for their time away from the paid labor force, and this penalty extends to their own access to care as well as to employment.

LINKING HEALTH CARE WITH EMPLOYMENT

In the struggle to attain economic self-sufficiency, an important value in American society, women are held back by the expectation that they value caring for others above their own employability. Yet in the United States, access to health and medical care has been linked with employment. This link constitutes a major threat to women's access to health care by restricting their access to benefits and insurance. Women are two-thirds of the contingent work force, which means that they are more likely to work part-time or part of the year, or to work for or operate a small business where they are not covered by benefits (American Association of Retired Persons, 1991).

Middle-aged women are particularly disadvantaged in access to employment. In the United States, the employment rate for women in their fifties is sharply lower than for women in their forties, suggesting that a combination of age discrimination in hiring along with a demand for family caregiving may force some women to retire early, further reducing their Social Security and pension income (Older Women's League, 1991). Women face age discrimination in employment at an earlier age than men do, frequently in their forties, while for men it is rare before age fifty (Rayman, Allshouse, & Allen, 1993).

When medical insurance is linked with employment, women's health and medical choices are reduced along with their employment prospects. The group at greatest risk of lacking coverage is women aged fifty-five to sixty-four (Lamphere-Thorpe & Blendon, 1993). Middle-aged women are more

likely than middle-aged men to face age discrimination at the point of hiring
(Rayman et al., 1993) and to face longer periods of unemployment when laid
off (U.S. Department of Labor, 1992). They often become "discouraged
workers" who give up the job search and are no longer counted among the
unemployed (Doress-Worters & Siegal, 1994). Yet, because they are too
young to be eligible for Medicare, under the present system they may face up
to a decade of uninsured status.

At every attempted return to employment, women face an upward-spi-
raling cycle of age discrimination in hiring. This makes it especially difficult
for those entering or returning to the work force after divorce or widow-
hood. Because older women are also less likely to remarry than are older
men, their access to health insurance through marriage to a wage earner is
also reduced.

Lack of health insurance clearly reduces access to medical care (Lamphere-Thorpe & Blendon, 1993). Uninsured women in the 1980s were
screened significantly less often for four major illnesses, despite the fact that
as low-income women they were at higher risk of these and other illnesses
(Woolhandler & Himmelstein, 1988). A system that limits access to preventive care is practicing short-sighted economy, increasing the need for long-
term care in the future. When low-income people must forgo treatment of
chronic conditions, such as diabetes and hypertension, disabling illnesses
leading to the need for continuing care may result (Lamphere-Thorpe &
Blendon, 1993). Such lack of preventive care may account for the preponderance of women in institutions providing care for chronic conditions.
Women are 75 percent of nursing home residents (Lanspery, 1994).

WHY LOW-INCOME MIDDLE-AGED WOMEN
LACK ACCESS TO MEDICAL CARE

Because medical care has been marketed as a commodity, rather than provided as an entitlement, poor and uninsured women have lacked access to
care and have been undertreated. Many women, especially women of color,
have been poor or without health insurance throughout much of their lives.
Some women at mid-life lose their benefits due to job loss, divorce or wid-
owhood, and then face pervasive sex and age discrimination that limits their
reemployment opportunities. Under these circumstances, federal legislation
now offers the opportunity to maintain coverage through an employer's
group plan for between eighteen months and three years if the woman can
afford to pay for it herself.

For women a lifetime of reduced opportunity and a gender gap in wages results in double discrimination, a compounding of ageism with sexism. The gender gap in wages actually increases by the time women reach middle age. Women earn 80 percent of men's salaries in the young adult years, but only 61 percent in the middle years (U.S. Bureau of the Census, 1991). As a result, women's rates of poverty and of near poverty over the age of sixty-five are twice as high as those of men over sixty-five (Doress-Worters & Siegal, 1994). Women are 58 percent of the aged, but 71 percent of the aged poor. African American women are 5 percent of the elderly, but 16 percent of the elderly poor (Taeuber & Allen, 1993).

The average woman's Social Security check was 76 percent of that of the average man in 1990 (Smith, 1992). Women were more likely to depend on their Social Security check for their entire income; only 22 percent of women over sixty-five receive any income from public or private pensions (Quadagno & Meyer, 1990).

Many women's incomes cluster just above Medicaid eligibility level, leaving them without coverage during the period when their age (55 to 64) is just below Medicare eligibility level (Taeuber & Allen, 1993). While 15.4 percent of older women fell below the poverty line, nearly a third had incomes within 150 percent of poverty level, and fewer than one in twelve had incomes of $25,000 or more (Malveaux, 1993). The majority of African American older women, nearly half of Latina older women, and nearly 30 percent of white older women were near poor (Malveaux, 1993).

Women must manage longer lives and greater risk of chronic diseases and conditions with fewer resources due to their lifelong disadvantages in the labor force and consequent reduced retirement income. In the absence of health insurance coverage, access to medical care may be paid for privately, but many middle-aged women lack the means to do so. Indeed, poverty may be one of the greatest causes of the health problems of older women (Doress-Worters & Siegal, 1994). For example, five-year survival rates for cancer are much higher for women with incomes over $30,000 than for those with incomes of less than $15,000, or 78 percent compared to 63 percent (Hardisty & Leopold, "Cancer and Poverty: Double Jeopardy for Women," pp. 219–236). Low income may increase breast cancer morbidity and mortality in two ways: greater exposure to environmental causes of breast cancer in low-income communities, and reduced access to early detection and treatment. Racial differences in access to health care underscore the effects of income on morbidity and mortality. Overall cancer death rates for black and white women are fairly similar, but this similarity obscures important differences. Black women are more likely to die of breast cancer younger than age sixty-five, while white women's death rates from breast cancer are higher in their sixties, seventies, and eighties (Fahs, 1993). Black women's cancers are more advanced at the time of detection (U.S. Department of Health and Human Services, 1991), in part also reflecting reduced access to medical care services.

Research agendas have been framed without adequate attention to middle-aged and older women's health concerns. Heart disease has been erroneously viewed as a man's disease. In the young adult years, women are less likely to have heart attacks than men of their age group, but by five to ten years after menopause the rates for women and men converge, and for both women and men continue to increase with increasing age. Yet, women and the aged are two groups most often left out of studies of heart disease (Doress-Worters & Siegal, 1994).

Because of the near-exclusive focus on men in heart research, little is known about how heart disease presents in women, and physicians may fail to diagnose women properly. Strategies to prevent heart disease have been tested only on younger men (Fahs, 1993), and may not be effective in treating middle-aged and older women. Consequently, women's heart attack survival rates are lower than men's. The death rate of older black women aged sixty-five to seventy-four from cerebrovascular diseases is twice as high as that of older white women. Yet black women have not been targeted as a high-risk group (Fahs, 1993). No one has investigated the factors that may put middle-aged black women at such increased risk in their young-old years, ages 65 to 74, typically a period of good health. This oversight is typical of the neglect of the medical concerns and needs of women of color at the research and policy level.

THE PROFIT MOTIVE LEADS TO TARGETING WOMEN OF MEANS FOR OVERTREATMENT

While poor and low-income women often lack access to care and cannot get the services they need, women with money or insurance coverage, privately or publicly funded, may be targeted by the medical care system because caring for them is profitable. They constitute a desirable market for services, tests, and drugs.

Women learn very early in life to consult obstetrician-gynecologists (ob-gyns) about normal life events, such as menstruation, sexuality, and reproduction (Boston Women's Health Book Collective, 1992). Under many of the new health care reform proposals, ob-gyns will be designated as primary care providers, even though none of the leading health maintenance organizations consider this acceptable practice, and even though the training of ob-gyns is focused on surgery rather than primary care.

By the time women arrive at the mid-life transition of menopause, it may seem natural to consult the ob-gyn, and to look to medicalized solutions to avoid the changes and minor discomforts of that time of life. Although much research on menopause is based on clinical samples, the majority of women, according to a community study of 2,500 women, manage without medical intervention and regard the cessation of menses with neutrality or relief (Avis & McKinlay, 1991). However, most of the research on menopause is designed to demonstrate the desirability of medicalized interventions. As a result, the marketing of exogenous hormones is relentless.

Hormone therapy has rightly been called a product in search of a market. Although the use of hormones to help women cope with common signs of menopause, such as hot flashes, has been known since 1937, hormone treatment was popularized to a mass market in the 1960s with the publication of books by medical doctors who declared menopause a "deficiency disease" and urged women to be "feminine forever" through the use of estrogen (Bell, 1987).

Too many physicians give out hormones indiscriminately to women at mid-life, instead of carefully evaluating who is likely to benefit and who may not, and despite the fact that the risks and benefits of such treatment are still a matter of controversy. Promoted as a panacea for the "psychological problems" attendant to the change of life, such claims were unproven and promoted a stereotyped view of postmenopausal older women as asexual, neurotic, and unattractive (National Women's Health Network, 1993).

Without adequate testing, exogenous estrogen became one of the five top-selling prescription drugs, until, in the mid-1970s, several studies tied the use of estrogen to an increased rate of uterine cancer, and sales plummeted. To bolster sagging sales figures, drug companies began to promote hormone treatment for preventing "diseases" that are largely normal effects of aging, such as the thinning of bones in older women. The women's health movement is critical of promotions that imply that all women need to be worried about osteoporosis, rather than those who are likely to be at particular risk (Coney, 1994; Doress-Worters & Siegal, 1994; National Women's Health Network, 1993).

Marketing of hormones to prevent heart disease is an even more questionable practice, since women who take hormones are thinner, healthier, and wealthier (Rosenberg, 1993), and would have less heart disease in any case. In addition, the possibility looms that taking hormones increases the risk of breast cancer (Colditz, Egan, & Stampfer, 1993). While medical science knows how to reduce heart disease, and rates of heart disease are falling, no one knows how to prevent or effectively treat breast cancer (Rosenberg, 1993). Almost 80 percent of women who develop breast cancer eventually die from it or with it, a rate that has not changed significantly since the 1930s (Boston Women's Health Book Collective, 1992).

An individual woman who buys into this regimen becomes increasingly dependent on the medical care system. Women who take hormones are subject to increased medical visits and are at increased risk of medical procedures and surgeries (National Women's Health Network, 1993). Medical practitioners, taught that all of a mid-life woman's problems stem from menopause, overtreat what is really a normal life transition while frequently undertreating and misdiagnosing chronic diseases in this same population. This results in a lack of choice for poor and uninsured women, who, because of the expense, are rarely offered hormone treatment even when appropriate, and a bogus choice for women with wealth or coverage, who are encouraged to believe that hormones are the answer to their medical, emotional, and social problems. Instead of having choices, women's care at mid-life is defined by their coverage.

Low-income women are unlikely to be offered expensive hormone treatment, but may be overtreated or inappropriately treated in other ways. Women with publicly subsidized coverage may be at risk of receiving treatments geared to their coverage or lack thereof, rather than what is indicated by their condition. For example, a plan may cover surgery but not a series of office visits or medication. Clinic patients may be targeted for surgical procedures needed for training medical students. African American women at mid-life undergo an exceptionally high rate of hysterectomies; it is not known how many are unnecessary (Miles, 1993). Women of color have not been represented in the large, major National Institutes of Health–funded menopause studies; information about their health and medical needs is seriously limited (Doress-Worters & Siegal, 1994).

Women of means are targeted for elective surgery even when it is not covered by their insurance. Too many doctors are practicing cosmetic surgery because of its profitability, and some with only minimal qualifications. The number of plastic surgeons has nearly quadrupled since 1960, increasing at more than twice the rate of physicians generally. Almost one-third of physicians who practice plastic surgery are board certified in another specialty or are not board certified at all (Roback, Randolph, & Seidman, 1993.) They all need employment and are now free to advertise. The marketing of "cosmetic" surgery as if it were simply a superficial beauty routine rather than a medical treatment entailing risks has become a big business, especially as the baby boomers, the generation that was supposed to be young forever, approaches menopause. The double standard of aging (Sontag, 1979) increases women's susceptibility to such advertising and promotions.

Because medical care in the United States has been more responsive to market forces than to human needs, there are no mechanisms to control which specialties medical school graduates choose to enter. Only 13 percent of physicians are primary care providers. The Clinton administration has expressed an intention to grapple with this problem. In the meantime, we find ourselves with a lack of primary care providers in underserved inner-city and rural areas, and an oversupply of practitioners in lucrative specialties of questionable value such as cosmetic surgery. This shortage of primary care providers will only get worse in the next decade, since half of all primary care providers are close to retirement age.

MANAGING CHRONIC CONDITIONS
OF AGING UNDER MEDICARE

Despite unequal disadvantages and burdens, women live longer than men do. Upon reaching age sixty-five, many women breathe a sigh of relief at becoming eligible for Medicare benefits and escaping the status of the uninsured.

At age sixty-five most women today are energetic and healthy, with a life expectancy of twenty more years. Preventive health care and health promotion in the young-old, years ages 65–74 can forestall many of the problems that occur in the old-old years, ages 75 and older. (Fahs, 1993). Yet Medicare rarely covers preventive care and health promotion that could improve the quality of life in the older years. Physical exercise restores flexibility of joints, strengthens muscles, improves the functioning of the cardiovascular and digestive systems, and enhances alertness and well-being (Doress-Worters & Siegal, 1994). Health promotion can be successful even for the oldest and frailest among the elderly. For example, body-building programs for nursing home residents have been remarkably successful in restoring muscle strength and functioning. It has been most successful with the most debilitated (Doress-Worters & Siegal, 1994). If we had a health care system that took prevention seriously at all ages, elders would not end their lives in long-term care institutions due to conditions that could have been prevented.

Most elders in need of care prefer to remain in their own homes, and current health reform proposals recognize this by promising wider availability of at-home care. Yet, Medicare does not always cover care to help manage chronic conditions, such as home care services. At-home and community care have only been available as part of a patchwork of services that varies from state to state and from community to community. Some coverage of nursing home care has been available under Medicare for a limited time in special circumstances, while long-term care is only available by private payment or by qualifying as indigent under Medicaid, which carries the risk of pauperization for older women who need care for themselves or a spouse. Lack of long-term care coverage, whether at home or in a long-term care facility, severely limits the choices of elders in need of care and of their caregivers.

Concerns about health spending often seem to blame the elderly without taking into account the ways that aging has been medicalized. Treating all the problems of the elderly as medical events is excessively costly. Many of them can be more successfully ameliorated through social rather than medical interventions. Managing the chronic health and medical conditions of an aging population should be viewed in the context of needs for housing, assistive devices, caregiving, and social services. These can help elders live independently despite minor disabilities, and should be covered as a way of improving quality of life while reducing medical costs. Alternatives such as group or congregate elder housing can help older women manage two of the greatest challenges of aging without a partner—inadequate income and isolation (Doress-Worters & Siegal, 1994).

Creative and flexible programs, which are available in a few communities, can help. For example, funding the purchase of a microwave oven for an elderly person no longer able to cook enables her to continue preparing food at home and thus avoids institutionalization. Better use of "assistive technology" can prevent secondary disabilities or the worsening of conditions. For example, air conditioning can prevent respiratory problems from worsening. But typically funding is available for medical care or equipment, not for cooking equipment or air conditioning.

THE RIGHT TO DIE:
CAN IT BE A WOMAN'S CHOICE?

Concern is growing that too great a percentage of Medicare expenditures occur in the final months and years of life (Lamphere-Thorpe & Blendon, 1993.) Advocates for elders argue that the money could be better spent to improve the quality of life in the five or ten years preceding a final hospitalization.

Yet we cannot simplistically assume that all expenses at the end of life are wasteful. The end of life is often when people are sickest. Many of us do not want high-tech interventions to keep us on life supports when no meaningful quality of life remains. But we may require significant and costly nursing care and pain management. The current reimbursement system favors hospitalization and costly, frequently futile interventions, instead of less expensive and more humane hospice care. The latter would be funded under most of the reform proposals.

When decisions are made as to where budgets should be cut, we cannot accept the view that life is less valuable at a later age. People must have choices at any age. We must be aware that the population in the later years is overwhelmingly female, and that cutting care at advanced ages would primarily affect women, who are disadvantaged throughout life in their access to medical care (Lamphere-Thorpe & Blendon, 1993). In a PBS panel discussion following a film on euthanasia, similar concerns were expressed by health advocates for people of color working in poor communities. They asked why the choice to die is the first real choice being offered to people in their communities ("Euthanasia in Holland," 1993). Can older women and other economically disadvantaged groups have true choice about dying and death in a context of unequal access to employment, health care, housing, and social services?

Most elders do not want to be a burden on their families, preferring to live in their own homes and have access to social services as needed. Older women may strongly identify with their caregiver role and feel shamed or devalued by being a receiver of care. They know from personal experience the human costs of caregiving and may not want to make such demands on family members. Older women may lack the power to make such demands. Older men are more likely than older women to insist on being cared for at home. Thus, women may feel more internalized or family pressure to make the choice, if it were available, for euthanasia. It should therefore not surprise us that the overwhelming majority of Dr. Kevorkian's "patients" have been women.

Given that there are such gross inequalities in income, and in access to health and medical care, we must be especially careful that any mechanisms put into place to provide choice in death and dying do so in a context of universally available health and medical care, including long-term care for elders.

Clearly women need more choices throughout their lives, not just at the end. Without adequate health care and social supports for all Americans, the choice of euthanasia can only take older women from the uneven playing fields of their lives to a possibly premature death in an unevenly plotted burial ground.

POLICY IMPLICATIONS

Caregiving Policy

In order to level the playing field for mid-life and older women, significant changes are required in two major policy areas: health care policy and family policy. Mid-life and older women are beginning to organize for recognition of the contribution their unpaid caregiving labor makes to the health care system.

Women's caregiving work should be supported and compensated as the linch-pin of a combined health and caregiving policy that acknowledges the needs and concerns of both the care receiver and the caregiver.

A reasonable family caregiving policy must help caregivers who want to continue providing care and also those who can no longer do so. We need programs that will help women obtain and keep their jobs even while pro-viding care to family members, whether they are young, old, or disabled. At the very least, Social Security credits and other benefits should be provided to caregivers on unpaid leave. At best, caregivers should be compensated for their caregiving work, and given priority for retraining and re-employment if desired. Needs for support services must not play off one age group against the other. All generations are part of our families and our society.

We must support the full continuum of caregiving services to help frail elders and people with disabilities of any age, whether they have family sup-port or not. Services should be provided in a way that acknowledges and re-spects the care family members provide. Long-term care at home, in institu-tions, and in the community must be integrated into the health care system for the young as well as the old. Most health care needs are chronic rather than acute and require care in nonhospital settings (Zola, 1993). The Clin-ton administration's 1994 health care proposal would have strengthened at-home and hospice care but did not fully address the funding of long-term in-stitutional care. Women must have a true choice about providing care, which includes the use of nonfamily options for caregiving.

By signing the federal Family and Medical Leave Act upon taking office, President Clinton made a bold statement in recognition and support of care-givers who want to remain in the workforce. With an unpaid leave and a full range of support services, a caregiver can manage a family member's short-term illness without fear of loss of employment and benefits. Yet, this law provides only partial relief. It leaves out too many caregivers-those who work for companies with fewer than fifty workers, as the majority of women do, and those who cannot afford to take an unpaid leave. We must develop a plan for meeting the nation's health, medical, and caregiving needs, irre-spective of whether sick persons have family members available to care for them, and without impressing women into unpaid and frequently involun-tary labor as caregivers.

Health Care Reform Plans

This chapter has documented the disadvantages faced by midlife and older women under the present health care system. When this chapter was begun, many health care reform proposals were under debate across the nation and in Congress, yet the 1994 Congressional session ended with the defeat of President Clinton's proposal and with reduced momentum toward any more far-reaching proposals. Indeed, the 1995 Congress mainly concerned itself with cutting taxes for the wealthy by attacking entitlements, and reformers were forced to turn their attention to defending Medicare and Medicaid, rather than breaking new ground. As we develop strategies for the congressional session of 1996, it is becoming clear that the 1995 freshman class of "Newt Republicans" has overreached. The polls and media report that the public is increasingly disenchanted with the mean-spiritedness of an approach that is resulting in a massive transfer of resources from the poor and middle class to the wealthy. We may therefore be entering a period of opportunity to resurrect some old reform proposals or bring forth some new ones that would bring greater equality in access to health and medical care. As new and old proposals are put forth in the coming year, how can we evaluate their ability to remedy the disadvantages faced by midlife and older women?

An excellent tool for this analysis is William Ryan's "Fair Shares" theory of equality. Ryan (1981) argues that a crucial difference between Fair Shares, which conserves resources for public use, and Fair Play, which is the popular American conception of equal opportunity, is the question of what should be considered a commodity. "Fair Shares equality means removing from the category of commodities the basic necessities of life as well as significant services such as health care and education. These are to be redefined as resources to be held in common and shared in such a way that everyone has an equal right of access to them" (p. 191).

The Clinton administration's 1994 proposal put forth "universal" health care coverage as a bottom-line objective, yet failed to attain universality even in its stated objectives. A truly universal health care plan must provide equal access to all, irrespective of age, gender, income, or employment, marital, or citizenship status. Yet even as proposed, the Clinton plan had significant gaps, such as care for elders in need of long-term care, undocumented immigrants, and certain Medicaid recipients.

Yet, for mid-life women who are typically "too old" to obtain quality full-time employment with benefits, too young to qualify for Medicare, too poor to pay for insurance coverage, and not poor enough to qualify for means-tested programs such as Medicaid, the Clinton administration's proposed standard benefits package would have provided significantly improved coverage. Indeed, most women would benefit substantially from the central feature of the Clinton plan, universal coverage with a standard benefits package that included essential aspects of women's health care (Norsigian, 1993).

Universality of coverage does not by itself guarantee that the same quantity or quality of health and medical care will be equally available to all. Continuation of a private market in health care plans is a major source of inequality in the Clinton administration's proposal. Those who could afford it would be able to purchase "premier" plans that offer a greater range of choices, thus establishing at the outset multiple-tier plans of health care. Universal coverage is only a first step toward achieving equality in the provision of care. It is a precondition for equality in health care, but will not by itself automatically lead to equality of access to health and medical care.

Another source of inequality in many of the proposed reform plans, compared to single-payer plans, those paid for through tax revenues, is financing through a premium-based system that is inherently regressive. The Massachusetts Women's Health Care Coalition notes that a secretary supporting herself and her two children on a salary of $20,000 would, under the Clinton administration's 1994 proposal, pay the same premium as her boss who earns $80,000. They recommend that just as small businesses are being offered a percent of payroll cap on their contributions to the Health Alliance, low-paid and part-time employed women need such a limit on their contributions (Sherry & Lui, 1994).

The Coalition also warns that requiring co-payments and deductibles limits access for poor and low-income women by discouraging visits for preventive care, thus leading to disabling chronic conditions (Sherry & Lui, 1994). The well-respected Rand study found that co-payments discouraged visits for low-income people, irrespective of how medically necessary the visit was thought to be (Sherry & Lui, 1994). It is a cruel fallacy that requiring co-payments will make poor people "more responsible" about their health care utilization.

Ultimately, plans that rely on multiple funding sources, such as third-party reimbursements, incur enormous administrative costs, money that could be better spent directly on health and medical care. A single-payer plan, such as the American Health Security Act of 1993 (the Wellstone/McDermott/Conyers bill), would be less cumbersome, less expensive, and more likely to provide care in a manner that is truly universal and equitable. An important feature of single-payer plans is that the consumer retains choice over provider and health care facility.

Special interests, such as the insurance industry, lobby for offering "more choice," by which they mean more choice among competing insurance companies and, under many of the congressional plans, the choice to be without any coverage at all. Profit-making companies have ample resources to flood the airwaves with their perspective, thus distorting public debate. Their contributions to political campaigns assure that their views will not be overlooked in Congress.

Regrettably, partisan politics and loyalty to those who finance congressional and presidential campaigns have triumphed over concern for the health of the public. Consequently, the focus on maintaining private enterprise in health care coverage has dominated the discourse even among advocates of universal coverage, while government supported "single-payer" systems were not seriously considered by most of the public, the media, or Congress.

The failure of the Clinton administration's initiative may be substantially due to its inability to convince the public, 85 percent of whom are insured, that their health care coverage would remain the same or improve. Rather than raising substantive issues of concern, such as choice of provider and facility, they focused on devising arcana of cost-cutting approaches and bureaucracies to be interposed between consumers and funders of health care. At this writing, movements to pass single-payer systems at the state level offer the most promise for working toward equal access to health care. If the Congress would remove some of the impediments to action at the state level, the nation may yet have an opportunity to compare outcomes of different states with different systems (White, 1994).

We have discussed at some length the effects on mid-life women of regarding types of medical care as commodities to be marketed for profit. Regrettably, in the 1994 debate health care coverage itself was defined as a commodity to be tailored for different markets with differing abilities to pay. Even if some type of health care reform is passed in the next congressional session, many of the inequities and lack of choice will continue for middle-aged women. Whether or not low-income women gain access to the system through universal coverage, they will continue to have fewer choices at mid-life than wealthier women. The private market in health care will no doubt continue, offering affluent mid-life women opportunities to choose tests and procedures not covered by a standard benefits package, while placing them at continued risk of unnecessary and often hazardous treatments and practices, and continued overdependence on physicians. As the baby boomer generation ages, more technological innovations in health and medical care will be developed and offered to the public. Will they lead to better quality of care? Will they be cost-effective? To control costs in a way that improves rather than threatens quality of care, better technology assessment is needed.

Even if health reform is brought back to the table in Congress, even if something similar to the Clinton administration's proposal is passed in the next Congressional session, and near-universal access achieved, the fight for equality in the provision of quality care will continue to be one of the great challenges of the twenty-first century.

ACKNOWLEDGMENTS

Portions of this essay grew out of conversations with Diana Laskin Siegal, my co-author of *The New Ourselves, Growing Older* (1994), and Norma Meras Swenson of the Boston Women's Health Book Collective in preparation for revising our chapter on women's health and reform of the medical system. I am grateful to Norma for reading and commenting on an early draft of this essay, and to Diana, Ramsay Liem, Michael Morris, Judy Norsigian, and Irving Kenneth Zola for thoughtful comments and helpful suggestions on later drafts.

REFERENCES

American Association of Retired Persons. (1991). *The contingent workforce: Implications for mid-life and older women.* Washington, DC: AARP Women's Initiative.

Avis, N. E., & McKinlay, S. M. (1991). A longitudinal analysis of women's attitudes toward the menopause: Results from the Massachusetts Women's Health Study. *Maturitas, 13,* 65–79.

Bell, S. E. (1987). Changing ideas: The medicalization of menopause. *Social Science and Medicine. 24*(6), 535–542.

Boston Women's Health Book Collective. (1992). *The new our bodies, ourselves.* New York: Simon & Schuster.

Colditz, G. A., Egan, K. M., & Stampfer, M. J. (1993). Hormone replacement therapy and risk of breast cancer: Results from epidemiological studies. *American Journal of Obstetrics and Gynecology, 168,* 1473–1480.

Coney, S. (1994). *The menopause industry: How the medical establishment exploits women.* Alemeda, CA: Hunter House.

Doress-Worters, P. B., & Siegal, D. L. (1994). *The new ourselves, growing older.* New York: Simon & Schuster.

Euthanasia in Holland [PBS special]. (1993, March 13). *Frontline.*

Fahs, M. C. (1993). Preventive medical care: Targeting elderly women in an aging society. In J. Allen & A. Pifer (Eds.), *Women on the front lines: Meeting the challenge of an aging America.* (pp. 105–132). Washington, DC: Urban Institute Press.

Gibeau, J. L. (1989). *Adult day health services as an employee benefit.* Washington, DC: National Association of Area Agencies on Aging.

Lamphere-Thorpe, J., & Blendon, R. J. (1993). Years gained and opportunities lost: Women and health care in an aging America. In J. Allen & A. Pifer (Eds.), *Women on the front lines: Meeting the challenge of an aging America.* (pp. 75–104). Washington, DC: Urban Institute Press.

Lanspery, S. (1994). Nursing homes. In P. B. Doress-Worters & D. L. Siegal (Eds.), *The new ourselves, growing older.* (pp. 249–261). New York: Simon & Schuster.

Malveaux, J. (1993). Race, poverty, and women's aging. In J. Allen & A. Pifer (Eds.),

Women on the front lines: Meeting the challenge of an aging America. (pp. 167–190). Washington, DC: Urban Institute Press.

Miles, T. P. (1993, March 22–24). *Menopause and African-American women: Clinical and research issues.* Paper presented at a National Institutes of Health Workshop on Menopause, Current Knowledge and Recommendations for Research, Bethesda, MD.

Miller, J. B. (1976). *Toward a new psychology of women.* Boston: Beacon Press.

National Women's Health Network. (1993). *Taking hormones and women's health.* Washington, DC: Author.

Norsigian, J. (1993). Women and national health care reform: A progressive feminist agenda. *Journal of Women's Health, 2*(1), 91–94.

Older Women's League. (1991). *Paying for prejudice: A report on mid-life and older women in America's labor force* [1991 Mother's Day Report]. Washington, DC: Author.

Quadagno, J., & Meyer, M. H. (1990, Summer). Gender and public policy. *Generations.*

Rayman, P., Allshouse, K., & Allen, J. (1993) Resiliency amid inequity: Older women workers in an aging United States. In J. Allen & A. Pifer (Eds.), *Women on the front lines: Meeting the challenge of an aging America.* (pp. 133–166). Washington, DC: Urban Institute Press.

Roback, G., Randolph, G., & Seidman, B.(1993). *Physician Characteristics and Distribution in the U.S.* Chicago: American Medical Association, Physician Data Services, Division of Survey and Data Resources.

Rosenberg, L. (1993, December). Hormone replacement therapy: The need for reconsideration. *American Journal of Public Health, 83*(12), 1670–1673.

Ryan, W. (1976). *Blaming the victim.* New York: Vintage.

Ryan, W. (1981). *Equality.* New York: Pantheon.

Sherry, S., & Lui, M. (1994, March). National health care: A feminist primer. *Sojourner, 19*(7), Health Supplement, p. 6H.

Smith, M. (1992). *Statement of the American Association of Retired Persons on Women and Social Security before the Subcommittee on Social Security, Committee on Ways and Means, U.S. House of Representatives, Apr. 8.* Washington, DC: American Association of Retired Persons.

Sontag, S. (1979). The double standard of aging. In J. Williams (Ed.), *Psychology of women* (pp. 462–478). San Diego: Academic Press.

Spalter-Roth, R. M., & Hartmann, H. M. (1988). *Unnecessary losses: Costs to Americans of the lack of family and medical leave, executive summary.* Washington, DC: Institute for Women's Policy Research.

Stone, R., Cafferata, G., & Sangl, J. (1987). Caregivers of the frail elderly: A national profile. *Gerontologist, 27*(5), 616.

Swenson, N. M. with editors. (1994). Women's health and reforming the medical-care system. In P. B. Doress-Worters & D. L. Siegal (Eds.), *The new ourselves, growing older.* (pp. 221–248). New York: Simon & Schuster.

Taeuber, C. M., & Allen, J. (1993). Women in our aging society: The demographic outlook. In J. Allen & A. Pifer, (Eds.), *Women on the front lines: Meeting the challenge of an aging America.* (pp. 11–46). Washington, DC: Urban Institute Press.

U.S. Bureau of the Census. (1991). *Money income of households.*

U.S. Department of Health and Human Services. National Institutes of Health, National Cancer Institute, (1991) *SEER [Surveillance Epidemiology and End Results].* Washington, DC: U.S. Government Printing Office.

U.S. Department of Labor, Bureau of Labor Statistics. (1992). *Employment in perspective: Women in the labor force* (Second Quarter Rep. No. 831). Washington, DC: U.S. Government Printing Office.

Waithe, M. E. (1989). Toward a gender undifferentiated moral theory. In M. M. Brabeck (Ed.), *Who cares? Theory, research, and educational implication of the ethic of care.* (pp. 3–18). New York: Praeger.

White, J. (1994, September 28). Let 50 flowers bloom. *The New York Times.* p. A21.

Woolhandler, S., & Himmelstein, D. U. (1988). Reverse targeting of preventive care due to lack of health insurance. *Journal of the American Medical Association, 259*(19), 2872–2874.

Zola, I. K. (1993) Disability statistics: What we count and what it tells us. *Journal of Disability Policy Studies, 4*(2), 9–39.

Chapter 11

Cancer and Poverty: Double Jeopardy for Women

•*Jean V. Hardisty and Ellen Leopold*

IT WOULD BE UNUSUAL TO MEET A WOMAN OVER THIRTY WHO HAS NOT BEEN touched either directly or indirectly by an episode of cancer or a cancer scare that has been mishandled in some way by the medical profession. Tales are legion of misdiagnosis, misinformation, and carelessness that, at best, have inflicted unnecessary additional suffering and, at worst, have cost women their lives. Even women with comprehensive insurance coverage who are well informed and assertive have often fared poorly in the hands of the cancer establishment. Their mistreatment, coupled with the relatively higher incidence of breast cancer among educated white women, has tended to reinforce our image of cancer as the great leveler. But while it is true that socioeconomic status may not necessarily determine how well a woman faces her cancer, how well she survives it, or how well she understands it, poverty is a powerful predictor of late diagnosis, poor treatment, and high mortality.

Women in the United States are disproportionately poor; women of color are the most disproportionately poor. The recent mobilization of women against decades of silence and indifference to women's cancers must, therefore, actively incorporate poverty and its interaction with racism and sexism as a primary focus, since poverty so clearly influences women's experience of disease and their expectations of survival.

POVERTY

It is widely acknowledged that health care in the United States is unevenly delivered and inadequate by the standards set by other industrialized countries. Great Britain, Canada, and Australia all have national health insur-

219

ance; in contrast, the United States has 36 million uninsured persons (without private insurance, Medicare, or Medicaid coverage) and another 50 million underinsured. The uninsured in the United States include 13 percent of the white population, 30 percent of African Americans, and a combined statistic for Asian Americans and Native Americans of 20 percent. Of all Hispanics, 35 percent are uninsured: one-third of Mexican Americans, one-fourth of Cuban Americans, and one-fifth of the Puerto Rican community (Trevino, Moyer, Valdez, & Stroup-Benham, 1991).

A disproportionate number of the uninsured are women, and many of these women are single heads of households. According to the 1990 Census, almost three of every five female-headed households live below the poverty line. Of course, poverty is associated with lack of health insurance, but even employed women are more likely than men to hold low-income jobs that provide no health insurance. In 1990, 85 percent of the uninsured lived in families headed by employed workers; nearly 50 percent of all uninsured workers were either self-employed or working in firms with fewer than twenty-five employees (Doress-Worters, "Choices and Chances," pp. 201–218; Employee Benefit Research Institute, 1992).

Lack of insurance becomes a health threat in itself when a woman receives a diagnosis of cancer. Uninsured women are more likely to die of breast cancer and less likely to receive appropriate care at the appropriate time, making lack of insurance an important risk factor. A study carried out at the Harvard Medical School and the Brigham and Women's Hospital (Ayanian, Kohler, Abe, & Epstein, 1993) demonstrates a clear link between insurance coverage and health outcomes. Using data from the New Jersey State Cancer Registry on women diagnosed with breast cancer between 1985 and 1987, the study brought to light a sharp contrast in patterns of breast cancer between women who were privately insured and those who were either uninsured or covered by Medicaid. The latter group had breast cancers that were significantly more advanced at the time of diagnosis than were those of the group of privately insured women. Women covered by Medicaid were more than twice as likely as privately insured women to be diagnosed with late-stage disease. Equally, survival rates among those lacking private health insurance were much lower than for those who did have private coverage.[1]

Significantly, the contrasts that emerged from this study—between those *with* some form of private health insurance and those *without*—lumped together women covered by Medicaid with women lacking any form of coverage, public or private. In fact, there was no appreciable difference in the rates of survival between these two groups of women, for any stage of the disease. In other words, the provision of a safety net in the form of guaranteed payment could not, on its own, overcome the more pervasive and persistent consequences of economic disadvantage on the course of the disease.

Of these disadvantages, limited education is certainly one of the most significant. It tends to restrict access to information about cancer prevention and warning signs, and it often makes interpretation of that information more difficult. These drawbacks often reinforce each other and contribute to delays in diagnosis that, in turn, are directly linked to higher cancer mortality rates (Baquet & Ringen, 1986). There is considerable evidence from research into other diseases (Winkleby, Jatulis, Frank, & Fortmann, 1992) to support this correlation.[2] Educational attainment is, in fact, often used as a surrogate for socioeconomic status in epidemiologic studies of health outcomes.[3]

One attempt to estimate preventable breast cancer death rates (Farley & Flannery, 1989) concludes that the rate for women with lowest educational attainment is 2.5 times higher than the comparable rate for women with the highest. Another estimates the five-year survival rate among white women who did not finish high school as 64 percent, compared with 81 percent among those who graduated from college (Gaiter, 1991).

The difficulties presented by inadequate education are, of course, compounded by an increase in the use of written patient education materials, such as brochures and handouts. B.D. Weiss, G. Hart, and R. Pust (1991) review a number of studies that conclude that these materials, including consent forms, are written at a reading difficulty level too high for the average American. This problem is compounded for those women who do not speak English as a first language. For poor immigrant women, language barriers that inhibit access to medical care are aggravated by cultural barriers that may subject women with admitted breast cancer to shame or loss of status, by fatalism based on past experiences, by the threat of deportation that may arise during any contact with service providers, by the lack of doctors willing to practice in the inner-city areas where many poor immigrant women live, and by the women's inexperience in negotiating their way through the complex tangle of public health services. Further, nearly all women living in poverty are increasingly forced to rely on emergency rooms, overtaxed clinics, and underfunded and inadequately equipped public hospitals. This is one result of the withdrawal of federal funds from urban clinics, which once provided the basic health care that more affluent people get from their family doctors ("City Plans," 1992; "Escape," 1992).

In New York City, for instance, a 1990 report released by Elizabeth Holtzman, then New York City Comptroller, revealed that eight of the eleven municipal hospitals offered no programs for the detection of breast cancer, and that 65 percent of breast cancers diagnosed in city hospitals were not picked up until the cancers had reached an advanced stage. This contrasts with a national figure of advanced stage diagnosis of 20 percent to 25 percent. Further, of those who were diagnosed with possible breast cancer, 30 percent were "lost to follow-up." As Elizabeth Holtzman put it, this "means that thousands of poor women will suffer and die from a very treatable disease" (quoted in Lee, 1990). And they do. According to the National Cancer Institute, the five-year breast cancer survival rate for women earning less than $15,000 is 63 percent for white women and 64 percent for African-American women, compared with 78 percent for white women earning more than $30,000 (Gaiter, 1991).

A review of the research on women, socioeconomic status, and cancer confirms our worst suspicions about a health care system in which the social "safety net" has been decimated: low income correlates with late diagnosis and a higher rate of death from cancer. The risk posed by poverty may be even greater for rural poor women, who suffer from the same severe cutbacks in federal funding of health care services as those in urban areas. The great distances to be traveled to obtain health care in rural areas, the inability of rural hospitals to reap the economies of scale that would allow them to maintain an infrastructure of expensive advanced equipment, and the drastic shortage of either specialists or general practitioners outside urban areas, all make the health care situation of low-income rural women even more precarious than that of poor urban women ("Rural New Englanders," 1992).

RACISM

Although the links between poverty and illness are well established, most of the historical and current studies of these links do not include specific reference to cancers, concentrating instead on conditions such as infant mortality, tuberculosis, and heart disease. The disturbing contrast between death rates for rich and poor in these areas are regularly highlighted in the media. Cancer statistics, on the other hand, have traditionally been handled differently. Here, the attempts to break down the global figures have commonly been based more on *race* than on income, and in particular, on the markedly higher rates of cancer among blacks when compared with whites. Linde Clayton and Michael Byrd (1993), analyzing this comparison, have called the incidence of cancer among blacks a "contemporary African American cancer crisis" (p. 84), noting that this higher rate among blacks was documented during the 1970s by medical researchers at Howard University and is even more severe today. The practice of comparing cancer rates by race rather than by socioeconomic status has often produced the impression that African Americans are genetically predisposed to cancer.

According to Dr. Harold Freeman (1989), a past president of the American Cancer Society, this view is untenable; There is "no known genetic basis to explain the major racial differences in cancer incidence and outcome. . . . Within one race, economic status is the major determinant of cancer outcome. Therefore the target for correction is poverty, regardless of race." (pp. 329, 332).[4] In fact, cancer statistics for middle-class blacks show a pattern similar to those for middle-class whites. And once the raw statistics are adjusted for age and income differences between the two populations, whites show higher incidence rates for some cancers, particularly lung cancer (Baquet, Horm, Gibbs, & Greenwald, 1991).

Because blacks are disproportionately poor, and suffer from housing discrimination, job and wage discrimination, and other effects of racism, black culture is often used as a proxy for poverty. All those aspects of life that contribute to reduced survival—such as lack of education, lack of access to health care, unemployment, substandard living conditions, poor nutrition, and an inadequate social support network—are most accurately described as symptoms of poverty rather than as characteristics of black culture. To confound poverty with black culture encourages the public to lose sight of the role of racism in creating poverty. With a few exceptions, race itself is not a known cause of cancer.

The exclusive comparison of rates of cancer between blacks and whites can obscure the threat that cancer poses to other minorities who are also disproportionately poor. Native American women, for example, have a higher rate of cervical cancer and a lower survival rate from breast cancer than African Americans or white Americans. Hawaiian and Japanese Americans both have higher rates of stomach cancer than whites or African Americans (Freeman, 1989). Hispanic women have higher than average rates of stomach and gall bladder cancer, and twice the rate of cancer of the cervix as white, non-Hispanic women (National Cancer Institute, 1988).

Most statistics presented to the general public fail to make any adjustments to accommodate demographic or socioeconomic differences. The results—which show blacks and other people of color dying more often of all cancers—inevitably carry with them an unstated but nonetheless powerful imputation of blame. This could create the impression that people of color are genetically or behaviorally more prone to cancer. Patterns of behavior that are known to be harmful—such as smoking, diet, and occupational exposure to toxins—are identified as the cause of higher rates of cancer. These practices are viewed as forms of willful self-destruction that characterize the life styles of low income people, instead of being viewed as a response to lack of employment options, stress, chronic economic recession, or, in the case of smoking, the relentless campaigns by tobacco advertisers targeting poor communities. Explanations for the restricted educational and job opportunities that are both cause and effect of poverty are rarely sought. Instead, the focus is placed on the individual.

The idea of individual responsibility for health through the pursuit of a healthful life style and lowered stress is without doubt a boon to the health of the nation as a whole. However, the positive effects of changes in individual behavior on overall health and longevity are often overstated (with the exception of cigarette smoking), and the ability to comply with current wisdom on a healthy life style depends on a wide range of external factors, both environmental and social. Responsibility for health can tend, if we are not careful, to be privatized without regard for the unequal ability of people to "follow the rules." Living near toxic dumps, working in chemical plants, and coping with job insecurity, low income, poor diet, and inadequate medical insurance are all factors that can easily overwhelm the most valiant efforts of the individual to take charge of her health.

It has been known for some time that toxic waste, radioactive materials, and pollutants are related to cancer. Since the 1970s, people of color have become more politically aware that their communities are disproportionately the targets of toxic dumping and the location of the most hazardous industrial operations. Both are harmful to their health, and both are indirectly attributable to the consequences of poverty and racism—low political visibility, lack of clout with environmental organizations, and low property values.

As early as 1979, studies linking environmental hazards to the race of those exposed to them revealed that all the city-owned landfills built in Houston since the 1920s were located in black neighborhoods, even though Houston was once an overwhelmingly white city ("Pollution-weary Minorities," 1993). A 1987 study found that this pattern is a national one; three out of the five largest commercial hazardous waste landfills in the United States are located in mostly black or Hispanic communities, accounting for 40 percent of the nation's estimated commercial landfills (Alston, 1990, p. 9; Lee, 1987).

This sort of injustice has inspired grassroots organizing within communities of color, notably a national conference in October 1991, the First National People of Color Environmental Leadership Summit. The raised awareness of environmental racism has also led to a dramatic increase in the number of lawsuits and protests against local, state, and federal agencies, often arguing that blacks and Hispanics are more likely to be found in areas with high concentrations of cancer (cancer clusters) caused by toxic pollutants.

The crucial contribution of this new movement is that it integrates an analysis of environmental racism with broader issues of social and racial justice. Thus, environmental degradation is not seen as one "issue area," but is redefined as part of the larger pattern of exploitation and victimization of poor urban and rural communities, especially communities of color and indigenous communities.

The concerns of the environmental racism movement overlap with those of the burgeoning women's cancer movement. Within the women's cancer movement, it is the grassroots groups that are most interested in forging a link with similar grassroots groups in communities fighting environmental pollution. Similarly, among the "Big 10" groups within the environmental movement, only Greenpeace has reached out to grassroots groups working on pollution in their communities and work sites. In fact, Greenpeace has played a crucial role in building bridges between the two grassroots movements by co-sponsoring, with the Women's Environmental Development Organization (WEDO), a meeting in Austin, Texas, early in 1994. The meeting brought together environmental groups, environmental justice groups, women's groups, and women's cancer groups to launch a campaign called Women, Cancer, and the Environment: Action for Prevention. Greenpeace has also published a report (Thornton, 1993) that marshals evidence that organochlorines—chlorine-based synthetic chemicals that are accumulating in the air, water, and food chain—may be an important factor in the escalating rate of breast cancer.

Pressure from both movements may be required to spur long overdue research on the relationship among environmental toxins, race, poverty, and cancer. We need to know much more, for instance, about the effect of chemical pesticides on men and women farm workers, the causes of cancer clustering, and the relationship among workplace hazards, the race and gender of employees, and cancer incidence (Arditti & Schreiber, 1993; Brady, 1991; Hofrichter, 1993).

SEXISM

One of the first issues explored by the contemporary women's movement was sexism within the medical establishment. The patronizing attitude of doctors, the overuse of hysterectomy and mastectomy, and the medication of women deemed "nervous" were all practices exposed through feminist activism. Feminists resurrected the practice of midwifery and changed the norms of childbirth.

More recently, feminists have taken up the issue of increasing rates of cancer among women, particularly focusing on the marked increase in the rate of breast cancer. According to the American Cancer Society, one in twenty women developed breast cancer in 1940. The incidence of breast cancer has grown by a rate of 1.4 percent every year since; now one in every nine women is at risk of getting the disease.[5] In the late 1980s, grassroots groups began to emerge across the country arguing that indifference to these alarming changes is part of a pattern of sexist neglect of women within the medical establishment (Foley, 1990; Gross, 1991). Writing in *Sojourner* in 1989, Susan Shapiro, a Boston area writer and feminist activist, analyzed her own and other women's experience of cancer as a feminist issue. This was the catalyst for the founding of the Boston/Cambridge-based Women's Community Cancer Project. Earlier that same year, in *Outlook* magazine, Jackie Winnow (1993) described the founding of the Women's Cancer Resource Center in Berkeley: "I took some of what I learned doing AIDS work and a lot of what I learned from feminist organizing and women's liberation, and with other women, created the Women's Cancer Resource Center" (p. 27). Both Shapiro and Winnow have died of breast cancer, but their efforts and similar efforts have now spawned at least a dozen grassroots groups across the country that organize, protest, and research the neglect of women's cancers and angrily demand that more research money be allocated, especially for breast cancer.

Much of the energy that propelled organizing efforts during the early period of the women's cancer movement came from lesbians who had experienced cancer or whose lives were touched by it in other ways. As a result, a number of the women's cancer projects are explicitly lesbian projects, providing services for lesbians with cancer and working with gay and lesbian clinics to lobby for the inclusion of lesbians in cancer research. Recent research indicates that lesbians may be at increased risk of breast cancer and other women's cancers, perhaps due to a low rate of childbirth, which reduces their exposure to medical attention, and/or reluctance to use health services that often are insensitive or hostile to lesbians.

In 1990, just as this women's cancer movement was emerging, a U.S. Government Accounting Office (GAO) report documented continued sexist neglect within medical research at the National Institutes of Health, despite the existence of a 1986 policy intended to correct it. Women, the GAO reported, have been systematically excluded from controlled experiments, long-term studies, and clinical studies of new drugs ("Health Research," 1990; "Our Bodies," 1990).

Also in 1990, the Physicians Insurers Association of America chided doctors for not taking women seriously when they report self-discovered breast lumps. The cost of dismissive and/or patronizing medical attention has been high in terms of claims paid in malpractice suits; in 69 percent of cases where malpractice insurance claims were paid in response to charges of unnecessarily delayed diagnosis, the female patient discovered the breast lump herself but had not been taken seriously by her physician.

In large part due to the activism of feminist health groups, Congress in 1993 allocated over $400 million to breast cancer. The 1993 allocation to the National Cancer Institute of $197 million represented an increase of $60 million over the previous year's award. An additional $210 million was awarded to the Department of Defense (DOD), raising total new appropriations to $270 million. By early 1994, the DOD funding had already attracted more than 7,000 proposals from prospective researchers across the country.

Although this is an extremely impressive beginning for the young and vigorous women's cancer movement, it does not address the practical impacts of cancer on the lives of women, and, more especially, on the lives of poor women. For women who are the caretakers of children, the elderly, and the ill, as well as the principal homemakers, a diagnosis of cancer, whatever the woman's income level, imposes enormous practical as well as emotional burdens. Poor women, however, are less likely to find relief from these burdens as they pursue their treatment options. When there are no family members available to help with caretaking, there is rarely money to hire a substitute. The significant commitment of time that must be made to pursue a course of radiation therapy may make such an option prohibitive for a woman without savings or family support, who may also be a single parent or the only breadwinner. The debilitating effects of chemotherapy may equally discourage women from submitting to recommended treatment if it takes too much time away from work or family obligations.

For many women in these circumstances, the most immediate threat may be the loss of their ability to care for their children; their own loss of life may appear as a more shadowy terror further down the road. In other words, while the lives of overburdened women are governed by short-term considerations, a proper understanding of cancer and the likely outcomes of available treatments demands a longer perspective. Poverty necessarily imposes a more limited frame of reference and so might be said to dictate the course of treatment even when the consequences of such decisions are understood and appreciated.

WOMEN AND THE HEALTH CARE MARKETPLACE

Racism, sexism, and poverty all conspire to make women more vulnerable as they face the danger of a cancer diagnosis and make their way through the health care system. In response to these obstacles, women are now being encouraged to apply market principles to their relationship with their doctors. They are urged to become well-informed "consumers" of medical care, to "shop around" for the best treatment—comparing services, surgeons, and fees.

In this model, women move from being victims (of both the disease and the medical establishment) to the more empowered role of in-charge consumers. In keeping with the axioms of the self-help movement, women are advised to seek information (the market ideal of "perfect information," if possible) about medical facilities, personnel, and treatment options. In this model, women become their own case managers, interviewing potential providers and keeping an eye on the bottom line of each fee-for-service medical experience.

This well-intended analogy between consuming goods and consuming medical care is, however, at cruel variance with the actual situation of most women. By construing the process as a personal quest prompted by individual necessity, the consumer model substitutes a view of personal responsibility for a more collective approach to health care that is based on a network of shared responsibilities. It assumes that the provision of medical treatment can be reduced to a series of transactions orchestrated by the patient. In fact, a more realistic model is a team approach, in which the goal is to achieve a consensus between the patient and various health care providers. In this case, the patient is neither the uninformed victim of medical paternalism, nor the hero of her individual, isolated health crisis.

In reality, there are many reasons why women cannot possibly obtain perfect information or make the rational choices about value for money suggested by the advice to "shop around." In the case of seeking information, it is nearly always unrealistic to expect a patient to be in a position to discover all the relevant facts about the treatment options she faces within the time available to her. The newly diagnosed cancer patient is unfamiliar with the medical concepts and jargon she encounters, and usually does not have the resources to recognize the treatment biases of different consultants or to make sense of often conflicting information. Here lack of education becomes an even greater burden, effectively eliminating the possibility that women with low education can fully participate in the process.

Further, advising women to consider the cost of their treatment and to compare and contrast the cost of various options open to them is sadly congruent with the situation faced by uninsured women in our current health care system. Knowing that their health care will be paid for out of their own savings or future earnings, they are already at the mercy of the marketplace, which excludes them. Increasingly, market considerations dictate even the medical decisions of the insured; third-party payers, such as insurance com-

panies or HMOs, are applying cost-effectiveness criteria to maintain profitability.

Surely it is preferable for women diagnosed with cancer to make decisions based on medical rather than economic criteria. They must, of course,
participate fully in the decision-making process, but this task should be approached with a realistic view of what can be achieved. Women should not
be given responsibility for managing their medical care when they do not
have the resources to carry out that assignment.

Whatever the form of health care delivery system—government owned,
single payer, mixed public and private, or free market, for profit—it must be
monitored constantly for inadequacies in its system of delivery. Equitable
distribution is a critical social goal that must remain visibly in the forefront
of health care policy. To be vigilant in pursuing that goal is the responsibility of all health care advocates, activists and clients, whether well or ill.

ADDRESSING THE INEQUITY

Frequent stories in print, television, and radio media tell of families bank-
rupted by the crushing burden of medical debt. Families in which the parent
or parents are unemployed are particularly vulnerable, but 80 percent of children who have no health insurance have at least one parent who is working
("At Risk," 1992). After years of neglect and foot dragging by Republican
administrations, popular support for major reform of the health care system
has forced the issue onto the legislative agenda. It would be comforting to
think that, should a system of universal health care be instituted, the problem of unequal access to quality health care according to socioeconomic status would be solved. However, what is needed is an affirmative action health
care program for low-income people and people of color, especially women.
This is necessary because, even when universal health care is provided, obstacles remain to taking full advantage of its services.

In Great Britain, which has operated a universal health care service since
1948, cancer incidence rates of those in the lowest socioeconomic group remain consistently and significantly higher than those in the highest income
group (Leon and Office of Population Censuses and Surveys, 1988). Four different cancers among women—invasive and *in situ* cervical cancers, stomach
cancer, and lung cancer—showed the greatest difference in rates between rich
and poor, with cervical cancer showing the greatest difference. Mortality
rates follow the same pattern (Doyal & Epstein, 1983, p. 13). Evidence from
Britain (Griffin, 1994) also reveals differences between those in different
socioeconomic groups in their ability to understand a diagnosis and to absorb

and retain advice given them by their family doctor. The higher the income group, the longer the consultation with the doctor and the more extensive the information exchange between the two.

The long-term persistence of these disparities suggests that, even when there is less economic discrimination in treatment after a diagnosis of cancer, delayed diagnosis of otherwise curable cancers may remain the overriding determinant of long-term survival rates. This in turn is a reminder that the repercussions of poverty (through restricted education and employment opportunities) affect the way women approach health care. Even if free and in principle universally available, timely and appropriate health care may nevertheless continue to elude women who are poor. Less likely to be registered with a primary care physician, they are less likely to learn of the benefits of mammography or to be encouraged/reminded to undergo regular screening for cancer of any kind. There is evidence to suggest (Hayward, Bernard, Freeman, & Corey, 1991; Zapka, Stoddard, Costanza, & Greene, 1989) that having a primary care physician is strongly associated with the use of mammography.

But even where some link to primary care has been established, obstacles remain. Many women are simply boxed in, without access to a car or a babysitter or a sympathetic employer. Further, fatalism may complicate a woman's relationship with the medical establishment. Hampered by limited knowledge of the system, or faithful to religious tenets to follow God's will, a woman may see cancer itself as a death sentence, leading to overwhelming fear of the diagnosis and of any possible treatment.[6]

Those who do manage to get to the doctor's office often face additional hurdles. Health care may be delivered in a way that stereotypes and alienates patients. The physician, who serves as the gateway to treatment, may not be sufficiently qualified to distinguish between patients who should be referred for diagnostic tests and those who should not. He or she may also be unaware of the most recent changes in clinical practice. But even the most conscientious family doctor cannot overcome the shortages of staff and/or equipment at the hospitals to which patients often must be referred; these may simply lack the resources to employ an oncologist or to purchase radiation equipment. Their own "poverty" sets clear limits on the type of treatment they can offer.[7]

This web of obstacles facing poor women with cancer does not, of course, minimize the absolute necessity of universal health insurance. Although it seems as remote a prospect as ever, the provision of universal health care nonetheless remains an essential first step toward a more equitable distribution of health care resources. It represents a radical challenge to the laissez-faire philosophy that justifies our current system of provision, so dominated by the ability to pay on one side and by the need for profitability on the other. But universal care on its own will not completely eliminate the impact of poverty, racism, and sexism on either the incidence or mortality rates of women's cancers.

It is a measure of the way the current health care debate has been conducted—and reported—that all critical issues have been reduced to their impact on total costs. The debate has been more a test of the limits of market economics than a threat to them. Questions of access, on the other hand, may be more explicitly political than economic. In principle, universal health care would not require any direct intervention to overcome the inequalities imposed by poverty, race, or gender. It would make health care, at least theoretically, available to all. In practice, however, universal health care necessarily must confront the problems of access on the ground. These problems require profound changes in the *delivery* of health care in order to overcome intractable maldistribution of resources. As we have tried to demonstrate, they involve biases, both personal and institutional, that affect the outcome of every health-related transaction. For women with cancer, a more systematic recognition of these inequalities is needed, conveyed through well funded, culturally informed cancer education and outreach efforts especially tailored to meet the needs of low-income women.

Many of those who study and advocate for reform of the U.S. medical system understand this need (Dalen & Santiago, 1991; Ginzberg & Ostow, 1991; Menken, 1991). Even mainstream organizations such as the American Cancer Society see a need for culturally specific outreach and education in poor communities about the risk factors and warning signs of cancer. More farsighted advocates see the additional need for people to organize to oppose criminal profiteering by pharmaceutical corporations, governmental indifference to the health needs of all the people, and the poisoning of the environment that leads to increased cancer rates. Universal health insurance without accompanying legislation to end environmental degradation and environmental racism will not bring an end to the rapidly increasing rates of cancer we are now experiencing. Similarly, universal health insurance will not end corruption within the medical system unless accountability to the public in the areas of profit-making and public health care policy are established. Finally, greater access to expensive drugs and medical procedures must be accompanied by a reassertion of the role of primary care and preventive care.

The devastation to women's health caused by poverty does not mean that women with money, education, access, and private insurance are never misdiagnosed or treated carelessly and stupidly, or even that they do not occasionally have cancer at higher rates. Nor does it mean that we should not care about men, who sometimes have cancer at higher rates than women. It does not mean that we advocate decreasing the federal budget allocation to AIDS research and treatment. This must be stressed since the conservative media often stir up discord between groups of activist women and sometimes play off AIDS advocates against cancer advocates. It is *not* a matter of pitting one against the other, but of recognizing and supporting multiple layers of demands that must be promoted simultaneously.

CONCLUSION

Statistical research speaks a painful truth about health care for women with cancer in the United States. To a shocking extent, a woman's health reflects her ability to pay for it. Surely this is morally indefensible for a society that advocates even a basic level of equality. Adequate health care should be a service that is universally available and accessible. A movement for women's health must demand not only health care reform that equalizes access to medical care, but also insist on affirmative outreach to those women who have been paying with their health—even their lives—for their race, their socioeconomic status, and their gender.

ACKNOWLEDGMENTS

Jean V. Hardisty and Ellen Leopold are members of the Women's Community Cancer Project, 46 Pleasant Street, Cambridge, MA 02139. They would like to thank the members of this group for their assistance.
Earlier versions of this article (both titled "Cancer and Poverty: Double Jeopardy for Women") were published in *Sojourner: The Women's Forum,* vol. 18, no. 4 (December 1992), pp. 16–18; and in Midge Stocker, ed., *Confronting Cancer/Constructing Change* (Chicago: Third Side Press, 1993), pp. 213–231.

NOTES

1. The contrast in survival rates may be distorted to some extent by what is called "lead-time bias." The earlier detection of more lethal forms of breast cancer (picked up in routine screening mammograms paid for by insurance) gives the impression that the patient has survived for a longer period of time, even though treatment has been completely ineffective.
2. In a pertinent 1992 study of the effect of socioeconomic status on cardiovascular

risk factors, level of education is identified as the most important parameter predicting high-risk factors (Winkleby et al., 1992).

3. The media, however, prefer to use income and race as surrogates for poverty. This creates distortions, as discussed in the section on racism below.

4. Recently, however, a cluster of studies has suggested that black women may suffer from a more deadly form of breast cancer, one that strikes earlier (under the age of 45) and that is more likely to be fatal. According to Dr. Brenda Edwards, an associate director of the surveillance program at the National Cancer Institute, although the higher death rate among black women may reflect poor access to medical care, it can only account for about half of the increased rate (see Kolata 1994). If this proves to be true, it may have implications for the future of health policy recommendations for women under 50.

5. The reasons for the rise in incidence are complex and not well understood. For a start, before the 1980s, less than 15 percent of American women had regular screening mammograms. Second, because the disease can grow very slowly, a recent rise of breast cancer among women in their sixties may reflect behavioral or environmental changes that first occurred 30 or 40 years ago. Third, although the rise in incidence of very small tumors has been an expected consequence of increased screening, there has been *no* decrease in the incidence of later-stage, larger tumors or disease. For a fuller discussion of the changing incidence rates, see Jay Harris, Marc Lippman, Umberto Veronesi, & Walter Willett. (1992).

6. This point was made in the findings of regional hearings conducted by the American Cancer Society in May and June 1989 in 7 states (American Cancer Society, 1989).

7. In an excellent account of one family's struggle with poverty and lack of medical insurance in one of Chicago's poorest neighborhoods, an experienced medical journalist followed the day-to-day medical problems and treatment of four generations of an African American family. The author discusses not only the family's difficulties but also those of the overburdened, underfunded public hospitals that serve the poor of North Lawndale (Abraham, 1993).

REFERENCES

Abraham, L. K. (1993). *Mama might be better off dead: The failure of health care in urban America.* Chicago: University of Chicago Press.

Alston, D. (Ed.). (1990). *We speak for ourselves: Social justice, race, and environment.* Washington, DC: The Panos Institute.

American Cancer Society. (1989). *Cancer and the poor: A report to the nation.* Atlanta: Author.

Arditti, R., & Schreiber, T. (1993). Killing us quietly: Cancer, the environment, and women. In Midge Stocker (Ed.), *Confronting cancer, constructing change* (pp. 231–260). Chicago: Third Side Press.

At risk: Middle-class families often lack insurance for children's health. (1992, June 5). *The Wall Street Journal,* p. 1.

Ayanian, J. Z., Kohler, B. A., Abe, T., & Epstein, A. M. (1993). The relation between health insurance coverage and clinical outcomes among women with breast cancer. *New England Journal of Medicine, 329,* 326–331.

Baquet, C. R., Horm, J. W., Gibbs, T., & Greenwald, P. (1991, April 17). Socioeconomic factors and cancer incidence among blacks and whites. *Journal of the National Cancer Institute, 83*(8), 551–557.

Baquet, C. R., & Ringen, K. (Eds.). (1986). *Cancer among blacks and other minorities: Statistical profiles* (Publication No. 86–2785). Department of Health and Human Services Bethesda, MD: (National Institutes of Health).

Brady, J. (Ed.). (1991). *One in three: Women with cancer confront an epidemic.* Pittsburgh: Cleis Press.

Cimons, M. Health research largely excludes women, GAO says. (1990, June 19). *Boston Globe,* p. 3.

City plans $3m cut in health-center aid. (1992, May 23). *Boston Globe,* p. 21.

Clayton, L. A., & Byrd, W. M. (1993). The African-American cancer crisis, part I: The problem. *Journal of Health Care for the Poor and Underserved, 4*(2). 83–101.

Dalen, J. E., & Santiago, J. (1991). Insuring the uninsured is not enough. *Archives of Internal Medicine, 151,* 860–862.

Doyal, L., & Epstein, S. (1983). *Cancer in Britain: The politics of prevention.* London: Pluto Press.

Employee Benefit Research Institute. (1992). *Special report: Sources of health insurance and characteristics of the uninsured.* Washington: Author.

Escape the emergency room trap. (1992, May 4). *The New York Times,* p. A16.

Farley, T., & Flannery, J. T. (1989). Late-stage diagnosis of breast cancer in women of lower socioeconomic status: Public health implications. *American Journal of Public Health, 79,* 1508–1512.

Foley, M. J. (1990, May–June) Cancer organizers push feminist agenda. *New Directions for Women, 19*(3), p. 1.

Freeman, H. P. (1989). Cancer in the socioeconomically disadvantaged. *Cancer, 64 (supplement),* 324–334.

Gaiter, D. (1991, May 1). Although cures exist, poverty fells many afflicted with cancer [citing unpublished NCI SEER data]. *The Wall Street Journal,* p. 1.

Ginzberg, E. (January 9, 1991). Access to health care for Hispanics. *Journal of the American Medical Association, 265*(2), 238–241.

Ginzberg, E., & Ostow, M. (1991, May 15). Beyond universal health insurance to effective health care. *Journal of the American Medical Association, 265*(19), 2559–2562.

Griffin, J. (1994). *Health information and the consumer.* (Briefing No. 30). London: Office of Health Economics.

Gross, J. (1991, January 7). Turning disease into political cause: First AIDS, and now breast cancer. *The New York Times,* p. A12.

Harris, J. R., Lippman, M. E., Veronesi, U., & Willett, W. (1992). Breast cancer. *New England Journal of Medicine, 327,* 319–320.

Hayward, R. A., Bernard, A. M., Freeman, H. F., & Corey, C. R. (1991). Regular source of ambulatory care and access to health services. *American Journal of Public Health, 81,* 434–438.

Hofrichter, R. (Ed.). (1993). *Toxic struggles: The theory and practice of environmental justice.* Philadelphia: New Society.

Kolata, G. (1994, August 3). Deadliness of breast cancer in blacks defies easy answer. *The New York Times,* p. C10.

Lee, C. (1987). *Toxic waste and race in the United States.* New York: United Church of Christ Commission for Racial Justice.

Lee, F. (1990, October 30). Needless breast cancer deaths reported among New York's poor. *The New York Times,* Section B, p. 1.

Leon, D. A., and Office of Population Censuses and Surveys. (1988). *Longitudinal study: Social definition of cancer.* London: HMSO. Her Majesty's Stationery Office

Menken, M. (1991). Caring for the underserved. *Archives of Neurology, 48,* 472–475.

National Cancer Institute. (1988). *Cancer in Hispanics.* Bethesda, MD: National Institutes of Health.

Office of the Comptroller, City of New York. (1990, October). *Poverty and breast cancer in New York City.* New York: Author.

Our bodies, their selves. (1990, December 17). *Newsweek,* p. 60.

Physicians Insurers Association of America. (1990, March). *Breast cancer study,* Lawrenceville, NJ: Author

Pollution-weary minorities try civil rights tack. (1993, January 11). *The New York Times,* p. A1.

Rural New Englanders find medical care in short supply. (1992, March 22). *Boston Globe,* p. 1.

Shapiro, S. (1989, September). Cancer as a women's issue. *Sojourner. The Women's Forum,* pp. 18–19.

Thornton, J. (1993). *Chlorine, human health, and the environment.* Washington, DC: Greenpeace.

Trevino, F. M., Moyer, M. E., Valdez, B., & Stroup-Benham, C.A. (1991, January 9). Health insurance coverage and utilization of health services by Mexican Americans, mainland Puerto Ricans, and Cuban Americans. *Journal of the American Medical Association, 265*(2), 233–237.

Weiss, B. D., Hart, G., & Pust, R. (1991, Spring). The relationship between literacy and health. *Journal of Health Care for the Poor and Underserved, 1*(4), 351–363.

Wenneker, M. B., Weissman, J. S., & Epstein, A. M. (1990, September 19). Association of payer with utilization of cardiac procedures in Massachusetts. *Journal of the American Medical Association,* 1255–1260.

Winkleby, M. A., Jatulis, D. E., Frank, E., & Fortmann, S. P. (1992, June). Socioeconomic status and health: How education, income, and occupation contribute to risk factors for cardiovascular disease. *American Journal of Public Health, 82*(6), 816–820.

Winnow, J. (1993). Lesbians evolving health care: Our lives depend on it. In Midge
    Stocker (Ed.), *Cancer as a women's issue* (pp. 23–35). Chicago: Third Side Press.
Zapka, J. G., Stoddard, A. M., Costanza, M. E., & Greene, H. L. (1989). Breast can-
    cer screening by mammography; utilization and associated factors. *American
    Journal of Public Health, 79,* 1499–1502.

Chapter 12

The Challenges Facing Community Health Centers in the 1990s: A Voice from the Inner City

•*Elizabeth Sparks*

AFRICAN AMERICANS IN THE UNITED STATES HAVE BEEN OPPRESSED, AS A group, since they were brought as slaves to the shores of this country in the early seventeenth century. Racism has historically affected the health of those being discriminated against, as evidenced by the indifference to health care for African American slaves and freed men, and the treatment of black soldiers in the Civil War who died in large numbers in hospitals because of neglect (Glatthar, 1989). The effects of racism have also been seen historically in the mental health system. When mental hospitals were initially established in the 1800s, only a few northern facilities admitted African Americans to segregated units; the majority of psychiatrically ill African Americans were sent to almshouses or placed in jail (Prudhomme & Musto, 1973; Wilson & Lantz, 1957). While gross abuses of the human and civil rights of African Americans have mostly disappeared due to changes in federal and state laws, racism and discrimination remain beneath the surface and effect both life and death for ethnic minorities.

There continue to be significant differentials in the rates of serious illness (both physical and mental) and mortality between whites and African Americans (Otten, Teutsch, Williamson, & Marks, 1990). Since the 1960s, various social reform efforts have been undertaken to alter this state of affairs. One such effort was the community health center movement, which began in the late 1960s. It was designed to provide comprehensive health care services to underserved poor communities with the hope of eliminating the inequalities that existed for the poor. In this chapter, I will examine the impact of this movement on the health status of African Americans and will argue that, despite some areas of success, community health centers have had little effect on reducing the gap between the health status of African Americans and that of whites. I will examine the factors that have contributed to this situation through the case study of one such center—the Boston Community Health Center (BCHC).[1] I will explore the macrolevel factors that are negatively affecting BCHC and suggest ways that community health centers can deal with these factors in order to enhance their fiscal viability and the effectiveness of their services.

HISTORICAL CONTEXT: THE COMMUNITY HEALTH CENTER MOVEMENT

The Boston Community Health Center, which is located in an ethnic minority neighborhood of the city, grew out of the community health center movement that began in 1965, when the federal government funded neighborhood-based health clinics as demonstration projects of the then-new War on Poverty. The movement took place within a sociopolitical context that emphasized a revitalized humanistic concern for the disadvantaged, the oppressed, and the powerless (Hersch, 1972). In the health care profession, there was a shift from the conservative viewpoint, which saw the primary cause of physical and mental problems as residing within the individual, to one that located at least some portion of the cause for these problems in the environment and that was focused on reform. At the core of the community health center movement was a shift in the underlying professional ideology from a strict clinical (i.e., individual and intrapsychic) perspective to a public health frame of reference.

Community health centers were originally funded through the federal Office of Economic Opportunity (OEO) grants, and were later transferred to the Bureau of Community Health Services within the Health Services Administration. Increased funding was made available to the community health centers in 1966 with an amendment to the Economic Opportunity Act that made comprehensive health center programs an established part of the federal budget (Patton, 1990). These centers were to be located within designated poverty areas to provide comprehensive health, social, and environmental services to "medically underserved" populations. BCHC opened its doors in 1969 with an OEO grant under the auspices of a major university medical center. As with other community health centers developed during this period, the purpose of BCHC was twofold: (1) to provide primary health care services to a medically underserved population; and (2) to facilitate community empowerment by providing employment opportunities for residents and establishing community control of the center's management (Hersch, 1972; Patton, 1990). BCHC was designed to provide primary health care services to a predominantly African American clientele that are accessible, affordable, and reflective of the community's cultural values.

With regards to the second purpose, BCHC initially experienced difficulties in establishing community control since the staff and clientele were predominantly ethnic minorities, while the administrators (through the medical center) were predominantly white. Changes in federal regulations made it possible for BCHC to become a freestanding clinic by 1972, and the board of directors (which included community residents) gained the authority to independently manage the center's fiscal resources and to make policy decisions. Currently, BCHC is a private, nonprofit clinic that has an operating budget of over $4 million, with substantial grants from the federal government, state contracts, specific program grants, and third-party reimbursements from insurers.

INSTITUTIONAL RACISM IN THE HEALTH CARE SYSTEM

When the community health center movement was initiated, it was anticipated that community-controlled health centers would reduce, or eliminate, the differences between the health status of poor ethnic minorities and that of whites. During this era, many of the social reform programs had similar expectations; however, these proved to be unrealistic since they did not sufficiently take into account the complex nature of the problems that were being addressed. Not surprisingly, community health centers have not been able to attain their primary goal. Currently, statistics indicate that the overall health status of African Americans has continued to decline, relative to whites, despite general improvements in health care standards and practices (Dutton, 1981; Mullings, 1989; Payne & Ugarte, 1989; Starr, 1986; U.S. Department of Health and Human Services [HHS], 1991). African Americans have been found to have a shorter life expectancy than whites (69.6 years compared to 75.2 years, respectively), and there is a striking gap between African American and white populations in terms of mortality (Mullings, 1989; Rice & Winn, 1990). There are also differences in the infant death rate as well as in the proportion of minorities who die of heart disease, cardiovascular disease, and cancer, compared with the white population (Sullivan, 1989). Minorities also suffer from higher rates of debilitating and chronic diseases and have been found to have less protection against infectious diseases, a situation that is seen most clearly in the racial differences in the epidemiology of acquired immunodeficiency syndrome, or AIDS (Hutchinson, 1992). These conclusions are based on national statistics; however, similar patterns exist in each of the states.

Differences between these two ethnic groups have also been noted in mental health. Prior to the 1960s, the psychological functioning of African Americans received considerable negative attention in the research literature (McAdoo, 1992; Nobles & Goddard, 1985; Wilson, 1986). The behaviors of African Americans were perceived as being deficient, and there was little effort made to identify strengths and resilience (Billingsley, 1968; Hill, 1972). Researchers have only recently begun to examine seriously the role that culture plays in the therapeutic process (Carter, 1991; Jones & Korchin, 1982; Ridley, 1984; Sue & Sue, 1990). Most theories of counseling have been based on the experiences of white, middle-class clients and therapists, which has led to mental health facilities having a Eurocentric orientation. Many believe that this has contributed to the underutilization of mental health services by ethnic minorities (Campinha-Bacote, 1991; Sue, 1977; Sue & Zane, 1987). There also appears to be racial bias in psychiatric assessment and diagnosis (Mukherjee, Shukla, Woodle, Rosen, & Olarte, 1983; Wade, 1993). Research has suggested that African Americans are rated as more psychologically impaired by white therapists, and that they are more likely to be labeled as having a chronic syndrome, rather than an acute episode, when diagnosed with psychotic or affective disorders (Jenkins-Hall & Sacco, 1991; Jones, 1982; Sata, 1990).

These differences between African Americans and whites with regard to illness, mortality rates, and psychiatric diagnosis and treatment suggest the continuing existence of some form of institutionalized racism within the health care system. Possible explanations for these differences can be found in the structural and institutional systems that are associated with health care for the ethnic minority poor. Such conditions as the unequal access to health care services, lack of culturally relevant services, and the multifaceted problems in the physical environments where most ethnic minorities live contribute to the lowered health status of this group. Clearly, a community health center cannot be expected to address all of these conditions, particularly those related to the environment. However, even when the centers do address the other conditions, their effectiveness is further hampered by the federal budget cuts and funding restrictions that have increasingly become a part of the national health care scene.

In 1981, a Select Panel for the Promotion of Child Health, sponsored by the U.S. Congress and the Secretary of Health and Human Services, conducted a national survey to determine the status of health care for poor women and children. The study concluded that despite numerous programs, a large number of infants, children, adolescents, and pregnant women *still do not receive essential health care services.* The Select Panel suggested that public programs have not been more successful in overcoming these problems because of inadequate access to services, the absence of basic program information, the lack of coordination among programs providing different levels of care and different types of services, and insufficient resources to support even essential maternal and child health services (U.S. Department of HHS, 1981).

A similar study conducted by the National Institute of Mental Health [NIMH] found an underutilization of community mental health services by minorities and a lack of culturally sensitive programs in community health centers (Campinha-Bacote, 1991). The NIMH surveyed programs for mental health services, with a special emphasis on minorities, and the results demonstrated the need to "develop model programs and clinical treatment standards that were culturally and ethnically appropriate" (Martin, 1988, p. 1).

The findings from both the Select Panel for the Promotion of Child Health and the NIMH suggest that community health centers have not been able to meet effectively their mandated purpose of providing comprehensive, culturally sensitive, primary health care services to the ethnic minority poor. These findings, however, do not offer an explanation for this state of affairs. Nor do they help us understand what might need to be changed in order to improve health care services to the poor. An exploration of the dilemmas faced by BCHC, as an example of a typical community health center, will provide at least one perspective on how these questions can be answered.

THE BOSTON COMMUNITY HEALTH
CENTER: EFFORTS TO OVERCOME
BARRIERS

For over twenty years, community health centers such as BCHC have struggled to meet their original goals of being sites of empowerment and self-efficacy for low-income communities, while also providing health care services to medically underserved populations. They have attempted to accomplish these goals from a marginalized position within the larger health care delivery system and with limited economic resources. Despite these handicaps some of the centers, such as BCHC, have had success in providing the community with primary health care services that overcome many of the barriers to care that have historically been experienced by African Americans.

POVERTY AS A BARRIER TO HEALTH CARE

In general, African Americans have less access to health care services regardless of their economic circumstances (Sullivan, 1989). However, those
who are poor are even more unlikely to receive the health care that they need.
Between 25 and 35 million people, about 15 percent of the U.S. population,
do not have access to adequate health care. These individuals, who are often
below the official poverty level, can be found in all ethnic groups; however,
recent statistics indicate that a disproportionate number are ethnic minority
children and their families. Of the 33.6 million Americans in poverty during
1990, 10.7 percent were white, 31.9 percent were African American, and
28.1 percent were Hispanic (U.S. Bureau of Census, 1992). The U.S. Department of Health and Human Services has concluded that both black and
Hispanic heads of households were more than twice as likely as their white
counterparts to be below the poverty level, and that more than one-half of
black and Hispanic female-headed households were below the poverty level
in 1987 (U.S. Department of HHS, 1990). The figures for Massachusetts and
for Boston are comparable to these national statistics (U.S. Bureau of Census, 1994).

BCHC, which is located in a densely populated area where over 23 percent of Boston's total population resides, provides services to a predominantly low-income, ethnic minority clientele. The racial composition is 55
percent African Americans, 12 percent Hispanic, 12 percent other ethnici-
ties, and 21 percent white. BCHC's patient population reflects a similar ethnic breakdown: 84 percent African American, 10 percent Hispanic, and 6
percent other ethnic groups and whites. At any given time, over 90 percent
of the residents in this neighborhood have incomes that are well below the
poverty level, and approximately 47 percent receive government assistance
as their sole source of income.

BCHC's clients live with various stresses associated with poverty, including welfare dependency, discrimination, lower levels of educational and
vocational skills, and an inequitable distribution of the city's resources. As a
result, they have a disproportionate number of major medical and mental
health problems, such as high rates of infant mortality, teen pregnancy, substance abuse, heart disease, cancer, AIDS, sexually transmitted diseases, and
homicide. BCHC has attempted to address these various problems directly,
and has been relatively successful in securing funding to establish a range of
general and specific medical and psychosocial services. These include ambulatory health care services in pediatrics, adolescent medicine, adult medicine,
and gynecology, and a number of support services to augment its medical
care of patients. BCHC is equipped to provide early detection and compre-

hensive treatment for many routine medical and mental health problems. However, the center is limited in its ability to provide care when a patient's illness is more complicated and/or serious, such as when diagnostic procedures and maintenance medical care utilizing specialized equipment are required. Physicians in community health centers must rely on hospitals to provide this level of care for patients, and it is standard medical practice to refer patients for these procedures. This, however, can pose problems for community health centers, because their marginalized status makes accessing hospital-based services and maintaining adequate communication between providers quite challenging. Patients referred to the hospitals for diagnostic testing often have difficulty getting appointments, and the feedback to the referring physician is at times delayed, or in some instances, does not occur at all. This situation negatively affects BCHC's ability to insure continuity of care for its patients and can interfere with its efficiency in treating illnesses.

INACCESSIBILITY AND CULTURAL
INSENSITIVITY AS BARRIERS
TO HEALTH CARE

Other factors that negatively influence the quality of health care services provided to the poor are inaccessibility (i.e., travel time to services and office waiting time; availability of convenient office hours and appointments), the cultural insensitivity of staff, and the extent to which the services provided are culturally relevant (Green 1982, Wells, Golding, Hougn, Burnam, & Karno, 1989). These barriers influence both patient satisfaction with services and continuity of care, which in turn can influence health status by reducing the possibility that an ethnic minority individual will initiate and/or follow through with the care that is available. In terms of accessibility, BCHC is located in the community that it serves and is easily accessible by public transportation. The center also provides van pick-up for patients who are unable to get to appointments due to illness or problems with mobility. A system of follow-up contact has been established for "no show" appointments, and efforts are made to offer evening clinic hours to accommodate working clients and those who have child care responsibilities.

BCHC's ability to overcome barriers connected with cultural insensitivity is a particular area of success and can most clearly be seen in the services provided by its Mental Health Department (MHD), which offers comprehensive mental health services to children and adults, including diagnostic evaluations; individual, family, and couples therapy; psychopharmacology; and psychological testing. MHD staff are predominantly ethnic minorities, and include a psychiatrist, licensed psychologists, social workers, and masters' level mental health clinicians, and they utilize a theoretical perspective that incorporates much of the existing research on the role of culture and ethnicity in the development and treatment of psychopathology. Clinicians are trained to conduct culturally sensitive assessments in such a way that they can overcome biases in the diagnosis of psychological problems that have been noted in the literature (Adelbimpe, 1981; Spurlock, 1975, 1982; Thomas & Sillen, 1972). Clinicians are also aware of the ways in which life circumstances (e.g., poverty, noxious environment, and racism) influence the etiology of psychological problems in African Americans. They identify strengths in the clients and emphasize these in the therapeutic process, instead of subscribing to the traditional perspective that inner-city African American families are "culturally deprived" (Adelbimpe, 1981; Chess, 1969; Stevenson & Renard, 1993).

This theoretical approach utilized by MHD is based on research results that have identified the relationship between life stress and the development of psychopathology among African Americans (Myers, Lindenthal, & Pepper, 1974, 1975; Smith, 1973). Essentially, this research suggests that racism and other social stresses resulting from discrimination represent a heretofore unacknowledged source of stress, termed "acculturative stress" (Anderson, 1991). Acculturative stress is the result of efforts made by African Americans to adjust to the threats and challenges to racial identity, cultural values, and patterns of living posed by the environment. The way in which these stresses are mediated by individuals can either exacerbate or ameliorate the detrimental impact of this stress (Myers, 1989). In working with African American clients, the theoretical perspective utilized by MHD suggests that the therapist should follow three basic steps: (1) identify the source(s) of stress a client is facing; (2) analyze the mediating (both external and internal) factors of stress and the stress-resistant forces within an individual and within the culture; and (3) decide upon a method of delivering services to the client (Atkinson, Thompson & Grant, 1993; Smith, 1985). In accomplishing these steps, MHD clinicians must be able to function in many different roles, including being an adviser, advocate, facilitator of community support systems, consultant, change agent, and psychotherapist.

Clinicians in MHD recognize that clients may initially have levels of mistrust that interfere with the establishment of a therapeutic alliance, and they are trained to establish credibility with clients during the initial stage of treatment by understanding and supporting the clients' world view—techniques that have been found to increase rapport and trust with African American clients (Stevenson & Renard, 1993). The overall goal of MHD's intervention services is to provide the type of assistance that clients need to address problems in their lives, whether these problems have an internal or external etiology.

MHD also provides service programs to meet the high-priority needs of their client population in a manner that respects the cultural values and norms of the African American community. Three such programs are: (1) a substance abuse prevention program for youth; (2) a homicide survivors support program; (3) a family-based intervention program for young children and their parents who are recovering from alcohol and/or other drug use. These programs grew out of identified needs in the client population, and demonstrate the way in which the center adapted its programming to be responsive to the ever-changing needs of the community.

The substance abuse prevention program, which was implemented in 1988, was designed to respond to the high incidence of substance use in African American youth. Its school-based prevention education program is Afrocentric, and includes a focus on the effects of poverty and discrimination on the use of substances. The program was originally funded for five years by a federal demonstration grant, which ended in 1993. Evaluations of the program suggest that its prevention education was successful in changing the students' attitudes toward the use of substances and in making them more aware of the inherent dangers of substance abuse. BCHC has identified an alternative source of funding to continue to provide substance abuse prevention services to the community; however, the resulting program is more limited in scope because of reduced fiscal resources.

The homicide survivors program (HSP) was instituted in 1989, at a time when the homicide rate among young African American males in the community serviced by BCHC was the highest in the Boston area. The program provides supportive services to family members and friends of homicide victims, and reflects an understanding of the sociopolitical conditions surrounding homicide in the African American community. It is funded through a state contract, which is renewable on an annual basis. The HSP reflects a culturally sensitive perspective through its acceptance and validation of clients' perceptions of racial bias in the criminal justice system and their concerns about the larger society's lack of commitment to stopping the violence in the inner city. The program is cognizant of the research that has been conducted on bereavement practices and customs in the African American community, and structures its services to meet the needs of these clients. For example, the mourning period that is normative in the African American culture is relatively brief, since there is a value placed on accepting the inevitability of death (Eisenbruch, 1984). The HSP accepts that clients may utilize direct supportive services for only a limited period of time, and it provides ongoing contact through telephone calls, cards, and a bimonthly newsletter.

The family support program for substance-abusing parents and their young children also grew out of a recognized need in the community. The program was developed in 1990, when the largest percentage of MHD's referrals for family therapy were coming from the Massachusetts Department of Social Services and involved children who were being reunited with recovering (formerly addicted) parents following foster care placements. BCHC received federal funding for a five-year demonstration project to provide services that would utilize a culturally sensitive approach to working with these parents and their children. Services are based on a model that takes into account the role of ethnicity and poverty in addiction, and program staff not only provide parenting training and family therapy, but also help clients with such concrete needs as obtaining housing and adequate financial resources.

Each of these programs has had some demonstrated success in providing effective, culturally relevant services to its target population. Under the federal demonstration grant funding (prior to 1993), the substance abuse program provided services for approximately one thousand adolescents each year through its various prevention education activities. The homicide survivors program serves approximately one hundred family members and friends of homicide victims each year, while the family support program provides assistance annually to approximately thirty families. Evaluation reports are submitted to the program funders each year, and the results demonstrate that those clients who are active participants in the programs gain some degree of positive change in the targeted problem areas. Clients also indicate their satisfaction with the services and with the staff (Gibney, 1993). Thus, BCHC has been successful in developing health care services that overcome many of the barriers to health care that African Americans encounter when they approach traditional facilities. Yet, there are still impediments to its effectiveness as a result of two factors: (1) the marginalization of community health care centers within the health care system; and (2) the politics of funding.

IMPEDIMENTS TO EFFECTIVENESS

Marginalization

BCHC functions within a medical community that has pushed community health centers into a marginalized position where they have little power to access resources readily or to effect change. The center must face the challenge of maintaining its fiscal viability and its capacity to provide the type of comprehensive services required to meet the ever-increasing needs of its service community with little or no support from the well established medical community. For instance, it has clearly been demonstrated in the research literature that African Americans are at extremely high risk for such conditions as cardiovascular disease, hypertension, and diabetes, and many of the large teaching hospitals in Boston obtain grants to study these illnesses. However, the community health centers who treat a majority of the African American patients with these conditions are rarely invited to participate in these well-funded projects as full collaborators. A similar situation can be found in mental health services for children and families. At times, the mainstream facilities secure grant funding for programs that are similar to ones being provided to clients in the community health centers, but again, there is little collaboration, and the centers are unable to share in the increased resources that result from the grants.

The Politics of Funding

For BHCH the complexities in funding for health care to the poor have become one of the principle impediments in its efforts to provide services that meet the changing needs of the community. Factors contributing to this situation are: (1) the realities of institutional funding for health care to the poor; and (2) problems that arise when there is a mismatch between the needs of the ethnic minority community as seen through the lens of culturally sensitive theoretical approaches and the perspectives of institutional funders. A majority of the center's funding is received from a federal grant to community health centers, which funds all of the primary health care services, except for mental health. Since the early 1990s, this funding has not significantly increased, while the health care needs of the African American community have intensified. BCHC, like other community health centers, has received level funding for the last few years, which means that there has been no increase in funding despite increases in the general cost of living and the cost of medical care. The center has had to increase physician salaries in an effort to recruit and retain them, since they are competing with the higher salaries being offered by hospitals and large health maintenance organizations. These circumstances pose a fiscal dilemma for BCHC—proportioning a larger percentage of the budget for personnel costs compromises the center's ability to maintain services.

In the area of mental health, BCHC's principal source of funding is through Medicaid reimbursement for clinical services rendered directly to clients. The Medicaid program has provided financing for health care for the

poor since the 1950s and has historically been placed within the public assistance framework. To receive Medicaid assistance, recipients must pass eligibility requirements based on income (to determine poverty status), and a
"means test" is given at regular intervals to insure continuity of coverage in
the program. Contrary to common perception, Medicaid is not a broad entitlement program that assures all poor persons access to health care services
(Dutton, 1981). Eligibility regulations are complex and are determined separately for each state, which results in the program varying widely across
states. It has been estimated that only about half of the poverty population
is covered under Medicaid at any one time due to eligibility restrictions and
other factors. This means that at any moment, approximately 12.5 million
poor people, including 5 million poor children, are not covered under Medicaid (Dutton, 1981). Fiscal pressures on the Medicaid program began in the
early 1980s, and by 1990, there was a net enrollment reduction of approximately 5 percent (U.S. Department of HHS, 1990). It is estimated that about
half of all persons who lose Medicaid eligibility remain uninsured.

In Massachusetts, all families who are eligible for Aid to Families with
Dependent Children (AFDC) benefits and whose income places them below
the poverty level receive Medicaid coverage. However, once the family's income rises above the poverty level, Medicaid coverage is provided only for
children under six years of age. And, a family looses its Medicaid coverage
when it has earnings of $10,000, day care benefits of $2,528 (Employment
Incentive and Training Commission program), and food stamps benefits with
a cash value of $2,208 (U.S. House of Representatives, 1994). National sta-
tistics indicate that individuals who are uninsured are generally young adults
from ethnic minorities (black and/or Hispanic), living in families where no
one is employed (U.S. Department of Health and Human Services, 1990).
The same is true for Massachusetts, where single adults are not eligible for
Medicaid unless they have been determined to be "disabled" (either physically or mentally). All other single adults are regarded as able-bodied and
capable of gainful employment (Douglass & Torress, 1994). In the community served by BCHC, only 60 percent of the residents are in the labor force,
and of that number, almost 16 percent are unemployed (CACI Marketing
Systems, 1991). The remaining 40 percent of the adult population have
dropped out of the work force and are no longer actively seeking employment. This suggests that approximately 56 percent of the residents in this
community are uninsured, and state regulations destine those who experience chronic joblessness and who are not disabled to remain ineligible for
Medicaid assistance.

Thus, the financing of health care for the ethnic minority poor takes
place within an institutional context where many individuals will remain

uninsured and have restricted access to health care. BCHC does receive a limited amount of state and federal funds to subsidize medical services for the uninsured poor; however, the need has greatly exceeded the available funding. As the center has become more effective in its outreach efforts in the community, it has created another difficult dilemma. Many of those who respond to the outreach efforts are uninsured, and since they may have not received consistent health care in the past, they often require special medical and social support services. These clients generate minimal revenue and essentially need free health care. This dilemma is difficult to resolve, because the center has a strong commitment to providing quality health care services for community residents; however, it does not have sufficient fiscal resources to provide free care for these clients.

There are also increasing problems with reimbursements, even for those clients with Medicaid coverage, as a result of the implementation of managed care. In the past, BCHC was able to provide comprehensive services to Medicaid recipients in a cost-efficient manner, despite the fact that Medicaid reimbursements have never fully covered the cost of services. Under the current managed care system, it has become increasingly difficult for the MHD to maintain a balanced budget, since its exclusive reliance on third-party reimbursements for its revenues means that as reimbursements become more limited, the gap between costs and revenues is widening. BCHC's status as a private, nonprofit clinic with limited state mental health funding has helped it avoid many of the problems experienced by state-supported inpatient and outpatient mental health facilities in Massachusetts (for a thorough discussion of this problem, see Matthew P. Dumont, "Privatization and the Global Economy and Mental Health in Massachusetts," pp. 258–271). The center is concerned, however, about possible changes in regulations governing Medicaid reimbursements that would place more stringent restrictions on the number of sessions allowed and/or on the range of diagnostic categories that will be approved for reimbursable services. To date, the most significant impact of managed care on the MHD has been the increased documentation that clinicians are required to submit (either in the form of telephone contacts with the insurer or written reports) to obtain approval for continued treatment. This process is both time-consuming and administratively cumbersome. It requires that clinicians spend many hours completing paperwork, which is not reimbursed by Medicaid, thereby causing the number of billable (i.e., direct client contact) hours to be reduced. This will ultimately affect the MHD's capacity to offer services, as it will be forced to reduce expenditures (e.g., personnel costs) in an effort to maintain a balanced budget.

In addition to these complications surrounding Medicaid, another impediment to effectiveness lies in the process by which BCHC must seek funding for its social service programs. Generally, funding is obtained from private foundations and state and/or federal grant programs. At times, the interests of a funding source are not consistent with the center's understanding of the needs of clients in the community, creating a theoretical and ideological "mismatch" that makes it difficult to compete for funding successfully. BCHC is often faced with the task of developing programs that both fit the requirements of the funders and are consistent with their cultural understanding of the problem. At times, this can become a daunting endeavor. For example, the MHD had long recognized the need to provide a program for children living in an area housing project where gang activity is pervasive. When a request for proposals was issued by the federal government for programs that would "gang-proof" young children, the staff decided to respond. The government's definition of what an adequate program should contain was based on a conceptualization of the problem that BCHC staff did not share. The government hypothesized that gang activity could be prevented in young children by strengthening their decision-making skills and by providing them with structured, alternative activities. They decided that such programs should be designed to "inoculate" children against peer and environmental pressures to join gangs by working directly with children to increase their coping and refusal skills. The MHD staff, by contrast, viewed the problem from a culturally specific theoretical perspective, and although they agreed with the need to boost children's internal resources, they also acknowledged the importance of poverty and environmental conditions as contributing factors to youth involvement in gangs. The program designed by the MHD staff not only focused on the children, but also included the parents in an intensive and comprehensive set of activities designed to enhance their ability to provide for their children and to facilitate healthier family functioning. The program included not only the development of decision-making skills in children that had been identified by the traditional, Eurocentric theoretical approach, but also job training workshops for parents and training to increase their feelings of control over the environment—an approach that highlights the importance of parents' being able to provide adequately for their families as a means of deterring gang involvement in their children.

This type of ideological and theoretical mismatch often occurs between community health centers and mainstream funding sources, and it is unlikely that this problem will improve in the near future. The marginalized status of community health centers in the health care system gives them limited access to the larger, majority-run institutions where policy and funding decisions are made. As a result, the voices of their administrators and boards of directors have very little impact on the setting of priorities in the national health care agenda for the poor or in determining the regulations governing funding.

The procedures and regulations that control reimbursements under federal programs also contribute to the problem. The bureaucratic setting within which BCHC delivers its services is one that, by definition, has standardized policies, procedures, and regulations. Although there is nothing inherently wrong with regulations, a problem arises when this standardization reflects values and norms of the dominant group that are not consistent with those of the minority. Some measure of discrimination is inevitable when this occurs, and the minority group will be the one that suffers (Wallen, 1992). Currently, the policies underlying federal funding to community health centers and Medicaid reimbursements have created a situation where the uniform application of standards and regulations often do not meet the special requirements and needs of ethnic minority communities. By mandating that only basic medical care and family planning services are covered by federal community health center funds, the federal government determines which services will be considered "essential" in health care for the poor. When utilizing a theoretical perspective that is culturally sensitive to African Americans, however, the impact of social and environmental conditions on both *physical and mental health problems* makes these important factors to be addressed in health care services. Yet, the federal government continues to hold to the position (as reflected in its regulations) that mental health and psychosocial programs designed to alleviate problems related to such conditions as homelessness, adolescent pregnancy and parenting, and homicide should not be paid for with federal dollars distributed through the community health center grants.

A similar type of restriction is placed on the services that are reimbursable under the Medicaid program. Under current regulations, Medicaid funding is only available for clinical services that are provided to clients whose difficulties meet the criteria for a psychiatric diagnosis. If there is the need for supportive intervention in order to *prevent* the development of a psychiatric disorder, this service is not reimbursable. When this restriction is applied within the African American cultural context, it is not consistent with the theoretical approaches utilized in mental health services. For example, in a situation where a family has been reunited after the parents' addiction treatment and the children's return from foster care, services are only reimbursable under Medicaid if there is evidence of a level of dysfunction that is diagnosable in psychiatric terms (i.e. one that meets the criteria for a diagnosis under the Diagnostic and Statistical Manual of Mental Disorders, Fourth Edition [DSM-IV]; this manual contains the diagnostic classification system used by most thrid-party reimbursers of mental health services as criteria for payment). However, the theoretical perspective utilized by BCHC encourages working with a family's strengths in collaboration with indigenous support systems to enhance healthy functioning. Therefore, if the health center wants to provide preventative services (as opposed to psychiatric intervention), it must seek alternative funding.

This dilemma is seen clearly in the areas of substance abuse and violence prevention. African American youth have been found to be at very high risk for both of these psychosocial problems; however, *prevention* services are not covered under Medicaid in either area. Centers do receive funding for intervention services, but in order to provide prevention services that might reduce the incidence of substance abuse and violence, it must find alternative sources of funding (usually from private foundations or specific government grant programs). Staff must constantly submit grant proposals, only some of which are funded, for different components of a comprehensive program. BCHC's capacity to provide on-going programs that link prevention and intervention services is hampered as a result of the standardized policies and regulations inherent in these institutional funding sources, and efforts to bring about changes in these regulations have been relatively unsuccessful.

FUTURE CHALLENGES

Community health centers were originally designed to provide culturally sensitive primary health care services to poor residents, and to establish a forum whereby community residents would have control of management and resource allocations within these centers. In the case of BCHC, the administrators and board of directors have identified the community's most pressing health care service needs. However, the almost complete control of the center's funding by federal, state, and private bureaucracies has made it difficult to obtain sufficient funding for programs that have a possibility of making a *real* difference in the lives of community residents. This is the case even in those instances when the perspectives of the center and the federal government are in agreement, such as in the area of adolescent sexuality. Grant funding has been secured for adolescent programs that are focused on the problems associated with sexually transmitted diseases and teen parenting; however, the funding is usually short-term (1–3 years in duration). This does not allow sufficient time for the programs to have a significant impact on such pervasive and multifaceted problems. Further, the total amount of funding and restrictions on the types of activities that can be reimbursed by the different grants generally limit the scope of the services to such an extent that their effectiveness in ameliorating the target problems is questionable.

To meet the challenges that lie ahead, community health centers will need to move away from their marginalized position in the heath care arena and gain a voice at an institutional level in the bureaucracies that control funding for health care to the poor. They must find a way not only to advocate for the needs of the African American community, but also to have a significant influence on the federal and state agencies that determine the direction and fiscal support for public health services. BCHC and other community health centers must continue to advocate for changes in these regulations through collective political action and civic assertiveness. It will be helpful to build alliances among different interest groups, a process that seems to have had some positive results in the efforts made by state hospital psychiatric patients, family members of psychiatric patients, clinicians, and public service unions in the wake of the proposed privatization of state hospitals in Massachusetts. Unless community health centers and the voices of the oppressed minorities that they service can begin to have more of an impact on the larger sociopolitical system, public financing for health care will continue to be insufficient to meet the needs of the ethnic minority poor. At some point in the near future, the constraints on funding will force community health centers to curtail their services, thereby reducing further their ability to improve the health status of ethnic minorities.

In addition to increasing their political activism at an institutional level, community health centers should also consider approaches to community economic self-development and public health/private industry collaborations in an effort to identify sources of funding that will help them break away from a total dependence on institutional financing. It is only by having a more powerful voice in the mainstream health care delivery system and by increasing control over their own fiscal resources that community health centers will be able to meet the ever-changing needs of the ethnic minority communities that they serve into the twenty-first century.

NOTE

1. This name is a pseudonym for a composite of 4 community health centers that provide services to the ethnic minority community of Boston. The author is familiar with these centers as a result of a 19-year career as a mental health clinician and administrator in this community.

REFERENCES

Adelbimpe, V. R. (1981). Overview: White norms and psychiatric diagnosis of black patients. *American Journal of Orthopsychiatry, 20,* 305–310.
Anderson, L. P. (1991). Acculterative stress theory of relevance to black Americans. *Clinical Psychology Review, 11,* 685–702.

Atkinson, D. R., Thompson, C.E., & Grant, S.K. (1993). A three-dimensional model for counseling racial/ethnic minorities. *The Counseling Psychologist, 21(2)*, 257–277.

Billingsley, A. (1968). *Black families in white America.* Englewood Cliffs, NJ: Prentice-Hall.

CACI Marketing Systems. (1991). *The sourcebook of zip code demographics* (1990 Census ed). Arlington, VA: Author.

Campinha-Bacote, J. (1991). Community mental health services for the underserved: A culturally specific model. *Archives of Psychiatric Nursing, 5(4)*, 229–235.

Carter, R. T. (1991). Cultural values: A review of empirical research and implications for counseling. *Journal of Counseling and Development, 70*, 164–173.

Chess, S. (1969). Disadvantages of "the disadvantaged child." *American Journal of Orthopsychiatry, 39*, 4–5.

Csapo, M. (1991). Post-traumatic stress disorder in children: Recognition of behavioral signs. *Boston College Journal of Special Education, 15(2)*, 111–125.

Douglass, R. L., & Torress, R. E. (1994). Evaluation of a managed care program for the non-Medicaid urban poor. *Journal of Health Care for the Poor and Underserved, 5(2)*, 83–98.

Dutton, D. (1981). Children's health care: The myth of equal access. In U.S. Department of Health and Human Services, (Ed.), *Better health for our children* (Vol. 4, pp. 357–441). Washington, DC: Public Health Service.

Eisenbruch, M. (1984). Cross-cultural aspects of bereavement: Ethnic and cultural variations in the development of bereavement practices. *Culture, Medicine and Psychiatry, 8*, 315–347.

Gibney, K. (1993). *Living after murder program: An evaluation of psychological services in an African-American community.* Unpublished doctoral dissertation.

Glatthar, J. (1989, November 2). *The costliness of discrimination: medical care for black troops in the Civil War.* Paper presented at the National Archives, Washington, DC.

Green, J. W. (1982). *Cultural awareness in the human services.* Englewood Cliffs, NJ: Prentice-Hall.

Hersch, C. (1972). Social history, mental health, and community control. *American Psychologist, 27*, 749–754.

Hill, R. B. (1972). *The strengths of black families.* New York: Emerson Hall.

Hutchinson, J. (1992). AIDS and racism in America. *Journal of the National Medical Association, 84(2)*, 119–124.

Jenkins-Hall, K., & Sacco, W. P. (1991). Effect of client race and depression on evaluations by white therapists. *Journal of Social and Clinical Psychology, 10*, 322–333.

Jones, E. E. (1982). Psychotherapists' impressions of treatment outcome as a function of race. *Journal of Clinical Psychology, 38*, 722–731.

Jones, E. E., & Korchin, S. J. (1982). *Minority mental health.* New York: Praeger.

Martin, M. (1988). Differences form the basis for inclusion. *Community Support Network News, 4(4)*, 1–2.

Mays, V. M., & Cochran, S. D. (1987). Acquired immunodeficiency syndrome and black Americans: Special psychosocial issues. *Public Health Reports, 102,* 224–231.

McAdoo, H. P. (1992). Upward mobility and parenting in middle-income black families. In A. Burlew, W.C. Banks, H.P. McAdoo, & D.A. Azibo (Eds.), *African American psychology: Theory, research, and practice* (pp. 63–86). Newbury Park: Sage.

Mukherjee, S., Shukla, S., Woodle, J., Rosen, A.M., & Olarte, S. (1983). Misdiagnosis of schizophrenia in bipolar patients: A multiethnic comparison. *American Journal of Psychiatry, 140,* 1571–1574.

Mullings, L. (1989). Inequality and African American health status: Policies and prospects. In W. Van Horme (Ed.), *Race: Twentieth-century dilemmas—Twenty-first century prognoses* (pp. 155–182). Madison: University of Wisconsin, Institute on Race and Ethnicity.

Myers, H. F. (1989). Urban stress and mental health in black youth: An epidemiological and conceptual update. In R. Jones (Ed.), *Black adolescents* (pp. 123–152). Berkeley, CA: Cobb & Henry.

Myers, J. K., Lindenthal, J. J., & Pepper, M. P. (1974). Social class, life events and psychiatric symptoms: A longitudinal study. In B. S. Dohrenwend & B. P. Dohrenwend (Eds.), *Stressful life events: Their nature and effects* (pp. 191–205). New York: John Wiley.

Myers, J. K., Lindenthal, J. J., & Pepper, M. P. (1975). Life events, social integration, and psychiatric symptomotology. *Journal of Health and Social Behavior, 16,* 421–429.

Nobles, W., & Goddard, L. L. (1985). Black family life: A theoretical and policy implication literature review. In A.R. Harvey (Ed.), *The black family: An Afrocentric perspective* (pp 24–36). New York: United Church of Christ.

Otten, M. W., Teutsch, S. M., Williamson, D. F., & Marks, J. (1990). The effect of known risk factors on the excess mortality of black adults in the United States. *Journal of the American Medical Association, 263,* 845–850.

Patton, L. T. (1990). Community health centers at twenty-five: A retrospective look at the first ten years. *Journal of Ambulatory Care Management, 13*(4), 13–21.

Payne, K. W., & Ugarte, C. A. (1989). The office of minority health resource center: Impacting on health-related disparities among minority populations. *Health Education, 20,* 6–8.

Prudhomme, C., & Musto, D. F. (1973). Historical perspective on mental health and racism in the United States. In C. V. Willie, B. M. Kramer, & B. S. Brown (Eds.), *Racism and mental health* (pp. 25–57). Pittsburgh: University of Pittsburgh Press.

Rice, M. F., & Winn, M. (1990). Black health care in America: A political perspective. *Journal of the National Medical Association, 82,* 429–437.

Ridley, C. R. (1984). Clinical treatment of the nondisclosing black client. *American Psychologist, 39,* 1234–1244.

Sata, L. (1990, April). *Working with persons from Asian backgrounds.* Paper presented at the Cross-Cultural Psychotherapy Conference, Hahnemann University, Philadelphia.

Smith, E. J. (1973). *Counseling the culturally different black youth.* Columbus, OH: Charles E. Merrill.

Smith, E. J. (1985). Ethnic minorities: Life stress, social support, and mental health issues. *The Counseling Psychologist, 13*(4), 537–579.

Spurlock, J. (1975). Psychiatric states. In R. Williams (Ed.), *A textbook of black-related diseases* (pp. 688–705). New York: McGraw-Hill.

Spurlock, J. (1982). Black Americans. In A. Gaw (Ed.), *Cross-Cultural Psychiatry* (pp. 163–178). Littleton, MA: PSG.

Spurlock, J., & Norris, D. (1992). The impact of culture and race on the development of African Americans in the United States. *Review of Psychiatry, 10,* 595–607.

Starr, P. (1986). Health care for the poor: The past twenty years. In S. Danziger & D. Weinberg (Eds.), *Fighting poverty: What works and what doesn't* (pp. 107–132). Cambridge, MA: Harvard University Press.

Stevenson, H. C., & Renard, G. (1993). Trusting ole' wise owls: Therapeutic use of cultural strengths in African American families. *Professional Psychology: Research and Practice, 24*(4), 433–442.

Sue, D. (1977). Community mental health services to minority groups. *American Psychologist, 32*(8), 616–624.

Sue, D. W., & Sue, D. (1990). *Counseling the culturally different.* New York: John Wiley & Sons.

Sue, S., & Zane, N. (1987). The role of culture and cultural techniques in psychotherapy: A critique and reformulation. *American Psychologist, 42,* 37–45.

Sullivan, L. W. (1989). Shattuck lecture—The health care priorities of the Bush administration. *New England Journal of Medicine, 321,* 125–128.

Thomas, A., & Sillen, A. (1972). *Racism and psychiatry.* New York: Brunner/Mazel.

U.S. Bureau of Census. (1991). *Poverty in the United States: 1991 (Current Population Reports, Series no. 181).* Washington, DC: U.S. Government Printing Office.

U.S. Bureau of Census. (1992). *Statistical abstracts of the United States: 1992.* Washington, DC: U.S. Government Printing Office.

U.S. Bureau of Census. (1994). *County and city data book.* Washington, DC: U.S. Government Printing Office.

U.S. Department of Health and Human Services. (1981). *Better health for our children: A national strategy* (Vols. 1–4). Washington, DC: Public Health Services.

U.S. Department of Health and Human Services. (1990). *Health status of minorities and low-income groups.* Washington, DC: Public Health Services.

U.S. Department of Health and Human Services. (1991). *Health status of the disadvantaged.* Washington, DC: Public Health Services.

U.S. House of Representatives. (1994). *The green book.* Washington, DC: U.S. Government Printing Office.

Wade, J. C. (1993). Institutional racism: An analysis of the mental health system. *American Journal of Orthopsychiatry, 63*(4), 536–544.

Wallen, J. (1992). Providing culturally appropriate mental health services for minorities. *The Journal of Mental Health Administration, 19*(3), 288–295.

Wells, K. B., Golding, J. M., Hough, R. L., Burnam, M.A., & Karno, M. (1989). Acculturation and the probability of use of health services by Mexican Americans. *Health Services Research, 24,* 237–257.

Wilson, D., & Lantz, E. (1957). The effect of cultural change in the Negro race in Virginia as indicated by a study of state hospital admissions. *American Journal of Psychiatry, 14,* 25–34.

Wilson, M. N. (1986). The black extended family: An analytical consideration. *Developmental Psychology, 22,* 246–258.

Chapter 13

Privatization and the Global Economy and Mental Health in Massachusetts

• *Matthew P. Dumont*

A GROWING NUMBER OF STATE GOVERNMENTS HAVE EMBARKED ON A policy of privatizing their mental health programs. This has profound implication for mental health professionals, our clients, and our communities. Subjecting mental health to market forces amounts to a repudiation of a public and collective responsibility for the care of the most helpless and disabled people in this society. It transforms our activities into commodities, forcing us to practice in unethical and professionally unsound ways as we become increasingly subordinate to business managers unconcerned with our true purposes.

While some professional organizations and public service unions have been engaged in *ad hoc* and local struggles with privatization, there has been little discussion and less understanding about its origins and implications on a larger scale. My purpose here is to offer a sketch of the international economic influences at work behind privatization and to describe the struggle against one particular manifestation of it in one locale: the privatization of public mental health services in Massachusetts. The source of the information for the more general issues is readings in economic history; for the particular, my personal experience. The latter was described in greater detail and depth in my book *Treating the Poor* (1992b), written after I was laid off from my job as a psychiatrist employed by the state at a newly privatized community mental health clinic in Chelsea, Massachusetts. In addition, I observed the effects of the privatization process in two Massachusetts state mental hospitals where I subsequently worked.

Even "leftists" these days have difficulty understanding a Marxist analysis of economic events. The manipulations of the media and the seductions of complexity have conspired to render what is simple and straightforward to an illiterate peasant in Haiti, esoteric and elusive to a college professor in Cambridge. I cannot hope to overcome such resistance in this space (or, perhaps, in any), but I am compelled to try. The Cassandra curse of the social critic is not in that he or she sees the future and is not believed but rather in the nagging, unrelenting thought that if one had only tried harder or been more skillful in describing one's vision, it would be shared by others.

The profits of capitalism reside very simply in the gap between something's use value and its market value. The utility of a spool of thread to make, mend, or embroider has a certain economic value. Call it X. What capitalism does is to hoard and later sell that spool, instead of using it, so as to extract an economic value greater that X. Call it Y. X is a good or service, an apple or a systems analysis, a thing more or less useful. Y is a commodity, an item of exchange that may or may not be useful. The greater the exchange value (Y) and the less the use value (X), the greater is the profit. Marx called this gap between the two (Y − X) the *surplus value,* and this theory is the central, simple transaction of the economic system that now rules the world.

To say that the profits in capitalism are inflationary is to miss the point. Profit *is* inflation. Anything that artificially inflates exchange values through monopoly or marketing is profitable, like tulips in the seventeenth century or designer jeans in the twentieth. And conversely, anything that suppresses use value also enhances profits, which is why economies are driven by luxuries, not by the basic necessities of life. War is profitable because it destroys use value, creating a sucking, murderous, terrestrial "black hole" of utility. It destroys rather than creates and, until recently, has been the quickest method of capital accumulation during the last five hundred years.

The conquest of the "New World" brought some vigor to the already decaying markets of Europe. The later invasions of Africa and Asia did the same. And now, after two world wars and several derivative ones, capital is again running out of things with which to expand. For it is precisely the expansion of capital that fuels its profitability, the illusion that there is something that remains to be done with it. The system cannot use such capital to house the homeless or feed the hungry because the returns are not great enough to warrant the investment. The other shore to which capitalism is forever building a bridge is forever receding. To achieve levels of return commensurate with the costs of the capital invested, the system can only build a bridge to nowhere.

Always incapable of reform, capitalism has become a system beyond repair. While in the past it was the inflated value of goods and services that provided the returns on investments (so-called productive capital), it is now the inflated value of credit itself ("finance capital") that fuels profits. The wealth of the world is now in its banks rather that in its factories and store-rooms. A bank's wealth is based on the illusion that its money is "working," that is, generating more money. It does not want its loans forfeited, nor does it want them paid off at once. Like a juggler who creates the illusion that there are more balls in the air than actually exist, the bank's loans can neither be "caught" nor "dropped," for the show is over either way.

The political dimension of all this juggling cannot be overemphasized. The Marxist axiom that all power is ultimately economic has been magnified by the distortions of the global economy. A former chairman of Citicorp stated in an offhand way that two-hundred thousand monitors in trading rooms all over the world conduct a "kind of plebiscite" on the policies of governments that issue currency—"there is no way for a nation to opt out" of this system. He described what happened when this "market" looked at the proposed programs of the newly elected "ardent socialist" François Mitterand of France in 1981: "within 6 months the capital flight [induced by the market] forced him to reverse course" (Brecher, 1993, p. 685). This shows where the world's power now rests and how even a *soi-disant* socialist becomes an even more ardent proponent of privatization.

One survey of eighty countries (Martin, 1994) where privatization was adopted as a public policy found that not only were the social costs evident but the promised economic benefits of a more efficient, market-based system did not materialize. The most immediate effects were in the laying off of public service workers and the destruction of their unions.

In Argentina, two-hundred thousand workers lost their jobs as result of privatization, and those who remained employed experienced a 20 percent reduction in income. Prime Minister Margaret Thatcher's vigorous privatization policies caused one-hundred thousand English workers to become jobless. In Peru, a law passed by President Alberto Fujimori's hand-picked, post-coup legislature gives sentences of three years to any worker in state-owned enterprises who actively opposes privatization. The sentence is doubled for trade union activists. And in New Zealand, privatization legislation specifically denies workers in previously publicly owned enterprises the right to form trade unions.

There is growing evidence describing the deterioration of public services once they are in private control:

•   After it was privatized, the water supply system in London suffered an increase in the frequency of breakdowns, and the reported incidence of water-borne infections tripled.

- In several Third World countries, when education programs were placed in private hands the ratio of teachers to students decreased, with some schools closing and others falling into disrepair.
- According to the International Labor Organization, the privatization of pensions in Chile resulted in employers failing to contribute to the pension funds, some of which failed, with a subsequent deterioration in the living conditions of pensioners.
- In South Africa, in anticipation of a government led by the African National Congress, the party formerly in power dramatically increased the pace of privatization so that a postapartheid government would have less control of the economy.

These are not random or merely "coincidental" situations. They are the systematic expression of the "new world order," the neoliberal confluence of social, economic, and political realities by those who define and control them through the manipulations of finance capital.

The World Bank and the International Monetary Fund (IMF) are the combined, governmentally controlled banking interests of the developed world, primarily its five richest countries. With their interlocking directorates they not only act in concert but point the direction and set the pace for the conjoined lending practices of private banks throughout the world. It is not only the giants of international banking like Citicorp and Bank of America that invest in Third World countries, for the small, friendly banks at the corner, which were supposed to invest their assets in their own communities, discovered during the 1980s that it was more profitable to join the stampede of credit to other nations. These "development loans," while couched in the socially conscionable terms of a shared responsibility for the economic well-being of the entire planet, are the major reason for the current misery of the "developing world."

There was never any question about the true purposes of such loans within their post–World War II origins: they were designed to create a dependence on the U.S. economy and to prevent war-torn and newly independent nations from turning to communism. They served to prop up the most corrupt and murderous elements in the Third World. In Haiti, Jean-Claude Duvalier, whose Ton-Ton Macoutes and their heirs are still committing murder and torture, was seen by John F. Kennedy as a "bullwark against communism in the Caribbean." The military killers who later drove out President Jean-Bertrand Aristide were armed and trained by the United States, and continued to be trained in this country even after the coup that was publicly condemned by the United States.

Throughout Latin America and the Caribbean, fascist dictators were "aided" by the United States with counterinsurgency military and police training in what became a series of wars fought by governments against their own citizens. Not only did this serve U.S. interests by suppressing left-wing revolutionary activity, but the "capital flight" of these dictators resulted in billions of dollars being invested in the banks of the United States and other developed countries. As tax burdens fall disproportionately on the American working poor, the system amounted to the poor of rich countries giving money to the rich of poor counties, to be given back to the rich of the rich countries for safekeeping. In nine developing countries surveyed during one ten-year period, a total of $150 billion of capital flight was estimated to have leaked back to the lending banks by corrupt politicians getting international loans (Hancock, 1989). The servicing of these loans involves austerity measures with cutbacks in social services such as health and education, with the result that it is the poor who are the ultimate debtor and the rich who are both creditor and beneficiary.

But this is not the most destructive feature of these loans. By "development" it is meant industrial and urban development with the implicit, inevitable, and systematic purpose of destroying rural economies. The local production of food is discouraged by the importation of cheap rice and cereals from the United States, which undersells the produce of native farmers who go out of business. Millions of rural people, whole populations from the countryside, are forced to seek jobs in the cities of the Third World. There, as a new army of the unemployed, they compete for scarce jobs in factories owned by international capitalists in situations where union organizing is suppressed. Giant corporations thus have a cheap, unorganized industrial labor force without having to be concerned with workplace safety and health issues as demanded by the unions in the developed world. The crowded shantytowns around every city of the Third World are the direct result of international lending practices. With a tidal wave of children turning to prostitution, the worldwide epidemic of AIDS becomes yet another direct result of international "development" loans.

While the IMF and the World Bank once gave such loans for specific and individual projects, they now focus on what is called "structural adjustment." This is the quickest and surest way of creating a desperate and impoverished industrial work force ready to serve capital. Along with austerity measures, including the elimination of food and fuel subsidies, of price controls, and wage reductions, these structural adjustment loans require that all publicly owned enterprises and utilities be privatized. This package of measures is now being applied in every single country that accepts IMF and World Bank credits. This state of affairs is the end result of a long process in the history of commerce. It is the story of the ultimate destruction of any social function of capitalism as a consequence of the inflated value of finance capital, when credit itself has become the sole source of profit and the only substance of exchange.

Fernand Braudel's (1984) exhaustive history of capitalism finds that profitability expands like an inverted pyramid as investments move inexorably from agriculture to manufacture to commerce and finally to credit. It is more profitable and less risky to make olive oil than to grow olives. It is still more profitable to be involved in the trade of olive oil than in its production. But it is most profitable of all to lend the money so that others can do the growing, manufacturing, and trading.

The trend over time for more investment to be made in banking and credit, rather than in other levels of business activity creates an increasingly inflated and unstable situation. Like an inverted pyramid expanding ever more rapidly at the top, it is destined to collapse, and once it does, it is beyond repair. Our current economy is one in which automobile companies make higher profits by lending the money for the buying of their cars than in their actual sales. The distribution of credit cards, like a gigantic "Ponzi" scheme, is the most profitable activity of banks. The consequence of lowered interest rates is not greater investment in manufacture and trade but the leveraging of buy-outs by one company of another, or worse, the absolutely inflationary and absolutely meaningless investment in currency itself. Each day the trillions of dollars exchanged in currency markets alone represent more goods and services than actually exist in the world.

This is what is unique about this era of capitalism: that so much capital is invested at so high a return in profit in so much insubstantial fluff, so far removed from human need or appetite. It is no longer possible for even a war to give it the semblance of vigor. War used to be "good" for capital because profit resides in the gap between use value and exchange value, and nothing expands the latter or destroys the former more effectively than war. But when an economy such as ours is so completely involved at the level of credit, even a war, costly as it is, cannot breathe life into it. In short, after about five hundred years, capitalism is now choking to death on an oversupply of overinflated credit.

This is why the privatization of public service is so desperate an initiative. Banks must keep their capital moving if the economy is to appear alive. No longer able to invest in factories for a useless war machine and with the housing market exhausted, they turned to education, health, transportation, waste management, prisons, and mental health.

But does not the government have an ongoing responsibility for basic human needs? Apparently not. It is not that the government lies, although it does. It is not even that the government lies all the time. Government *is* a lie. This is one of the implications of Braudel's history. What has masqueraded as an instrument for dealing with shared human needs or at least for moderating among various interest groups in some approximation of human need is actually always and everywhere, the instrument of commerce. Government, in a capitalist society, *is business.*

When business became so desperately dependent on credit manipulations that traditional public "responsibilities" had to be privatized in order to justify the further expansion of credit, government accommodated by merely selling those responsibilities. The private corporations taking them over have to borrow money, at prevailing interest rates, to develop the mechanisms and personnel for their execution. The media, itself an instrument of capital, cooperates by depicting public agencies as inept and their employees as corrupt, lazy, and self-indulgent. The lowering of taxes is presented as the major justification for privatization, and in the process public service unions (the most vigorous sector of the dwindling labor movement) are systematically destroyed, but the driving force and major purpose of the privatization of human services are to give banks something to do with their capital.

The fact that so-called non-profit institutions are given contracts for what were once public administrations of schools, highways, clinics, and prisons should not confuse the issue. Institutions that are not apparently or nominally for profit have always functioned as the conduit for funds to be transferred from the public into banks and other lending institutions that are very much *for* profit. The trustees of universities, medical centers, and foundations control billions of dollars of investment capital, and they themselves are generally the directors and executives of enterprises deeply involved with the direction of that money.

This complex ecology of deception and greed surrounds and dictates the function of individuals and institutions that are unconsciously in the service of finance capital. The traditionally defined responsibilities of local and state government are everywhere being put up for sale in tune with the same banking interests that control the destiny of the rest of the world. When schools, highways, prisons, waste disposal, and water supply systems are taken over by private enterprise (profit or "nonprofit"), loans must be floated to the contractors for start-up and sustaining expenses, which are paid back to the lenders (always for profit) at prevailing interest levels out of the pockets of the people.

I watched the process and effects of one small rivulet of this tidal wave of change in the form of the privatization of mental health services in Massachusetts. As always, the social costs of this initiative were massive, immediate, and obvious, as was the protest against them. A coalition of public service unions, patient advocacy groups, patients themselves, and their clinicians devoted two years to organizing, educating themselves and the public, and lobbying legislators, which resulted in the enactment in 1994, over the governor's veto, of a bill that significantly slowed the process of privatization.

While not the total moratorium desired by some of us, the law, drawn up as the Pacheco Bill, imposes on the state the obligation to demonstrate that actual cost savings would occur with a private contract, and permits public servants through their unions the opportunity to compete with the private sector in cost containment and quality of services. There is also, for the first time, a legislative monitoring function imposed on those private contracts that are signed.

Despite these minimal constraints on privatization, the legislation was bitterly opposed by lobbyists for private interests and by the governor himself, whose philosophy of "entrepreneurial government" was based on the assumption that market forces brought efficiency, economy, and quality to public services. The leadership of his Department of Mental Health (DMH) operationalized his philosophy with a program based on "downsizing" (i.e., consolidating and closing) mental hospitals, laying off clinicians working in outpatient settings, and contracting out as many direct or indirect services as quickly as possible. The central office of the DMH insisted that privatizing its programs would make them "equal or better" than those provided by its own employees. The realities told a different story. The privatization of outpatient clinics in Massachusetts was associated with the laying-off of nine hundred publicly salaried professionals. Contracts to private providers involved at least a 25 percent reduction in clinical personnel. In some cases whole clinics were closed and others consolidated. Patients accustomed to local, easily accessible centers or to home visits when they were house-bound were often referred to larger and more distant facilities. It is not known how many patients subsequently dropped out of treatment, but observations from several facilities suggest that the number was considerable. Those lost to treatment were often those most in need: the elderly, the disabled, and the socially incompetent.

Community clinics used to be the first places to be contacted when a patient became suicidal or psychotic. In their absence, the emergency wards of general hospitals become the only recourse. There, after as much as a six-hour wait, a psychiatric resident who does not know the patient must evaluate a suicidal risk or other potential for violence. Errors are more frequent in such settings, with the attendant financial and human costs. This is on top of the inflated cost of any emergency ward visit itself, which, through Medicaid or other insurers, is passed on to the general public.

The closing, consolidation and privatization of state mental hospitals in Massachusetts have been even more devastating for patients. A century after the pioneering reforms of Dorothea Dix, the impoverished mentally ill are once again being found in the Commonwealth's streets, jails, and shelters (the "almshouses" of the day). In a nine-month period in 1992, at least 170 people were found to have been discharged to two major shelters for the homeless in Boston, and following the closing of one state hospital, one shelter reported a 40 percent increase in the number of mentally ill people seeking admission (Massachusetts Human Services Coalition, 1992).

The private psychiatric hospitals or inpatient units of general hospitals expected to replace the state hospitals are themselves intolerant to these patients. They are disinclined to accept "disposition problems" who strain their utilization review guidelines, and in some situations have already revealed their capacity to abuse public contracts through "creative accounting" and "case-mix management" techniques of questionable legality.

In any case, even when private facilities accept violent, disorganized, or homeless psychiatric patients, they do so for brief periods, which means that more patients are stuck in a useless, expensive, and demoralizing pattern of repeated admissions. The consequence is greater numbers of psychotic people in the streets and more deaths from exposure, suicide, or homicide. A major study of over nine thousand patients with schizophrenia admitted to Danish psychiatric hospitals between 1970 and 1988 resolved that the effect of shortening the stay of admission for the first episode from an average of fifty days to an average of thirty days was a *doubling* in the suicide rate of such patients (Goleman, 1993, March 26).

It is hard to convey the depth of individual misery that resides in these realities. One year after I was laid off by the Massachusetts Department of Mental Health from a clinic in which I had worked for sixteen years, one of my former patients committed suicide. I had seen him through a series of crises for fifteen years. He lived an isolated and paranoid existence. I may have been his only social contact, his only friend. He accepted my departure matter-of-factly but refused to go across the bridge from Chelsea to Boston to the mental hospital where he was told to "get his medicine." The home visits, the encounters in the street, the waves from the window, the whole pattern of informal and easy access that adds up to a community mental health program was lost to privatization. I believe the loss killed him.

In August of 1994, when hospital and clinic "downsizing" was already well established, the Boston news was dominated by the shooting of two police officers in separate incidents. One of them was killed. There were pictures of grieving families and fellow officers. Just behind the pathos and bitterness of these events was the information that in both cases the shootings were by "mentally deranged" people whose access to mental health care had been compromised by "lack of insurance" and unavailable public services. Privatization is a killer ("Police Killings in Boston," 1994, August 31, p. C9).

The phasing-down period in state mental hospitals scheduled to close is highly stressful for that population least easily discharged, the most violent and helpless. They may be transferred from one ward to another repeatedly before relocation to another institution. The staffs are facing lay-offs or a confused and demoralized "bumping" procedure. They tend to be dispirited, angry, and less motivated. In one institution the consequence was a dramatic rise in the number of serious incidents such as assaults, fires, suicides, and accidents, some resulting in death. The overall frequency of incidents declined with the numbers of patients (a fact reported with pride by the Department of Mental Health), but percentages of *dangerous* incidents rose precipitously.

With state hospital closing, there are also growing numbers of exhausted, guilt-ridden, and furious family members (generally mothers) trying to cope with the demands of former patients. In addition, increasing numbers of psychotic and homeless people in the streets and shelters are accompanied by a greater risk of random violence and the spread of infection.

But these are not the only burden to the community resulting from privatization. Community-based mental health clinics are capable of detecting clusters of complaints that may be the first expression of a point source of heavy metal or organic solvent toxicity (Dumont, 1989). Larger and more centralized clinics cannot so easily determine that workers in a local factory are being exposed to neurotoxic substances whose earliest effects are irritability, insomnia, anxiety, depression, or acute psychosis. A community source of poisoning, such as the dust in a playground under a lead-painted bridge, may be detected through an unusual clustering of learning or behavior problems presented at a local clinic and missed entirely by the staff of a more remote medical center.

In addition, when staff in privatized outpatient settings are paid on the basis of their direct encounters with patients, they are less likely to devote the time needed to explore the source of a cluster of complaints. It is more remunerative for a private program to place people on antianxiety drugs than to meet with community leaders, industrial hygienists, or union representatives about a focus of heavy metal or organic solvent toxicity. It is far more expensive to the community, however. The lifetime costs of a single case of lead poisoning may be greater than the entire annual budget of a community mental health clinic. The smallest effort of prevention and advocacy can save millions of dollars and avoid endless misery and disability. However, such efforts are not encouraged in private clinics (Dumont, 1990, 1992a, 1992b).

This is only one of the constraints under which mental health professionals are now operating. Practitioners face joblessness in greater numbers than ever. Graduate programs in social work, psychology, and nursing continue to generate eager clinicians anticipating careers as psychotherapists.

But jobs are less available, the private practice marketplace is already flooded, and private clinics are turning away from long-term psychotherapy in favor of brief, time-limited treatments dictated by third-party payment schemes. Managed care programs arbitrarily limit the number of sessions available to clients, and case management and drug therapy have replaced supportive psychotherapy for more seriously disturbed patients.

The increasingly scarce jobs for mental health professionals are themselves becoming more routinized, less thoughtful, less in their own control—in short, less professional. At the very moment when a therapist, after many slow, painful hours, has been able to establish a relationship with a brutalized child, who is just beginning to open to another human being, then, suddenly, an arbitrary, third-party constraint on the number of sessions paid for may force the termination of treatment.

Diagnosis related groups (DRGs) are clusters of disease categories organized on the basis of the nature and duration of treatment. This and other formulas for controlling the costs of privatized treatment do not permit a professional judgment to be made. Case discussions, when they take place at all, become meaningless exercises about arbitrary and fictive diagnostic categories (Dumont, 1987). There is no opportunity for a real and shared discussion about patients as human beings. Deliberations about ethics, mutual support, and peer supervision are out of the question.

Clinicians in privatized settings are often paid on a fee-for-service arrangement that compels them to think in terms of billable hours of direct service rather than the actual requirements of a situation. Telephone contacts or discussions with family members, teachers, or other professionals are systematically discouraged. When incentive practice arrangements are built in, the clinician is actually paid on the basis of how much money he or she generates. This imposes a demeaning and demoralizing piecework mentality. Physiological measures of stress are higher when a task is rewarded on the basis of piecework rather than a salary (Johnson, 1989). In the absence of mutual support, this translates into higher rates of coronary heart disease, peptic ulcers, and hypertension as well as simple "burn-out."

A professional may try to keep his or her behavior independent of financial considerations. However, a weekly or monthly "productivity" report relating to income or job security is hard to ignore, particularly when transmitted by an officious supervisor. Such a regular feedback system may even represent an operant-conditioning situation in which the clinician unconsciously makes decisions based on productivity reports while still believing that ethical or clinical considerations are the guiding ones.

In private mental hospitals, insurance and utilization review criteria result in patients being kept only so long as the coverage lasts and often being discharged *on the day* it runs out. Clinical staff must interrupt their treatment and swallow their anxiety about a possibly suicidal or homicidal patient being discharged prematurely. The burden of legal and ethical responsibility remains with the clinicians, but business managers are making the decisions.

Privatization comes with a bit of contemporary cultural garbage, the mythology of management. Suffused with the arrogance and self-righteousness of a newly acquired vocabulary, holders of an MBA degree act like field marshals when confronting clinicians. They are armed with computers that generate and demand more information than is actually needed. They create their own reality and justify their own existence. Everything is reduced to millions of bits of yes-no decisions that are a mockery of the complexity and ambiguity of human suffering and its relief.

Computerized information is a matter of counting and organizing isolated units. Mental health does not reside in such fragmented bits of data. The treatment of mental illness cannot be understood within them. An hour with a person on the verge of suicide is not the same as an hour with a chronically psychotic patient or with an abused child. Managers and their computers redefine mental health considerations as financial ones. All patient sessions are seen in the same way and generate the same amount of money, and the more money a clinician generates, the more competent he or she is thought to be.

This is all couched in a double-think mystification that can itself drive a clinician crazy. During the hospital and clinic closings and lay-offs in Massachusetts, central office managers were talking about "right-sizing" the system, "spreading hope," "accentuating the positive," and being "consumer driven." They instituted a "quality management" system relying on computerized print-outs and slogans that belied the facts of homelessness and violence that they had caused. Indeed, despite the Disneyland, happy-face vocabulary it used, the Department of Mental Health successfully argued in court that it should have no responsibility for the care of patients who where thrown into the community after decades of residence in the state hospital system.

Along with the growing body of experience about the devastating consequences of privatization on the mentally ill and their families, there were widely reported instances of overt fraud in privatized settings (Alliance for the Mentally Ill of Massachusetts, 1993). In addition a Post Audit and Oversight Committee report by the Massachusetts Senate revealed that reported "savings" of privatization did not, in fact, materialize (Massachusetts Senate, 1993). Such information, along with case histories and expert opinions, were part of an organized and eventually successful campaign to enact the Pacheco Bill.

As in all such campaigns, this victory was made possible by the building of alliances among interest groups that were not naturally affiliated. Patients in a state mental hospital are usually a culture apart from and often in conflict with the clinical teams responsible for them. When privatization threatened to close a unit or result in lay-offs in one state hospital, patients mobilized along with staff to sign petitions, confront managers, and call legislators. The process was active, cooperative, and effective, and while not defined as a "mental health" activity, it had obvious benefits for the patients, who experienced a sense of participation in something outside themselves as well as a burst of self-esteem in its outcome. The discussions about mutual responsibility and the political economy governing their treatment (who decides and why) were not only a process of political education but a variety of psychotherapy.

The Alliance for the Mentally Ill (AMI) of Massachusetts, an organization of family members of psychiatric patients, was not previously in a confrontational position with the DMH and indeed was dependent on DMH funds for some of its staff expenses. In addition, it had so completely bought into the biological determinism of current psychiatric opinion that it tended to deemphasize the psychosocial and rehabilitation activities of state hospital care. However, after many meetings the AMI found itself in a solid alliance with clinicians and public service unions in a challenge to the privatization policies of the DMH.

The building of such alliances is happening all over the world. Throughout Latin America, in particular, student groups, trade unionists, intellectuals, and peasants are recognizing their common ground in opposition to the forces of international finance capital. This is being expressed in electoral politics as well as in revolutionary guerrilla activity.

In Venezuela, a man who began as a union militant in an underground political party became the mayor of Caracas. Only months before he had been in a fist fight with bank guards during a protest over the selling of the state-owned telephone company to a North American consortium. Now Aristobula Izturiz runs the major city and capital of the second largest supplier of oil to the United States. He believes that basic and strategic services . . . should remain in the hands of the state.

This is part of a growing understanding of the destructive effects of international banking, global corporate behavior, and trade alliances such as North American Free Trade Agreement (NAFTA) and General Agreement on Tariffs and Trade (GATT). The destruction of rural economies, mass unemployment, migration, and urbanization and the threats to the very survival of peasants, workers, and the world's ecology are crystallizing around the issue of privatization. And, at last, the responsibilities and self-interest of mental health professionals in such places as Massachusetts have found their common path with the revolutionary activities of the most deprived people in the world.

REFERENCES

Alliance for the Mentally Ill of Massachusetts. (1993, March). *Alliance for the Mentally Ill of Massachusetts Newsletter,* No. 44.

Braudel, F. (1984). *Civilization and capitalism: XV–XVIII centuries* (Vols. 1–3). New York: Harper & Row.

Brecher, J. (1993, December 6). Global village or global pillage? *The Nation,* p. 685.

Dumont, M. (1987). A diagnostic parable: A review of DSM-III-R—Readings. *American Orthopsychiatric Association,* 2(4), 9.

Dumont, M. (1989). Psychotoxicology: The return of the Mad Hatter. *Social Science and Medicine,* 29(2), 1077.

Dumont, M. (1990). Managed care, managed people, and community mental health [Editorial]. *American Journal of Orthopsychiatry,* 60(2), p. 166.

Dumont, M. (1992a). Privatization of mental health services: The invisible hand at our throats [Editorial]. *American Journal of Orthopsychiatry,* 62(3), p. 328.

Dumont, M. (1992b). *Treating the poor: A personal sojourn through the rise and fall of community mental health.* Belmont, MA: Dymphna Press.

Goleman, D. (1993, March 26). Gold mine of psychiatric data discovered in Danish registry. *The New York Times,* p. A4.

Hancock, G. (1989). *Lords of poverty: The power, prestige, and corruption of the international aid business.* New York: Atlantic Monthly Press.

Johnson, J. (1989). Collective control: Strategies for survival in the workplace. *International Journal of Health Services,* 19 p. 469.

Martin, B. (1994). *In the public interest.* London: Zed Books.

Massachusetts Human Services Coalition. (1992, December 16). *State House Watch,* 10(19), p. 1.

Massachusetts Senate. (1993). *A review of DMH policy planning and implementation during the closing of Northampton State Hospital.*

Police killings in Boston by mentally deranged. (1994, August 31). *The New York Times,* p. C9.

Part V

Consciousness-Raising, Action, and Community Change

Chapter 14

Women's Abortion Experiences as Sources of Political Mobilization

• *Abigail J. Stewart and Sharon Gold-Steinberg*

POLITICAL CONSCIOUSNESS AND IDEOLOGY PROBABLY ALWAYS BEAR SOME relationship to personal experience, although the connections may be complex (see Clayton & Crosby, 1986). For some people that relationship originates in broad-based distress over their own privilege, or anger and frustration over their own (and beloved family members') disadvantage. For example, when Winifred Holtby, the English feminist novelist of the early twentieth century, went to South Africa, she was shocked and moved to action by the poverty and discrimination suffered by so many Africans as a result of British colonialism (see several of Holtby's articles from 1927 to 1934, reprinted in Berry & Bishop, 1985). Indigenous leaders like Nelson Mandela may be moved to action by their rage and determination to end the oppression suffered by their own people. Sometimes specific experiences may catalyze the development of political consciousness. For example, Mahatma Gandhi was first moved to critique and act against British colonialism by his own searing experience of discrimination and racism on a South African train (Gandhi, 1929/1957). Similarly, political mobilization may result from direct exposure to charismatic leaders like Mandela and Gandhi (or, for Bill Clinton, to John F. Kennedy) or to political ideology. The impact of exposure to political ideas is described by Malcolm X, when he recounts his prison reading and discussions of Elijah Muhammad's teachings (Haley, 1965), and by Vera Brittain in her account of first reading about feminism in the writings of feminist theorist Olive Schreiner (Brittain, 1933/1970, p. 41). Because leaders and ideas can be such potent mobilizing tools, political movements and political parties try to use them to increase political consciousness.

Other kinds of experiences may also be important sources of political mobilization. These experiences may be fairly abstract yet deeply felt at the individual level. Thus, some persons respond to acts of violence undertaken by their nation with deep sadness and passionate objection; others respond with intense identification with the cause. Both of these responses can create, intensify, or sharpen political consciousness, as they did in civilian and military responses to the Vietnam War. Similarly, individuals may be directly involved in a large- or small-scale collective event (e.g., during the early 1990s, the violence in Los Angeles following the acquittal of the police officers involved with the beating of Rodney King), or may observe that event at a distance and still find it profoundly important (e.g., the confirmation hearings for Clarence Thomas in 1991). These events, too, may affect political consciousness. Cross (1971) suggests that the assassination of Martin Luther King, Jr., was an important politicizing event for many black Americans. Similarly, many observers (see, e.g., Bordo, 1993; Morrison, 1992) have suggested that watching Anita Hill's attempt to challenge Clarence Thomas's qualifications for the Supreme Court—as well as the public response to her—raised feminist consciousness among women in an unprecedented way. Ann Lopez (1993, July–August) reported that formal sexual harassment complaints filed at the Equal Employment Opportunity Commission (EEOC) numbered 10, 532 in 1992, up from 6,883 in 1991. A spokesperson from the EEOC is quoted as commenting, "It's pretty clear that the increase is due to the Hill-Thomas hearing." (p. 87). Finally, individuals may become politically engaged as a result of their exposure to social movements, such as the civil rights and women's movement; (see Echols, 1989; Evans, 1979; Giddings, 1984).

Personal events can also be experienced as having implications for political consciousness. For example, being denied medical treatment at a hospital, being mugged, being raped, and being assaulted because of your apparent race, ethnicity, or sexual orientation are all physical experiences that also carry potential political meaning. For some people, under some conditions, experiencing these situations mobilizes political consciousness and action (see Estrich's 1987 account of her rape). If the events are felt to result from individuals' acts or failings, they are unlikely to result in political action or ideology. According to several different theories (Crosby, 1982; Gurin, 1985; Ryan, 1971), though, if the events are seen as a function of social forces or systematic inequities, and those inequities are seen as amenable to change, then individuals may be moved to collective action. Under these conditions, "private troubles" get recognized as public issues. As Mills (1959) put it, "Both the correct statement of the problem and the range of possible solutions require us to consider the economic and political institutions of the society and not merely the personal situation and character of a scatter of individuals" (p. 9).

In the early 1970s and now again in the 1990s, abortion was and is being experienced by many women as a physical event with a substantial political meaning. In the early seventies, abortion was illegal in most places and therefore difficult to obtain (see Lee, 1969; Messer & May, 1988; Petchesky, 1990; Tatalovich & Daynes, 1981, for accounts of abortion in this period). Women who experienced unwanted pregnancies were forced by the legal situation to consider breaking the law and jeopardizing their own health and safety. Because abortion was illegal, many women went through abortions with little community support or publicly sanctioned help. However, as changes in the law became the focus of women's movement activity, a feminist community did provide support to women who wanted abortions. Later abortions were legal, although in the early period after *Roe v. Wade* (1973), some clinics were insensitive to the personal and moral dilemma abortion presented to many women who nevertheless sought them.

ABORTION AND POLITICAL MOBILIZATION

In her study of activists who were either pro-choice or anti-abortion, Ginsburg (1989) found that both groups linked their political activism with their own personal reproductive histories, including abortion experiences. She argues that "for almost all of the activists . . . reproduction is a key turning point, not as a biological occurrence but as a class of life-cycle events that forced an encounter with the inequalities of a gendered social world" (pp. 143–144). Ginsburg suggests, then, that women's personal experiences of pregnancy, abortion, and birth may lead them to political analyses: "because procreation in American culture is so deeply connected to asymmetrical understandings of male and female, any question raised about procreation is, necessarily, also one about gender identity and cultural reproduction" (p. 144).

Ginsburg posits a general tendency for women to find political meaning in reproductive experience (although her sample is limited to abortion activists). She argues, though, that the particular meaning found in abortion and other reproductive events depends not only on an individual woman's history and situation, but also on her generation and age at the time of the experience. Drawing on Mannheim's (1952) notion of generations, Ginsburg points out that the pro-choice activists were generally born between 1942 and 1952, while the pro-life activists were mostly born between 1950 and 1964. The critical issue for their reactions to reproductive experiences is not their date of birth but their transition to adulthood. Ginsburg suggests that the older cohort reached adulthood in the late 1960s and early 1970s, "at a time when feminism and reproductive rights activity were culturally ascendant" (p. 140). In contrast, the younger cohort became mothers later, when "feminism was on the wane as an active social movement and pro-life and anti-ERA [Equal Rights Amendment] activity were on the rise" (p. 140).

Stewart and Healy (1989) have similarly argued that the intersection of a cohort's coming of age with a period of dramatic social change is likely to result in more individuals consciously constructing personal identities in terms of social or political events. Thus, the pro-choice activists in Ginsburg's sample, who came of age during the turbulent late sixties, would be expected to develop political ideologies and personal identities in terms of the most personally relevant social events of that time. In contrast, individuals who come of age in periods of relative social stability are less likely to formulate identities in terms of political events. However, powerful personal experiences could (as Ginsburg found) provide a different basis for developing a politicized identity.

It seems clear, then, that the political and social context can provide a political shape to personal experiences. In this chapter we will explore how and when abortion experiences were sources of political mobilization for a sample of women not selected as activists but chosen instead because they had experienced abortions during the years surrounding the transformation of abortion itself from an illegal to a legal procedure. In the fall of 1989, Gold-Steinberg gathered questionnaire data from seventy-three women who had had abortions in the fifteen-year period between 1963 and 1978 (see Gold-Steinberg, 1991, for detailed descriptions of measures and sampling procedures). Half of these women had had legal abortions; half had had illegal abortions. All of the women in the sample were European American. Gold-Steinberg's primary goal was to assess the similarities and differences in the long-term implications of having had legal or illegal abortions. In this chapter we will focus on the similar and different political (versus mental health and other) implications of those two different experiences.

LOOKING BACK ON ABORTION
EXPERIENCES

The questionnaire asked women to describe their abortion experience in considerable detail, and also asked a variety of open- and closed-ended questions about women's mental and physical health, their lives since that time, their political views and activities, and their feelings about their own abortion and abortion policies in general. The women were recruited by advertising at women's organizations and political demonstrations, and by "snowball" sampling from early respondents. Because the sample was obtained in this way, it included women who, although not necessarily activists, were generally political, feminist, and pro-choice. Even so, we anticipated that the experiences of having had legal or illegal abortions, although similar in some respects, would be different in their political ramifications. Several women in the sample also participated in lengthy open-ended interviews exploring their abortion experiences in more depth. We will draw both on the questionnaire and interview data in exploring the political meaning of legal and illegal abortions in the period surrounding *Roe v. Wade*.

Abortion is not a simple experience, whether legal or illegal. It includes the experience of pregnancy—specifically pregnancy that is either unwanted or untimely. For all women faced with an unwanted pregnancy, certain aspects of their social situation, including inequality between the sexes, are highlighted. The decision about what to do—and the consequences of that decision—weigh unequally on the two sexual partners whose activity resulted in the pregnancy. For every woman   regardless of the legal, moral, and community context of abortion—this difference is likely to raise her awareness of the meaning of her gender in her life and relationships. Thus, untimely pregnancy, regardless of its outcome or the legal context of abortion, has the potential to remind all women in a powerful way of the degree to which they face different fates from men and share in the situation of all women. It should heighten gender consciousness and a sense of "common fate" with other women. In addition, it should enhance the tendency to blame the system rather than the individual for women's lower status. These are all preconditions for political mobilization, according to Crosby (1982), Gurin (1985; see also Gurin & Townsend, 1986), and William Ryan (1971).

Having any abortion (as opposed to an unwanted pregnancy) in twentieth century U.S. culture raises both medical and moral issues for women (Petchesky, 1990). For women who experienced illegal abortions, abortion carried with it in addition both the stigma of crime and the danger of an unregulated medical procedure. The possibilities of arrest, of complications followed by difficulty obtaining medical treatment, and of mistreatment by those performing the abortions all served to heighten the anxiety associated with the experience and the woman's sense of vulnerability. Obviously these factors increased the likelihood of abortion being traumatic and having certain psychological effects. In addition, though, in the political domain, illegal abortions underlined women's specific powerlessness under a legal and medical system that constrained the safe alternatives for handling an unwanted pregnancy. Illegal abortions revealed the importance of political change to reduce the unfair burden carried by women when an unwanted pregnancy occurred. For that reason we expected that illegal abortions, while not necessarily more likely to be saturated with political meaning, were more likely to result in women connecting their personal experience with a feminist ideology and political activism.

POLITICAL CONSCIOUSNESS
AFTER ABORTIONS

Consistent both with the nature of our sample and our expectation that all abortions would raise gender consciousness, we found no differences between the two groups of women on gender identification, or on individual or system blame for women's lower status. As expected, both groups scored relatively high on gender identification (means of 5.3 and 5.5 on a scale from 1 to 7) and system blame for women's status (means of 3.1 and 3.2 on a scale from 1 to 4), and low on individual blame (means of 1.2 and 1.3 on a scale from 1 to 4). Overall, 45.2 percent of the women, regardless of the type of abortion they had experienced, reported that having had an abortion changed their feelings about being a woman. More than half of these women said that the nature of that change was that they became more aware of inequalities between the sexes. As one woman who had had a legal abortion said, "It made me more aware of women's rights, or lack of them." Another, who had had an illegal abortion, also focused on the biological vulnerability associated with being a woman: "I felt that I had been victimized, and became more aware of how vulnerable women's biology can make us if we are not allowed access to abortion and birth control." However, another focused more on the political issues: "I felt oppressed as a woman. It was one of the first real incidents of harm done to me by a system not made by me." Another woman wrote: "As a result of not being able to get an abortion, I felt like I was totally controlled by a male-dominated world of politicians and AMA doctors. I felt persecuted for my sexuality."

Many women indicated that having an abortion changed their views on other women's issues. For example, one woman who had had a legal abortion described how needing an abortion made her aware of women's special vulnerabilities and strengths: "I became a feminist shortly after having had an abortion. I began realizing how vulnerable women are in this culture and in the world in general. I decided that to change that, I had to learn to love myself and appreciate other women for what they have accomplished and survived in their lives." Similarly, a woman who had had an illegal abortion described its effect on her: "It pissed me off that I had to go through the fear, the humiliation, the expense that I eventually became an activist regarding women's rights. "Another wrote: "It made me determined to do whatever I could to prevent other women from having a similar dreadful experience! I worked with groups which were trying to legalize abortion, and testified before a special commission that the governor [of my state] convened to explore the need for legalization."

Virtually all of the women in the sample were pro-choice at mid-life; half of them said that their abortion had changed their political stance on abortion. Thirty of the thirty-seven women who said this, said that the abortion had made them more liberal in their beliefs. As one woman who had had an illegal abortion put it: "It's difficult to judge how having an abortion may have affected my life, but I suspect it didn't do much to alter the course of my life except to increase my awareness of and commitment to pro-choice politics." Another, who had had a legal abortion, similarly commented that "it made me more aware of the necessity for women to always have this option legally available to us." One woman did report that she had become more conservative (pro-life) since her legal abortion, although she attributed this change in her political consciousness to a powerful religious experience two years after she had terminated her pregnancy rather than to the abortion per se. The others said it had made them more sensitive to the implications of abortion decisions. For one woman, the experience of a legal abortion led her to be "more sensitive to the plight of poor women," while another said: "I think it's made me a very tolerant person. I know very well that even the best plans of the 'smartest' people can fall through and cause awful problems. I know now that each situation is unique and should be treated as such."

There were also some clear, and statistically significant, differences between the two groups.[1] Women who had experienced illegal abortions reported that they had felt less control over the options they had (mean = 4.81 versus 6.00 for those with legal abortions); that they thought others did not view abortion as acceptable (mean = 2.65 versus 3.55); that it had taken them longer to arrange their abortions (mean = 3.8 weeks versus 1.5); that their abortions had occurred significantly later in the pregnancy (mean = 11.7 weeks versus 8.9 weeks); that their abortions had cost more (mean = $487 versus $218); and that their abortions had taken place farther away from their home (mean distance was closer to 100 miles, while for legal abortions it was under 50). Only about one-third of the women in either group was accompanied by anyone to her abortion; however, many more of the women who had had legal abortions reported that they had received counseling about what to expect (75% versus 31%), about making whatever decision was in their own best interest (51% versus 11%), and about birth control (78% versus 11%).

In addition, as we expected, women who had had illegal abortions recalled much higher levels of anxiety about the dangers associated with the abortion. Specifically, they were more worried about being hurt (mean = 3.78 versus 2.51), dying (mean = 3.17 versus 1.60), getting arrested (mean = 2.89 versus 1.00), becoming sterile (mean = 2.57 versus 1.73), and being molested during the procedure (mean = 1.54 versus 1.00). One woman simply described it as "a barbaric procedure" that had left her "emotionally scarred." Another said: "I felt isolated, anxious, fearful. I felt angry at having to go through such a horrible thing by myself. In some ways, I felt numb—I was really trying to deny the possibility of death. . . . I did develop complications after." Still another reported that

> after I began to lose so much blood that my husband was filling Turkish bath towels with it, he decided to take me to the hospital. My mother stood in his way (he had to carry me because I was too weak to walk) and tried to stop us because she said it was illegal and we would be in terrible trouble. But my husband pushed her aside, because he said he didn't want me to die. The doctors refused to give me any pain medication to try to force me to tell who had done the abortion. I didn't tell them.

Overall, then, the women's retrospective reports suggest that both legal and illegal abortions had raised their consciousness about gender inequality. However, illegal abortions also carried with them greater difficulty, stigma, and isolation along with an intensity of recalled fear and danger. Coping with these features of their experience not only intensified it, but may also have encouraged the women's politicization. Women whose experiences were more dangerous and aroused more intense affect were faced with a more powerful stressor. Their efforts to master or cope with the experiences demanded more of them, both in terms of an explanation (perhaps to be found in feminism) and instrumental action to restore a sense of personal efficacy. For these reasons, we expected that frightening abortion experiences, when they cried out for a system-level explanation (that is, when they took place in an illegal context), were more likely to politicize women than either more affectively neutral abortions in an illegal context or frightening abortions in a legal context. We returned to the original data set and conducted more extensive analyses to explore this issue further.

TRANSFORMING PRIVATE TROUBLES

We assessed politicization in terms of a variety of forms of political participation in the recent past (from giving money and writing letters for causes
and campaigns to giving speeches and actively lobbying). We expected that
women who had had illegal abortions that were especially frightening would
be likely to seek to transform their personal experience of gender-based helplessness and vulnerability into political efficacy. In contrast, we expected that
women who had had legal abortions or less frightening illegal ones would be
much less likely to base their political activism (or ideology) on their personal
experience of abortion. Path analyses tested our hypothesized connection between personal experience and political activism for the two groups. According to our model, preconditions of political activism for all the women
should include strong gender identification as well as low levels of self-blame
and high levels of system blame for women's status. For women who had had
illegal abortions, we expected that personal experience would be linked to
these ideological measures that would, in turn, be linked to political activism.

For women who had had legal abortions in the early period after *Roe v.
Wade,* there was no connection between personal experience and either political ideology (gender identification or self- or system blame for women's
status) or political activism. In contrast, in Figure 14-1 we can see that for
women who had had illegal abortions, there was a relationship between personal abortion experience and gender ideology, and a clear connection between that gender ideology and political activism.

For both groups, there was a close, inverse linkage between individual
and system blame for women's status, and a positive connection between system blame and gender identification. For the women who had experienced

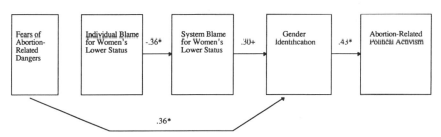

Figure 14-1   Path analysis showing links among the circumstances of abortion, aspects of gender consciousness, and political activism among women who had illegal
abortions. *First asterisk* indicates ($p < 0.05$) high scores on individual blame predict
low scores on system blame. *Cross* indicates ($p < 0.10$) high scores on system blame
tend to predict high scores on gender identification. *Second asterisk* indicates ($p <
0.05$) high scores on gender indentification predict high scores on political activism.

illegal abortions, other connections were equally close. Women who recalled having had many fears at the time of the abortion had higher levels of gender identification, and stronger gender identification in turn predicted political activism. In short, for women in this sample who had had illegal abortions in the late sixties and early seventies, that experience was deeply connected with their general and specific political beliefs as well as their political actions. For even the politically active women in this sample who had had legal abortions in the early and mid-seventies, that experience was not connected with either their general or particular political beliefs or their activism. The availability of legal, medically safe abortions appeared to be a permanently secured right for women; women might suffer personal pain as a result of the moral, emotional, relational, or medical problems they faced, but they did not experience their abortions as carrying political meaning. By exploring two particular cases, we can articulate more specifically how and why political connections were made for women who had experienced frightening illegal abortions, but not for women who had experienced even very difficult legal abortions. We will also briefly explore why some illegal abortions—which were not particularly frightening—also did not result in politicization.

ILLEGAL ABORTION AND COLLECTIVE ACTION

Sarah's illegal abortion occurred in 1968 in Chicago. She was twenty-eight years old at the time, and considered herself to be an antiwar and civil rights activist committed to the cause of social justice. An analysis of Sarah's story demonstrates, however, that it was her experience of illegal abortion that sparked her political awareness and activism regarding women's issues. Ironically, when Sarah discovered she was pregnant, friends on the police force helped her make contact with an underground organization of women (which came to be known as the Jane Collective; see Boston Women's Health Collective, 1984, for an account) who helped arrange illegal abortions. Sarah's experience of illegal abortion and her later involvement with "Jane" ultimately contributed not only to her politicization about women's health care but also to her professional identity.

Sarah recalls both the clandestine nature of the procedure and the month wait until her abortion could be performed as the most trying aspects of the experience. She later learned that "Jane" took elaborate precautions to scout out and secure safe homes and apartments in which to carry out abortions on any given day. There was a backlog at the time that Sarah made her call to

"Jane." During the wait, "Jane" provided Sarah with counseling, as they routinely did, about what to expect in the abortion procedure. Nonetheless, the delay was difficult: "It was the waiting that was the worst, absolutely. You don't know what is going to happen. You don't know whether it will actually come into being. You're really anxious about—well, it's illegal, so you're doing something that's not aboveboard. . . . The longer you waited the more anxious you became. And I can't explain that experience, but it's awful."

Finally, after a month's wait, Sarah received a phone call at 5 P.M. confirming her appointment at 7 P.M., to take place in her own apartment. In the following description of that evening, Sarah recounted not only the pain of the procedure but her incessant fear of being discovered:

> And so my doorbell rang and a woman comes in and starts creeping around my apartment, looking behind the doors and seeing if anyone was hiding in the closet. And that was rather unsettling. And then she said, "Alright, go in the bedroom and I'll close the door." So I went into my bedroom and I had a big dog—she wouldn't have hurt anybody but she made a lot of noise. And she wasn't about to be shut out of any room, so she started jumping against the bedroom door to be let in. In the meantime, [the man performing the abortion] got his instruments together in the bathroom and I was blindfolded. I was on the bed. The woman opened the door enough to let the man in from the bathroom. Then, during the whole procedure the dog kept barking and jumping on the door. I kept thinking, [the man performing the abortion]'s going to get scared, and somebody will hear us and come down and investigate, and then it'll be over and I'll be right in the middle of this. And I was calling to my dog to shut up; [the man doing the abortion] was reciting poetry; his assistant was holding my hand. It was a zoo, and it hurt like hell. It really hurt.

Sarah was recontacted by the Jane Collective to check on how she was doing. Sarah informed them at that point that her own physician had refused to provide follow-up medical care after her illegal abortion. She was reassured to learn that "Jane" was compiling a list of helpful, and not so helpful, physicians for women to seek out (or avoid) in these circumstances. Sarah was relieved that by getting her doctor's attitudes documented on Jane's list, her difficult experience might help to ease the trauma of other women. She remembers feeling at the time that taking that action "counterbalanced the bad experiences. And it made me say, 'Can I help you? You know, I really want to help other women like you helped me.'" As a result, Sarah joined the collective.

As well as providing her satisfaction in helping other women, Sarah's involvement in the Jane Collective contributed to her sense of empowerment and politicization about women's health care issues. As the women in "Jane" became frustrated with arranging for male professionals to perform the actual illegal abortion procedures, they eventually trained themselves in the techniques of dilation, curettage, and the administration of appropriate medications. Throughout their existence, the Jane Collective emphasized counseling as part of the services they offered so that women would know and understand what was happening to them despite the atmosphere of illegality.

Over time, Sarah found that the group reinforced her personal beliefs about women and abortion. She stated with wonderment, "All these women thought like I did." Sarah's involvement with "Jane" led to broader political interest in women's health care:

> Because of working with the women's groups you became politicized about the whole health care system that way. We were in contact with a lot of health activists. . . . So I was right in the middle of a very politicized environment about women's health. Just having been near and around women who thought in very political terms about women's issues in general, and the groups I was with, drew that parallel with the health care system.

In reflecting back on her experience of illegal abortion, Sarah concluded that its biggest impact was on her political and professional development. As an academic researcher after the legalization of abortion, Sarah investigated the structure and success of the new legal abortion clinics. She has also studied other aspects of women's health care networks, such as the services provided by midwives, and has worked internationally to investigate and improve women's health care. Sarah's abortion had much less impact on her personal life, as the pregnancy had occurred in the midst of an already faltering relationship. Sarah stated, "It did a lot for me in terms of getting me involved in political groups. And my whole professional career got turned around. So it did have a large effect, but not a personal one."

In Sarah's experience, illegal abortion was associated with danger. Perhaps her confidence in the Jane Collective and its efforts to provide counseling limited the degree to which Sarah (compared with other women who had had illegal abortions) worried about the medical consequences of the procedure. Nonetheless, Sarah's narrative highlights the intensity and pervasiveness of her worries about the dangers of being caught or abandoned without receiving the care she desperately needed. Sarah knew that she was not alone in her fears and was moved to assist other women in the way she was helped by the Jane Collective. Her awareness that her experience was not unique sparked her desire to empower women, especially around their own health. Ultimately, her involvement with a group of organized and highly politicized women contributed both to her development of a political ideology that identified the problem as in the social structure, and to a professional commitment to change that structure and enhance the health care available to women.

LEGAL ABORTION: A PERSONAL CRISIS

Alexandra had a legal abortion in 1976 at the age of sixteen. Like Sarah, in subsequent years she also was motivated to help her peers to cope with the experience of unwanted pregnancy and abortion. However, because Alexandra's abortion was legal, her helping efforts were associated with neither politically empowering other young women nor developing a political ideology about women or abortion. In her era, abortion was a legal right nearly taken for granted. Her involvement with abortion felt entirely personal to her, although it also enhanced certain relationships in her life. Whereas the Jane Collective took on a political mission to help women cope with a dangerous and clandestine experience, Alexandra and other women of her cohort tried to help friends feel supported in dealing with a painful, and sometimes shameful or embarrassing, medical procedure.

Alexandra's pregnancy at sixteen resulted after her boyfriend promised to "pull out" instead of using a condom during one of her first sexual experiences. Suffering from intense morning sickness, she confessed her pregnancy, first to a younger sister, then to her parents. She was surprised by their basically calm and rational response, although she knew that the idea of abortion was distressing to her mother, who had experienced a number of pregnancy losses subsequent to Alexandra's birth. Although her mother helped Alexandra to obtain a pregnancy test at a local clinic, her father ultimately accompanied her to a neighboring state for the abortion procedure.

Alexandra's abortion occurred in a women's health facility. She received counseling and information on birth control. She viewed the staff at the facility as sympathetic and progressive. A nurse held her hand during the procedure. Despite this generally supportive environment, Alexandra's experience of unwanted pregnancy and abortion led to much anger about her relationship with her boyfriend, and a reexamination both of teenage sexuality and of male-female relationships. She was keenly aware that the pregnancy affected only *her* body and *her* life, not that of her partner: "I was really angry that I was the only one. I mean there were two of us that were involved in this, my boyfriend and I. . . . I felt like there were two of us at that point [of having sex], and only one of us suffered any consequences."

Alexandra felt the injustice that she was the only one forced to cope with morning sickness, disappointing her family, and undergoing an abortion. Furthermore, she felt the act of sex had been for his benefit. He had taken advantage of her at a time she felt alone and vulnerable. For Alexandra, there was little romance, glamour, or pleasure involved in the experience. Alexandra remembers agreeing to have sex with him, even without a condom, out of a fear of losing him. She recalled, "I knew it was dumb. . . . I just crossed my fingers and did stair laps—running up and down the stairs to prevent the sperm from swimming up."

Alexandra's analysis of the dynamics in this relationship opened her eyes to other inequalities between the sexes. Soon after the abortion, she remembers a conversation in which she asked her mother about someday joining the family business. She explained the family business was fine for summer jobs, but that her uncle would "never hire a woman salesperson." Again she felt personally confronted with a norm of unfairness or discrimination just because she was female. She remembered, "I had to discover about men and the way they set [the world] up after I had left home. The . . . abortion, all that, brought it home real unfair." Still, Alexandra kept her analysis very much at the level of personal relationships rather than a larger social system. She recognized unfairness in her family relationships and in relationships between individual women and men, and she tried to support individual women in their unfair situation. Thus, Alexandra's legal abortion heightened her sense of gender identification without motivating her toward political action.

Moved by the recognition of her own hurt and naïveté, Alexandra soon saw herself as a resource person for other young women confronting similar dilemmas. When a roommate confessed a fear that she was pregnant, Alexandra offered to help her obtain a pregnancy test in the manner in which her mother had helped her. Alexandra and her mother became known among students at Alexandra's school as people to turn to in such a crisis. Alexandra explained: "I became, along with my mother, the underground link to Planned Parenthood at my school. The school gave no counseling or birth control advice to students. Girls who got pregnant and tried to go through the school for help got expelled. We helped girls stay in school."

In addition, Alexandra became very outspoken on the topic of sex and birth control among her peers. She would recite to vulnerable women: "If you can't do anything else, don't ever believe what he says. Even if he is the nicest person in the world, he either wears one [a condom] or else. You find

some way or you just don't do it. You don't want to go through the other."
On one occasion, hoping her sister's youthful sexual experiences would be
happier than her own, she sent her younger sister a locked box containing
condoms, gel, a sexually explicit romantic magazine, and candles. This story
underlines the degree to which Alexandra saw her abortion experience as
carrying significance for young people's sexual and relational lives rather
than women's broader social situation. She also was impressed with how her
abortion experience enhanced her relationship with her parents. In fact, she
acknowledged that this was the greatest impact of her abortion on her life.
She was amazed by her mother's ability to set aside her own pain over past
pregnancy losses and ongoing longings to have another baby to support her
daughter in the action that was best for her. Alexandra was also grateful for
the opportunity it gave her and her parents to come to know each other in a
different way. She recalled: "The three of us all learned new things about ourselves and each other. I learned that my mother and father were human, that
they were more supportive and less condemning than I'd feared. They
stopped reacting to me as their 'good little girl.' They trusted me less, but
questioned me less also. . . . I found an inspiring strength in my mother."

Alexandra's abortion shaped her feelings about herself as a woman, her
relationship with her parents, her attitudes about male-female relationships
and adolescent sexuality (particularly heterosexuality), and her identity as
someone who helped to enhance the assertiveness and to protect the self-re-
spect of her women friends. However, it did not motivate her at this stage of
her life to an analysis of structural obstacles associated with gender (she did
not, for example, define herself as a feminist), nor to political action. Alexandra learned how to cope with sexism in relationships, but she did not feel
moved to challenge or change the system that produced those relationships.

COMPARING THE ILLEGAL AND LEGAL
ABORTION EXPERIENCES

A number of interesting comparisons can be drawn between Sarah's and
Alexandra's abortion experiences. Both women indicated that these were significant, and in some ways formative, episodes in their lives. However, the
specific meanings of those episodes differed, in part because of the legal context in which they occurred. Sarah felt betrayed by a legal system that marginalized her and jeopardized her health and emotional well-being; Alexandra felt betrayed by her boyfriend, but supported by her parents and a
well-intentioned clinic staff. Ultimately, Sarah's abortion experience was
transformed in her own mind from a personal to a political one. Her efforts

to help other women took the form of collective political action. In contrast, Alexandra—equally sympathetic with other women's problems—was moved to help young women in private settings and through interpersonal connections. Rather than seeing her personal experience in political terms, Alexandra commented that her abortion made a distant political debate a personal issue. She stated: "I really started to think about women's issues from a personal perspective. I could finally see that they were related to my life, not a news headline or party topics."

In comparing these two experiences, we have focused on an illegal abortion experience that was frightening and a legal abortion experience that was less so. This makes sense, since women generally experienced illegal abortions as more frightening than legal ones. However, since the degree of fear and anxiety experienced was an important factor in women's politicization after an illegal abortion, it is important briefly to consider the experience of a woman who did not find her illegal abortion frightening or politicizing. Marcia only developed her strong pro-choice perspective recently, despite an illegal abortion fifteen years ago at age twenty-three. She explained: "I really can't even say at the time that I was aware that it was illegal. All I was aware of was that there was no place to go. . . . I mean, I must have known that it was illegal, but I wasn't conscious of that. . . . There was never the thought that I could get arrested. Or that I could legally be in trouble. It never occurred to me."

Marcia's abortion was performed by a licensed physician in his private office after hours. Although Marcia had to travel over two hundred miles by car and paid over $500 for the procedure, she had made the connection to this doctor quickly and easily through a friend. She knew he used sterile instruments to perform the abortion. As she pointed out, "When I drove down there there was no dread, there was no fear, nothing. Just like, well, okay, whatever this is, it'll be whatever it is, and then we'll go home, and that will be whatever that is."

Her memories of the period afterward were similarly free of distress:

> There was no trauma for me. . . . I drove home and I didn't know what to expect. I thought maybe I'll be in pain, maybe I'll be in bed for a week, and I didn't know, and maybe I'll be fine. And I was fine. I went home and washed and waxed the floor. End of story. [Interviewer: And went on with your life.] Yeah. Just nothing to it. No dilemma, just relief, relief, relief.

Despite the actual illegal context in which Marcia's abortion occurred, she did not experience the context consciously at all. The ease with which she obtained a safe, albeit illegal, abortion worked against her developing either a sense of common fate with other women or a political analysis of her abortion experience. She concluded, "I didn't suffer for being a woman." The abortion allowed her, like her boyfriend, not to suffer the consequences of an unwanted pregnancy. Marcia reflected, "I think I'd have felt women are victims if I hadn't been able to obtain an abortion." Moreover, her abortion was not bracketed by periods of intense and painful emotions. Perhaps because of these factors, and because her abortion itself was not particularly frightening or painful, Marcia perceived no social dimension in her experience. Her eventual politicization is still not closely connected with her abortion experience. It is important to note, then, that it is not the mere fact of illegality that made illegal abortions so politicizing for many women; rather, the social and political meaning of the experience was carried in the details of what happened to each individual woman. When illegal abortions were not frightening or painful, as sometimes they were not, they did not sharpen women's consciousness of their physical vulnerability and their political powerlessness, nor their sense of connection with each other. Additionally, we can see why even legal abortions that were frightening would not necessarily be politicizing. If the fear and anxiety some women experienced in the course of a legal abortion were attributed to immediate and idiosyncratic circumstances (an unsympathetic doctor, a coercive boyfriend or parent, etc.), then those women would be unlikely to view their experiences in social or political terms.

WHEN ABORTIONS POLITICIZE WOMEN

In the years before *Roe v. Wade,* it was easy for women to see the political implications of their abortion experiences. In order to have an abortion, women were forced outside the law, and many risked physical injury and death; the fact that this experience was specific to them as women was hard to overlook. It is clear, though, that it was not the sheer illegality of abortion that made it politicizing; it was the combination of intense fear, the asymmetry in their experience and that of their male partners, along with the danger and pain they suffered, that made illegal abortion a politicizing experience. There may have been other factors as well; in particular the social context immediately following the abortion, and the woman's own developmental stage.

Sarah's illegal abortion took place when she was working in Chicago in 1968. She had recently returned to the United States after time abroad, and was appalled by the country's involvement in Vietnam. Although she was self-supporting, her political and professional identities were still in early stages of development. Not long after her abortion, she pursued further education and committed herself to a career path. Sarah was clearly in the period that Stewart and Healy (1989) identify as "late adolescence/young adulthood," or the time before constraining life commitments (to career, relationships, and/or parenthood) preclude dramatic identity changes for a while. Stewart and Healy suggest that dramatic social events in this period are likely to shape an individual's identity formation, particularly in the context of a strong cohort identification. In the period following Sarah's abortion, the antiwar and civil rights movements continued to build, and, perhaps more crucially, the women's movement (partly exemplified in the Jane Collective) developed. Sarah's individual experience during these years included linkage with a face-to-face community of supportive living partners, a community of activists for women's reproductive rights, and a larger, more diffuse community of political activists worldwide. Her connection with these communities certainly supported her in her choices and her experiences, and offered her broader political perspectives through which to understand what happened to her; they also offered her opportunities to take actions she felt were redemptive (like listing her doctor as one to avoid and helping other women). Marcia's illegal abortion occurred during the same period of turbulent social change and during a similar stage of individual development. Nonetheless, because her personal experience of abortion was not particularly constrained by social factors, it did not prove to be politically mobilizing.

Alexandra was only sixteen—still a child, at least in terms of this experience (her parents actually made all of the decisions and arrangements about her abortion). Her abortion took place in 1976, not only after *Roe v. Wade,* but after the Vietnam War had ended and Jimmy Carter was in the White House expressing a national commitment to human rights. Alexandra was embedded in a set of family relations that underlined the relational aspects of her experience as well as her own lack of adult status. There was no ready community of politically conscious peers at either the face-to-face or a more abstract level, and there was no contextual pressure to see her experience in ideological terms (although there were other women needing abortions). Alexandra's own stage of development combined with the social context in which her abortion occurred to make her experience one that allowed her to see the individual and relationship dimensions of abortion, but not the social and political ones.

It is important to note, though, that more than ten years later, Alexandra's perceptions had changed. There was a different political climate that included the *Webster* (1989) decision allowing individual states to limit women's abortion rights, eight years of the Reagan presidency, and women (including Alexandra's sister) being harassed by demonstrators while seeking legal abortions. At this point in her life (age 29), Alexandra found herself reexamining her views: "It seemed like *Roe v. Wade* was written in stone. . . . It was not going to be questioned. . . . And then things started looking darker and darker. It just finally woke me up that if you wanted the opportunity for choice and freedom to stay around that it meant the individual had to do something."

Alexandra began attending pro-choice rallies. Through these experiences, she felt herself to be further politicized. After many years of thinking of herself as a middle-of-the-road Republican, Alexandra started seeing herself as a feminist and as a Democrat. She has volunteered at a local clinic to escort women past anti-abortion protesters and now sees her family's experiences with abortion no longer as personal events but as political ones. She says that now "I'm going to do all I can to see that our right to decide is protected."

Interestingly, although Alexandra had made constraining life commitments at the time of her sister's abortion (she was married, had become a parent, and had organized her own small business), she was nevertheless moved by social and personal events to a transformation of her political identity at age twenty-nine. Although Stewart and Healy (1989) suggest that this is relatively rare at this life stage, what may be important in Alexandra's case is that she, like many women, saw a substantial threat to one of her core values (women's right to choose) in the *Webster* decision. While developmental factors may be important in enhancing or limiting individuals' potential for politicization, Alexandra's example makes it clear that threats to core values may move individuals at any age (although it may help if those values are linked with powerful personal experiences from a formative period). Moreover, her awakening political consciousness and commitment were supported by the availability of a community of pro-choice activists created in part by the more conservative social climate and the invigorated anti-abortion movement.

Overall, then, the quantitative and qualitative evidence we have explored here combines to suggest that women's abortion experiences were sometimes sources of political mobilization. Although women who had experienced legal and illegal abortions were equally likely to identify with other women, to hold the social system responsible for women's lower status, and to take political action, there were important differences in their attitudes. Women who had had illegal abortions felt they had less control over their experience and knew that they were doing something that was socially unacceptable. They had more difficulty arranging their abortion, traveled further, and paid more for it. Most of all they suffered much more anxiety, particularly about being hurt, molested, arrested, and dying. These anxieties were associated with feeling identified with other women, which was in turn associated with political activism. This set of relationships did not hold for women who had experienced legal abortions. By examining the case material, we were able to understand why these differences might have occurred.

One woman who faced an illegal abortion was a young adult surrounded by peers who were politically conscious and aware. Moreover, her abortion was one she personally had arranged and sought through a collective dedicated to helping women who needed abortions. After her abortion, she herself participated in collective action with that group. In contrast, another woman who had a legal abortion was a teenager in a period when young people were not especially politically active. Moreover, her abortion was arranged for her by her parents and experienced within a familial rather than peer context. The experience surely underlined her dependent status as much as her gender. Years later, though, her safe, legal, and apparently apolitical abortion provided an important personal contrast to the dangerous and politicized abortion her sister sought. The combination of that contrast and her increasing exposure to the community of pro-choice activists helped her transform her compassionate efforts to help individual women into a politically conscious collective action to resist Operation Rescue. These cases underscore the crucial role that a visible activist community can play in helping individuals not only to recognize the public issues that have shaped their "private troubles," but also to see why "the economic and political institutions of the society and not merely the personal situation and character of a scatter of individuals" (Mills, 1959, p. 9) must be implicated in the solutions they seek.

NOTE

1. All differences reported produced statistically significant chi squares or t-tests; $p < 0.01$.

REFERENCES

Berry, P., & Bishop, A. (1985). *Testament of a generation: The journalism of Vera Brittain and Winifred Holtby.* London: Virago.

Bordo, S. (1993). Feminism, postmodernism, and gender skepticism. In *Unbearable weight: Feminism, Western culture, and the body* (pp. 215–339). Berkeley, CA: University of California Press.

Boston Women's Health Collective. (1984). *Our new bodies, ourselves.* New York: Simon & Schuster.

Brittain, V. (1970). *Testament of youth*. New York: Wideview. (Original work published 1933)

Clayton, S., & Crosby, F. J. (Eds.). (1986). Social issues and personal life: The search for connections [Special issue]. *Journal of Social Issues, 42*(2).

Crosby, F. J. (1982). *Relative deprivation and working women*. New York: Oxford.

Cross, W. (1971). The Negro to black conversion experience: Towards a psychology of black liberation. *Black World, 20*, 13–27.

Echols, A. (1989). *Daring to be bad: Radical feminism in America, 1967–1975* Minneapolis: University of Minnesota Press.

Estrich, S. (1987). *Real rape*. Cambridge, MA: Harvard University Press.

Evans, S. (1979). *Personal politics: The roots of women's liberation in the civil rights movement and the new left*. New York: Vintage.

Gandhi, M. K. (1957). *An autobiography: The story of my experiments with truth*. Boston: Beacon Press. (Original work published 1929)

Giddings, P. (1984). *When and where I enter: The impact of black women on race and sex in America*. New York: Bantam.

Ginsburg, F. (1989). *Contested lives*. Berkeley: University of California Press.

Gold-Steinberg, S. E. (1991). *Legal and illegal abortion: Coping with the impact of social policies on women's lives*. Unpublished doctoral dissertation, University of Michigan, Ann Arbor.

Gurin, P. (1985). Women's gender consciousness. *Public Opinion Quarterly, 49*, 143–163.

Gurin, P., & Townsend, A. (1986). Properties of gender identity and their implications for gender consciousness. *British Journal of Social Psychology, 25*, 139–148.

Haley, A. (1965). *The autobiography of Malcolm X*. New York: Ballantine.

Lee, N. H. (1969). *The search for an abortionist*. Chicago: University of Chicago Press.

Lopez, A. (1993, July–August). Clippings. *Ms. Magazine*, 86–88.

Mannheim, K. (1952). The problem of generations. In *Essays on the sociology of knowledge* (pp. 378–404). New York: Oxford University Press.

Messer, E., & May, K. E. (1988). *Back rooms: Voices from the illegal abortion era*. New York: Simon & Schuster.

Mills, C. W. (1959). *The sociological imagination*. New York: Oxford.

Morrison, T. (Ed.). (1992). *Race-ing justice, en-gendering power*. New York: Pantheon.

Petchesky, R. P. (1990). *Abortion and women's choice: The state, sexuality, and reproductive freedom*. Boston: Northeastern University Press.

Roe v. Wade. (1973). 410 U.S. 113.

Ryan, W. (1971). *Blaming the victim*. New York: Pantheon.

Stewart, A. J., & Healy, J. M. (1989). Linking individual development and social changes. American Psychologist, 44, 30–42.

Tatalovich, R., & Daynes, B. W. (1981). *The politics of abortion: A study of community conflict in public policy making*. New York: Praeger.

Webster v. Reproductive Health Services. (1989). 492 U.S. 490.

Chapter 15

Rethinking Social Action and Community Empowerment: A Dialogue

•*Bill Berkowitz and Tom Wolff*

EMPOWERMENT ATTEMPTS HAVE LARGELY FAILED

BILL: Let's start with a story, one that still upsets me. I was in New York City last summer, visiting my cousin Barbara, near Columbia University. She works for the city, as an assistant commissioner in economic development; a lot of professional people live on her street. But across from her apartment, and this is relatively new, there are also clusters of people who appear to be homeless or drugged out and not doing very well at all.

We go to sleep, with the windows open. The people across the street are talking, and sometimes yelling, and sometimes screaming all night long, straight through till dawn. Barbara is adapted, she apparently tunes it out; I can't. Maybe it's about 6:00 A.M., and I hear a woman's cry that fills the whole block: "I don't have a nickel for a cup of coffee; I don't have a nickel for a fucking cup of coffee." There's no response, nothing. Barbara, who is as devoted as they come, gets up and goes downtown to build local economies. I take notes, and write from a distance.

So when we talk about empowerment, about injustice, a generation after William Ryan's *Blaming the Victim* (1971), this is part of what's going on. Disparities in empowerment and in social justice are at least as profound as they were twenty years ago. And personal connectedness to the problem seems at least as hard to find.

TOM: It's not just more disparities. I've got a story, too. There's a rural mill town in Massachusetts where we've been active for many years. Someone proposed converting a downtown factory into subsidized housing for the working poor in the community, who couldn't afford to buy. But others in the community said, "We don't want THOSE people living here"—even though many of these same opponents were not much better off. They were concerned with outsiders, but they also opposed this housing option for their own neighbors.

So this created a powerful local conflict. We had a hard time getting these different groups to hear each other, to understand their common concerns—and the housing did not get built. It goes beyond the simple economic disparities in your story. The psychological distances are just as strong. Intolerance runs deep where we've been working. And in this case, social class was the underlying cause.

BILL: So what lessons do we draw? Are these just isolated instances we've recalled? Or do these stories reflect some general truths about the impact of social action over the last few decades?

TOM: General truths; at least for the communities we work with in Massachusetts. For them, economic discrepancies have gotten much worse since the 1970s. Intolerance and indifference have grown. Citizen participation and sense of community have declined. Alienation has risen. Mediating institutions have weakened. Many people in the community are much worse off. And so many individuals and institutions feel disempowered and unable to have an impact on their lives or on their communities.

There is another side, though, because we also see enormous efforts at caring within these same communities, at pulling people together, at wanting things to heal. Some people really wanted to build affordable housing. These forces exist at the same time.

BILL: There is caring, even though some recent evidence suggests that levels of volunteerism have peaked or declined (Hodgkinson & Weitzman, 1994). But I would argue that empowerment efforts over the past generation or so have largely failed. That generally speaking, people have not been empowered—poorer people certainly not; that social conditions and inequalities are worse than they were a few decades ago; and that community action attempts have had isolated and limited success at best. That's a tough indictment. We need to face it, straight up.

If the stories aren't convincing, look at the numbers. Income disparities have grown, we've already noted that (e.g., Cassidy, 1995). There's a national Index of Social Health, which tracks progress on sixteen well-being indicators—such as children in poverty, average weekly earnings, health care coverage; the latest overall index score was one of the lowest in twenty-four years of recording (Miringoff, 1995). There's a Harris poll, which measures alienation yearly, alienation as perceived; the 1995 level was at an all-time high (Taylor, 1996). People certainly don't *feel* empowered, regardless of levels of caring.

TOM: I agree we should distinguish caring from empowerment. Empowerment is about self-determination. Empowerment means gaining access and control over those resources that allow you to master your life, or, for a community, to have control over what happens in its domain (Minkler, 1989; Rappaport, Swift, & Hess, 1984; Wallerstein, 1992). And in this sense I would agree, compared to when *Blaming the Victim* came out in 1971, that overall levels of empowerment have declined.

BILL: But why have they declined? What's behind the failure? That's the next big question. Then we can figure out what to do about it.

FAILURE HAS MULTIPLE CAUSES

TOM: Why have we failed? I think we can certainly see over twelve years of the Reagan and Bush administrations how there was license from above to have institutions act in disempowering ways. Many institutions became much more systematic about suppressing efforts of citizens to achieve a voice for social and economic justice. When we go to communities now to help give people a voice, we see that people have been socialized to be quiet. We're working hard to reverse that. But I think that there's been a serious decline in institutional accountability and that to an extent it's been systematically planned.

BILL: You mean political leaders *wanted* people to be less empowered?

TOM: Not just political leaders. There have been industry and union leaders who've wanted workers quieted. We've seen it in schools—as a local school committee person, when I once said, "Let's give students a voice in the evaluation of faculty," everybody in the room was outraged at such a bizarre idea. I was told to not even raise this issue in public because the teacher's union would go crazy. So most people in power felt they had license to silence the voices of people with less power. The political environment was ripe; but there were many levels of society where this happened, not just the political.

BILL: Failure has multiple causes; there are other reasons we could put on the table. One might be that for all our talk about empowerment, we really don't know how to go about it. As helping professionals or as social scientists, our track record of empowering people isn't very good. So an alternate hypothesis is that we're lacking something ourselves. Maybe we don't know the right techniques, for example.

TOM: Truthfully, I think we've got a lot of techniques. If you look at any psychology textbook, there are pages full of well-validated knowledge about how to change attitudes and behaviors, how to lead groups, how to reduce stereotyping and conflict, the primary formal skills we need to know. It's mostly there.

BILL: And I know you've developed additional coalition-building techniques in your own work. But generally, when it comes to putting techniques into *practice,* that's where we've come up short. Exactly why, I'm not sure. Possibly something gets lost in the translation. Or, another possibility, we simply haven't tried hard enough. When it comes down to cases, we as professionals may not be particularly motivated to empower. It threatens us. The distances between "us" and "them" are too great. That is scary. Or maybe it's something else about professionals that gets in the way.

TOM: I'd say any discussion that focuses on professionals and then starts to talk about empowerment is in trouble. I don't think that professionals had much of an empowering role in the past. The mediating institutions that gave people a voice—the unions, the local political club, church groups, community schools—were mostly there before professionals came on the scene.

And there are structural difficulties for professionals as key actors in creating empowerment now, because the role of professional today is often to have more power over other people. I've been strongly influenced by the work of John McKnight. He suggests that professional human service approaches overemphasize the deficits and needs of individuals in communities, rather than their capacities and assets. Professionals "push out the problem-solving knowledge and action of friend, neighbor, citizen, and association" (McKnight, 1989, p. 9). McKnight believes that there really is a role for professionals, but not "until the capacities of people are recognized, honored, respected, and lifted up" (McKnight, 1990).

BILL: And our job is to do the lifting. But there's at least one more possible reason for failure to empower, which is that most people may not be concerned about empowerment at all. It's our agenda, not theirs.

For example, a recent poll asked, "What is part of the good life as far as you are personally concerned?" Here are the top ten responses, in order: a home of your own, a happy marriage, a car, children, college education for the children, an interesting job, a well-paying job, a yard and a lawn, a lot of money, and a color TV (Roper Organization, 1991). Empowerment, or anything remotely like it, is nowhere to be found. And the poorer the person, the less the manifest concern. It's not a priority. It's not even close.

TOM: My view is different. I would say we don't see empowerment in the polls because we don't *ask* about it. When we do ask, it shows up. Once I was involved in a needs assessment of elders in a rural area. We asked people about new services they might use or not use. And one of the services we called "advocacy," defined as "helping elders have their voices heard on issues that affect them." More elders wanted this than any other service proposed. It's only one survey, but it certainly illustrates that citizens can value generalized empowerment over very hard, concrete services that would make a day-to-day difference. But only if we ask can we find out.

BILL: Point well taken, although some scholars claim that empowerment itself is a limited and not always desirable social goal. Stephanie Riger, for example, has recently argued, "The underlying assumption of empowerment theory is that of conflict rather than cooperation"; and consequently empowerment "tends to deny or overlook the role of connectedness in human life" (Riger, 1993, pp. 285, 286). Strong language, and a strongly defended position.

TOM: Empowerment and connectedness are both important. Riger is right in that respect. And they're not exclusive. As far as empowerment goes, though, I need to call you on all this pessimism, for we want to move to positive examples, directions that will make a difference. They way you're talking, it sounds as if there are no examples of empowerment at all, that it's been all downhill for the past twenty years. We both know that's not true. I can point to examples of empowering community programs and activities, and so can you.

BILL: You're right; new directions are what we're after. Why don't you start, because your coalition work is one good model of an empowering community approach. Then I'll give some other examples, and we'll see what generalizations we can draw.

WE KNOW EMPOWERMENT CAN BE CREATED

TOM: Our starting and continuing goal has been to create competent helping systems in communities. If you look at typical community helping systems, you will find they are fragmented, competitive, duplicative, detached, crisis-oriented, unplanned, professionally dominated, and culturally insensitive. Instead, we aim for systems that are coordinated, collaborative, comprehensive, accessible, preventive, planned, holistic, and culturally relevant. They emphasize community assets; they deal with emergent problems; they maximize both informal and formal helping. And they are integrated in the community so as to promote the individual's and the community's capacity to solve their own problems (Wolff, 1992).

That's the theoretical framework. How does it operate in practice? We began this work ten years ago, when we were invited in to help a small town in Massachusetts with 17 percent unemployment. A group had gathered, including the clergy, the chamber of commerce, the local hospital, the local mental health center, and business people: they wanted to do something about the enormous distress and disorganization stemming from the unemployment plus a massive plant closing. We persuaded them to join into a coalition, our first one. We defined a coalition, then and now, as a structured and inclusive gathering of diverse community members to solve some community problem—and by so doing to generate the competent helping system I mentioned.

At the first meeting, we heard issues people were concerned about and the services they thought were needed. Then we helped them set up an information and referral service, and later an emergency shelter in a church basement. It became clear to us that working with communities in this collaborative way was very effective in stimulating the community's capacity to solve its own problems. And we learned a great deal about how to mobilize community resources around identified community issues, in ways most communities could not do on their own.

BILL: Can you point to the specific accomplishments?

TOM: For one thing, our coalition-building expanded into ten other Massachusetts communities. The specific accomplishments vary, depending on local community goals. For example, in the Northern Berkshires, people identified the issue of homelessness yet felt quite unable to do anything about it, but a coalition quickly rallied community forces. It designed a new program called a Family Life Support Center to prevent homelessness, and successfully lobbied the state and federal government for resources. The private sector came up with matching money; the newspaper editor, along with the city councilors, slept out on the street to raise funds and awareness around the issue; a local restaurant had a lasagna dinner with a male stripper as an innovative form of fundraising. The coalition was not only able to create an innovative homelessness prevention program, but also to show the community and the state that this community could mobilize around issues and provide services. This was a major triumph in terms of giving voice to the community.

Other accomplishments? In Athol, we created a child sexual abuse prevention program for the schools. On Cape Cod, we developed a house-sharing program with the Interfaith Housing Council. In other communities, we've started a Parent's Place for teaching parenting skills, three neighborhood organizations, and a community development corporation. And I think of our Latino Coalition in Worcester, which persuaded hospitals and HMOs to provide interpreter services for an underserved population. That same Latino Coalition later met with its legislators, who said, "But your people don't vote. Why should we listen to you?" So the coalition turned around and launched an intensive voter registration campaign.

BILL: Impressive. Would you say there are common guiding principles behind your successes?

TOM: Definitely. Here are five: (1) We believe that everyone in the community has a potential role in the coalition, and that it's only a matter of time before we bring them in. (2) We address key issues of organizational competence: coalition leadership, decision-making, staffing, planning, communication, and effective use of resources. (3) We have a very clear commitment to advocacy and action. (4) We commit to our communities for the long haul and stay with them. (5) Finally, we focus on celebration and hope; coalitions need to include fun, and must affirm the strengths and joys of the community (Wolff, 1992; see also National Assembly, 1991).

BILL: All right—if coalitions have generated so much progress in so many different communities, how far do we extend this? We could say that every community should do the same. The universal empowering structure would be the coalition, a coalition in every community.

TOM: That is a concept that immediately terrifies me. Because one would need to look very carefully at the value base of these coalitions to make sure that they really work *with* the community in solving its problems, as opposed to solving problems *for* the community. Calling yourself a coalition does not guarantee a commitment to empowerment (Wolff, 1993).

This is especially true when you have too much emphasis on just the health and human service providers, without sufficient citizen participation and control. You can end up with a coalition that amasses power among the providers, and that becomes more efficient at doing *for* people—and not empowering the community at all, either the citizens or even other caregivers. The providers become more empowered, and the clients can get blamed. We're still blaming the victim. Power is sticky. Shifting it is hard.

Arthur Himmelman's distinction between collaborative betterment and collaborative empowerment strategies is important here (Himmelman, 1992). He argues that collaborative betterment can produce policy changes and service improvements, but tends not to produce long-term ownership. On the other hand, collaborative empowerment means setting priorities and controlling resources that are essential for increasing community self-determination. Applying this to our coalitions, we have evolved into doing much more work with neighborhoods, trying to figure out more ways to involve the average citizen. And we have added the goal of a mobilized and empowered citizenry to the goal of a competent helping system.

BILL: That sounds right, including the citizenry as partners. But suppose every coalition were inclusive and had the right value base.

TOM: There's another limitation to what coalitions can do. In the mill town we originally went into, one of the plants closed; the other major employer gained control. In this case, the owner is a very conservative individual who describes his politics as well to the right of Reagan, who has strong feelings about keeping schools underfunded, and who has been dominant in oppressing workers, who I believe then openly go ahead and oppress their families. We have had no impact on the power of that corporate leader. Community coalitions as we've operated them can create local community empowerment, but not larger-scale social and economic transformation, at least not directly—although of course change at that level clearly also has to occur. That's a different level of action, however—the political dimension of what Ronald Labonté has called "the empowerment holosphere" (Labonté, 1994).

BILL: It's good that you acknowledge the limits honestly, and that's an issue we'll have to come back to. I think your coalition work has broken new ground. But there are other local empowerment models that involve citizens more directly. I'll mention two prominent ones—I want to preview by saying there are reservations and drawbacks about each of them.

Recently I visited the offices of the Dudley Street Neighborhood Initiative (DSNI), in the Roxbury area of Boston. Ten years ago, this neighborhood was so poor it didn't have a name. But some residents got together, formed an organization, attracted some money, and for a combination of reasons, things took off from there.

They built thirty-three affordable homes this past year, and rehabbed eighty other units; they won eminent domain authority; they've got millions of dollars in grants and loans. They've cleaned up the neighborhood, put trash barrels down and street signs up. They are painting murals. They've got a neighborhood youth commission, a child care network, a trilingual newsletter, a multicultural board of directors, about three full-time organizers, and a growing membership—all this and more. They're light years ahead of most neighborhood organizations. Their work has gotten national attention. That's an example of empowering community action, wouldn't you agree? (See also Medoff & Sklar, 1994.)

TOM: Yes, DSNI is a great example of collaborative empowerment, which illustrates economic development as well as community ownership. For some dilemmas, getting citizens involved in the solutions may be the only way out. And I remember reading about their organizing principles: residents are the best spokespeople for their neighborhood; residents are the leaders for planning and implementation; anything is possible.[1]

BILL: And here's another strong example—less economic, more psychological—the Block Booster Project in New York City. In the mid-1980s, the Citizens Committee for New York City hired trainers to teach organizational and leadership skills to residents on forty-eight city blocks, the goal being to strengthen individual block associations. And this was conducted as an actual experiment; there were control blocks that didn't get the training. The block associations that were trained, or "boosted," held together longer, and showed lower mortality rates, presumably because of the leadership training they received. The distinctiveness here is the combination of grass-roots empowerment with research backing (Florin & Wandersman, 1990). And the research shows it really works.

So we know it can be done. *We know community empowerment can be created.* There are lots of examples like this, even if they're small. They are scattered. They're not always well publicized. Their effects are limited. They come and go. But if we put our minds to it, we could make a catalogue of local empowerment successes without too much trouble—and in fact there are about a dozen data bases around the country that have done just that (Berkowitz, 1991).

TOM: So the next step, in theory, would be publicizing these examples and replicating many more. Unless there are problems we haven't identified.

BILL: There are lots of problems. The biggest one is sustainability. For example, Block Booster as such isn't around anymore, even though no one promised it would last forever.[2] There are many, many smaller empowerment actions that simply haven't stayed alive. They weren't institutionalized. They may have been terrific while they lasted, but they haven't lasted. Not that every action *should* last indefinitely, but too many die before their time.

It's sad. They're like fireworks—they flare and burn out—where we really need a steadier light.

There are related problems, such as professionalism again, for much of local empowerment work is still professionally driven, as it was in both these examples. Even Dudley Street's operating budget is well over $500,000. But if the professionals pull out, and if a good program is not institutionalized, and if the community is insufficiently motivated or insufficiently trained, there's nothing left. This still happens, even though we know better.

Then, there's the connected issue of money. Much successful local empowerment action is funded from outside the community. Block Booster had major foundation funding; Dudley Street still has. That means the work is externally motivated, and externally controlled, to a degree. Most successful coalitions, the ones you've been talking about, have paid staff. When the money stops, the music dies—not every time, but most of the time. How many successful and lasting citizen-led and zero-budget actions do we know of? Not many.

TOM: I'm not that pessimistic. We can create empowerment programs, get external funding, bring people in, teach leaders new skills, and create new neighborhood organizations. Then we back out and leave people to continue the work without us, and they actually continue it. New money, if needed, can be generated from within. That's good strategy, and it's good work. It can be done.

There are also smaller-scale projects with lasting effects. For example, we know one in the Boston area, The Right Question Project, which trains low-income mothers to become advocates for their kids—to go into schools and ask the right questions about education. Once you have trained and supported that mother, and she has gone to her child's school a couple of times on her own, she is going to continue, and she is going to be able to do more over time, by herself.[3]

On the other hand, I can flip right around and tell you that in building health and human service coalitions, we have sometimes been in communities for up to ten years and haven't left. Because to make really significant changes in communities is a long-term process. Maybe we shouldn't always be going in with the expectation that it's going to be short-term and that we'll be pulling out soon. So I guess I can hear both sides of the issue.

BILL: Then some "right questions" here are, "How do you institutionalize empowerment?" and "How do you get more?", and "What kind of structures do you set up to make empowering actions last?" If we had the right answers to those, we'd be in good shape.

TOM: I think we have answered part of this. But I'm not so sure it would concern me greatly if each community had a commissioner of Empowerment, whose job it was to make sure that more and more people were learning leadership development skills, and that more and more groups were organizing to make sure their needs were met. My only regret would be the title.

But no such person is in the cards. And many communities are not empowered at all. So it would definitely help if we could find other strategies.

BILL: That's a challenge. Let's first set some strategic criteria: we're looking for directions that are relatively simple, that don't cost a whole lot of money, that don't require a whole lot of technical expertise, that build participation, that just about anyone can pull off, that are replicable across a wide variety of community settings, that should last, that are fun to do—and that are something different from what's been tried before. Any others we should add?

TOM: Of course, they must actually produce empowerment, which means we've got to measure it too. Are we ready to take this on?

THE NEIGHBORHOOD IS AN UNDERVALUED EMPOWERING STRUCTURE

BILL: Let me offer an approach that's worth developing further. It has to do with geography, with the place where community action naturally occurs, and this time without external training or funding or impetus—that's the key difference from our previous discussion. I've come to believe more and more in the power of the neighborhood, and even of the individual street block, as a self-generating empowering structure. Neighborhoods are underutilized and undervalued resources in American society. But they have so many advantages!

In the first place, they are close to home, they are right where people live; when you walk out the door, you're there, no commuting. Second, most people know at least a few other people where they are, even if only to say hello, so there's a base for developing other activities. Third, the odds of success for smaller-scale neighborhood actions are generally higher than for town-wide or regionwide campaigns, where there's less direct control; success is reinforcing, and this ups the chances of similar actions in the future. Fourth, you can *see* the results of neighborhood actions—the cleaner streets, the new playground—and that's reinforcing too. Fifth, many neighborhood actions can succeed with very little money or no money at all. And finally, it can be a lot of fun to come together and work with people and get to know them, so there is an added interpersonal value to the activity, and that will strengthen community connections too, sometimes in indirect, unpredictable, and wonderful ways.

So neighborhood activities—*internally generated* activities—clearly meet the criteria we just stated. They are convenient, inexpensive, nontechnical, nonbureaucratic, easier to do, easier to succeed at, replicable, open to everyone. The irony is that neighborhoods have been there all along. It's just that on a policy level we've never paid full attention to them.

TOM: It makes sense to me. But if there are so many reasons to do this, how come we see so little of it?

BILL: A good question, Tom. To begin with, there's a lack of political leadership from the top down, from elected officials and policy-makers on federal, state, and even local levels. Neighborhood-based programs are not on the national agenda, and never have been. In recent presidential campaigns, not just the last one, you never heard a whisper about improving the quality of life on a neighborhood level, on a street-by-street level—that type of thinking is just not in the national consciousness.

And I think that's a very large mistake. We know, and this is only for starters, that strong interpersonal connections keep people healthier and living longer (see review in Aneshensel, 1992). If I were president, one of the key cost-saving and health-promoting features of my national health policy would be the strengthening of local neighborhood life. Who in government is talking about this? But if they won't, we must.

TOM: Let me stop you there. Can a national agenda drive neighborhood organizing?

BILL: No doubt about it. There are at least two national mechanisms. One is through moral leadership; it still means something. That means first *believing* in local-level action possibilities, and then educating people about them, making speeches about them, getting them into the media, and instructing one's deputies to do the same. The other is through action incentives. In the Clinton administration, HUD's [Department of Housing and Urban Development's] heart has been in the right place. But the dollars set aside for neighborhood development are so tiny that for all intents and purposes government backing is missing here.

TOM: I do have doubts about how far you can go with this. Expecting empowerment to happen on a neighborhood level may be romanticizing an old-fashioned idea. Is it really possible in the 1990s? Aren't people too much into their work and their private lives to get involved in neighborhood activity?

BILL: I don't believe it. I'm thinking of another poll, a Gallup poll in 1990. When a national sample was asked: "Would you like to be involved in volunteer work with local and community problems—definitely, perhaps, or not?," only 22 percent said they were already involved, and 38 percent had no interest. But 7 percent reported they "definitely would like to be" involved, and 33 percent said "perhaps" (George H. Gallup International Institute, 1990, p. 7). So I'm looking at the Wannabes and the Perhapses, 40 percent of the American population—40 percent! 100,000,000 people. Our job is to go out and capture that 40 percent. We can do it, national policy or not.

TOM: Tell me how you do it. What are the operating principles?

BILL: The simple and compellingly powerful principle is, "You ask them." Why do people volunteer? In surveys, the most common answer frequently given is, "Somebody asked me" (Hodgkinson & Weitzman, 1988, p. 6). This makes perfect psychological sense: influence is strongest when the source is someone you know, like, and respect, and when the requested action is seen as do-able and impactful (e.g., Cialdini, 1992). Translated into practice, we don't do enough targeted asking, and neighborhood connections often aren't strong enough for that asking to be optimally effective. But there's plenty of running room, even at present. Even if we increased levels of neighborhood involvement by 5 to 10 percent, or engaged another 5 to 10 percent of people in local community life, that would be a giant step forward.

TOM: I think we've got to do more than just ask. I think we need the training of neighborhood residents in capacity-building and community-building skills—training in all the nuts and bolts of community organization—planning, publicizing, getting people hooked in, running meetings, building a record of success, the whole works. It's got to be delivered on the scene, in a vivid, informal, down-to-earth collaborative way that responds to stated needs, builds on people's experiences, and has immediate meaning for people's lives.

BILL: Okay, but I'd make three qualifications. First, I hesitate at the word "training": it sounds too formal, bureaucratic, and top-down. I might prefer to use "education," and to stress the more informal and collaborative aspects you mention. Second, much training can be internally rather than externally generated; it can come from inside the community—from schools certainly, from churches, from local media, from civic groups, and even from government itself. If it's internally generated, it's more likely to become institutionalized and therefore ongoing.

And third, education or training is vital, is essential, but it's only part of the answer. Training will be most attractive and useful when there are clear community issues, real and immediate problems that people can organize around. If you've got drugs, crime, trash, toxins, rats, roaches, gangs, guns on the street—these are problems that leap right at you, they can hurt you or kill you, and they need to be dealt with right now, today. The problem is that in many neighborhoods, nothing leaps. Issues are conspicuous by their absence. There aren't any particular neighborhood problems. There's nothing going on.

Take my own neighborhood, for example. I live in a metropolitan suburb, the kind of place that's home for close to half the U.S. population (U.S. Bureau of the Census, 1992). My neighborhood isn't wealthy, but it is comfortable; it's a relatively safe haven. Most people I've spoken to like it well enough. And maybe one reason why they like it is *because there are no issues* here. Crime is reasonably low. The streets are drug-free. The sidewalks are relatively clean. There's nothing to mobilize around. And it's not just my neighborhood, either (e.g., Baumgartner, 1988).

TOM: Wait a minute. Big red flags here. Is the empowerment of suburbanites something we ought to get wrought up about?

BILL: There are plenty of hardscrabble suburbs. And it's not only suburbanites. Many lower-income urban neighborhoods will have no dominating issue at a given moment. There's also recent research indicating that neighborhood satisfaction levels of suburban residents are not higher than those of people living in the city (Adams, 1992).

Now, we can choose to disregard these people, suburbanites and those who may have more economic advantages. Yet I'd hesitate to call them empowered, either. Many of them are struggling, except their struggles are played out in private. Their economic futures are hardly secure. They beat up on each other, behind closed doors. They're poorly connected to supporting structures. They're jerked around by political and economic forces they can't control. They're just like the alienated people in the Harris poll we mentioned before, or rather, they *are* those people. Do we want to ignore them in shaping social policy? I don't.

This isn't in any way to suggest that they are just as badly off as people in poverty. And poor people participate less, that can't be ignored either (Verba, Schlozman, Brady, & Nie, 1993). But it is to suggest that empowerment issues cross class lines. Neighborhoods should empower everyone, on all socioeconomic levels. It's not either-or. It's time, though, to turn to the substance, to what empowering activities should go on there, as a consequence of asking, and educating, and training.

TOM: The activities would have to vary, depending on the setting and its needs.

BILL: They would. And if there are live local issues, great; let's work on them. But I feel the key to empowerment in many neighborhoods and small communities is through people's *interests*. Not every place or every person has *issues*, but just about everyone is *interested* in one thing or another. It can be flower-planting, or going to church, or caring for children, or baking bread. The interest can be social, recreational, political, economic, or spiritual—it can take any form. The idea is to bring people with common interests together.

TOM: And so what? What on earth does this have to do with empowerment and with reducing social injustice?

BILL: Quite a bit, although it's gradual and indirect. By linking people with common interests, the first thing that happens is that they meet each other. When they meet each other, they talk with each other. When they talk with each other, they get to know each other. When they know each other, they come to like each other. When they like each other, they come to trust each other. And when they trust each other, they are much more likely to act together for a common cause, when and if one arises, and eventually one will.

The events on this chain are governed by tested social-psychological principles. They apply to rich and poor. They form both the empirical and the theoretical basis for organizing activity of any kind. Applied to small community settings, these are stages of gradually tightening interconnectedness. They lead people to collective action that will collectively empower them. Those empowering actions are partially self-sustaining, for in and of themselves they strengthen the connections—by the process of action and through the results.

But the prior interconnections are almost essential. It's really hard for people to work together on issues when they have no previous ties to each other. You need some glue. Interest organizing can create those ties, can be the glue. Putting it another way, interest organizing can make subsequent issue organizing more successful.

TOM: It seems like we're talking about two different models here. One is more direct, focusing on stated social needs. The other is more indirect, focusing on other social commonalities. Maybe they overlap, although they really seem quite different. But I'd like to hear some examples of how common interests lead to empowerment.

BILL: Here's one simple example. In my neighborhood, people walk their dogs in the local park. Dog walking is a common interest, right? These dog-walkers have come to know each other; they've become connected, pretty tightly as it turns out. If an issue arises—park maintenance, to pick one—there's a natural constituency already behind it. Or they might *make* the issue arise. Either way, the prior interest constituency fosters issue-oriented success. Its very existence empowers it to act, and its action can empower it further. In fact, I've seen this actually happen, on just this issue.

In a sense, this example is atypical. The interests here are already out in the open. But a lot of the time, most of the time, people don't know who's interested in what, because they don't know each other in the first place. The interests need to be drawn out.

TOM: And how do you do that?

BILL: Well, basically, once again you ask. It's not hard to do on a neighborhood level, and there are many ways to do it. You can interview, in living rooms or on doorsteps. You can use mailed questionnaires or newsletter surveys. You can conduct "community concerns meetings" (Schriner & Fawcett, 1988). You can take a slightly different tack, emphasize capacities instead of interests, and construct community capacity inventories (Kretzmann & McKnight, 1993). You can do focus groups, block meetings, coffees, or, in Latino communities, "house chats"—whatever makes the most sense, given the local culture and your own resources. All this takes time, and someone to get things started. But it costs next to nothing.

And when it's done right, the data collection *itself* can be an empowering process. The very acts of asking and being asked can and should generate mutual warmth, respect, and connectedness, over and above the content that's revealed through the asking or the effects that might come out of it.

Then you've got to find some way of making these interests at least semipublic, so that those with common interests have the chance to link up. Again, there are plenty of choices—newsletter publication, directories, bulletin board postings, community meetings, public events, and so on. Ideally, it's good if one person with a given interest can be motivated to take the lead in convening a one-time meeting of similarly interested people. Or, alternatively, one person in a given microneighborhood can organize a one-time meeting of people in that area who may have complementary interests and skills.[4] In either case, something bigger may happen, or something related may surface in the future, in a different form, in an unanticipated way. We don't need, or want, complete control here. Our task is to start balls rolling. We look for downhills, where they can pick up speed.

None of this is direct or conventional issue organizing. But conventional organizing is limited, as we've said before. And an interest-based strategy is potentially very powerful. Its power rests on what sociologists sometimes call "the strength of weak ties." What this means is that when connections get formed, even weakly, they can grow, largely by themselves, without our direct intervention. We may be like surgeons, attaching the severed connections at the beginning. But when we've made that initial reattachment, that's some-

times the biggest part of the job. Nature may take over. Basic social laws of
reciprocity and equity may then apply. In other words, once you get people
talking—just as we are talking here—other things will follow, in their own
way. That's a big load off our backs, if it works.

"PEOPLE WANT TO DO MEANINGFUL CIVIC WORK"

TOM: Well, I remain a skeptic that this form of interest organizing and support leads to empowerment. I can see how it could increase a sense of community. But it can also just lead to self-centered local contentment and isolation that does not involve concern for the outside world, much less acting
on it. What's more, getting together around simple interests has no inherent
value base, or built-in social justice content, or intrinsic political agenda.
Even when it does, that agenda could be unrelated to, or even antithetical to,
what we're striving for.

BILL: You're right. It could be. And granted, we don't know for sure if
this strategy will work. It's never been systematically *tried* for an extended
period of time. If it does work, it may work imperfectly, for weak ties can
yield weak networks with short lifetimes. Even if it works wonderfully, there
are still miles to go before we are looking at measurable reductions in social
inequality and injustice.

And I can hear not just your skepticism but much harsher criticism too.
We began with income disparities and class conflict. I conclude with neighbors talking about their interests. Some others, not just you, might see this
approach as misplaced at best, as abdicating as turning one's back from the
fundamental problems.

TOM: I understand their point. What you've said doesn't address the
need for major social change, or how one can redistribute power and capital to lead to a more just and equitable society. David Chavis and J. R. Newbrough have put it nicely: what citizens say they need are the "3 Cs"—cash,
community, and control. Your approach may strengthen a sense of community. Coalitions can build local control. That leaves us to find the cash—or
the jobs, or the housing—and that may take another strategy altogether,
(Chavis & Newbrough, 1986).

BILL: And how do we do this, Tom? Let's be as honest as we can about
it. The goal of correcting social and economic inequalities is hardly new. It's
thousands of years old. What do we do as human service professionals and
as social scientists to make this happen—in our lifetimes?

Recent strategies haven't worked well, let's just say it. We certainly can't wait around for government to take the lead. And simply calling for redistribution won't do the job. Sure, we can keep on doing more of the same—more advocacy, more letters to the editor, more calls to legislators, more campaigns—but however admirable this is, the bottom-line results have fallen far short.

On the other hand, when you have local cohesion, that's a precursor of effective action, social and also economic. Many empowerment attempts ultimately fail because the organizational base is simply too weak. It can't be strengthened by a one-time exercise. Instead, we need to reach down to the smallest building blocks—two neighbors talking to each other—and make these our foundation. The poorer the community, the more important that foundation becomes (cf. McDougall, 1993). It comes back to the meeting-knowing-liking-trusting-acting dynamic we spoke about before. If we can stimulate movement along this natural chain, and strengthen local interconnectedness, and replicate this process in neighborhoods across the United States, then I begin to get optimistic (cf. Berry, Portney, & Thomson, 1993).

TOM: I question the payoffs of just meeting and talking, but I am most optimistic about local solutions. We need to find the local-level experiments that people are engaged in, to disseminate their findings, and to let neighborhoods be the incubators for the ideas that the nation as a whole will finally embrace. We're seeing this now, as police, schools, and human service programs turn to communities and say, "Come be partners in innovation with us"—whether it be community partnerships against substance abuse (e.g., Hawkins, Catalano, & Associates, 1992) or neighborhood-based child abuse prevention programs (e.g., Barry, 1992), or community policing, or interventions designed by gang members themselves. That's where hope lies. And I have a lot of faith that if we invest both patience and resources in those experiments, we are going to find some surprising results.

BILL: I'd go further and say that local cohesion and local solutions set the stage for local economic change. As collaboration grows, and the web of interconnectedness grows tighter, people experience common fate. They begin to acknowledge and value and motivate and care for each other more (Pilisuk & Parks, 1986). This will translate into more equality in how local economic resources are distributed in practice, even if not yet into more equality in formal resource ownership itself. But it's a start. We move from there.

TOM: For this to happen means we need an active community policy, with funding and with specific incentives for community-building. It will not happen on its own. It means that individual citizens, families, neighborhoods, and communities must have the core roles in all community development and coalition-building efforts, including defining the issues, driving the agenda, becoming significant partners in implementation, and evaluating the effort on their terms.

But it also means local actors have to move beyond their community arenas to trigger the larger political and policy changes needed for a more just and equitable society. For us as professionals, we have to figure out how to support and catalyze all of this activity, as opposed to creating professional caring and dependence as a substitute. And that's going to require understanding and building upon natural community strengths, and upon natural community modes of helping.

BILL: All of this rests on a high assumption—that citizens and community members will want to and will be able to take this on. I think they can. As one of my mentors taught me, "People want to do meaningful civic work" (Shonholtz, 1987). I believe this. People have to be asked, face to face, by people they respect, to do meaningful tasks they can personally relate to. Under those conditions, when you ask them, they will come. All ages, all races, all income levels, across the demographic spectrum. Not everyone. Not all at once. But a very large number. And if they find fulfillment, others will follow them.

TOM: That's all fine, Bill. But I hope they will also follow into civic work aimed at changing the larger system, at redistributing the resources of civic society itself. That's Bill Ryan's message in *Blaming the Victim,* and it can't get lost.

BILL: Ryan's message still holds true. Social action and community empowerment are universally needed. Yet the basic strategy for generating both of them may be universal too; it rests on local community activity. Local actions add up, and their effects ripple out. As the noted Worldwatch Institute scholar Alan Durning has written in summarizing research from across the world: "The work required . . . will involve an unprecedented outpouring of human energy. The tasks are far from mysterious; in fact, millions have been engaged in them for years. But achieving a just and sustainable global [society] will require an enormous number of simple acts. Grassroots groups, whose membership now numbers in the hundreds of millions, may be able to show the world how to tap the energy to perform these acts" (Durning, 1989, p. 7).

NOTES

1. These principles are adapted from DSNI program literature. For further information, contact Dudley Street Neighborhood Initiative, 513 Dudley Street, Roxbury, MA 02119.
2. Block Booster has been succeeded in part by a Neighborhood Leadership Institute, offering training in each New York City borough. For further information, contact Citizens Committee for New York City, Inc., 305 Seventh Avenue, New York, NY 10001.

3. For further information, contact The Right Question Project, 167 Holland Street, Somerville, MA 02144.
4. For information on one successful current microneighborhood example, contact The Neighborhood Exchange, 21 Linwood Street, Arlington, MA 02174.

REFERENCES

Adams, R. E. (1992). Is happiness a home in the suburbs? The influence of urban versus suburban neighborhoods on psychological health. *Journal of Community Psychology, 20*, 353–372:

Aneshensel, C. S. (1992). Social stress: Theory and research. *Annual Review of Sociology, 18*, 15–38.

Barry, F. (1992). *Neighborhood based approach—What is it?* (Background paper for the U.S. Advisory Board on Child Abuse and Neglect). Ithaca, NY: Cornell University, Family Life Development Center.

Baumgartner, M. P. (1988). *The moral order of a suburb*. New York: Oxford University Press.

Berkowitz, B. (1991, Summer). Sources of community-action ideas. *Whole Earth Review, 71*, 16–17.

Berry, J. M., Portney, K., & Thomson, K. (1993). *The rebirth of urban democracy*. Washington, DC: Brookings Institution.

Cassidy, J. (1995, October 16). Who killed the middle class? *The New Yorker, 71*, 113–124.

Chavis, D. M., & Newbrough, J. R. (1986). The meaning of "community" in community psychology. *Journal of Community Psychology, 14*, 335–340.

Cialdini, R. B. (1992). *Influence: Science and practice* (3rd ed.). New York: Harper Collins.

Durning, A. B. (1989). *Action at the grassroots: Fighting poverty and environmental decline* (Worldwatch Paper No. 88). Washington, DC: Worldwatch Institute.

Florin, P., & Wandersman, A. (1990). An introduction to citizen participation, voluntary organizations, and community development: Insights for empowerment through research. *American Journal of Community Psychology, 18*, 41–54.

George H. Gallup International Institute. (1990). *America's cities and communities: Problems and people power* (Survey for National Civic League). Princeton: Author.

Hawkins, J. D., Catalano, R. F., Jr., & Associates. (1992). *Communities that care: Action for drug abuse prevention*. San Francisco: Jossey-Bass.

Himmelman, A. T. (1992). *Communities working collaboratively for a change*. (Available from Himmelman Consulting Group, 1406 West Lake, Suite 209, Minneapolis, MN 55408)

Hodgkinson, V. A., & Weitzman, M. S. (1988). *Giving and volunteering in the United States: Summary of findings from a national survey* (1988 ed.). Washington, DC: Independent Sector.

Hodgkinson, V. A., & Weitzman, M. S. (1994). *Giving and volunteering in the United States: Findings from a national survey* (1994 ed.). Washington, DC: Independent Sector.

Kretzmann, J. P., & McKnight, J. L. (1993). *Building communities from the inside out: A path toward finding and mobilizing a community's assets.* Chicago: ACTA Publications.

Labonté, R. (1994). Health promotion and empowerment: Reflections on professional practice. *Health Education Quarterly, 21,* 253–268.

McDougall, H. (1993). *Black Baltimore: A new theory of community.* Philadelphia: Temple University Press.

McKnight, J. (1989). Do no harm: Policy options that meet human needs. *Social Policy, 20*(1), 5–15.

McKnight, J. (1990, November). *The community way.* Address presented to the New Haven Foundation, New Haven, CT.

Medoff, P., & Sklar, H. (1994). *Streets of hope: The fall and rise of an urban neighborhood.* Boston: South End Press.

Minkler, M. (1989). Health education, health promotion, and the open society: An historical perspective. *Health Education Quarterly, 16,* 17–30.

Miringoff, M. L. (1995). *The Index of Social Health: Monitoring the social wellbeing of the nation.* Tarrytown, NY: Fordham Graduate Center, Fordham University Institute for Innovation in Social Policy.

National Assembly of National Voluntary Health and Social Welfare Organizations. (1991). *The community collaboration manual.* Washington, DC: Author.

Pilisuk, M., & Parks, S. H. (1986). *The healing web: Social networks and human survival.* Hanover, NH: University Press of New England.

Rappaport, J., Swift, C., & Hess, R. (Eds.). (1984). *Studies in empowerment: Steps toward understanding and action.* New York: Haworth Press.

Riger, S. (1993). What's wrong with empowerment. *American Journal of Community Psychology, 21,* 279–292.

Roper Organization. (1991). *Roper Reports* (No. 92–1). (Reprinted in part in *The American Enterprise,* 1993, 4(3), 87).

Ryan W. (1971). *Blaming the victim.* New York: Random House.

Schriner, K. F., & Fawcett, S. B. (1988). Development and validation of a community concerns report method. *Journal of Community Psychology, 16,* 306–316.

Shonholtz, R. (1987). [Interview]. In B. Berkowitz, *Local heroes* (pp. 60–77). Lexington, MA: Lexington Books.

Taylor, H. (1996). *Americans more alienated than at any time in the last 30 years.* (The Harris Poll, 1996, No. 2). New York: Louis Harris & Associates.

U.S. Bureau of the Census. (1992). *Statistical abstract of the United States: 1992* (112th ed.) Washington, DC: U.S. Government Printing Office.

Verba, S., Schlozman, K. L., Brady, H., & Nie, N. H. (1993). Citizen activity: Who participates? What do they say? *American Political Science Review, 87,* 303–318.

Wallerstein, N. (1992). Powerlessness, empowerment, and health: Implications for health promotion programs. American Journal of Health Promotion, 6, 197–201.

Wolff, T. J. (1992). *Coalition building: One path to empowered communities.* (Available from Community Partners, 24 South Prospect Street, Amherst, MA 01002)

Wolff, T. J. (1993, October). *Coalition building: Is this really empowerment?* Paper presented at the meeting of the American Public Health Association, San Francisco.

Chapter 16

Art as Community Narrative: A Resource for Social Change

•*R. Elizabeth Thomas and Julian Rappaport*

THIS CHAPTER IS ABOUT HOW NARRATIVES, THE SHARED STORIES OF A COMmunity that are often expressed in its art forms, both shape and reflect individual and social life. We argue that what is typically thought of as "art" is a powerful means for communicating the narratives that interpret experience and shape our collective understanding of ourselves.

Despite its portrayal as the bastion of avant-garde social change, much of what is legitimated as art is controlled by the most powerful and conservative forces in government and the private sector. In a quest for equality and social justice, or what William Ryan (1981) called a "Fair Share," the arts can be, however, both a powerful tool and a concrete product. In using the term "arts," we imply a broad spectrum of creative expression, visual and verbal, written and performed, "no-tech" and mass media (O'Brien, 1990). We recognize the arts as both product and process, and include the intended and actual audiences as participants in the arts. We suggest that engagement in local arts projects is a way for communities that are typically excluded from control over the means to uncover, interpret, and create their own identity to obtain access to a powerful resource. The arts serve as a means by which a society reminds itself of the stories it wants to remember.

In the face of what we will call dominant cultural narratives about them, many communities can uncover and create their own stories, expressed through artistic performance owned by the people themselves, rather than by an elite class of artists and patrons. By working with artists and local communities, social scientists have the opportunity both to foster empowerment and to learn about identity development and personal and social change. The

317

goals and methods of such work are congruent with the aim of those who are concerned with empowerment, which is defined as "an intentional, ongoing process centered in the local community, involving mutual respect, critical reflection, caring and group participation, through which people lacking an equal share of valued resources gain greater access to and control over those resources" (Cornell University Empowerment Group, 1989, p. 2).

STORIES ABOUT US VERSUS STORIES BY US

The stories a society tells about itself are the glue that holds its citizens together. Shared holidays, heroes, and retold events mark the vision of a nation, often captured and indexed in the work of its artists, writers and performers. These indexes serve as reminders of who we are. Did Columbus discover America, or did he begin its invasion? Does it matter to social scientists or to local communities how historians answer this question and how artists portray it? Does the answer inform present-day social policy? Does the designation "African American" signify more than a fashion, or is there some larger story about Africa, Europe, and today's North Americans that lies behind it? Why is it important to have access to tools for telling how one's daily life connects to others in our past, present and future? Who has the right to speak for themselves? Who has the right to speak for others?

Much of William Ryan's work life has been devoted to uncovering the implicit rationales and rituals of his most well known phrase—"blaming the victim"—that have justified the unequal distribution of what he called, with characteristic directness, "loot and clout" (Ryan, 1971). His analysis of our most cherished beliefs in internal, individual differences, as opposed to the power of collective similarities and external social and economic realities, taught that much of what we come to take for granted about ourselves and others is a product of interpretation.

> We come to believe those ideas and . . . assumptions that appear to be consistent with our own experiences or—and this is most important—that someone can *interpret to us* as being consistent with our own experiences. . . . Complicated mental processes take place. Some of them might use prior experience to formulate interpretations; some of them might use earlier interpretations to shape the experience and its perception. (Ryan, 1981, pp. 200–201 [italics in original])

We suggest here that the "complicated mental processes" Ryan points to are carried by largely the dominant cultural narratives of a society, that is, the stories a society tells and retells about its members. These stories become the common-sense understanding people have of themselves and others.[1] By "dominant cultural narratives," we mean those stories that are so pervasive as to be unquestioned, yet so powerful as to carry with them assumptions about character, attributions of motivation, and expectations about behavior. Psychologists studying stereotypes sometimes get a handle on this when they ask participants to endorse adjectives that characterize a group of people (Ashmore & Del Boca, 1981; Brigham, 1971; Katz & Braly, 1933). But what are the sources of these endorsed adjectives? We suggest that they are like visual images, indexes that serve as "shorthand" for the stories that are often learned in school, in the popular media, and in the oral traditions of a society. These dominant cultural narratives, once indexed, feel to us like our own experiences, in part because good stories mimic the way the world is taken in, that is, as temporal sequences that entertain and capture our attention (Brewer & Lichtenstein, 1982). Once the stories are indexed in our memory, they function in ways similar to the ways our own experiences, also indexed in our memory, function.

Ironically, the dominant cultural narratives are usually believed by those who both benefit from and are hurt by them. For example, most Americans, raised in the context of stories, pictures, and songs that venerate the lone cowboy and the individual entrepreneur, or that link shared resources with the loss of individuality (think of George Orwell's *1984* or *Animal Farm*), remain repulsed by the thought of socialized medicine, despite their own insecurity about health care. In the face of violent crime and the reality that the use of a handgun increases danger to one's self, we evoke stories of self-defense and the right to own weapons in part because these are reinforced by the narratives we have heard many times and in many contexts. Underneath our beliefs, attitudes, and values are a set of well-learned stories conveniently indexed as visual, verbal, and other shorthand devices of memory.

For people who are part of an organization or a community with a well-developed narrative of its own, there are alternatives to the dominant cultural narrative. For example, membership in a mutual-help organization or a religious community can provide clear alternative stories around which identity is formed or changed (Cain, 1991; Rappaport, 1992, 1993). Similarly, neighborhood, ethnic, and grass-roots organizations have the potential to provide a story that tells their members who they are, where they have come from, and what they can be.

Individuals live in specific social contexts. Within these contexts are relationships of power between people and groups of people that have real consequences for how individuals are able to engage that world. How we define, and who defines, these relationships may or may not reflect past or current realities, but these processes certainly play a role in shaping future realities for individuals and communities. Our thesis is that these relationships, often more accurately called struggles, are defined in the stories that we tell about the communities we belong to: stories about who we are, how we got to this place, and where we are going. In other words, the shared narratives that people tell again and again about their own and other communities are instrumental in maintaining these communities and in shaping the way that people think about themselves in these communities.

For those who are outside the mainstream of access to power and material resources, there is often a conflict between the dominant cultural narrative about them and their own community narrative. For indigenous leaders, community organizers, and social scientists who are action researchers and advocates (Weber & McCall, 1978), finding ways to give voice to stories that not only challenge the dominant cultural narrative but also celebrate the community members' own construction of reality is often a basic but unarticulated aim. How can our way of understanding ourselves be presented, first to ourselves and then to others? How can we obtain control over the right to speak our own history, our own identity, and our own future? What we suggest here is that one powerful resource available to people with such concerns is the use of visual and performance art. Because it serves as a collective memory device, storytelling in the visual and performing arts is among the most powerful tools for stabilizing or changing communities and their relationships to one another.

We shall first present our analysis of how and why narratives are powerful. We discuss how they are used by mainstream and legitimated authority to construct a reality that is usually taken for granted. We then briefly describe several examples of how visual and performance narratives have been used in the service of local community organizing, and conclude with suggestions for future work by the social science community in collaboration with grass-roots and artistic communities who share a common sense of mission and values.

HOW AND WHY NARRATIVES
ARE POWERFUL

In a classic study of stress and coping, conducted some thirty years ago, Richard Lazarus and his colleagues demonstrated that the verbal indexes accompanying filmed events could change the meaning as well as the emotional experience of those events (Lazarus & Alfert, 1964; Lazarus, Speisman, Mordkoff, & Davison, 1962; Speisman, Lazarus, Mordkoff, & Davison,

1964). He showed two groups of observers the same film of circumcision rites among an African tribe. One group listened to a narrator describe the trauma of the procedure. A second group saw the same film accompanied by an "anthropological" sound track in which the events were described in a very matter-of-fact way. Lazarus found that the first group experienced significantly greater physiological and psychological signs of emotional distress. This effect has many counterparts in the day-to-day experiences of people.

When a video recording of policemen beating an African American man named Rodney King was broadcast on national television many people believed that it told an obvious story. For some this was a shocking and remarkable event. It was not the presentation of a beating on television, an all too commonplace occurrence, that was remarkable, but rather its recording and repeated presentation by newscasters as an act of obvious illegal violence by the police. Many assumed that the story told by video pictures and initial news reports was straightforward. However, we were soon to learn that it was not. Much to the surprise of those who believe in common-sense notions of objective reality, many stories can be told about the same behaviors. What surprised people about the aftermath of this event was that its recording actually made it easier for different observers to tell different stories while watching the same video. It is not unusual for eyewitnesses, relying on memory, to tell different stories about the same event. Such differences are easy to attribute to psychological factors. But in this case it was possible to seem to observe the identical event many times and yet still see different things, depending on what indexed stories were invoked. Here we have a case of life imitating art. It is a common device for films and novels to provide different interpretations of the same events through the eyes of different characters, yet when this occurs in "real life," it continues to surprise us.

Much of the meaning of the recorded behavior in the Rodney King incident was determined by the narrative index applied to it by various storytellers. To the residents of south-central Los Angeles, where the event took place, there was a readily available index based on their own daily experience. The video recorded the events in a story they believed to be less an exception than an example of the everyday reality of police officers interacting with neighborhood residents. It could be indexed as "police brutality." Yet according to police accounts the video was indexed as a story about public servants performing a difficult job that required them to restrain a dangerous person who resisted arrest. To prosecutors it was a case of excessive force, and to the defendants, their lawyers, and at least one jury, it was a story about the dangerous people the police must control. As subsequent events revealed (one jury acquitted the police of criminal charges, leading to large-scale civil disturbances, physical violence, and property damage; a latter jury found some of the officers guilty of violating King's civil rights), it takes much more than a video recording to change the social constructions of reality held by the various actors. Different people quite literally see different things in the same behaviors. What they see is in large measure a function of the narratives they have acquired and how these are indexed in their memory.

Although the exact definition of a story is hotly debated by cognitive psychologists and linguists (Brewer & Lichtenstein, 1982; Labov, 1982; LeGuin, 1990; Schank, 1990; Stein, 1982; Wyer, 1995), most agree that people seem to recognize one when it is presented, and narratives seem to provide an ordering of sequential events that help us to remember and interpret those events (Mandler, 1984). Here we accept Roger Schank's (Schank, 1990; Shank & Abelson, 1995) theoretical formulation, which emphasizes the importance of the index as an aid to memory. The story index may be in the form of a verbal narration, a shorthand adjective, a picture, or a performance that serves to remind us of a story we already know. Art can serve as such an index, and it can also teach us new stories. The more well known the story, the more briefly it can be indexed. New stories require greater detail. Stories already told many times can be indexed in a more symbolic shorthand.

Mark Salzer (1992) asked a sample of undergraduates to write stories about housing project residents. With no information other than the names and ages of the characters they were asked to write about, individual respondents constructed a common story emphasizing drugs, single parents, violence, and irresponsibility. He also spent several months attending meetings at a local housing project, where he found a very different picture. Although residents knew of the stories that others were likely to tell about them, their own stories about themselves emphasized the poor maintenance of their physical environment, the lack of respect they received from managers of their housing project, their arbitrary treatment by police, and their negative expectations for their children in the public schools. They also emphasized their own knowledge that many of them engaged in responsible and caring behavior, motivated by a concern for their children and their neighbors. As the residents expected, the stories that undergraduates told, most of whom had never met a housing project resident, were the same ones told by the media. The stories the residents themselves told were unlikely to be heard by anyone, including other residents. Herein lies a potentially powerful tool for community organizing, empowerment, and the fostering of positive identity among members of a local community.

Community residents, including those in the poorest and most excluded sectors of our society, hold a vast knowledge of stories about themselves. In this knowledge is the potential power to define themselves for themselves and for others. What communities usually lack, however, is the means to make known their own sense of history and self-definition. The use of art as a vehicle for indexing, defining, presenting, and amplifying a community's own voice is a powerful tool that can be used in the service of community identity development and organizing. Unfortunately, art as a resource for organizing, like most other resources in our society, tends to be distributed so that those who need it the most have it the least. This inequitable distribution of artistic power is psychological as well as material. It is in part determined by what we have come to define as art.

PUBLIC NARRATIVES AND LOCAL CONTROL: WHO OWNS THE ARTS?

Many of the narratives that define a community are indexed in the form of visual and performance arts, domains usually dominated and controlled by legitimated authorities, patrons, and governments. Yet these same artistic vehicles have the power to transform and energize local communities through the stories communities tell, or are permitted to tell, about themselves. There are excellent examples of the power of local arts projects, some of which we shall mention below, to assist people in obtaining control over their own history, identity, and future. However, these are few and far between. In order to foster such projects, and to see their power and relevance to everyday life, it is necessary to have a conceptual framework that acknowledges, indeed, covets the arts as a resource. However, what is usually taught by our public schools and authorized institutions is exactly the opposite.

On the one hand, artistic expression and the development of artistic skills tend to be relegated to a place in the educational curriculum for "extras," which are not so important as other, "real" subjects. At the same time, there is a tendency to teach that art, as opposed to mathematics or science, is a "natural skill," one that cannot be developed or even appreciated unless someone has a special talent not possessed by ordinary people.

Thus, creating art is something most persons do only as young children. They stop creating when they "learn" that they are not creative. Seymour Sarason (1990) notes this decline of artistic activity by elementary school in all but a few people. He asserts that it is extinguished in most due to a feeling that they are inadequate at representing reality and to a perceived gulf between themselves and great artists. Additionally, our culture implies that artistic activity has little developmental significance, and we do not nurture artistic development as we do language development and reading.

This lack of anticipation and reinforcement for art continues in the classroom and beyond, as students are not often encouraged to connect artistic activity to their own experiences and communities. As adults, we are often embarrassed and intimidated in our response to art (Lippard, 1990), and see ourselves as incompetent creators and viewers.

We often think of art, then, not as a creative process in which we are able to participate, but as a finished product, produced only by artists of great genius. Art is made up of rarefied objects or performances that can only be found in museums and concert halls; it cannot happen anywhere else. It is consumed and produced only by a small, elite group. Thus, this privileged group's notions of good taste and quality can be used to justify ethnocentrism (Lippard, 1990) and retain class divisions. Norms requiring the use of legitimate language, images, genres, and forms can be used to keep control around a select group of people. If we do think of art, we think of it as a special experience and an escape from daily life instead of as representations drawn from a variety of sources that are accessible, both as process and product, to a variety of persons. In global terms, the making of art is not a part of our everyday lives. This restricted definition leaves most of us separated from the conscious process of creating or defining our own symbols, rituals, and stories.

These restrictions may arise in part from thinking of ourselves in terms of our roles in a market economy: we are producers and consumers of products. A large part of who we are is determined by what we do "to earn our keep" and what we own. Dislocations arising from this economic system result in a general separation of art and art-making from daily life and an emphasis on product rather than process (Dewey, 1934; Sarason, 1990; Trend, 1992). As we deny the connections between art and life, we also deny that all classes of people can experience art and that all topics can be subjects of art (Klein, 1984; Trend, 1992). We thereby give up the power of art as a means to index our own life stories.

The denigration of art as irrelevant to everyday life is not a message believed by the most powerful members of society with respect to their own class interests. Rather, they recognize art as a resource by which they can define reality. Loss of control over that definition is not taken lightly by those in power, as can be seen most easily by recalling the art of Soviet Realism or Nazi Germany. The democratization of art is even a threat to the powerful in a society that prides itself on democratic political participation, such as the United States. It is exactly this threat that prevents the National Endowment for the Arts from widespread funding of community-based, as opposed to elite, arts projects. Disguised as an argument for "standards," our educational system and our government work hard to prevent our students from becoming conscious of their own power to use art to define themselves. Rather, these institutions prefer to create passive recipients of "culture" that the students sense is irrelevant to their own experiences, an irrelevance that they are encouraged to see as due their own lack of intellect, talent, or family upbringing.

The public portrayal of historical narratives, traditionally connected to religious consciousness, has in modern times been used to solidify national identity. These narratives take the form of public sculpture, architecture, and ritual that are the background of our lives and are often invisible as story or ideology. For example, in the United States, children grow up seeing pictures of Washington, D.C.'s architecture and public sculpture accompanying the stories they learn about the country's history in required texts. News reporters regularly use these capital sites as backdrops for stories, lending legitimacy and authority to the news source and to the news makers. Additionally, many people make pilgrimages with their families or on school trips to "see heroes," to gain a sense of history, or to connect to the stories of their past. They may leave feeling a renewed sense of respect, confidence, and loyalty to the country. They often do not recognize their experiences of these artistic forms as indexes for a narrative that is imposed or purposefully created, but instead think of this contact as getting in touch with something they already know to be true, that they in a sense "own."

In this example, art forms experienced through various media (e.g., television or history books) or in a more immediate context (e.g., a visit to the city) provide a vital supplement to a primarily textual narrative. They serve as concentrated symbols, representations, or indexes of the idealized stories that our nation wants to tell about itself. The artworks reveal the essence of a larger story and presume cultural currency, or knowledge, of that story. Their effect is ultimately political; it says something about how we stand in relation to each other now and how we should stand in the future.

Bernice Johnson Reagon (1990), founder of the vocal ensemble of black women singers Sweet Honey in the Rock and curator at the National Museum of American History in Washington, D.C., describes the importance of form as a rhetorical strategy by saying that the content goes "beyond text." Here, she is talking about the importance for leaders, or agents of change, also to be cultural artists of great power. The virtuosity of the delivery of a message depends on both what is said (the gist of the story) and whether the teller can purposefully craft a form that allows his or her storytelling to connect with the affections of a given audience. The form, or *how,* of the story helps tie information to our emotions, and our senses. This is why art can be such a powerful way to index the stories we want to remember.

In using the Washington, D.C., example above, we do not suggest that most of us live in a state of false consciousness or that we have all been duped by the orchestrators of culture. We do, however, suggest that before we can begin to tell alternative stories about ourselves and our communities, we must know that the stories captured in our urban and rural landscapes, in the spaces around us, are, like those landscapes, not natural. Instead, they are created and maintained to serve particular purposes. They are guarded as material resources.

These powerful stories told and indexed for memory by the arts, like the ones we have in the United States about our country as a land of opportunity and the powerful righteous leader of the world, serve many purposes, one of which is the limiting of the range of alternative stories that are available or considered legitimate. Communities can be trapped by the mostly negative or socially degraded dominant narratives told about them by powerful others, as in the case of the public housing residents mentioned earlier. Of course, no unified history or perspective captures the story of complex communities. The history of the interaction of cultures as in the United States is full of appropriation, degradation, violence, and blocked possibilities. It is, however, also rebellious and creative (Clifford, 1988).

While all of us will be deeply influenced by the dominant cultural narratives of our society, to the extent that local communities have alternative ways to index their own experiences, they will be more likely to think of themselves in ways other than those forced upon them. To the extent that people participate in the creation of indexes to remember their own stories, they are more likely to become creators of their own history, their own future, and their own identity. This is the type of resource that local arts projects can provide. Although the details of each individual project are beyond the scope of this paper, below we shall point to the kinds of projects that illustrate our point.

COMMUNITY ARTS PROJECTS

Community arts projects, while not an everyday phenomenon, have emerged often enough to catch the attention of newspaper writers. Michael Kimmelman (1993), in an ambivalent *New York Times* article about such projects, remarked that they often look more like social work than artwork. In the context of artistic sensibilities, such an evaluation was not intended as a compliment. He nevertheless described several such efforts in New York and Chicago. Among the most interesting are those that involved youth from different neighborhoods working on the same project, including making and showing videos, organizing costume parades, and creating gardens. Although he sympathetically described some of these projects, the questions Kimmelman raised focused on asking if the money might not be better spent for "established" social programs, and if programs such as these tend to "ghettoize" art for the poor and assume that museums are "irrelevant to such people." What seems to be missed in this way of conceptualizing such activities is an awareness of their power to create shared group consciousness among the creators and the community residents. The aim is not to provide services for people but rather to create contexts for people to learn about themselves and their community, and to use art as a means to index and therefore to remember their own stories.

It is perhaps important to note that a locally produced artwork may not have the same kind of impact that a popular culture text or performance may have. A display of photographs at the local library will obviously not have the same breadth of impact or appeal as the release of a popular film. In thinking about local community change, we focus less on television, film, and other forms of mass, or popular, culture not because we do not think that they can and should be used progressively, nor because we wish to perpetuate a false "high art" versus "low art" distinction, but because those media are less accessible to most local groups who are interested in engaging in creative work with community members. Many community groups are familiar with budgets of tens of dollars rather than tens of millions of dollars. While they are not wealthy, these local groups may have a wealth of creative resources in their community. The key to such efforts is artists collaborating with members of a local community to tell the stories of their lives, their histories, and their experience.

Judy Baca and the Social and Public Art Resource Center (SPARC) have done visual storytelling in the Los Angeles area since the late 1970s. Baca is a professor in fine arts at University of California at Irvine, a Chicana spokesperson, and an activist who has directed several mural projects involving children from various ethnic communities in the Los Angeles area. She began her work by spending time in city parks and gaining information from youth about their visual subculture (graffiti and tattooing). These young people, some of whom were recruited through the juvenile justice system, were hired as mural painters and collaborators in Baca's projects. Under the direction of various artists, they have painted a series of murals, including *The Great Wall of Los Angeles,* which is one of the longest murals in the world and depicts the role of different ethnic groups in the settlement and development of California. Over 250 youth and 70 artists, historians, and resource people worked on the wall through five summers from 1976 to 1983. The wall is painted in sections organized chronologically. Examples of events depicted include the 1940s struggle against covenant laws that denied blacks access to equal housing in south-central Los Angeles, the forcible internment of Japanese Americans during World War II, and the division of a tightknit Los Angeles Chicano community by a freeway that split it in two.

Tim Rollins is another teacher and artist who has used painting and collage in collaborative work with young people in public schools. He has worked in New York with students who have been labeled as having emotional and behavior problems; they are known as KOS, or Kids of Survival. They begin their collaborative process by reading together a text, such as a newspaper clipping, story, or novel, that has been assigned as part of the curriculum and creating a work that "translates the themes of these texts through their own related experiences into visual images" (Kaplan, 1990, p. 120). One example of their work is a 1988 mural covering one side of Central Elementary School 4 in the South Bronx, entitled *Amerika—For the People of Bathgate*. Its images of twenty-eight golden horns, created by the students and staff of the school working with KOS, were inspired by a section from Franz Kafka's unfinished novel *Amerika*. KOS tells us that each horn is an individual vision collaboratively joined into mural design, representing the beauty and challenge of democracy.

The Little Flag's Theater in Boston works to eliminate some of the barriers between the lives and stories of the performers and the audience. Maxine Klein (1984) directs the project, teaching public school students the technical and creative aspects of producing a play. The students, meeting in groups, begin the work of choosing and refining stories gathered from oral histories told to them by parents and grandparents. The children then perform these stories for their families and community.

In our own community, Cheryl West, a playwright from Champaign, Illinois, worked with the local Planned Parenthood to produce a play about teen-parent relationships and communication. Set in an African American community, the play dealt with issues of rape and pregnancy for teens. Persons from the local community served as actors and technicians. The performances were free and held in appropriate, accessible community locations. Many people stayed for planned discussions after the performances.

Persons such as Baca, Rollins, Klein, and West are not the inventors or discoverers of a new tool for community education and development. Rather, they are making obvious a process that is occurring all around us in our daily lives. They are making explicit the notion that stories have always been and continue to be shared in our culture to affect the way people think about their lives and their relationship to both their local communities and the larger society. They recognize and act on the fact that these stories and those who do their telling matter.

ART, SOCIAL STABILITY, AND
SOCIAL CHANGE

As discussed, the power of the arts to index and therefore to remind us of a different, unsanctioned story has long been recognized by church and state authorities, as demonstrated by actions ranging from the strict regulation of icons, or images of the holy, to the very purposeful way that nations fill their public spaces and depict their histories in art. The processes of defining and renewing the cultural representations of communities continue to have implications for the formation of social identity and the possibilities of self- and community transformation (Dewey, 1934; Giroux, 1992; O'Brien, 1990).

The most obvious examples of this recognition of the radical potential of art are found when those in control explicitly curtail or deny certain artistic expression by censorship or the destruction of artwork. A recent example is the government-sponsored eradication of popular murals in Nicaragua that were commissioned by the Sandinista government of the 1980s. In the early 1990s, most of these murals were painted over or destroyed (Kunzle, 1993). We have seen this occur most recently in the United States with the Reagan and Bush administrations' attempts to dismantle the National Endowment for the Arts. They met popular and congressional resistance, but were quite effective in reducing expenditures for community art programs and outreach programs. They have also been effective in frightening curators and artists into self-censorship, particularly of work that has dealt frankly with homosexuality (Kresse, 1991).

Much of this discourse about art and culture in the last decade has explicitly focused on aesthetic or moral "standards" and their noteworthy decline. Although the struggle may actually be about who has power and who wants it, it is important to recognize the form these power struggles are taking and to address this concern with "standards." Recognizing and developing everyday, or democratic, forms of culture does not mean abandoning all notions of quality or excellence in our judgment of works of art. Lucy Lippard (1990) notes that art does not become worse as it spreads out and becomes accessible to more people: "the real low ground lies in the falsely beneficent notion of universal art that smoothes over all rough edges, all differences, but remains detached from the lives of most people" (p. 8) David Trend (1992) echoes this notion in describing this process of opening up the way we think about how art is produced and received: "this is not a process of ignoring the very important objective ways that people form groups or discarding the classics of culture. But it does mean making these structures prove their continuing relevance to our lives. By doing this one accepts the task of critically evaluating the ongoing nature of social contracts" (pp. 102–103).

What is exciting, or frightening—depending upon where one is standing—about the types of creative projects discussed above is that they are both a criticism of the existing social order and a suggestion of an alternative vision. These projects are critical in the sense that they contradict what has become familiar, what we thought we already knew.

John Dewey (1934) claimed that the first stirrings of dissatisfaction with the present and an intimation of a better future are always found in art:

> The impregnation of the characteristically new art of a period with a sense of different values than those that prevail is the reason why the conservative finds such art to be immoral and sordid, and is the reason why he resorts to the products of the past for aesthetic satisfaction. . . . Change in the climate of the imagination is the precursor of the changes that affect more than the details of life. (p. 346).

Local art projects can work to turn stereotypes around by reversing frequently used images (Lippard, 1990) or by juxtaposing common symbols in an uncommon way (Clifford, 1988), and can serve to reclaim the vocabulary through which struggle is expressed: the family in the Little Flag's Theater, the community in the Los Angeles mural, democracy in the KOS project. In contradicting what is familiar in the dominant narrative, they set the boundaries of discourse as extreme, disrupting the existing social text and leaving more room for dialogue. Thus, we see relationships between people and communities in a different way, breaking the sense that reality is petrified or that the way things are is the way things will always be.

Community art projects are about claiming one's right to tell existing stories about self and community and to create new ones. They are about reclaiming a history and filling in a past that helps to make a whole person. Restorations of community histories are important for forming and informing the human subject and developing community solidarity. They are not only exercises in nostalgia (Lippard, 1990) or in feeling good. The political project may be quite radical, resuscitating narratives that celebrate emancipatory struggles and social justice (Trend, 1992), or that document injustices, as in *The Great Wall of Los Angeles*.

Stories of the past, or memories, inform present experience and feed present observation. They are a "nutriment that gives body to what is seen" (Dewey, 1934, p. 89). Memory is liberating as it is used as a resource for reconstructing ethics from the conflicts, discourses, and stories of those who have lived before. It is "dangerous" when it reveals stories that differ from those most often told in dominant discourse. It says that "my people are central to what is the main cultural power and fabric of this society" (Reagon, 1990, p. 4). Thus, the process of real social change is engaged in this development of alternative narratives indexed through art.

Community art projects are also about reclaiming spaces—public spaces from which we determine what it means to be a self and a community (Morales, 1990). Maxine Greene (1984, 1986) extends this theme to a community level as she calls for public spaces where people may choose to appear before one another as the best they know how to be. It is essential that neighborhoods contain public spaces that are truly public—sites for democratic debate and cultural expression. Shopping malls and corporate lobbies are not those kinds of community spaces. They do not want, nor are they obligated, to meet the social needs of residents in a community (Deutsche, 1990).

Public spaces indicate that the people who live and work in these spaces participate in the process of planning, designing, and maintaining these spaces (Goleman, 1992). An example that highlights differential notions of community access and control is the official festival "Mexico: A Work of Art," sponsored in part by the Mexican government, that included twenty art shows and traveled to several major U.S. cities, including Los Angeles. In addition to artwork, the festival included cooking demonstrations, business conferences directed toward U.S. investors with an interest in "free" trade, and a tourist show featuring Mexican products set up in a giant mall.

The Mexican and Chicano communities in Los Angeles originally wanted to complement this festival with locally organized events and more recent artwork. When they received no support from the planners of the official exhibit, they began organizing their own community-based festival, "Artes de Mexico." Over 180 events were staged in Mexican and Chicano communities, including art exhibitions, film and dance festivals, conferences, and typical Mexican fiestas. The two festivals thus represented two distinct cultural agendas and approaches to public celebration and art (Hollander, 1992). Locally controlled and produced celebrations, public performances, and public murals all take up space—space to develop and share resources, space to tell our stories.

"Telling our stories" may involve the telling of many different—and sometimes conflicting—stories. Communities are not monolithic or essential in nature; instead, they are comprised of a multiplicity of voices and concerns. Issues of diversity and relations of power apply within as well as across communities.

COMMUNITY ART AND ACTION RESEARCH

For all the above reasons, social scientists engaged in community action and research may be interested in the "action art" that occurs (or perhaps does not occur very often) in particular communities. Action researchers will want to understand why and when the projects are powerful for those involved. Activists will want to fill the role of facilitator for future projects in spaces where the community has yet to become conscious of itself and in spaces where resources and strategies are wanting. Both activists and scientists who want to serve as advocates for the least powerful, rather than as consultants for the most powerful, can collaborate with local artists. This is a vehicle that can enhance both the small wins (Weick, 1984) and the genuine collaboration that is the crux of empowering relationships (Rappaport, 1990).

Community arts projects can be a vehicle for social scientists to take the role of collaborator in these "do-able" projects. Because we do not see ourselves as primarily artistic resources, we can more easily be less arrogant in our approach to change and collaboration in such situations. We may be more apt to look for existing community resources (such as artists, young people, and available spaces) and to listen to community members in working for a mutually desired goal. Working together with local artists and would-be artists from the beginning of a project encourages the development of untapped talents, builds leadership and community cohesion, and engages a broad spectrum of potential community (audience) members. This organization is essential for further community talk.

Most people engaged in community arts projects explicitly recognize the political implications of the projects, but are coming from disciplines, or backgrounds, that have led them to the representations (art products) as a focus, or justification, for their study. The social, psychological, and interpersonal impact of such work is not well understood. Mark O'Brien (1990) commented on the growth of this type of progressive cultural work over the last decade:

> This is unquestionably a cause for celebration. It also calls for some form of evaluation. For while it is readily apparent that "content" is streaming into cultural arenas and, far from destroying the standard of the arts, is invigorating them, it is less apparent what, if any, reciprocal effects this increasingly politicized cultural activity is having in generating action in other spheres. (p. 9–10)

Social scientists interested in evaluating and amplifying the possible strengths of these projects might focus specifically on their effects for the people who participate in them, for the community in which they take place, and on the communities around them who might also be learning new stories about the target community. Can we document changes in social identity, community cohesion, and solidarity? Can we demonstrate the transgenerational communication of cultural and historical narratives? Do such projects lead to a different sense of control over one's self-definition? Are there consequences for other, more directly political action, for educational outcomes, and for proactive behavior? What are the conditions that make art liberating as opposed to oppressive? These are questions for action research.

For empirical scientists these ideas, while politically sensible, remain logical hypotheses, untested by research. The notion that participation in such work changes participants' and observers' views of the community and its members can be empirically tested. On the one hand, we would expect to see different stories told and different characteristics attributed to oneself and by others. We might also expect different views of and by children as well as an influence on local institutions, including the schools. The behavioral consequences of local arts projects remain to be analyzed. Both the political and the psychological consequences can be documented by researchers willing to engage in participant observation, community surveys, and public opinion polls designed to serve rather than merely to observe or exploit the local community.

If art leads to disruptions in the social order and in the stories told by dominant groups, it also has the power to heal. It can rehabilitate the role of communal imagination by fostering an understanding of differences rather than simply smoothing over them. At the same time, it may lessen the threat of differences and offer a "vision to those whose mirrors are clouded by social disenfranchisement or personal disempowerment" (Lippard, 1990). Art can be visionary, predicting what we can be as individuals and communities. Most importantly, the development of alternative narratives through art can engage and document the process of real social change.

ACKNOWLEDGMENTS

Thanks are extended to the members of our research group, Susan Carpenter, Karen Horneffer, Keith Humphreys, Mellen Kennedy, Bret Kloos, Eric Mankowski, Mark Salzer, and Robert Wyer, who have played a major role in shaping many of the ideas presented here.

NOTE

1. The question of how information obtained in story form is processed, stored, and retrieved is an interesting one for psychologists to ponder (see, for example,

Schank, 1990). For one analysis of the process by which community narratives may become incorporated through cognitive information processing, see Robert Wyer (1992; Wyer, 1995). Roger Schank and Robert Abelson (1995) have argued that all important knowledge is in storied form. They suggest that stories told and retold are indexed in memory. These indexes are shorthand devices that enable the recall of a great number of details that would otherwise be forgotten. In this paper we assume that art, in its various forms (visual, performance, verbal) serves a similar function: it indexes the important stories of a society. Art, in this view, is the keeper of a society's memory.

REFERENCES

Ashmore, R. D., & Del Boca, F. K. (1981). Conceptual approaches to stereotypes and stereotyping. In D. Hamilton (Ed.), *Cognitive processes in stereotyping and intergroup behavior* (pp. 1–35). Hillsdale, NJ: Erlbaum.
Brewer, W. F., & Lichtenstein, E. H. (1982). Stories are to entertain: A structural-affect theory of stories. *Journal of Pragmatics, 6,* 473–486.
Brigham, J. C. (1971). Ethnic stereotypes. *Psychological Bulletin, 76,* 15–33.
Cain, C. (1991). Personal stories: Identity acquisition and self-understanding in Alcoholics Anonymous. *Ethos, 19*(2), 210–253.
Clifford, J. (1988). *The predicament of culture: Twentieth-century ethnography, literature, and art.* Cambridge, MA: Harvard University Press.
Cockcroft, E. S. (1992, June). Chicano identities. *Art in America,* pp. 84–91.
Cornell University Empowerment Group (1989, October). *Networking Bulletin, 1*(2).
Deutsche, R. (1990). Uneven development: Public art in New York City. In R. Ferguson, M. Gever, T. T. Minh-ha, & C. West (Eds.), *Out there: Marginalization and contemporary cultures* (pp. 107–132). Cambridge, MA: The MIT Press.
Dewey, J. (1934). *Art as experience.* New York: Minton, Balch.
Giroux, H. (1992). *Border crossings: Cultural workers and the politics of education.* New York: Routledge, Chapman & Hall.
Goleman, D. (1992, June 2). Architects rediscover the best city planners: citizens. *The New York Times,* p. C1.
Greene, M. (1984). The art of being present: Educating for aesthetic encounters. *Journal of Education, 166*(2), 123–135.
Greene, M. (1986). The spaces of aesthetic education. *Journal of Aesthetic Education, 20*(2), 56–62.
Hollander, K. (1992, June). Community access. *New Art Examiner,* pp. 57–61.
Kaplan, J. (1990). Tim Rollins & KOS. In M. O'Brien, & C. Little (Eds.), *Reimaging America: The arts of social change* (p. 120). Philadelphia: New Society.
Katz, D., & Braly, K. (1933). Racial stereotypes in one hundred college students. *Journal of Abnormal and Social Psychology, 28,* 280–290.
Kimmelman, M. (1993, September 26). Of candy bars and public art. *The New York Times,* p. B1.

Klein, M. (1984). Four minutes till midnight. *Journal of Education, 166*(2), 170–180.

Kresse, M. E. (1991). Turmoil at the National Endowment for the Arts: Can federally funded art survive the "Mapplethorpe Controversy"? *Buffalo Law Review, 39*(1), 231–274.

Kunzle, D. (1993, April). The mural death squads of Nicaragua. *Z Magazine*, pp. 62–66.

Labov, W. (1982). Speech actions and reactions in personal narrative. In D. Tannen (Ed.), *Analyzing discourse: Text and talk* (pp. 219–247). Washington, DC: Georgetown University Press.

Lazarus, R. S., & Alfert, E. (1964). Short circuiting of threat by experimentally altering cognitive appraisal. *Journal of Abnormal and Social Psychology, 69*, 195–205.

Lazarus, R. S., Speisman, J. C., Mordkoff, A. M., & Davison, L. A. (1962). A laboratory study of psychological stress produced by a motion picture film. *Psychological Monographs, 76*(553), 1–35.

LeGuin, U. (1990). *Dancing at the edge of the world: Thought on words, women, places.* New York: Harper & Row.

Lippard, L. (1990). *Mixed blessings: New art in a multicultural America.* New York: Pantheon Books.

Mandler, J. (1984). *Stories, scripts, and themes: Aspects of schema theory.* Hillsdale, NJ: Erlbaum.

Morales, R. I. (1990). In M. O'Brien, & C. Little (Eds.), *Reimaging America: The arts of social change* (pp. 16–24). Philadelphia: New Society Publishers.

O'Brien, M. (1990). Introduction. In M. O'Brien, & C. Little (Eds.), *Reimaging America: The arts of social change* (pp. 9–10). Philadelphia: New Society Publishers.

Rappaport, J. (1990). Research methods and the empowerment social agenda. In P. Tolan, C. Keys, F. Chertok, & L. Jason (Eds.), *Research community psychology: Integrating theories and methodologies.* Washington, DC: American Psychological Association.

Rappaport, J. (1992, May). Community narratives and personal stories: An introduction to five studies of cross-level relationships. In J. Rappaport (Chair), *Community narratives and personal stories.* Symposium conducted at the meeting of the Midwestern Psychological Association, Chicago.

Rappaport, J. (1993). Narrative studies, personal stories, and identity transformation in the mutual help context. *Journal of Applied Behavioral Science, 29*(2), 237–254.

Reagon, B. J. (1990). Foreword: Nurturing resistance. In M. O'Brien & C. Little (Eds.), *Reimaging America: The arts of social change* (pp. 1–8). Philadelphia: New Society Publishers.

Ryan, W. (1971). *Blaming the victim.* Random House.

Ryan, W. (1981). *Equality.* New York: Vintage.

Salzer, M. A. (1992). Stories, narratives, and community organizing in a public housing setting. In J. Rappaport (Chair), *Community narratives and personal stories.*

Symposium conducted at the meeting of the Midwestern Psychological Association, Chicago.

Sarason, S. B. (1990). *The challenge of art to psychology*. New Haven, CT: Yale University Press.

Schank, R. C. (1990). *Tell me a story: A new look at real and artificial memory*. New York: Schribrers.

Schank, R. C., & Abelson, R. P. (1995). Knowledge and memory: The real story. In R. S. Wyer (Ed.), *Advances in social cognition* (Vol. 8, pp. 1–85). Hillsdale, NJ: Erlbaum.

Speisman, J. C., Lazarus, R. S., Mordkoff, A., & Davison, L. (1964). Experimental reduction of stress based on ego-defense theory. *Journal of Abnormal and Social Psychology, 68,* 367–380.

Stein, N. L. (1982). The definition of a story. *Journal of Pragmatics, 6,* 487–507.

Trend, D. (1992). *Cultural pedagogy: Art, education, and politics.* New York: Bergin & Garvey.

Weber, G. H., & McCall, G. J. (Eds.). (1978). *Social scientists as advocates: Views from applied disciplines.* Beverly Hills: Russell Sage.

Weick, K. (1984). Small wins: Redefining the scale of social issues. *American Psychologist, 39,* 40–49.

Wyer, R. S., Jr. (1992, May). Ecological cognition: An approach to conceptualizing the comprehension and communication of community narratives. In J. Rappaport (Chair), *Community narratives and personal stories.* Symposium conducted at the meeting of the Midwestern Psychological Association, Chicago.

Wyer, R. S., Jr. (Ed.). (1995). *Advances in social cognition* (Vol. 8). Hillsdale, NJ: Erlbaum.

Chapter 17

Dismantling the Postwar Social Contract

•*Sumner M. Rosen*

WILLIAM RYAN'S *EQUALITY* (1981) DEMONSTRATES HOW THOSE WHO YIELD power exploit a straw man dubbed "Equal Shares" to sustain their dominance. Wealth ownership is highly concentrated in the United States. Those who hold it, and those who act for them, largely control what the British Labour Party once called the "commanding heights" of an economy, the scope of which now extends throughout the world through a relatively small number of large multinational corporations (Barnet & Kavanaugh, 1994).

American culture and rhetoric ostensibly honor equal opportunity, while economic and political forces replicate and intensify longstanding structures of inequality whether measured in income distribution, educational opportunity, or social status. Economists have largely neglected efforts to explain the degree to which these dimensions of inequality resist improvement because they reflect and incorporate inherent characteristics deeply embedded in the structure of the economy. Ryan's elegant, understated rationale for an analysis and policies based on the principle of "Fair Shares" provides a starting point for the reconstruction of economics that points the way toward public policies adequate to meet the challenge.

The climate for a more probing analysis and for policies that flow from it began to change in the early 1990s, as the evidence steadily mounted documenting the serious and continuing deterioration of the economic prospects of ever larger numbers of people. A society that defines itself through the work ethic is no longer able to ensure adequate numbers of jobs, with adequate levels of earnings and security, across the spectrum of economic and social classes. The pathology is most acute among urban blacks, Hispanics,

and immigrants, but waves of plant closings, job reductions, corporate con-
solidations, and the replacement of domestic products by cheaper and better
imports have affected ever wider concentric circles reaching into the suburbs
and the middle class. This failure erodes and undermines the popular faith in
the American belief system. If, as is argued here, this failure impeaches the
ideological foundations on which the structures of economic power and privilege depend, a new politics can begin to grow.

THE NEW DEAL AND POSTWAR AMERICA

The issues at stake were seriously engaged during the Depression of the
1930s, when the New Deal began to use new instruments intended to curb
and control the excesses of private economic power and to establish a legitimate and central role for public policy in the management of economic affairs. The Depression and the intellectual revolution in economics developed
by John Maynard Keynes discarded pre-Depression doctrines of laissez faire
that confined government's role to trade policy and central bank management of credit. The intellectual architects of the New Deal feared that the end
of World War II could result in a return to depression conditions unless the
government stood ready to ensure full employment with adequate pay, rising levels of mass consumption to absorb the products of mass production,
comprehensive health care, universal access to secondary and higher education, and adequate housing.

Although European governments had adopted many of these ideas, they
were new in the United States. Franklin D. Roosevelt's 1944 State of the
Union message called for a second, economic bill of rights as the United
States prepared for the postwar era. The prospect that economic rights might
establish a foothold and base of support posed a fundamental challenge to
the beneficiaries and political guardians of the old economic order, whose
loss of status and power had been reversed as war prosperity replaced mass
unemployment with full employment. The postwar years saw the most important ideological struggle of the twentieth century. The issue was whether
the still fragile instruments of economic planning—a central role for government in economic policy, a commitment to full employment, and comprehensive social protection—would become the normative priorities of government policy.

Conservative intellectual voices and business interests shared a stake in
the struggle to discredit these ideas. The real objective of the domestic cold
war waged in the name of anticommunism was not to combat a threat of
communist subversion (which was never plausible) but to silence and mar-

ginalize those who supported and advocated fundamental economic reform and valid provision of protection against the ravages imposed by economic insecurity and exploitation. The expulsion of the communist-dominated unions from the CIO—itself the fruit of New Deal policies and politics—emasculated the only institution with the mass base and the political stake adequate to combat this effort; the purge of university intellectuals marginalized and suppressed the voices best able to articulate the rationale for an American version of what the West knows as the social democratic welfare state, as seen in Scandinavia, Australia, New Zealand, West Germany (before the integration of the East Germany), and—in part—Canada. (Diamond, 1992). These are capitalist states, many prosperous over long periods, in which state policy and power anticipate, counter, and control market forces that otherwise can exert destructive effects on social well-being, and utilize some of the fruits of prosperity to protect and enhance economic security and social welfare.

THE POSTWAR SOCIAL CONTRACT

In the United States the conservative effort prevailed, halting progress or reversing past gains in virtually all spheres of social policy except for social insurance for the elderly, commonly known as Social Security, an effective program but one that exerts no control over private sector decisions; in fact, by socializing the risks of retirement, this program extended the decision-making scope of employers and increased the adaptability of labor markets to changing conditions of supply and demand for workers in the same way that a national program of universal health care would shift from the employer the burden of providing an important benefit. Social Security and unemployment insurance, by providing a countercyclical offset to declining purchasing power when workers lost their jobs, won favor with the emerging Keynesian orthodoxy that dominated economic ideas and policies in the postwar decades.

One of the first fruits of the conservative restoration after World War II was the cancellation of the large-scale programs of direct job creation pioneered under Harry Hopkins in the early and mid-1930s. At their peak these programs enrolled between five and six million people in a labor force less than half the size of today's (Harvey, 1992). Postwar Keynesian policies relied exclusively on fiscal and monetary tools. Even as evidence accumulated of long-term unemployment among specific groups and in specific areas—what some economists called "structural"—the high priests of the new Keynesian orthodoxy rejected calls for programs of direct job creation.

The unprecedented period of economic growth and prosperity in the thirty years following World War II solidified the ideological control and policy dominance of the Keynesians, and consigned to the sidelines the remnants of critical attention to the problems of corporate dominance of the economy. The studies undertaken by the Temporary National Economic Commission (TNEC) between 1938 and 1941 had been carried out in response to Roosevelt's message citing "a concentration of private power without equal in history," as a result of which "private enterprise is ceasing to be free enterprise and is becoming a cluster of private collectivisms" (Zinn, 1966). Its final report emphasized that concentrated economic power, wielded privately with no accountability to public authority, bore major responsibility for the onset, depth, and duration of the Depression; it proposed a range of legislative remedies designed to reduce concentration and prevent its restoration (Hawley, 1966).

By 1941, when the TNEC report was issued, mass unemployment had already begun to shrink in response to large-scale defense spending and the nation's focus—as well as Roosevelt's—had shifted from domestic problems to the challenge of Germany and Japan. Business leaders played an active role in the war effort, and their political influence gradually was restored. With their congressional and intellectual allies they successfully watered down the first bill in Congress that attempted to mandate a full employment policy as the central postwar economic program; between 1944, when the first draft was written, and 1946, when the Employment Act was enacted, the proposed mandate had been diluted into a set of preferences with no statutory teeth (Bailey, 1950/1980).

The combined effects of a neutered, impotent, and discredited left on the one hand and unprecedented prosperity on the other accelerated the exit from the political and intellectual stages of any serious attention to the phenomenon of concentrated economic power, which was left undisturbed and unquestioned. What emerged instead was the postwar "social contract." Under its terms, unwritten but widely understood, the control of the economy by large firms with close interlocks among them would remain intact. In return, business undertook to honor a set of obligations; among them the most important were: (1) acceptance of the legitimate role of labor unions, and the responsibility—codified in the National Labor Relations Act of 1935—to negotiate terms and conditions of employment, in effect a sharing of the fruits of growth; (2) acceptance of a level of national taxation sufficient to meet the social burdens imposed on workers and communities by economic change, and progressive enough to meet the test of fairness; (3) provision of adequate numbers of jobs at adequate levels of pay and job security; and (4) production of goods and services of good quality and at prices that consumers could afford.

This contract worked well in an economy that dominated world markets and in which the Keynesian inventory of policy measures operated reasonably well, sustaining high employment, steady growth, and low rates of inflation. The first thirty-plus years after World War II saw rising living standards for most people and decreasing inequality in income distribution. Regardless of the party in power, business influence remained strong because of the perception that business had lived up to its obligations under the contract.

CHANGING PRIORITIES: THE END OF PROSPERITY

In the early to mid-1970s these trends were reversed. Growth turned into stagnation; real incomes ceased to rise; unemployment rates steadily increased; poverty levels reached new heights; income distribution became increasingly unequal, weighted in favor of the upper income groups; and symptoms of social pathology and breakdown worsened, especially in the large cities. Labor market trends encapsulated these new realities as unemployment and underemployment rose, and as hidden unemployment took new forms: more discouraged workers, people working below the level of their skill and education, people working part-time who wanted and needed full-time work, and more families forced to rely on two earners simply to sustain a level of income previously provided by a single earner, usually male. Employers increasingly shifted to part-time, temporary, and intermittent workers as the "contingent" labor force reached new heights. Single heads of households, especially women, fell ever further behind in earnings.

Most union members were able to keep abreast or ahead of inflation, but their numbers fell steadily; by 1993 U.S. union density as a percentage of the nonagricultural labor force barely exceeded that of France, the lowest among industrialized economies. Were it not for steady union growth among public employees, the level would have approached 10 percent, below even the rate of the pre-Depression 1920s.[1] Employer efforts to limit union organizing and to "take back" benefits and concessions negotiated in earlier periods increased in effectiveness. These were serious moves by the corporate sector to redefine and reduce the scope of the postwar social contract.

Supported by academic and journalist advocates, employers advanced as their rationale the argument that union-imposed rigidities in the workplace and union-generated wage increases above the rate of productivity increases were responsible for the loss of American competitive ability to other economies in the increasingly global marketplace. Union leaders attempted to fight back, but they were outgunned and outmaneuvered. One reason was the sophisticated use by business of academic and media resources to discredit a generation of union leaders who relied on traditional methods of organizing, picketing, and pressure that no longer worked. Another was the growth of the union leader as a bureaucrat, a sharp contrast to a generation of leaders like John L. Lewis and Walter Reuther whose names were household words and who had dramatized the union struggles in terms that reached the hearts and minds of the larger public. A third reason was the increasing apathy at the top; when observers expressed concern about diminishing numbers and weakened union clout, AFL-CIO president George Meany dismissed their views as elitist and incorrect. A fourth was the preoccupation, bordering on obsession, of top union leaders with a rigid anticommunist world view that paid more attention to the struggles of Solidarity in Poland than to the changing domestic scene and its effects on workers and unions. The AFL-CIO largely stood aside during the climactic struggles for civil rights in the 1960s and actively opposed efforts to end the war in Vietnam in the 1970s. Its failure to respond to new forces among women, blacks, Hispanics, and others that were reshaping political life had the effect of marginalizing labor in the eyes and minds of journalists and scholars as well as the public; academic institutions focused on labor studies that had once flourished now languished with diminished support and a loss of purpose. Young scholars whose predecessors had embraced unionism as the arena for study and advocacy shifted their attention to other areas of interest and concern.

Business values influenced not only the larger public but workers themselves; many agreed with the arguments that unions were too strong, their negotiated wages too high, and their workplace protections too rigid. Strike frequency fell, and strike effectiveness weakened. Union-organizing campaigns failed more than they succeeded. Unions led by white males had difficulty reaching workers who were increasingly female, black, and Hispanic, while employer resistance grew stronger, abetted by probusiness administrations that weakened the enforcement of the labor statutes.

The focus of economic policy shifted from full employment to the control of inflation. The argument, simple but plausible, was that changes in the domestic and global economy, and in the composition of the labor force, had worsened the trade-off between employment levels and rates of inflation to the degree that previous levels of unemployment could no longer be achieved without unacceptably high rates of inflation, and that, after all, inflation hurts everyone, while unemployment affects relatively few. The shift from the production of goods to the production of services of necessity lowered productivity, went the argument; as a consequence, improvement in living standards must be slower in comparison to earlier periods. The choice offered was clear: higher real wages and living standards for some can be achieved only at the price of excluding others from sharing in affluence; these are the less educated, the less skilled, and the less experienced, who include large numbers of blacks, Hispanics, immigrants, and women. To seek full employment would mean smaller increases in living standards. The Darwinian subtext of this message comes directly from *Blaming the Victim* (Ryan, 1976): those who are at risk are those with less motivation to succeed; they are deviants from the work ethic and a threat to the standard of living of a white, nonurban majority. Much of the manipulative and cynical politics of recent decades has its roots in this soil of division. It survived in the rhetoric of welfare reform of a president, Bill Clinton, who won office campaigning for economic renewal and job growth, testimony to the enduring appeal of the impulse to blame victims when it is too difficult politically to confront the real problem.

THE BASE FOR RESPONSE

This posture became more difficult to sustain or defend as the inroads of joblessness and job insecurity spread in the 1980s and 1990s from the cities to the suburbs, from the hourly worker to the salaried middle manager, in ever wider concentric circles. Many of the victims blame themselves; print and electronic media reported examples of laid-off men and women, some with many years of well-paid employment, who expressed more sadness than anger, more desperation than solidarity with others like themselves. Insecurity erodes self-confidence as well as the capacity to see oneself as part of something larger, requiring a political analysis and response (Lerner, 1986). A counterrevolution of falling expectations, engineered by the corporate elite through mass communications and reinforced by real actions—layoffs, downsizing, shifts of activity to other places in the United States and abroad—has changed the response to job loss and economic difficulty from anger and the search for effective methods of correcting the causes to self-blame, isolation, and scapegoating. When people have been taught to believe that having a job is not a right but a matter of personal attributes, good luck, and good connections, they are not disposed to raise or respond to serious questions about the legitimacy of the structures of economic power and control.

Yet Clinton's election in 1992 and his focus on the economy opened a window of opportunity to new ideas and approaches. The middle–class victims of economic decline are part of the base of political support that could be developed around Ryan's model of equal opportunity and Fair Shares. The contradiction is growing between the expectations that came with a good education, commitment to the work ethic, and a deep belief that each generation would experience a standard of living above that of their parents, and the reality of stagnation and insecurity. In the past people might have felt compassion for the deprived and neglected victims of urban decay— blacks, Hispanics, single mothers, immigrants—but they did not see a connection with their own lives, families, and communities. As economic problems persist and their effects widen, the basis strengthens for organizing around a shared experience and perception of failure by the larger system.

This possibility could become an Achilles' heel for the corporate and financial elites who have abrogated the earlier social contract. Even friends and apologists of American business have expressed concern about its failure to understand and respond effectively to the new challenges posed by new international forces. The question remains whether this vulnerability can be exploited in order to restore and renew analysis of the contradictions between the affluence and power of the corporate system, and the damage and destruction it has inflicted on the economic and social order. The intellectual mainstream, long the beneficiary of corporate and financial largesse, so far has failed to respond to the challenge. We others, debtors to William Ryan's courage, vision and compassion, must take up the task.

THREE ISSUES: TOWARD A NEW POLITICS

Three struggles that began in the early 1990s illustrate both the possibilities and the limitations of efforts to address and control concentrated economic power. The first was the 1993 campaign to defeat ratification of NAFTA, (North American Free Trade Agreement). It marked the first time in more than a generation that organized labor demonstrated the will and ability to mobilize from both its own depleted ranks and a broader base of public support. While the effort failed, it came close and lost in Congress only because the president mounted a full court press for passage. As the issue of the World Trade Organization, successor to the General Agreement Tariffs and Trade (GATT), began to embody the possible effects of a global economic regime with the power to abrogate, modify, or annul domestic laws protecting social standards or environmental protection, new opportunities opened to build a broad base of understanding and support for measures to control corporate power in the name of social decency, national values, protection of nonrenewable natural resources, and respect for the legitimate needs and claims of developing economies for investment, market access, and the freedom to make their own decisions about their relation to one another and to the global economy. Criticism of the role of the International Bank for Reconstruction and Development (IBRD), the International Monetary Fund, and the large multinational corporations began to enlist advocates among economists and others. Larger scale struggles remained to be fought, but the early signs indicated greater receptivity among broad strata of the population than in the past.

The second issue illustrating the stakes and possibilities was the 1994 contest over the Clinton plan to reform and restructure health care, more accurately the provision of medical, hospital, nursing home, and other services to the ill, the frail, the aged, and the impaired. Despite widespread public recognition of the need for reform, little was accomplished. The political ineptness of the Clinton administration played a role; a far more decisive role was that of the organized interest groups that share a stake in the health care marketplace, an industry the accounts for one seventh of the gross national product and ten million workers. They spared no expense to ensure that a lucrative market dependent on major public funding would remain private; an estimated $100 million was spent in lobbying, advertising, public relations, and direct payment to key members of Congress who played key roles in the legislative process. Public concern about the costs, inequities, and failures of the existing systems of care remained fragmented and incoherent; the necessary organizing and mobilizing actions proved to be beyond the capabilities of the supporters of the single-payer model, although more than ninety members of Congress co-sponsored it. But this issue will not recede from public awareness far or for long, and the potential remains for development of a broad base of public support. Division among the unions was a major barrier to effective action; protection of their negotiated benefit plans outweighed the potential for major reform. In the future phases of this struggle, with new leadership and alliances, the balance could shift toward a stronger, more coherent role for labor.

The third issue only began to affect political and public activity in 1994, when the New York–based New Initiatives for Full Employment (NIFE) published a full employment program in book form (Collins, Ginsburg, & Goldberg, 1994), and began to develop a base of support for the task of drafting legislation that would remedy the limitations and failures of the 1946 Employment Act and the 1978 Full Employment and Balanced Growth Act ("Humphrey-Hawkins").

CONCLUSION

Each of these three activities represents a serious effort to redefine politics by mapping and exploiting the fault lines that embody and exemplify dimensions of the corporate and financial abrogation of the social contract and its consequences. The struggle over the control and direction of the global economy directly confronts the increased power and role of large multinational corporations not only in trade but, even more critically, in the flow of investment capital and the international division of labor. The health care struggle challenges the exploitation for profit of needs that are defined almost universally in the modern world as a social and public responsibility. The full employment effort seeks to reverse the systemic deterioration of income, security, and prospects for working people that were the central elements of the postwar social contract. Success in any of these areas will redefine and reconstruct the relationships among those who hold and wield economic power, the society in which they operate and whose sanction they need, and the public authority that embodies and expresses the views, needs, and concerns of the people. William Ryan's vision was always at root political. His spirit and insight will help to inform and energize the struggles that lie ahead.

NOTE

1. These data can be found in U.S. House of Representatives (1993, July 8); U.S. Department of Labor, Bureau of Labor Statistics (1991, March); U.S. Department of Labor *Monthly Labor Review;* Dembo and Morehouse (1994); and Center on Budget and Policy Priorities (1990).

REFERENCES

Bailey, S. (1980). *Congress makes a law: The story behind the Employment Act of 1946.* New York: Greenwood Press. (Original work published 1950).
Barnet, R. J., & Kavanaugh, J. (1994). *Global dreams: Imperial corporations and the New World Order.* New York: Simon & Schuster.
Center on Budget and Policy Priorities. (1990). *Rich–poor gap hits 40-year high as poverty rate stalls.* Washington, DC: Author.
Diamond, S. (1992). *Compromised campus: The collaboration between the universities and the intelligence agencies community, 1945–1955.* New York: Oxford University Press.
Collins, S. D., Ginsburg, H. L., & Goldberg, G. S. (1994). *Jobs for all.* New York: Apex Press.

Dembo, D., & Morehouse, W. (1992). *The underbelly of the U.S. economy: Joblessness and pauperization of work in America.* New York: Apex Press.

Harvey, P. (1992). *Securing the right to employment.* Princeton: Princeton University Press.

Hawley, E. W. (1966). *The New Deal and the problem of monopoly.* Princeton: Princeton University Press.

Lerner, M. (1986). *Surplus powerlessness.* Oakland: Institute for Labor and Mental Health.

Ryan, W. (1976). *Blaming the victim.* New York: Vintage.

Ryan, W. (1981). *Equality.* New York: Pantheon.

U.S. Department of Labor. *The Monthly Labor Review.* Published monthly.

U.S. House of Representatives, Committee on Ways and Means. (1993, July 8). *Overview of entitlement programs, 1993 green book, background material on programs within the jurisdiction of the Committee on Ways and Means.* Washington, DC: U.S. Government Printing Office.

U.S. Department of Labor, Bureau of Labor Statistics. (1991, March). *Employment, hours, and earnings, United States, 1909–1990* (Vol. 1, Bulletin 2370). Washington, DC: U.S. Government Printing Office.

Zinn, H. (1966). *New Deal thought.* New York: Bobbs-Merrill.

Part VI

A Conversation between William Ryan and M. Brinton Lykes

PHOTO OF WILLIAM RYAN BY BARBARA RUSKIN

M. BRINTON LYKES: I THOUGHT WE MIGHT BEGIN BY YOU SHARING SOME of your personal and political experiences and the relationships that contributed to the development of the ideas that you presented in *Blaming the Victim* [1971].

WILLIAM RYAN: It really goes way back. It goes back to the struggle for school integration in the early 1960s here in Boston—when Mrs. [Louise Day] Hicks was chair of the school committee. When the issue of integration was raised, the response was this "cultural deprivation" response. There was one guy, Bill O'Connor, I remember, who said, "We don't have inferior schools, we've been getting an inferior type of student." Another official said, "Well, the problem is with the parents. They're nothing but a pair of hands," things of that sort.

LYKES: These were school department officials?

RYAN: School committee members and high muck-a-mucks in the school department. Their response was that the problem wasn't segregation, the problem was cultural deprivation. I began to focus my attention on that issue—as a matter of fact, I recently ran across a newspaper interview with me way back in the early 1960s in which I used the phrase "blaming the victim" in discussing the effect of this idea of cultural deprivation. That's, I think, how it started. There was a "Blue Ribbon Commission" on school integration that the governor set up, and I did some background studies for them that involved replicating some of the studies that Kenneth Clark and Jim

351

Jones had done in Harlem in the Haryon Project. Then I think what really brought it into focus was when I started to hear about the Moynihan Report,[1] and somebody got me a copy of it, and then I wrote a critique of that. I think that was the beginning of *Blaming the Victim*. That critique was published in *The Nation* [November 22, 1965], and Carey McWilliams, the editor of *The Nation*, said "Does the same sort of thing happen in other areas?" and I said, "Yes," and he said, "So why don't you write a book about it?"

LYKES: And what were you doing at the time? Were you in the mental health field or were you teaching?

RYAN: I was working for an advocacy group, the Massachusetts Committee on Children and Youth. Officially, I was the senior mental health consultant, but it was pretty wide-ranging. I did work on child welfare. I worked on urban renewal and Model Cities[2] in Springfield. It was generally consistent with what I was doing in real life, that is, in the Civil Rights Movement. The woman who was chair of the board of this group was Dr. Martha Elliot. She was one of these heroines of the age—a knowledgeable health and welfare politician. She served as the second head of the Children's Bureau in Washington and as head of UNICEF when it got started. She encouraged me to get into this sort of thing. In fact, I spent some of my work time working on civil rights issues. . . . Then it seemed to me that everything fell into place. I saw the same thinking processes going on in the ways politicians, academics, and policy-makers were talking about poverty and talking about slum housing and so forth. That's how I happened to do it.

LYKES: The phrase "blaming the victim" actually has become synonymous with your name. Many people have approached you to learn more about your work after reading *Blaming the Victim*. It's had an enormous impact both in the social sciences and, more importantly, perhaps, in fieldwork, on practice. I'm wondering whether you identify that as your life work?

RYAN: Well, yes and no. I do reluctantly. Clearly, that's the thing that I've done that's had the most impact, and that's the thing that I've done that's brought me gratification, because, aside from its use in academic quarters, I've gotten so many responses from people in the community, activists of one kind or another, who have read it and have responded. Either they wrote me a letter or I ran across them or something like that, and their approval gave me a boost. Someone will say, "How did *you* know that?" I don't know how I know that. I don't think I ever *didn't* know that. I don't think I ever changed sides, so to speak.

LYKES: Well, back it up a little then, in terms of the question, "How did you know that?" What preceded your work in the Civil Rights Movement, or how did you end up in the Civil Rights Novement?

RYAN: Well, I guess without thinking of it, . . . I had always sort of been a person of the left. I grew up in the Depression. I had uncles who were teamsters who were out on strike, an aunt who was in the WPA. So I was always automatically prolabor, pro–New Deal, and so forth. Then in my teenage years I became aware of fascism, so I was pro-labor, pro–civil rights, pro–New Deal, and antifascist. I think I just sort of got set that way. And being in the army during the war—we stopped Hitler. I think you have a certain identification. I don't know. It was way back. My first political experience was in 1928: I'm five and a half years old. The kids in my family, me and my cousins, gather around the dining room table, and on the dining room table is the old *Record American,* with the picture of Herbert Hoover and Al Smith, and we all lined up to vote for Al Smith—at the age of five.

LYKES: Really! And you knew what you were doing?

RYAN: Oh, I don't think so.

LYKES: But you talked about it.

RYAN: Well, it was just assumed that there were Democrats and then there were the bad guys. I suppose in those days (my family was Catholic), if you voted Republican, it was sort of a matter for confession.

LYKES: You said that the war gave you a sense of being on the right side in terms of issues of fascism and antifascism. What was your experience in the war?

RYAN: I had a very easy war. I was a cryptographer in the air force, doing coding and decoding. I spent the whole war in the Caribbean. So I spent a year and a half in Miami, and a year or so in Trinidad, and time in British Guyana and then the last six months or a year in Dutch Guinea, which was the bad part, but, up until then, it was a breeze. I had a very lucky war.

LYKES: But you felt a part of some collective process?

RYAN: Oh, yes. Because what we were doing there was manning the supply route to North Africa and China.

LYKES: And how did you end up in the academy? How did you take up these kinds of concerns and interests?

RYAN: The GI Bill. I was the first person in my family to go to college, and I didn't go until I was twenty-four or twenty-five years old. . . . From high school I got a job, and then I went into the army. My generation—it wasn't that you said, "Are you going to go to college? No." It just never occurred to anybody. But then I decided I'd go to college since the GI Bill would take care of it. So at the age of twenty-five I became a schoolboy again, but I didn't like it. I was constantly about to drop out. And I just gritted my teeth and kept going, but by the time I had finished, I had gotten interested in psychology. It just seemed interesting. Clinical psychology seemed interesting to me.

LYKES: Do you see your studies in psychology as in any way connected to your political trajectory or your interest in labor or your interest in antifascism?

RYAN: No, and it wasn't until a couple of years after I got past the Ph.D. that I realized that clinical work really wasn't what I was interested in. I began then to get interested in social and community psychology and social issues and social problems and got back on track again.

LYKES: "Blaming the victim" continues to be a phrase that pops up over and over again in terms of writing and thinking, and in politics, and, to the extent that there is any activism today, in activist circles. I'm wondering: do you see it as meaning the same thing that you meant when you first used it?

RYAN: Well, from the beginning, it was used in ways that I didn't mean to use it. "Blaming the victim"—maybe it was an unfortunate phrase. What I had in mind was the process by which problems that are basically social in nature, that have to do with the social structure, in one way or another get defined as having the cause of the problem in the people who are enmeshed in the problem. But I didn't mean that in any individual sense. I'll give you a good example. A perfectly valid way to use the phrase is in a rape trial, when the defense attorney tries to impugn the virtue of the woman who got raped. That's blaming the victim, but that's not the way I meant it. That's blaming an individual person. I meant it more as a formulation explaining a whole social problem. And when it gets twisted that way, to refer to blaming an individual person, there are a lot of criticisms made that are legitimate. A very common criticism is that if you talk about blaming the victim, are you not justifying, are you not saying that the person is not responsible for what he or she does? On the one hand somebody says, "Poverty is caused by a bunch of shiftless, lazy people." But you can make the argument that's blaming the victim because that's *not* what causes poverty. Now that doesn't mean that there aren't shiftless, lazy poor people, or even that some people get poor be-

cause they're shiftless and lazy. It doesn't have to do with attributing particular characteristics to individual persons. It has rather to do with the analytic process. So I get criticized a lot by misunderstandings of the nature of
what I had in mind when I used the phrase.

LYKES: On the one hand, I see the distinction you're making. But, if we
look more closely at the rape example you gave, isn't the person who criti-
cizes the defense attorney trying to suggest that it's a system of patriarchal
power and gender inequities that contributes to the DA's behavior? Isn't it
also a similar line of reasoning—that is, that it's not just that the rape "victim" is not individually responsible but also that one needs to examine the
broader structural issues to understand the courtroom dynamic?

RYAN: Yes, I see what you mean. In fact there's a way to apply "blaming the victim" analysis to that in the way that I *did* mean it. Yes, that's right.
In a sense, it's probably true that rape is facilitated by the prevalence of this
kind of thinking, so that there are men who have been at least partially persuaded that a lot of women really would like to get raped, really are "looking" for it. And all the other things that you were implying, "Well, they're
men, so they have the right anyway because they're in charge."

LYKES: It's interesting. It makes me think in some way that as you're describing it, the core element of the analysis that the phrase "blaming the victim" has come to represent has everything to do with the individualistic tendency within our Western way of thinking, that is, of reducing collective
phenomena to individual causality.

RYAN: Yes, exactly. The first assumption is that, whatever it is, there has
to be some kind of explanation involving individual pathology or individual
deviance or individual character flaw or something of the sort. The popular
psychology of America is highly individualistic. . . . You see much more discussion nowadays of excessive individualism and how it's pushing beyond
the point where it's viable, because if you push individualism too far you're
going to get some kind of libertarian anarchy and nobody will be able to
function.

LYKES: Do you see the "blaming the victim" analysis as relevant for the
1990s as it was when you first developed it?

RYAN: I think so. I think, for example, the dialogue about "the underclass," about homelessness—they used to talk about illegitimacy, now they
talk about teenage pregnancy. All of these kinds of things are pretty much
analyzed in the same way—that there's something wrong with these people.

That they're crazy or they're addicted or they're incompetent or they're stupid, or whatever it might be. They describe the homeless and then make the usual *post hoc, propter hoc* fallacy, and say that's what causes it. And they do the same thing with other kinds of problems.

LYKES: Thinking again of the relevance of your analysis for the 1990s, one thing that has changed in the last twenty years is the U.S. population and the increasing diversity of what some call ethnic minority groups or peoples of color. In *Blaming the Victim* you clarify the ways in which a similarity-difference dimension underlies ideological differences and the extent to which a focus on differences tends to be associated with the individualistic tendency we were just discussing. Yet many individuals from excluded groups identify their particularity or difference as critical to their struggle for self-determination.

RYAN: Does that contradict what I was saying about difference-similarity? Is that your question?

LYKES: That's my question. If all of our ideas are embedded in some way in history, don't the demographic and historical changes in this country and the new formations of struggle that they envision, that rely in some way on articulating the legitimacy of difference, affect how you see the issue of difference?

RYAN: Generally speaking, it makes me nervous, because to me it's structurally very similar to other kinds of things that are far from progressive. Think of the received wisdom about racial struggles in Boston—that the center of opposition is South Boston, where people see themselves as together as a collective but as different, and that they emphasize their difference. Now to the extent that there's any truth in that story, it seems to me that it has a lot of negative consequences. Where I think it's applicable is in the notion of the legitimacy of difference, that is, what kind of a difference makes a difference with respect to some particular issue? What kind of difference is a significant difference with respect to the right to access to education or to jobs and so forth. For example, a group says: "Yes, we're different, we like the ways in which we are different. The ways in which we are different are legitimate, and they are not relevant to whatever it is, education, employment, anything on the equality-inequality dimension." Do you see the point I'm driving at? Because so much of this can get picked up and distorted. I'm sure you've seen what's developing now as a way of playing off Asian people against black people, saying: "Well, why can't black people be like Asian people? Asian people have strong family values," or whatever it might be. Asserted differences can be used in that way. So I'm not sure how safe it is to emphasize differences.

LYKES: But in that example the people who use them in that way are the people in power who in some way reduce the asserted difference to an individual characteristic or trait. In that sense I think that it's more similar to what you were saying earlier about the structural problem being reduced to an individualistic analysis.

RYAN: Yes, but those in power are very clever about that kind of thing. For example, I've heard the argument that African culture is more of an oral culture than a written culture. All right, I can see people in power saying: "That's right. These people depend on an oral culture; they're not interested in reading and writing. So, if you've got a job that involves reading and writing, you'd better not hire them." So the oral culture notion will eventually become another mark of "cultural deprivation." I think you've got to think very carefully when a group makes assertions of difference from other groups. I don't know. I haven't thought it through, and I haven't had occasion to interact with people about these kinds of issues.

LYKES: I agree with you that people in power are very clever about using these issues in divisive and controlling ways. On the other hand, if we're talking about similarities and we minimize important differences—it's also problematic. The first wave of the current women's movement in the United States might be a good example. It mostly emerged from and appealed to middle-class white women, and its agenda got articulated by them, and their priorities were initially yoked to notions of gender discrimination that had everything to do with middle-class values. They spoke as if all women shared these experiences and concerns. This began to change when African American women challenged early feminists, arguing that African American women have different experiences and different priorities. Don't we first have to understand what the diversity is in the experience before we can talk about unity?

RYAN: All right, but can't that kind of analysis get turned around by saying that those who were dominant in the Women's Movement were defining women falsely or inadequately? Their definition of what women were about and needed and wanted was limited to a particular group of women.

LYKES: Right. That's precisely the point—because "women" is a category that takes on a different set of social meanings depending upon the historical context in which it's used and the particular group to whom you are making reference.

RYAN: Yes. That has to be at least partially true. But I start running into feeling like I'm wandering in the woods.

LYKES: Well, go back to the women's issue and the statement of difference and similarity. I hear what you're saying when you say that you haven't been challenged to think about this issue in those terms.

RYAN: So for the Women's Movement the question is, or one question might be, is it more valuable to at least spend some time focusing on the ways women are different? Is that the question?

LYKES: Right.

RYAN: Well, my first response would be, Why? To what end? Is it an organizing thing, or would it have some kind of long-range implications? Would it have any programmatic implications?

LYKES: Enormous programmatic implications . . .

RYAN: I was thinking more in terms of what are the effects in real life. See, here's what I worry about. It seems to me that, broadly speaking, there is theoretically a pro-equality movement and that would include trade unions, the Civil Rights Movement, the Women's Movement, and so forth. That requires thinking about all of these issues as subcategories of a larger issue. The subcategories are differentiating themselves off in too marked a way. I'll give you an example. In the gubernatorial election in Massachusetts, people who were concerned about homosexual rights, people who were concerned about abortion rights, and others of that sort—so-called liberals—supported Bill Weld who is, at least, in my judgment, a terribly reactionary guy. The same thing happened in the Boston mayoral election. Those groups supported Tom Menino in the 1993 election. Now what happens when this process of emphasis on difference leads to a fracturing of what could be the potentially progressive coalition, the pro-equality coalition? I think that's what's happening.

LYKES: It's interesting the way that you see the question. I see those groups as sharing something in common, which I guess the media would refer to as a personal versus public liberalism. That is, a liberal position around individual rights, but not necessarily a liberal position around public rights that is, labor rights and the like.

RYAN: But it has gotten to the point where if you say, "I'm in favor of homosexual rights," or "I'm in favor of abortion," etc., then you are a liberal. But if you say, "I think labor unions should be controlled more," or "Taxes are too high," etc., you will never be defined as a liberal.

LYKES: Yes, but that's the problem that you yourself have pointed out multiple times with the categories "liberal" and "conservative." Those categories no longer have political meaning. I'm not sure the groups you mention are all part of a broad movement toward equality, if by equality we mean economic equality. I think those groups represent some move toward social tolerance and individual rights, and they do not necessarily participate in a broad movement toward economic equality.

RYAN: That's not progressive? Can we say that individual liberties are not part of the progressive agenda? I don't think so. It's fundamentally economic . . . but with redistribution of resources comes redistribution of life chances and access to social institutions. In other words, there's a lot of seemingly noneconomic, seemingly social things that are consequences of greater economic redistribution. The other thing about self-differentiation as a strategy is that I think that it runs the risk of identifying the opposition or the oppressor as "the totality" of those who are different. For example, if the distinction is in women, there's a tendency to say, "Well, the trouble is men in general, who have been oppressing women." Or, "It's whites in general." Well, there is some truth to that, because the oppressive mechanisms do spread throughout the whole population. But the real problems are a much smaller group, and they get hidden in the crowd, so to speak, so I think there's a misunderstanding of what the problem is by focusing too much on self-differentiation, assuming that we're this, this, this, and this, and they're something else, and they're doing a job on us.

LYKES: Yes, I would agree that the long-term goal is to build coalitions, but it's not easy to build coalitions if there's an enormous imbalance in power in the different elements in the coalition.

Ryan: Let's see if I can make a distinction between coalitions and something else. Let's take, at its best, the trade union. Now, at its best, the trade union movement included activity directed against racism and against sexism, because they were seen as a part of the barriers and handicaps that working people confronted, and it seems to me that that's not the same thing as a coalition.

LYKES: It's not, but . . . at its best, it is. On the other hand, let's look at the history of the experiences of women and blacks in trade unions.

RYAN: But that was my next point. At their worst, the trade unions were as racist and sexist as anybody else. To me that means that the area of struggle should have been the trade unions. Overcoming racism and sexism within the trade unions was a necessary component to making that movement more effective. To pull those issues off and make them separate dimensions was not the answer.

LYKES: Yes, but the issue is how you do that. In fact, many people found that part of the struggle necessitated forming their own organizations. Women had a difficult time getting any kind of voice in the trade union movement.

RYAN: But they've formed organizations within trade unions.

LYKES: Some organizations within the trade union movement, but some organizations like office worker organizations that entered later, after they were autonomous organizations—both were necessary.

RYAN: But they were supported by the labor movement.

LYKES: Sometimes, not always. And often it was very confrontational. And it still is in terms of leadership. Women have never had the kind of leadership men have.

RYAN: But that was true in the Civil Rights Movement. The Civil Rights Movement was very sexist.

LYKES: That's right.

RYAN: What does that mean? Women should form a separate Civil Rights Movement?

LYKES: Once the issue emerged around the sexism of the Civil Rights Movement and the continuing degradation of women, some women did, in that the Civil Rights Movement was a source of some of the women's rights movements. We learned out of our experiences of continually being marginalized—these are both black and white women in the Civil Rights Movement—that we needed other resources in order to be able to gain power and then move forward either in coalition or separately.

RYAN: Right. But it would never have worked if there were a men's civil rights movement and a women's civil rights movement. . . . Well, let me see if I can put it a different way. It seems to me that . . . some quantity of universality must be inherent in the goals, and the goals are greater equality. In the Women's Movement the goals are greater equality for women. One arm of the Women's Movement, in focusing on difference, focusing on differentiation, and so forth, might be saying, "Well, how do we get some women into the position of being bosses?"; that is, "How do we get other women not to push for equality but to share in the goodies of inequality?" It's the same thing among blacks. I had this kind of thing happen to me in my life before I began thinking of any of these things. For a while I worked as a part-time organizer when I was living in Washington, and I went to this plant, which seemed like a good target, and everything was going like peaches and cream, and everybody was signing up. We had a meeting two weeks after I arrived on the scene, and one guy said, "This is the greatest thing that ever happened; we can have us a union. We can get together, and we can make it into a branch of the Ku Klux Klan and keep all the niggers out." Well, what the hell was going on? I was absolutely set back on my heels. Now, I don't know, from some people's point of view, I may have done the wrong thing. I just pulled the plug on the whole thing and walked away, because I was so upset by that. But, do you see what I mean? The goal didn't get . . . it wasn't properly universalized. Somehow or another these guys were still thinking of how are we going to make life better for us white guys.

LYKES: I agree with you, on the one hand, but on the other hand, I think it's a whole different issue when the group in power is focused on, "How are we going to make life better for ourselves?" Whether it's relative power or not. I'm not saying that these workers were bosses, but they were whites in relationship to blacks, and they have certain privileges as whites.

RYAN: That's one of the mechanisms, and I don't know today what I should have done. I don't think I did the right thing. I think I should have managed it somehow. I think I should have confronted it somehow.

LYKES: Much of this discussion about similarity and difference and the universal or collective nature of the struggle presumes shared understandings of equality. I wanted to back up a bit, given that that's a title of one of your books, and ask you whether you could share some of the factors that contributed to your deciding to do *Equality* [1981], and what your objectives were when you began that process?

RYAN: Well, I think that somewhere along the line I stopped thinking about poverty and started thinking about it in more relative terms, that is, I began to see inequality rather than poverty. . . . I think if I went back to *Blaming the Victim,* I'd see that I was talking about inequality when I was making the ideological points, the things that maintain inequality.

LYKES: So how would you distinguish the two books if you were going to characterize them?

RYAN: Well, *Blaming the Victim,* I think, is more rooted in actual experiences of doing things, and *Equality* is perhaps more reflective, trying to grasp some things a little better. . . . But, to some extent it was a failure. I don't think I quite pulled it off, whatever I was trying to do. I don't think I quite got it, or I didn't put it in such a way that it made much of an impact. Maybe that's just comparing it to *Blaming the Victim,* which did seem to have more of an impact on people, but I think *Equality* was to some extent a failure.

LYKES: . . . A failure?

RYAN: Well, I think I was trying to underline what I thought was my own insight, namely that the goal was equality rather than the "abolition of poverty," and I think I was hoping that people would pick up on that, that people would pick up on the equality issue as the crucial one, and also, on all the ideological stuff, about how people get to certain ways of formulating their perception of issues.

LYKES: When you say you were hoping people would get the equality argument, what do you have in mind when you talk about equality?

RYAN: Well, the two basic points, I would say, the fundamental points, are first, that when we start worrying about so-called disadvantaged or oppressed categories of people who aren't doing well, who are discriminated against, who are poor, it's more useful to think of them on a continuum. They're offset, the poor are offset by the rich, so to speak. The definition of poverty requires some kind of background or description of wealth, and vice versa, so that the imbalances that exist, rather than simply the phenomena themselves, are in focus, so that we see poverty and wealth as being out of balance, as undesirable imbalances. The second main point was to try to illustrate how prior assumptions, so-called ideological factors, were the principal barriers against achieving equality. Those are the two points I think that I was trying to make.

LYKES: If you think of those points and look at the contemporary political situation—in something like the Clinton administration's health plan—how do you see his plan in relationship to your argument?

RYAN: It's a nonstarter. It's not a player. It's not in the discourse. The discourse is between us and those who don't have this or those who don't have that. We, those crafting or advocating the policy, feel for them, and we're compassionate. But we don't see the imbalance. We don't see how wrong it is that there are some people whose health, maybe even whose life, is to be dealt with in the marketplace—that you can buy health or that you can buy life. That seems to me blasphemous almost. But there's no sense of that in the discourse of health care reform.

LYKES: Why do you think that is?

RYAN: Because I think there's this habit of segmenting groups of people and seeing them in a fairly static way that these are, for example, the deprived, and not seeing the process of deprivation, always using the past participle of "the deprived," "the disadvantaged," and not thinking about the active voices, that is, that someone is doing the depriving, somebody is doing the oppressing, somebody is doing the disadvantaging. There's no sense of that kind of inequality representing an imbalance that should, and I think does, create some kind of a dynamic in the society. There's no recognition of that.

LYKES: Do you think we're any closer to that discourse than we were ten or twenty years ago, or do you think we're further away?

RYAN: I think we're further away. In the last fifteen years there has been, on the one hand, so much emphasis on individual achievement, individual genius, individual skills, and then, on the other hand, individual disorder and individual violent people, individual incompetent people. I think that kind of thinking has become much more predominant. There really isn't much being said against it.

LYKES: Do you see any signs of an alternative discourse?

RYAN: I haven't, and I don't see it in any of the so-called progressive movements. I don't hear the kind of stuff that I'm listening for at least.

LYKES: What would it sound like, for example, in the debate about health care?

RYAN: On health care it would sound like—well, first of all, health care is one of those inalienable rights, so we have to make sure that everybody has access to it. Then, it wouldn't get into who was deserving, and all this stuff about market forces and how are we going to work it out, can the government do it, all of this kind of policy junkie talk that immediately takes over. Nobody's jumping up and down saying, "People have a right to health, and that's what we have to try to figure out." Nobody dares say that, even people who believe that, I don't think they'd dare say it. Some of the criticism of Clinton's plan is that, "Oh, he's creating a new entitlement. People are going to want to suck on the public tit and get taken care of, and the costs are going to be unbelievable," and so forth. As if entitlement has become just as bad as welfare.

LYKES: Can you think of ways to mobilize that discourse? What could you recommend to students or community activists who were committed to that agenda?

RYAN: Only in the most general terms. It seems to me that an analysis of things suggests that equality is achieved by clear-sighted collective action. To me the model of how equality is achieved is still the trade union. That's the model. And I think maybe it is being applied in groups like ACORN[3] that are kind of working that way, but they're not growing the way I'd hoped they'd grow.

LYKES: When you say the trade union is the model, do you mean collective bargaining?

RYAN: Collective action. Or at least potential collective action. Collective bargaining doesn't mean anything unless there's some implicit action. It's all well and good to say, "Well, it's not necessary to strike but we'll do collective bargaining." But if you're going to do collective bargaining, you have to have a threat. It seems to me that, in the first place, it's organizing, and, in the second place, it's having the potential for job action, strikes, and so forth. Collective bargaining, that's just a process, to me. That's not the goal. That's just how it comes about.

LYKES: And what's the goal for the trade union movement?

RYAN: More, more for us.

LYKES: For the workers?

RYAN: Yes.

LYKES: And so how does that relate to what you were saying about the need not to focus on particularity?

RYAN: Well, there's always the problem about how universal can you get. How far can you reach? What is the particular universe you're embedded in? For most people, it doesn't go very far beyond the neighborhood and the workplace, maybe it goes up to some kind of religious or ethnic identity, to some extent. But the other thing is that the logic, if you will, or the ethos, of the trade union movement is: we're all in it together. It isn't just that these guys go on strike. People say that one of the terrible things that happened was when Reagan broke the PATCO[4] strike and fired the air traffic controllers. That's absolutely right; that was a dreadful thing that happened. But the other dreadful thing that happened was that the other unions didn't join in solidarity with the air traffic controllers. They let them go down the drain. In the old days, if they went on strike, then the pilots and the flight attendants and the mechanics wouldn't have crossed the picket line. So it's not just a particular group that's involved. Whenever one group went on strike, they expected the rest of organized labor to support them. So that there was solidarity. The issue is solidarity.

LYKES: If you were to describe your agenda for the 1990s, or what you would see as the agenda for activists and people in the university, how would you describe it?

RYAN: Save the labor unions and save social insurance! I think if we can manage that, we might survive.

LYKES: And is there a role for the academy in that process?

RYAN: Well, there's always a role for the academy to provide interpretation of what goes on. I think that's the main role that the academy can play—to interpret to people what's going on. To go back to the health care business again . . . I recently read a study of three groups of people: people whose care was in the traditional fee-for-service model; people who were in HMOs were the second group; and the third group was Medicare patients. Now the discussion was all about how there wasn't much difference between people in HMOs and people who were in the fee-for-service system. But there was hardly any discussion of the fact that the people in Medicare had a much higher level of satisfaction. It seems to me that we have twenty-five to thirty years of experience with Medicare. We know how it works. It's very efficient. It's no more bureaucratic, maybe less bureaucratic, than all the individual insurance companies. It costs so much less than the regular insurance companies. Why wouldn't we just go along in the same way? We started out in 1935 with Social Security, old-age pensions, and we've built on that step by step by step. Why not just take Medicare and expand it and have another social insurance program? Everybody says it's unacceptable, it's politically impossible, people won't buy that. But when you describe to people what it would be like—for example, if you describe the Canadian system to people, and ask, "How would you like it if this and this and this and this were true?"—about 80 percent of the people would say, "That sounds good to me," and something like 90 percent of Canadians are satisfied with the system. So that seems the logical way to go. That would be the social insurance way to do it. What they're doing now, it's going to end up with some kind of god-awful complicated plan that will be worse than anything. They're caving in to the insurance companies. Imagine, it's like going back thirty years—having state-granted monopolies. Imagine being in a business like the health insurance business, where a law is passed that everybody in the country has to buy what you're selling. What could be better, I mean that's heaven on earth. Whatever you're selling, everybody has to buy it.

LYKES: So the academy could interpret this?

RYAN: Of course they could.

LYKES: But they don't. Why?

RYAN: Who knows? I think there are two reasons: one is that the residents in the academy, as we well know, are not, on the average, terribly progressive people; and the other is that those who are, are wrapped up in other kinds of things. They're wrapped up in sexism in nineteenth-century Victorian novels, things like that. OK, that's all well and good, but it doesn't add much steam to the present situation. I don't think there are very many people in the world of universities who have social equality and justice on their agenda. They have other things on their agenda that they think are equally progressive and equally worthy, and they may very well be right.

LYKES: What would you say to somebody who presented him- or herself to you today, wanting to do a Ph.D. in psychology because they were interested in justice issues?

RYAN: I'm afraid I'd say, "Are you sure you want psychology?" I'm not sure that psychology is the best platform to deal with that kind of thing. If you're interested in social science in general, maybe you should go off a little bit into something more related to justice issues, because unfortunately psychology has become the science of understanding internal individual differences, which leads to kinds of ideological distortions that support inequality. I think we can blame psychology for a lot of things that have happened that are bad.

LYKES: Do you think it's that powerful?

RYAN: No, not in itself, but it's like a lot of other things. I don't want to sound paranoid, but let me just talk about the people in charge, the people with power. If you say what they like, they'll give you a boost. Take somebody like Charles Murray.[5] Nobody would call him a political scientist or a scholar; he really isn't very able at all, but he was saying things that people like to hear, so he got a big boost. He was supported, his ideas were pushed, and so forth. So I think psychology furnished ideas that some people liked, and they pushed it.

LYKES: And it continues to do that. And you don't see much place within the discipline for moving it?

RYAN: If you look at readings in social psychology in 1935, you'll see all kinds of stuff about prejudice, social class, stratification, inequality, etc. Social psychologists used to be interested in all of those kinds of things. All that stuff gradually dropped out. Nobody would recognize that today.

LYKES: What keeps you going, given the realities that we have been discussing? Lots of professionals talk about burnout or about having "gotten into" issues for a period of time and then "giving up."

RYAN: I don't know. I have no idea.

LYKES: So you haven't turned your inquisitive mind and your search for the causes of social problems on yourself?

RYAN: No, I haven't. I'm not interested, I really am not. That sort of thing seems very trivial to me. . . . On the one hand, it seems trivial; on the other, it seems one of those unknowable things, whether because we can't get at our own unconscious or because it's too big a thing for us to understand. Whatever. But I think it's trivial and kind of a waste of time. . . . I've always had a lot of interests. I have interests in horse racing and baseball and musical theater and other things. But, in terms of real-life activity, I think I've always been sort of oriented toward—what would we call it?—social justice? equality? Not in any systematic way, not to say, "Hey, look at me! I am the social justice guy around here." It's just the sort of thing I've always been interested in. So I'm Popeye. I yam what I yam.

NOTES

1. Daniel Patrick Moynahan (1965, March), *The Negro Family: The Case for National Action.* The full text and selected critical responses can be found in Lee Rainwater and Will Yancey's *The Moynihan Report and the Politics of Controversy* (Cambridge, MA: M.I.T. Press, 1967).
2. The Model Cities Program was one of the Great Society Programs of the Lyndon B. Johnson administration.
3. Association of Community Organizations for Reform NOW.
4. Professional Air Traffic Controllers Union.
5. Author, with Richard J. Herrnstein, of *The Bell Curve: Intelligence and Class Structure in American Life* (New York: The Free Press, 1994).

About the Contributors

George Albee is a professor emeritus of psychology at the University of Vermont, Burlington. In 1977–78 he chaired the Task Group on Prevention for the President's Commission on Mental Health. He is past-president of the American Psychological Association and the Division of Community Psychology, the author of many books and articles, and founder and for many years coordinator of the Vermont Conference on the Primary Prevention of Psychopathology.

Ali Banuazizi is a professor of psychology at Boston College and a fellow at the Center for International Studies at the Massachusetts Institute of Technology. His current research interests include problems of civil society in the Middle East and the social-psychological dimensions of political development and change. His recent publications include *The Politics of Social Transformation in Afghanistan, Iran, and Pakistan* (1994) and *The New Geopolitics of Central Asia and Its Borderlands* (1994) (both co-edited with M. Weiner).

Bill Berkowitz is a community psychologist who works with the Community Partners program of the Massachusetts Statewide Area Health Education Center, consults with other nonprofit community organizations, and serves as an adjunct faculty member of the Department of Psychology at the University of Massachusetts at Lowell. He has been teaching about, writing about, and engaged in local community development for the past twenty years.

Richard A. Cloward is a professor of social work at Columbia University School of Social Work in New York. He is the co-author, with Frances Fox Piven, of *The Politics of Turmoil* (1974), *Poor People's Movements* (1977), *The New Class War* (1982, rev. ed. 1985), *The Mean Season* (1987), and *Why Americans Don't Vote*. Their co-authored article in this volume is adapted from the 1993 updated edition of their book *Regulating the Poor: The Functions of Public Welfare*, first published in 1971.

Dennis P. Culhane is an assistant professor with the Center for Mental Health Policy and Services Research and a senior fellow at the Leonard Davis Institute of Health Economics at the University of Pennsylvania, both in Philadelphia. His most recent research has involved the analysis of administrative data bases that register and track shelter utilization in New York City and Philadelphia. He is also involved in several studies that examine the relationship between health care utilization and housing instability.

Paula B. Doress-Worters is a founding member of the Boston Women's Health Book Collective. Co-author with Diana Laskin Siegel, of *The New Ourselves Growing Older: Women Aging with Knowledge and Power* (1987), she is a consultant, lecturer, and advocate for health, work, and family issues of mid-life and older women in community and government settings, and teaches women's studies at Boston area colleges.

Matthew P. Dumont, M.D., is a psychiatrist at Westborough State Hospital in Massachusetts. He has published widely in the field of mental health, including *Treating the Poor: A Personal Sojourn through the Rise and Fall of Community Mental Health* (1992).

Michelle Fine is a professor of psychology in the Social Psychology–Personality Program of the Graduate School and University Center, City University of New York. Since 1988 she has served as a consultant to the Philadelphia Schools Collaborative Restructuring Comprehensive High Schools Project. Her most recent publications include *Disruptive Voices: The Transgressive Possibilities of Feminist Research* (1992) and a collection, edited with L. Weis, *Beyond Silenced Voices: Class, Race, and Gender in American Schools* (1993).

Herbert J. Gans is the Robert S. Lynd Professor of Sociology at Columbia University in New York. His latest book is *The War against the Poor: The Underclass and Antipoverty Policy* (1995). Among his other eight books are *The Urban Villagers* (1962/1982), *The Levittowners* (1967), *More Equality* (1973), *Deciding What's News* (1979), *Middle American Individualism* (1988), and *People, Plans and Policies* (1992). He is a past president of the American Sociological Association.

Toni Genovese is a Ph.D. candidate in Developmental Psychology and Women's Studies at the Graduate School and University Center, City University of New York. She has taught extensively and is currently investigating the silencing of the voices of incest survivors.

Sharon Gold-Steinberg is a clinical postdoctoral fellow at the Center for the Child and Family and a lecturer in the Department of Psychology at the University of Michigan, Ann Arbor. She has specialized in clinical training in the area of child abuse and neglect, and conducts therapy with incest survivors.

Jean V. Hardisty received her Ph.D. in political science from Northwestern University in Evanston, Illinois. In 1981 she founded Political Research Associates, a documentation, information, and publishing center studying the right wing. She is also a founding member of the Women's Community Cancer Project.

Sarah Ingersoll is a Ph.D. candidate in sociology and urban policy at the Graduate School and University Center, City University of New York. She has worked as an activist for educational and economic justice, serving as the vice president of the Organization for a New Equality in 1991. She also has extensive video, film, and photography experience.

Ellen Leopold completed a master's degree in economics at Birkbeck College of the University of London. She has served as a research associate and economic adviser on a wide range of policy and planning projects in London. Her book on social and economic theories of consumption, *The World of Consumption* (1993), was co-authored with Ben Fine. She is a member of the Women's Community Cancer Project.

Joan Huser Liem is an associate professor of psychology at the University of Massachusetts at Boston. Her research focuses on the psychological effects on individual and families of stressful events such as unemployment, divorce, and most recently, physical and sexual abuse. For the last five years she has contributed to the development of a new Ph.D. program in clinical psychology, emphasizing cross-cultural and life-span developmental perspectives on clinical work with underserved populations.

Ramsay Liem is a professor of psychology at Boston College. He has conducted longitudinal research on the psychological impact of unemployment and advocated support for worker initiatives to combat economic displacement. His current work includes teaching and research in Asian American studies with an emphasis on the historical roots of ethnic and racial identity. He is also engaged in studies of the cultural construction of the self and emotional experience.

M. Brinton Lykes, associate professor of psychology at Boston College, has worked since 1986 in the development of community-based psychological assistance programs in contexts of war and state-sponsored violence. Her writings explore the importance of culture and indigenous practices in the lives of women and child survivors and the dilemmas encountered in multicultural, engendered action research.

Pat Macpherson received a master's degree in women's studies from the University of Kent at Canterbury, and is currently a part-time English teacher and consultant to the Philadelphia Schools Collaborative Restructuring Comprehensive High Schools Project.

S. M. Miller is a visiting professor of sociology at Boston College and a senior fellow at the Commonwealth Institute in Boston. He is currently completing a book on social stratification that integrates class, race, and gender around the themes of money (income and wealth) and respect. He is a member of the board of directors of the Poverty and Race Research Action Council, which supports work that combats racism and poverty.

Michael Morris is a professor of psychology at the University of New Haven, where he serves as director of Graduate Field Training in Community Psychology. His recent publications have addressed such topics as welfare reform, ethical conflicts encountered by program evaluators, and training in evaluation research. His consultation work focuses on interagency collaborative efforts to achieve community and social change.

Frances Fox Piven is Distinguished Professor in the Political Science Program at the Graduate School and University Center, City University of New York. She is the co-author, with Richard A. Cloward, of *The Politics of Turmoil* (1974), *Poor People's Movements* (1977), *The New Class War* (1982, rev. ed. 1985), *The Mean Season* (1987), and *Why Americans Don't Vote*. Their co-authored article in this volume is adapted from the 1993 updated edition of their book *Regulating the Poor: The Functions of Public Welfare*, first published in 1971.

Julian Rappaport is a professor of psychology at the University of Illinois. He is past president of the Society for Community Research and Action and past editor of the *American Journal of Community Psychology*. His research focuses on the educational, mental health, and legal systems. Recent interests include the development of empowerment among members of mutual help organizations.

Rosemarie Roberts is a doctoral student in the Social Psychology–Personality Program at the City University of New York. She is the winner of numerous scholarships, awards, and grants (including the MARC, Charlotte Newcombe, and Phillip Siff Educational Foundation scholarships). She teaches Afro-Caribbean dance and music as vehicles to promote cultural identity and pride.

Sumner M. Rosen is a Boston native who organized and taught freedom schools with William Ryan in the 1960s. He was on the faculty of Columbia University School of Social Work in New York from 1975 through 1993. He is the author of *Economic Power Failure* and *Face of the Nation* (Encyclopedia of Social Work, 1987), and a founding member of New Initiatives for Full Employment and Jews for Racial and Economic Justice.

Elizabeth Sparks is an assistant professor of counseling psychology at Boston College. For over seventeen years she worked as a mental health clinician and administrator in the African American community, and this experience is reflected in her research interests and teaching. Her research focuses on understanding coping and resilience in youth who live in violent environments, and on multicultural counseling and training.

Abigail J. Stewart is a professor of psychology and women's studies at the University of Michigan, Ann Arbor. Her current research focuses on aspects of personal life experience, cohort-related historical events, and personality that shape political consciousness and political activism. She is also past director of women's studies at the University of Michigan, where the priority has been to shape a new agenda for the program based on the recognition of diversity among women, and current director of the Institute for Research on Women and Gender at the University of Michigan.

R. Elizabeth Thomas is a Ph.D. candidate in psychology at the University of Illinois, Champaign-Urbana. She is a graduate of Georgetown University with a degree in psychology and art history. She has worked in the Washington, D.C., area on projects for mental health, literacy, and human rights in Latin America. Her current research includes establishing dialogue between high school students and school administrators.

Tom Wolff is the director of community development of the Massachusetts Statewide Area Health Education Center Program of the University of Massachusetts Medical School. He is the principal investigator of a project developed by Area Health Education Center/Community Partners—Coalition Building: One Path to Empowered Communities—dedicated to building community coalitions across the state of Massachusetts.

Author Index

Subject Index

abortion: as catalyst for activism, 12, 277, 280–281, 283–284, 291, 294; comparison of illegal and legal, 289–291; effects on women of illegal, 277, 279–286; effects on women of legal, 277, 279–284, 287–289; fears of, 279, 281, 284, 287; Jane Collective, 284–287, 292; Operation Rescue, 294; personal accounts of, 280–282, 285–286, 290; pro-choice movement, 277–278, 281, 293–294; pro-life movement, 277–278, 293; self or system blame for hardships of, 279–280, 283

activist research. *See* social scientists' role

adolescents: deterrence from joining gangs, 250; substance abuse prevention for, 245, 252; sexually transmitted diseases (STDs), 252; teen pregnancy, 242, 251–252; violence prevention for, 245, 252

affirmative action, 4, 229

AFL-CIO. *See* labor unions

African Americans, 12, 18–20, 28, 29, 52, 53, 140, 205, 208, 220, 223, 233, 237–257, 318, 321, 328, 357. *See also* black Americans, income disparities, people of color, racism, underclass, welfare, women of color

ageism, 205

Aid to Families with Dependent Children (AFDC), 3, 21–22, 55, 77, 79–81, 248

antipoverty policies: the heterogeneity of poverty, 13; moral claims for, 23–25, 27; need for cohesiveness in, 96–98; proposals for decreasing economic inequalities, 21, 96–98; resulting in increased democratic participation, 6, 28–30, 96; role of social construction of unemployment in, 91–92; stereotyping of underclass as an obstacle to, 37–38, 40–42, 84, 91–94; work sharing, 98. *See also* Great Society; War on Poverty

Argentina, 167, 175, 260

art making: community arts projects, 326, 330, 332; community festivals as, 331; control of, 317–318, 323, 330–331; democratization of, 324; as empowerment, 317–318, 322; about homosexuality, 329

385